The **Journal** and **Major Essays**

of

John Woolman

Edited by
PHILLIPS P. MOULTON

Friends United Press
Richmond, Indiana • www.fum.org

First printing 1971
Eighth printing 2007

Friends United Press
101 Quaker Hill Drive
Richmond IN 47374
friendspress@fum.org
www.fum.org

Cover design by Shari Pickett Veach
Artwork of John Woolman's handwriting courtesy of Haverford College Library, Haverford, PA: Quaker Collection.

Library of Congress Cataloging-in-Publication Data

Woolman, John, 1720–1772.
    The journal and major essays of John Woolman / edited by Phillips P. Moulton
        p. cm.
    Originally published: New York: Oxford University Press, 1971, in series:
    A library of Protestant thought.
    Includes bibliographical references and index.
    ISBN 978-0-944350-10-2
        0-944350-10-0
    1. Woolman, John, 1720–1772. 2. Quakers—Biography. 3. Slavery—United States.
    4. Poor. I. Moulton, Phillips P., 1909–2002 II. Title.

BX7795.W7 A3 2000b
289.6'092-dc21   00-046626
[B]

❖

Originally part of the series:

A LIBRARY OF PROTESTANT THOUGHT

❖

A LIBRARY OF PROTESTANT THOUGHT

✤ ✤ ✤

EDITORIAL BOARD

✤ ✤ ✤

✤ ✤ ✤

To My Wife and Children
Mary, Larry, and Kathy Moulton

A Library of Protestant Thought

A LIBRARY OF PROTESTANT THOUGHT is a collection of writings intended to illumine and interpret the history of the Christian faith in its Protestant expression. It is as variegated in its literary forms and theological positions as is the movement its mirrors. Tracts, letters, sermons, monographs, and other types of literature comprising the heritage of Protestant thought find a place in this series. Works that were originally composed in English, whether in Great Britain or in the New World, and works that were originally written in other languages, many of them not previously translated into English, are included. But it is neither necessary nor desirable that every segment of Protestant theology, piety, and ethics receive equal space. The trite theology, the conventional piety, and the platitudinous ethics always bulk larger in any tradition, also in the Protestantism of the past four centuries, than does the creative output of the religious spirit. The latter is our primary interest in this Library. While we have not felt obligated to grant them equal attention, we have included works that are typical of the more commonplace literature of the Protestant tradition. On the other hand, some works which logically belong in this series have not been included because they are readily available elsewhere.

In keeping with the fundamental purpose of this Library, the voices of Protestantism are allowed to speak for themselves, with only as much introduction, commentary, and exposition as will in fact allow them to do so. Wherever feasible, documents are reproduced in their entirety. A few representative selections have been preferred to more numerous but shorter passages, for the Library tries to depict the structure of thought rather than the genetic development of a man or a movement. Nevertheless, the variety of Protestant forms precludes a uniform treatment throughout. Our aim has been to be representative rather than exhaustive and to employ the best available tools of critical historical scholarship. Despite its ambitious scope, A Library of Protestant Thought is not an encyclopedia of Protestantism. It is a series of volumes from which not only clergymen and theologians, but students of philosophy, history, literature, political science and other disciplines can gain a more balanced view of how the Protestant mind has thought and spoken since the Reformation.

The Board is grateful to the Hazen Foundation for an initial grant enabling it to begin its work; to the Sealantic Fund, Inc., for a grant making possible Board meetings, consultations, and editorial assistance in the prepartion of specific volumes; and to the Oxford University Press for undertaking the publication of the Library.

THE EDITORIAL BOARD

Preface

The significance of Woolman's writings and the need for a new edition are discussed, respectively, in the Introduction and in Appendix A of this volume. The major purpose of this edition is to reproduce with fidelity Woolman's final manuscripts: to include everything he meant to include and to exclude revisions made by others. The aim has been to produce a reliable edition, accessible to the general reader, yet sufficiently documented to meet the needs of scholars.

Editorial Methods

In editing Woolman's *Journal* and major essays, the method employed has been adapted from the best current examples of editorial scholarship in the field of American history. Particular reference was made to *The Papers of Benjamin Franklin*, now being published by Yale University Press. Two other models were frequently consulted: *The Papers of Alexander Hamilton* (Columbia University Press) and *The Papers of Thomas Jefferson* (Princeton University Press). Articles by Julian P. Boyd, L. H. Butterfield, Lester J. Cappon, Leonard W. Labaree, Waldo G. Leland, and Wilmarth W. Lewis, dealing with the editing of historical documents, have likewise been consulted. *The Harvard Guide to American History*, by Oscar Handlin, *et al.* (Cambridge, Mass., 1954, 95–104), proved especially helpful.

A study of the standards and methods of the Center for Editions of American Authors (CEAA) of the Modern Language Association of America contributed many useful insights. The *Statement of Editorial Principles* and the *Newsletters* published by the Center were examined carefully, as were articles by Fredson Bowers (who has developed and articulated the editorial principles followed by the Center) and essays by Lewis Mumford and Edmund Wilson on the work of the Center. Fruitful reference has also been made to volumes bearing the Center's imprint; these include works of Nathaniel Hawthorne, Ralph Waldo Emerson, and Walt Whitman.

The work of the Center has been especially useful to the present editor because of a common major aim: to produce (as nearly as possible) a text representing the final intent of the author. For the most part, to follow the principles of the Center has been consistent with using as a general model *The Papers of Benjamin Franklin* mentioned above. In one respect, however, the practice recommended by the Center has not been followed. The recording of every editorial change made in "accidentals"—punctuation, spelling, and capitalization—has been practically impossible. This is chiefly because Woolman's manuscripts were a product of the eighteenth century, whereas the holographs reproduced by the CEAA volumes nearly all date at least a century later. As Benjamin Franklin regretfully noted in one of his essays, the eighteenth century was a period of unsettling transition in English usage. This is reflected in Woolman's manuscripts. His different spellings of the same word are quite random and unconnected with his intended meaning. The same is true of his use of capitals and often of his punctuation. To document every change made in the process of modernization would have involved scores of notes per page, most of them serving no real purpose.

Moreover, one cannot always know, for example, where Woolman intended to end a sentence or paragraph. Where he did not appear completely indifferent to such divisions, he followed several practices that either might or might not indicate such a terminus. One cannot record all editorial emendations unless one is sure of the points at which changes are actually being made. To achieve with Woolman's eighteenth-century holographs what has been done effectively with nineteenth-century works, it would be necessary to print facsimile reproductions of the two parallel manuscripts of Woolman's *Journal* in the same volume. It should be added, of course, that emendations of the accidentals have been noted wherever ambiguity or some other problem has made this advisable.

Without describing in detail the procedure followed in transcribing the *Journal*, the chief guidelines can be noted. In order to produce a reliable edition, the editor has taken care that no words be added, substituted, or omitted. The rare exceptions to this rule consist of interpolations by the editor (in brackets) and the dropping of an occasional word or letter whose repetition by Woolman in the process of copying was clearly unintentional. Woolman's grammar has been left strictly intact; hence the reader will occasionally encounter such errors as lack of agreement between subject and verb.

In regard to dates, it may be recalled that before September, 1752,

England and its colonies followed the Old Style calendar, in which March was the first month and February the twelfth. Thereafter, January was the first month. Woolman's first entry in his journal after the change was in September, 1753. Since he had apparently adjusted to the New Style by then, no dates have been altered.

To remove barriers between the author and the modern reader, Woolman's erratic capitalization and spelling have generally been brought into accord with present-day usage. The spelling of proper names and geographical locations has been standardized, and Woolman's abbreviations have been revised to conform to contemporary models of style. However, where either of two forms of a word is correct, Woolman's has generally been retained so long as the meaning is clear, even though the alternative is more commonly used today. Examples are "betwixt" and "spake." More frequently than most writers of his day, Woolman ended third-person singular verbs in "th" rather than "s" (as e.g., in "doth" and "hath"). This practice testifies to the influence on his style of the King James Version of the Bible. The retention of these endings serves a scholarly purpose and conveys something of the flavor of the original. Indeed, the softer "doth" seems more consonant with Woolman's gentle character than today's equivalent. Use of the older endings does not seriously impede the reading process. Since there was more to gain than to lose, Woolman's usage has been followed.

Two special problems should be noted here. Three times in Chapter 7, referring to the Legislature, Woolman wrote "Legislator." If this had been thought of simply as the wrong word, it would have been allowed to stand, with consequent confusion for the reader; instead, it has been treated as a misspelling to be corrected, and has been rendered "Legislature." Throughout the *Journal*, Woolman generally wrote "God" and "Lord" in a special way. While capitalizing only the first letter, he often made the whole word much larger than other words and formed each letter individually, leaving space between the letters rather than connecting them as in ordinary script. Less frequently he accorded the same treatment to other references to deity, such as "Jesus Christ," "Most High," "His Love," and "Him." He did not always do this, however, even with "God" and "Lord." Moreover, there are many gradations in size and numerous borderline cases where it is uncertain whether the word is significantly larger. Woolman's varying treatment of such words generally appears to have no relation to the intended meaning or emphasis. The present editor and his advisers finally decided simply to call the reader's attention to the practice, rather than attempt to deal individually with the hundreds of instances.

Since the point at which paragraphs begin is related to meaning, Woolman's practice has generally been followed where it could be determined. The present editor has felt free, however, to combine short paragraphs or divide long ones where to do so would facilitate communication without altering Woolman's emphasis.

Punctuation posed a more difficult problem. Sometimes Woolman sprinkled many commas at random throughout a sentence. On the other hand, he occasionally omitted punctuation in complex passages where guidelines would have been helpful. He had certain habits of punctuation that tend to mislead modern readers, some of them peculiar to himself and others reflecting the usage of his time. In this edition the practice has been to use whatever correct punctuation would convey Woolman's meaning most clearly to modern readers. Specific decisions have taken account both of Woolman's punctuation and of twentieth-century usage. Occasionally Woolman's punctuation was such that the present editor could not be certain of the nuance of meaning intended. At these points his usage has been retained, since it seemed better to leave the meaning ambiguous than arbitrarily to restrict the range of interpretation available. It has generally been possible, however, to determine Woolman's meaning and to convey it by modernizing the "accidentals."

Brackets have been used in the main body of this volume (as distinguished from notes or appendices) to indicate material that Woolman clearly did not intend for the printer and/or did not incorporate into his final holographs. Any bracketed material not explained by a footnote is an interpolation by the editor. It should be noted that in the *Journal* the chapters were numbered by the original editorial committee, whereas in *A Plea for the Poor* this was done by Woolman. The present editor is responsible for the dates at the head of each chapter indicating the approximate period covered therein.

Woolman's Scripture quotations are from the King James Version. Sometimes they extend a verse beyond the reference he cites. Occasionally he omits or changes a word or two. To avoid unnecessary pendantry, the editor has not called attention to these instances. However, ellipsis points have been used to indicate longer omissions, and Scripture references have generally been supplied (in brackets) where they were lacking or where Woolman's citation was not adequate to identify the source.

In composing two holographs of the *Journal* plus a third copy of several portions, Woolman made a great many revisions. Significant alterations by Woolman in the final copy (MSS. B and S) have been indicated, and sometimes discussed, in the notes. Variant readings, omissions, or additions in preliminary holographs have generally been less fully documented. The aim has been to deal with such variants in a note (or appendix) when they reveal thought processes or character traits, provide historical context, illuminate Woolman's literary style, or clarify the relation of one manuscript to another.

Variations in MS. A have been documented less thoroughly than those in the other texts because they are so numerous and because MS. A is more accessible. (See Appendix B for descriptions of the manuscripts.) Chapter 11 has been documented more fully than the rest because preliminary manuscripts T1 and T2 are not readily available and vary widely from the final product. Much the same relation obtains between the first two chapters of MS. B and their parallel in MS. C; here all variant readings that seemed significant to the meaning have been recorded. Chapter 9 has been heavily documented because MSS. P and R3 are parallel to it and because unusual textual problems are associated with sections 7 through 9 of MS. B, which comprise much of this chapter. Throughout the *Journal*, revisions by those other than Woolman have been noted only when they impressed the editor as having special importance.

Although the documentation is much less extensive than in most projects associated with the CEAA, it is considerably more extensive than that of other volumes in A Library of Protestant Thought. This practice, made possible by the availability of holographs, has seemed advisable not only to explain the many departures of the present edition from earlier ones but also to provide serious students with the data needed to study Woolman's life, thought, and literary methods.

Acknowledgments

Bringing this work to completion has involved the cooperation and resources of more individuals and institutions than can be named here. While those mentioned have been of special service, none should be held responsible for final editorial decisions or for whatever limitations this volume may have. Recognition is due primarily to Henry J. Cadbury, Professor Emeritus of Divinity, Harvard University, who devoted a great many hours to detailed scrutiny of the sources and advised the editor at innumerable points, with particular regard to textual analysis. Other scholars whose counsel was frequently sought and gladly given are Edwin B. Bronner, Professor of History, Librarian, and Curator of the Quaker Collection at Haverford College; Thomas E. Drake, Professor Emeritus of History, Haverford College; Frederick B. Tolles, formerly Professor of Quaker History and Director of the Friends Historical Library at Swarthmore College; and Whitfield J. Bell, Jr., formerly Associate Editor of the Franklin Papers and now Librarian of the American Philosophical Society.

In addition, I am especially grateful to scholars connected with the Center for Editions of American Authors, notably to its former director, William M. Gibson; to E. Sculley Bradley, Professor Emeritus of English at the University of Pennsylvania; and to John Ashmead, Professor of English at Haverford College.

I am grateful as well to Wilbur D. Ruggles and Mrs. Elise Van Gerven of Oxford University Press, to Miss Amy Clampitt, copy editor for A Library of Protestant Thought, and to Robert T. Handy and Winthrop S. Hudson of its editorial board, for much advice and assistance.

At Haverford College, where the editor was twice awarded the T. Wistar Brown Fellowship, thanks are due to President John R. Coleman and to Hugh Borton, President Emeritus, for making all of the college facilities available. In particular, I had the help of Mrs. Mildred B. Hargreaves (chief typist) and, among many staff members of the college library, David A. Fraser, Associate Librarian, and those serving the Quaker Collection: Mrs. Elizabeth B. Tritle, Mrs. Frances S. Barnett, Mrs. Alice E. Whittelsey, and Mrs. Barbara C. Curtis.

At Adrian College, where the project has been made possible by Summer Study Grants and leaves of absence, my special thanks go to John H. Dawson, President; to James A. Dodd, Librarian, and his staff; and to Darrell H. Pollard, George C. Seeck, Howard C. Emrick, A. Douglas MacNaughton, Miss Marcella Miley, Mrs. Carolyn Roney, and Mrs. Sonja Hoffman.

The American Philosophical Society assisted the project with a Research Grant from the Penrose Fund, and Willman Spawn, Restorator, APS Library, aided in the identification of manuscripts. At the Friends Historical Library of Swarthmore College, I had the perceptive help of Miss Dorothy G. Harris, its Acting Director, and of Mrs. Eleanor B. Mayer, Mrs. Jane M. Thorsen, Miss Claire Shetter, and Mrs. Nancy Speers. Thanks are due as well to the staff of the Historical Society of Pennsylvania, particularly Nicholas B. Wainwright, Director; John D. Kilbourne, Curator; and Mrs. Vilma J. Halcombe of the Manuscript Department.

For very valuable assistance and making manuscripts available in England, appreciation is extended to Miss Joyce Blake, Headmistress of the Mount School in York, and to Edward H. Milligan, Librarian of the Society of Friends in London. The use of manuscripts in the depositories mentioned in Appendix B is also thankfully acknowledged.

For typing and other services I am grateful to Mrs. Jeanne Friebel, Miss Frances L. Gallagher, Mrs. Thelma MacNaughton, Philip Mayer, Miss Kathy Moulton, Larry Moulton, Miss Wendy Nash, Mrs. Judy Perloe, and Miss Linda Petty. Fruitful use was made of the work of the editors of previous editions, notably Mrs. Amelia Mott Gummere and Mrs. Janet Whitney. Mrs. Isabel N. Bliss first recommended that I read Woolman's *Journal*. James M. Read, Staff Consultant at the Charles F. Kettering Foundation, helped initiate the project. Finally, I wish to express my gratitude to Edwin and Anne Bronner, John Davison, and Richard and Clementine Jenney for sharing their homes with me and my family during periods of research at Haverford, and to my wife for unremitting aid and encouragement.

PHILLIPS P. MOULTON

Table of Contents

✤

THE JOURNAL AND MAJOR ESSAYS
OF
JOHN WOOLMAN

✤

Introduction

IN 1797 SAMUEL TAYLOR COLERIDGE COMMENTED: "I should almost despair of that man who could peruse the life of John Woolman without an amelioration of heart." [1] In the same year, the poet Charles Lloyd gave a copy of Woolman's *Journal* to Charles Lamb. Deeply moved by it, Lamb later remarked that it was the only American book he had read twice. Henry Crabb Robinson and other friends of Lamb and Coleridge were equally enthusiastic. High tribute was paid the *Journal* in the nineteenth century by Ralph Waldo Emerson and other writers both within and beyond Transcendentalist circles. Its literary standing was raised still further in 1871, when it was reprinted with a perceptive introduction and notes by John Greenleaf Whittier. In the twentieth century it had a powerful effect on Theodore Dreiser, for whom it opened avenues of thought beyond his customary naturalism; it figures prominently in his novel *The Bulwark*. As a personal revelation, the *Journal* rightly takes its place in American literature alongside such classics as Franklin's *Autobiography*, Thoreau's *Walden*, and Whitman's *Democratic Vistas*. [2]

Yet it is not just as a literary work (in the narrow sense) that the *Journal* has been kept in print for the past two hundred years. Time and again readers have noted the relevance of Woolman's insights to their own times. Especially in our day, his ethical convictions, rooted in religious experience, speak directly to the major issues of racial equality, economic justice, and the responsibility of the individual toward military and political authority.

Born in 1720, Woolman grew up in Burlington County, New Jersey, less than twenty miles from Philadelphia. The fourth of thirteen children, he came of a family that was neither wealthy nor poor. His father was a farmer and fruit grower. Friends of the family included leading business-

---

1. *Collected Letters of S. T. Coleridge*, edited by E. L. Griggs (London, 1956), I, 302.
2. See Edwin H. Cady, *John Woolman*, 171–172.

3

men and entrepreneurs of Philadelphia. John Woolman's formal education at the village school apparently lasted the usual ten years, beginning
at age four. Encouraged by his father, he continued a lifelong process of
self-education, using his family's library and the exceptional collections
of their Philadelphia friends. A strong Quaker influence at home, where
the Bible "or some religious books" were read aloud each Sunday, formed
the setting of the conflicts he experienced during adolescence. Apparently gregarious, he was torn between a life of frivolity and a serious
religious vocation. Eventually the latter won out; the foundation for his
life was established.

Leaving the farm at age twenty-one, Woolman moved to the town of
Mount Holly, five miles away, where he was hired to tend a retail store in
which bakery products and other items were sold. Later, as he set up shop
for himself, his sales grew and he began to prosper. The possibility of
commercial ventures in Philadelphia also beckoned. He had become successful without really intending to do so, and affluence lay before him.

But his very success was disturbing to Woolman. He had become so
much involved in business that the balance he had set for himself was
threatened. At first he cut back his trade. Later he gave up retailing
altogether in favor of tailoring, which he could control more readily. To
supplement his income as a tailor, he engaged in surveying, in drawing up
such legal documents as wills and deeds, in teaching, and in tending his
orchard. These services were integrated into a simple pattern that enabled
him to live in unhurried fashion and to pursue his real calling.

The Quakers had no paid ministry. On First Day (Sunday) the meeting (congregation) gathered for silent worship, during which any who
felt the moving of the spirit could rise and speak. It was common for
Quakers with an especially strong sense of vocation to speak more frequently than their companions and to travel to other meetings, sharing
their convictions during First Day worship. When a meeting agreed that
a member's witness was truly edifying, it could acknowledge his special
gift by making an appropriate record in the official minutes. Thus one
became a "recommended minister." When he embarked upon a specific
mission, the meeting facilitated his work by granting him a certificate for
the occasion.

At the age of twenty-three, having been recorded as a minister and
issued a certificate by his meeting, Woolman went on his first missionary
journey. During the remaining twenty-nine years of his life he made
some thirty excursions, ranging through the colonies from New England

to the Carolinas. He died while visiting England in 1772. Of the hundreds of itinerant Quaker ministers in America and England between 1655 and the Revolutionary War, Woolman was one of the most notable.

Although most of the *Journal* is devoted to his itinerant ministry, Woolman averaged only about a month per year away from home. The day before his twenty-ninth birthday he married Sarah Ellis, whom he seems to have known for over ten years previously. Of their two children, only Mary survived infancy. Letters to Sarah and references in the *Journal* reveal that he was "a loving husband, a tender father," as the Burlington Monthly Meeting expressed it in a testimony after his death. Being away from home was sometimes a trial for both him and his wife, and perhaps one reason he did not make a projected visit to the West Indies was the feeling that he should not be absent from home at the time.[3] Yet he and Sarah were in agreement over the other journeys, believing that so long as their decisions were in "the pure spirit of Truth," God would "be their guide and support."

When he was about thirty-six years old, Woolman began writing his *Journal*, to which he added intermittently until his death. He composed several essays, the most notable of which are included here. His works reflect the conviction, nurtured by his reading, that a man is first of all a spiritual being. The saturation of his thought with the Bible is attested by some seven hundred quotations or allusions ranging widely over both Old and New Testaments. This is particularly evident in the essays. The journals of several itinerant ministers, as well as classics of the Quaker faith by William Penn, Robert Barclay, and William Sewel made up a large part of his reading. He also studied devotional literature by authors of other denominations. Of special interest is his reading of non-Quaker mystics: *The Imitation of Christ* (attributed to Thomas à Kempis) and works by Jakob Boehme, John Everard, and William Law.[4]

3. See *Journal* (this volume), Chapter 9, note 58.
4. See W. Forrest Altman, "John Woolman's Reading," Chapter 2. Boehme (1575–1624) was a German mystic. Some of his works, translated into English between 1644 and 1662, were probably read by George Fox, founder of the Society of Friends. The Behmenist societies that came into existence during the seventeenth century eventually merged into the Quaker movement. Everard (ca. 1575–1650) was a Puritan influenced by Neoplatonism. He wrote *Some Gospel Treasures Opened . . . Whereunto is Added the Mystical Divinity of Dionysius the Areopagite,* which was widely read by the early Friends. Its continuing popularity a century later is suggested by Woolman's records: his copy was borrowed at least seven times. The Quaker doctrine of the Inner Light probably owed much to Everard's emphasis upon the immanence of God. Law (1686–1761) was a well-educated English divine, who served for many years as

With this background, it is not surprising that Woolman had a keen sense of God's presence in his life—and likewise at times of God's absence. On several occasions he had dreams and visions to which he attached religious significance. His prayer life was active, and his evident sense of divine guidance was enhanced by the Quaker emphasis on an Inner Light, available to those who silently wait for it. He also believed firmly in divine providence—that God directed the destinies of men and nations who trusted in him. God's hand he discerned in secular history as well.

Perhaps as a reflection of his early observations on the farm, Woolman had a strong sense that a principle of order and harmony pervaded the universe. The Creator, he believed, intended that man should share in this harmony. If one's relations with his fellow man were in accord with true wisdom, a divine proportion would be evident. For example, as conscience directed one away from lucrative but harmful employment, the desires for expensive luxuries would subside. Woolman's sense of order, harmony, and beauty is comparable to that found in Hesiod's *Works and Days* and in Plato.[5] Going beyond Plato was Woolman's conception of divine love permeating the universe.

Woolman's ethics issued naturally from his religion. He drew no sharp distinction between the classic values of goodness and truth. Evil deeds and customs were viewed as those that were without a foundation in truth. His frequent references to pure wisdom usually occurred in the course of a discussion of righteous dealings with one's fellow man.

Related to his belief in divine providence was his conviction that moral law was basic in the universe. Some ten times in the *Journal* he declared that if man continued to treat his fellows unjustly, retribution was certain to follow:

> Many slaves . . . are oppressed, and their cries have reached the ears of the Most High! Such is the purity and certainty of his judgments that . . . should we . . . neglect to do our duty . . . by terrible things in righteousness God may answer us in this matter.[6]

---

tutor to Edward Gibbon (father of the historian). His books on ethics and theology were of a high order. He is best known, however, for *A Practical Treatise upon Christian Perfection* and *A Serious Call to a Devout and Holy Life,* which deeply affected the Wesleys, George Whitefield, and other leaders of the Evangelical revival. His later works, in particular, reflect his admiration for Boehme. For à Kempis, see *Journal* (this volume), Chapter 5, note 6.

5. See Plato, *Republic*, Bk. 9, 588B–592B.

6. *Journal* (this volume), 93. Quotation immediately following: 129.

One hundred years before the Civil War he warned, "The seeds of great calamity and desolation are sown and growing fast on this continent."

Rooted in the love, goodness, and power of God, Woolman's ethical views were undergirded by a profound sense of security. God would certainly care for those who trusted in him and who lived in the power of that trust. Any sacrifice or risk could be accepted with courage by a person "united to him who hath all power in heaven and earth," for "a woman may forget her sucking child, yet he will not forget his faithful ones." [7] A striking testimony to Woolman's sense of security in God is contained in a letter by Esther Tuke,* who attended him during his last illness. After his death Mrs. Tuke wrote:

> The state of his mind throughout the whole of his unspeakable affliction was one continued calm; a firm trust in the Lord, with perfect resignation to his disposal, appeared throughout the whole; patient beyond description; his hope and confidence so firmly fixed, that no outward distress seemed . . . to discompose or ruffle him. [8]

This sense of security in the divine love provided a solid basis for the moral imperative—the conviction that one must do the right, come what may. Woolman's was not a prudential ethic, in which the judgment of right and wrong is determined merely by foreseeable consequences. In social action he was not so much a strategist working for specific goals as he was a faithful witness to the revealed truth of God. His imperative was not primarily to show results but to testify in what he said and did, trusting to open the hearts and lives of others to the disturbing power of God. Yet he held the conviction that doing right would somehow be validated in the total economy of the universe.

With the inner life of the spirit Woolman harmoniously combined the outer life of action. In surveying his major social concerns, one observes not only his relevance to crucial issues of the twentieth century, but also the centrality of his teachings to the Quaker tradition. The Quakers have always emphasized the equality of all men. Woolman's concern for equality was expressed in his opposition to slavery. Clues to his character are revealed when we examine the motives and goals of his efforts in this cause.

His primary aim, of course, was to ease the plight of the slaves. Sensitive to hardship of any kind, he was keenly aware of what they suffered.

7. "Considerations on the True Harmony of Mankind," in Amelia Mott Gummere, *Journal and Essays of John Woolman*, 441.
8. "Biographical Sketch," in Gummere, 148.

Yet he also sympathized with the spiritual plight of the slaveholders, believing that to treat a person as a slave dimmed the owner's vision and depraved "the mind in like manner, and with as great certainty, as prevailing cold congeals water." [9]

Further, he was concerned for the Society of Friends and its mission of fostering the eternal well-being of all men. He was distressed that participation in slavery by church members tended to prejudice slaves and other sensitive spirits against the faith, and to hinder their religious growth. He pleaded for a maximum consistency of practice with profession. When individuals and groups persisted in evil, he believed, they would answer for their conduct before "him who is no respecter of persons."

While he sought a way of eradicating the evils associated with slavery, Woolman also recognized that some slaves were well treated. He did not blame a person who retained them from "a real sense of duty and true charity." He was convinced, however, that such cases were exceptional. With clear insight he emphasized that despite good intentions, people were generally "biased by narrow self-love," and did not have sufficient wisdom and goodness to warrant being entrusted with absolute power over others. He recognized that their children, when they inherited the slaves, would be even less likely to rule with justice.

Because of his concern for slaves and slaveholders, for true religion, and for society at large, and because he saw no other solution to the evils associated with slavery, Woolman worked for the abolition of the system. As related in the opening chapter of the *Journal*, the first experience that brought the issue of slavery sharply to his attention caught him by surprise. The situation had all the ingredients needed to tempt him to evade responsibility, and he took a middle course—which he later regretted. From that time onward he did not waver.

Although Woolman's opposition to slavery was expressed in many ways, his preferred approach was a personal confrontation with individuals. This kind of social action had characterized the Quakers ever since 1656, when George Fox stood before Oliver Cromwell and bade him "lay down his crown at the feet of Jesus." For three decades Woolman visited slaveholders, urging them to consider seriously the unethical aspects of the system in which they were involved. To those who would evade the issue he was an effective gadfly. He did not self-righteously rail at them; quietly, but insistently, he urged them to examine their responsibilities.

9. *Considerations . . . Part Second* (this volume), 237.

Like other itinerant ministers, Woolman was given free board and lodging in the homes of leading Friends, many of whom owed their prosperity to the labor of slaves. In accepting their hospitality, Woolman not only observed the system of slave labor at first hand; he was also implicated in it. In order to avoid "the gain of oppression," he insisted on paying his hosts (or the slaves themselves) for services rendered. More important, he had serious talks with his hosts. In the *Journal* we find frequent references to friendly but urgent conversations in which he stressed the ill effects of slaveholding and its inconsistency "with the purity of the Christian religion." This was "hard labour," he confessed, but it often led to a deeper experience of the "nearness of true gospel fellowship."

The most striking instance of his personal influence occurred in Newport, Rhode Island, a major center of the slave traffic. After the New England Yearly Meeting met there in 1760, Woolman felt impelled to seek out and talk with prominent Quaker slaveowners.[10] With a local Friend who shared his concern, he enlisted the counsel of "one of the most noted elders who had slaves," indicating those with whom he wished to talk. The elder not only proposed the names of others but went personally to their homes, persuading them to attend a gathering where the evils of their practice were discussed! It is likely that Woolman engaged in this sort of personal confrontation more than any other Friend. Throughout his lifetime it was his most effective means of influencing Quaker opinion.

Closely related to the issue of slavery was Woolman's emphasis on voluntary simplicity. Although he did not advocate poverty, he believed one should moderate his desires and forego unnecessary material goods. Simple living by the individual was a corollary of his economic theory: God had so ordered the universe that the needs of all would be met insofar as each person was guided by universal love to seek only what he really required. Only in this way would there be time and opportunity for proper maturation and spiritual growth and for sharing with one's fellows. Woolman referred frequently to the harmful effects of striving for a standard of living higher than was really essential; he traced nu-

10. A Yearly Meeting is the largest basic geographical unit of the Society of Friends. The expression refers not only to annual gatherings but also to a continuing organization. It is composed of representatives of Quarterly Meetings, which cover smaller geographical areas and which convene every three months. The smallest unit is a Monthly Meeting, which gathers each month for business. It generally meets weekly for worship. Its representatives comprise the Quarterly Meeting.

merous evils to the pursuit of wealth, luxury, status, honor, or easy
living. A person seeking such ends, he pointed out, would tend to work
too hard—or drive his slaves or employees to greater toil than was consistent with "pure wisdom." Such a person would be likely to charge
excessive interest on his money or rent for his land. Those who had
to pay the interest or rent would be subject to the same kind of
pressure.

Woolman urged the wives of men engaged in whaling to shun costly
adornments, lest their husbands be tempted to take undue risks. On
several occasions he argued that when white men pursued excessive gain
in dealing with Indians, the result was bitterness and war. To live on a
material level beyond what was needed to do the will of God drew one
into a concatenation of harmful effects:

> One person . . . continuing to live contrary to true wisdom com-
> monly draws others into connection with him; and where these
> embrace the way this first hath chosen, their proceedings are like a
> wild vine which, springing from a single seed and growing strong,
> the branches extend, and . . . twist round all herbs and boughs . . .
> where they reach, and are so . . . locked in that without much la-
> bour . . . they are not disentangled.[11]

Another concern felt by Woolman was with the issues of war and
peace. During the French and Indian War, when the British sought the
full support of the American colonies, Woolman wrote the Philadelphia
Yearly Meeting Epistle of 1755, urging Friends not to waver in their
pacifism, but to "depend fully upon the Almighty arm." This counsel
was not based on the assumption that the faithful would escape injury;
he recognized the possibility of martyrdom. It rested, rather, on the
assurance that even suffering and death could not ultimately harm one
who lived "in pure obedience to God."

When taxes were levied to prosecute the war, Woolman learned that
respected Friends in both England and America paid readily. But he also
noted that the effect of this upon Quaker government officials was to
salve the consciences of those who took the easy way of cooperating in
the war effort. Not only did Woolman struggle with this issue; he stimulated other Quakers to do so, both individually and collectively. Of his
decision not to pay, he wrote: "To refuse the active payment of a tax
which our Society generally paid was exceedingly disagreeable; but to
do a thing contrary to my conscience appeared yet more dreadful."[12]

11. *A Plea for the Poor* (this volume), 258, 259.
12. *Journal* (this volume), 77.

A contribution to peace of a different sort was Woolman's hazardous journey of reconciliation to the Indians. Such face-to-face encounters were typical of his approach to social problems. In dealing with war, as with other issues, he was always realistic. He took account of the arguments on both sides, making his decisions with full awareness of the risks involved. He recognized, for example, the difficulty of being a pacifist when one's territory was invaded and when there was a real possibility of successful defense through war. Because he had examined such problems carefully, and because his pacifism was based on profound ethical and theological convictions, he did not waver.

In studying Woolman it is natural to wonder what effect his writings have had—on the spiritual and moral experience of mankind, on race relations, on economic life, and on issues of war and peace. His spiritual influence largely explains the continuous and wide dissemination of the *Journal* and the many references to him in Quaker literature throughout the past two centuries. A number of individuals both within and beyond Quaker circles have testified to the added spiritual and ethical dimensions derived from reading the *Journal*. Notable among these is Thomas Kelly, whose *Testament of Devotion* reflects the influence of Woolman and has brought many to a closer sense of communion with the divine.[13] A more recent instance is reported by George Willoughby, a crew member of the ship the *Golden Rule*, which sailed in 1958 to the Marshall Islands as a protest against testing atomic weapons. While he was jailed in Honolulu, a visiting Quaker lent him a copy of Woolman's *Journal*. He had read it before, but in his situation at the time, its message of comfort and challenge struck him with a new force and directness.

Theologically, Woolman stood in the main stream of the Christian evangelical tradition. His doctrine was orthodox. Yet his breadth and tolerance gave support to the liberal faction when the Quaker divisions came to a focus in 1827–28. The liberal leader Elias Hicks was deeply affected not only by Woolman's antislavery views (notably his refusal to use the products of slave labor) but also by his mystical tendencies, which transcended creedal formulations. In the 1830's Woolman's *Journal* was criticized by orthodox Quakers for giving insufficient attention to what for them were the essentials of their faith (symbolized by such phrases as "Christ crucified as the ground of . . . salvation" and "propitiatory sufferings and death").

In their "Introductory Remarks" to the 1840 edition of the *Journal*, James Cropper and his successor answered these objections. They as-

13. See Kelly, *A Testament of Devotion* (New York, 1941), 34, 42, 52, 117.

serted that Woolman held the same beliefs, but that the distinctive emphasis of Quakerism was upon "our duty as Christians, maintaining the truth as it is in Jesus not merely in its fundamental principles but in all its practical bearings." Further, they contended that

the character of John Woolman . . . was . . . an exemplification of the power of the grace of Christ to change the heart of man; and that his tender sympathy with the afflicted and oppressed, his unsparing self-denial and deep sense of the purity of the true Christian character, as well as his continued efforts to extend the mild and peaceable kingdom of the Redeemer, were genuine fruits of faith in that Saviour, "whose name," he says, "to me was precious." And such fruits must be considered as better evidence than mere words could give, however correctly framed, of the obedience of faith . . . which worketh by love to the purifying of the heart, producing righteousness and true holiness, to the praise of God and the good of our fellow creatures.[14]

John Greenleaf Whittier, in his introduction to the 1871 edition (a reprint of the one published in 1840), in phrases of surpassing beauty and clarity, gave essentially the same answer to these objections.[15] Woolman's purity of life and breadth of vision, unobscured by sectarianism, have commended him to thoughtful readers beyond the confines of Quakerism or of any particular age.

There can be no doubt of the very real effect of Woolman on the antislavery movement. From the beginning, sporadic Quaker voices had been raised against slavery. In 1696 and 1711 the leading American Yearly Meeting (Philadelphia) admonished its members not to be involved in the importation of slaves from abroad.[16] On several occasions between 1730 and 1743, the same Yearly Meeting took the further step of publicly disapproving "the buying of Negroes." The antislavery movement continued to grow; it needed only an inspired leader. At this juncture Woolman's witness bore increasing fruit.

The Philadelphia Yearly Meeting of 1754 sent a strong antislavery epistle, composed by Woolman, to all Quaker groups in Pennsylvania and New Jersey. Woolman's first essay, *Some Considerations on the Keeping*

14. *A Journal of . . . John Woolman*, edited by James Cropper (Warrington, England: Thomas Hurst, 1840), vi, viii–ix. The phrases quoted at the end of the preceding paragraph are from the same source (v, vi).

15. Whittier, Introduction to *The Journal of John Woolman*, 42–45.

16. The events noted in this and the following paragraphs are traced in detail by Thomas E. Drake, *Quakers and Slavery in America*, 20–24, 42, 50–84. See note 10 (above) for the meaning of "Yearly Meeting."

of Negroes, was published that year and distributed more widely than any previous antislavery work. Henceforth, his efforts in person were supplemented by the printed word. In fact, his essay was largely responsible for the progress against slavery made at the Philadelphia Yearly Meeting of 1755. With the Epistle of 1754 it was later sent to England where (according to Thomas E. Drake) it was one of the factors that influenced the London Yearly Meeting of June, 1758, to condemn the slave trade.[17] In turn, an epistle from the London gathering affected the Philadelphia Meeting in September of 1758. That crucial meeting, at Woolman's insistence, adopted a formal minute urging Friends to free their slaves, arranging for the visitation of slaveholders, and decreeing that anyone who bought or sold slaves was to be excluded from participating in the business affairs of the church.

The influence of Woolman's first essay was multiplied when Anthony Benezet * quoted from it in a widely disseminated pamphlet issued in 1759. The year 1762 saw the publication of *Considerations on Keeping Negroes: Part Second*—an even more forceful document. It made a strong impression in successive Monthly, Quarterly, and Yearly Meetings in Pennsylvania and New Jersey. Stimulated by these essays (more than by those of predecessors such as Ralph Sandiford and Benjamin Lay), the antislavery movement grew, and manumissions became common.[18] In 1776 (four years after Woolman's death) the Philadelphia Yearly Meeting took the decisive step of prohibiting the owning of slaves. Quaker meetings throughout the colonies, which had been making similar progress (often at Woolman's prodding), followed suit.

By the time the second essay was published, Benezet was engaged in the widespread distribution of antislavery writings. For example, he sent copies of both essays, the Epistle of 1754, and other literature to government officials in England.[19] Starting in 1774, the essays were generally printed along with the *Journal.* Because later references to Woolman seldom distinguished among them, it is difficult to assess the influence of particular works. Considerable evidence attests to the continued effect of his writings, however, not only in Britain and America but elsewhere.

Primarily among Quakers, Woolman's influence grew and extended to the antislavery movement as a whole. Thus Benjamin Lundy, a Quaker disciple of Woolman, was one of those who inspired William Lloyd

17. Drake, 60.
18. Cf. Sydney V. James, *A People Among Peoples,* 348.
19. George S. Brookes, *Friend Anthony Benezet* (Philadelphia, 1937), 382, 395-396.

Garrison to devote his life to the cause. In 1853, although most Quakers did not support the radical abolitionists, Governor Sterling Price of Missouri specifically blamed the *Journal* for contributing to what he saw as the evils of the movement in the United States, England, and the West Indies. Thomas Clarkson in England, Jean Pierre Brissot in France, and even Alexander II of Russia, in varying degrees, owed their efforts against slavery and serfdom to Woolman's writings.[20] This influence, of course, did not end with the abolition of slavery. It is significant that in 1969 and 1970, as a response to the mounting interest in black studies, Woolman's *Considerations* (on slavery) and the first (1774) edition of his *Journal* and *Works* have been reprinted.

Woolman's economic views, expressed chiefly in *A Plea for the Poor*, have inspired many individuals to live simply and without luxury. Some of his ideas—e.g., that each man has an inalienable right to land and other necessary material goods—were expressed by Thomas Paine and (a century later) by Henry George, but no direct influence is evident.

Although Woolman was no socialist, his sharp criticism of prevailing economic assumptions has given support to radical reformers. Whittier noted the relevance of his teaching to the "labor question" that was a source of agitation in 1870.[21] In 1897 the socialist Fabian Society in England distributed as one of its propaganda tracts a large excerpt from *A Plea for the Poor;* the next year it printed 10,000 more copies. While recognizing the spiritual basis of Woolman's concern, the editor of the tract, reading its message through Fabian glasses, asserted: "He perceived clearly that the question of slavery was but one phase of the labor question." [22]

A renewed interest in *A Plea for the Poor* and the *Journal* arose among Quakers in the early years of the twentieth century when their Social Order Committees dealt with economic issues. They frequently quoted Woolman's contention that the "seeds of war" take root in an unjust social order. A typical pamphlet in 1920 bore the title, *John Woolman: A Pioneer in Labor Reform*. Its author emphasized a sentence from *A Plea for the Poor:* "To labor for a perfect redemption from the spirit of oppression is the great business of the whole family of Christ Jesus in the

20. For Woolman's influence beyond Quaker circles, see Drake, 105–106, 155–156, 188–189; also Whittier, 31–32.

21. Whittier, 41.

22. John Woolman, *A Word of Remembrance and Caution to the Rich,* Fabian Tract no. 79 (London, 1898), 2. For an explanation of this title, see Addendum.

world." The pamphlet closes with the challenge: "Let such reformers come on now. The times are ripe for further work." [23] Twenty-eight years later, Reginald Reynolds observed: "In recent years the American saint has had something of a vogue among politically minded Quakers of the 'left.' . . . But," he continued, "there was nothing 'left' about his methods, whatever affinities may be discovered in the content of his teaching. He did not try to stir up feeling against those who had power or possessions, but endeavoured to arouse the feelings of those very people and to quicken their consciences. He did not stand apart and condemn society, but took upon himself the burden of its guilt." [24] Largely because Woolman cannot be confined within party lines, the message of *A Plea for the Poor* will be relevant for those in any age who strive for social justice.

As noted above, Woolman perceived the close relation between economic injustice and war. The influence of his peace testimony is less readily traced than his other concerns—partly because it played a lesser role in his experience. In opposing direct participation in war, he reflected the traditional Quaker witness. His distinctive contribution—a refusal to pay war taxes—for long elicited little response. During the past decade, however, as increasing numbers of Americans have wrestled with this issue, the journal of the War Resisters League has carried an article on Woolman as a tax refuser, and the Peace and Social Action Program of the New York Yearly Meeting has published excerpts from the *Journal* and *A Plea for the Poor* dealing with the seeds of war, including the section on taxes. The version of the *Journal* that follows contains (in Chapter 5) passages on this subject that have been omitted from other printed editions; their restoration makes it possible for the views of Woolman and his contemporaries to be more thoroughly understood.

Woolman's influence has extended far beyond his own generation and beyond the Society of Friends. The root causes to which he devoted his life are essentially timeless. Not typical of Americans or of men generally, his views and his character remain those of a minority. Yet certain of his attitudes have been absorbed into the cultural heritage of America. Some of these attitudes have been identified by Henry Seidel Canby in

23. Ann Sharpless, *John Woolman: A Pioneer in Labor Reform* (Philadelphia, 1920), 3, 22. The passage quoted from Woolman is the last sentence of the last chapter of his essay as it is usually printed. MS. W ends at this point, but MS. *Plea* contains three additional chapters. These are printed in the present edition.
24. Reginald Reynolds, *The Wisdom of John Woolman*, 62.

his *Classic Americans*. Affirming the *Journal* to be "of almost incalculable influence upon American culture," he singled out Woolman as exemplifying "the Quaker," whom he characterized as follows:

> He gave the widest diffusion to the optimistic humanitarianism that was the direct result of his theory of a beneficent Inner Light. Distrust of violence, a belief in the essential kinship of mankind, respect for the individual without reference to rank or estate, justice and mercy to prisoners and to slaves, dislike of pomp and circumstance, all these Quaker fundamentals have been American ideals also, held by many if by no means all, and strong enough to shape American history.[25]

Woolman is especially relevant to the late twentieth century. He is needed to point up the moral realities that hedonism and violence have tended to obscure. It must be recognized, however, that his works do present a few difficulties to modern readers. Now and then his language may sound quaint or archaic (thus calling for the glossary appended to this volume). Woolman's naïveté may bewilder those who are accustomed to a pose of sophistication. He developed a few idiosyncrasies that sometimes appear more like defects than virtues. Perhaps he was overscrupulous on occasion. Alerted to all this, the present-day reader can easily cut through such minor difficulties to perceive the lucid insights and the profound truths his writings convey.

What does Woolman say to us? As against those who are callous, he encourages the increasing numbers who are sensitive and compassionate. To anyone who is under pressure to turn his conscience over to a superior officer, an employer, or the nation, he brings a reminder of the responsibility owed to one's conscience, to society, and to God. To those who look only for immediate results, he reveals the ramifications and interconnections of our separate acts. For those caught up in sensory gratification, he offers an example—followed by many youth of the seventies —of simple living and concern for one's neighbors. To the pragmatist who adjusts his conduct as expediency dictates, he provides an instance of unswerving integrity. To nihilism and fanaticism he provides an antidote of balance and perspective. In an age of relativism, steeped in anxiety and beset by violence, he encourages those who believe in moral law, truth, love, harmony, and peace.

25. *Classic Americans* (New York, 1931), 4–5, 29. Canby, a professor at Yale University, was a well-known scholar and literary critic and one of the founders of the *Saturday Review of Literature*.

Woolman Chronology

(Journeys and visitations were with one or more companions, except as otherwise noted.)

1720   (October 19) Born at Rancocas, Burlington County, New Jersey.

ca. 1736–1739   Spiritual conflicts, culminating in firm religious vocation.

ca. 1741   Began living in Mount Holly, New Jersey, where he first attended to customers and kept books for a shopkeeper, and later became an apprentice tailor.

ca. 1742   Expressed his call to the public ministry by speaking in meetings.

1743   First religious journey, to points in New Jersey (2 weeks).

ca. 1746   Began working independently as a tailor, gradually developing also a retail trade.

              First southern journey, through Pennsylvania into Maryland, Virginia, and North Carolina (3 months, 1500 miles).

              Journey to points in New Jersey (22 days, 340 miles).

1747   First journey through Long Island and New England (4 months, 1650 miles).

1748   Journey into New Jersey and Maryland (6 weeks, 550 miles).

1749   Married Sarah Ellis, "a well inclined damsel."

1750   Death of his father, Samuel Woolman (1690–1750).

1750   Birth of his daughter Mary (1750–1797).

1751   Journey to upper part of New Jersey, probably alone (9
               days, 170 miles).

1753   Journey to points in Pennsylvania (2 weeks).

1754   Publication of *Some Considerations on the Keeping of
               Negroes.*

1754, 1755   Several weeks' visitation in Chesterfield, Shrewsbury,
and 1756   and Burlington areas of New Jersey (partly alone).
(winters)

1755   An epistle composed by Woolman and signed by four-
               teen Quakers, advocating the pacifist position, sent to
               "Friends on the Continent of America."

               An Epistle of Tender Love and Caution sent to Quakers
               throughout Pennsylvania by twenty-one Quakers, in-
               cluding Woolman, presenting the case for refusal to
               pay taxes levied principally to support war.

1756   Journey to points on Long Island (24 days, 316 miles).

               Gave up his too successful retail merchandising business,
               to rely on tailoring and orchard-tending as his chief
               gainful occupations.

ca. 1756   Began writing MS. A of the *Journal* (based upon MS. C
               and possibly other notes written earlier).

1757   Second southern journey—into Maryland, Virginia, and
               North Carolina (2 months, 1150 miles).

1758   Philadelphia Yearly Meeting adopts formal minute urg-
               ing Quakers to free their slaves, arranging for the
               visitation of slaveholders, and decreeing that any who
               buy or sell slaves are to be excluded from participating
               in the business affairs of the church.

1758 and   Visitation of many Quaker meetings, families, and slave-
1759   holders in Philadelphia and adjacent counties (partly
               alone).

1759	An epistle composed by Woolman sent by the Philadelphia Yearly Meeting to its constituent Quarterly and Monthly Meetings, urging Quakers to be true to their spiritual heritage.
1760	Second journey into New England, via New Jersey and Long Island (4 months).
1761–1763	Visitation of Quaker meetings, families, and slaveholders in and around Philadelphia and central New Jersey (partly alone).
1761	Decided to give up wearing dyed clothing.
1762	Publication of *Considerations on Keeping Negroes: Part Second.*
1763	Journey to Indians at Wyalusing, Pennsylvania (3 weeks).
1763–1764	Much of *A Plea for the Poor*—not published until 1793 —may have been composed around this time.
1764 and 1765 (winters)	Visitation of Quakers and others near Mount Holly and along the New Jersey coast.
1766	Journey on foot into Delaware and along the eastern shore of Maryland.
	Visitation of Quakers in upper New Jersey.
1767	Journey on foot, alone, into the western part of Maryland.
	Visitation of Quakers in Philadelphia and Mount Holly areas, partly alone.
1768	Journey on foot, alone, into Maryland (5 weeks).
	Probable date of publication of *Considerations on Pure Wisdom and Human Policy.*
1769–1770	Seriously considered making a religious visit to the West Indies; then decided to defer it, at least for the time being. Also considered, and deferred, a trip southwestward to Carolina.

1770	Severe attack of pleurisy.
	Publication of *Considerations on the True Harmony of Mankind.*
ca. 1770–1772	Revised and rewrote the *Journal,* preparing it for publication; also prepared his brother Abner's writings for the press.
1771	Marriage of Mary, John Woolman's daughter, to Samuel Comfort.
1772	Composed *Conversations on the True Harmony of Mankind,* not published until 1837.
	Composed, shortly before sailing for England, "An Epistle to the Quarterly and Monthly Meetings of Friends," a personal letter that was published later in the year, apparently in early autumn.
(May 1)	Embarked for England.
(June 8)	Arrived in London.
	At sea and in England, composed five short essays: "On Loving Our Neighbors as Ourselves," "On the Slave Trade," "On Trading in Superfluities," "On a Sailor's Life," and "On Silent Worship." These were published posthumously in 1773 under the title *Remarks on Sundry Subjects.*
(October 7)	Died of smallpox in York, England.

PART ONE

❖

The Journal of John Woolman

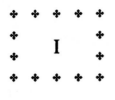

I

1720–1742

[MS. B, p. 1]

I HAVE OFTEN FELT a motion of love to leave some hints in writing of my experience of the goodness of God, and now, in the thirty-sixth year of my age, I begin this work. I was born in Northampton, in Burlington County in West Jersey, A.D. 1720, and before I was seven years old I began to be acquainted with the operations of divine love.[1] Through the care of my parents, I was taught to read near as soon as I was capable of it,[2] and as I went from school one Seventh Day, I remember, while my companions went to play by the way, I went forward out of sight; and sitting down, I read the twenty-second chapter of the Revelations: "He showed me a river of water, clear as crystal, proceeding out of the throne of God and the Lamb, etc." And in reading it my mind was drawn to seek after[3] that pure habitation which I then believed God had prepared for his servants. The place where I sat and the sweetness that attended my mind remains fresh in my memory.

This and the like gracious visitations had that effect upon me, that when boys used ill language it troubled me, and through the continued mercies of God I was preserved from it. The pious instructions of my parents[4] were often fresh in my mind when I happened amongst wicked children, and was of use to me. My parents, having a large family of children, used frequently on First Days after meeting to put us to read in the Holy Scriptures or some religious books, one after another, the rest sitting by without much conversation, which I have since often thought

1. MS. C adds: "and often found a care upon me how I should please him."
2. MS. C adds: "and it was even then of use to me."
3. MS. C adds: "and long for."
4. MS. C adds: "I esteem a great blessing. Their care over me was." Omitting these words caused the subject of the sentence to be changed from singular "care" to plural "parents." In copying, Woolman changed the first "was" to "were," but apparently overlooked the second "was."

23

was a good practice. From what I had read and heard, I believed there
had been in past ages people who walked in uprightness before God in a
degree exceeding any that I knew, or heard of, now living; and the apprehension of there being less steadiness and firmness amongst people in
this age than in past ages often troubled me while I was a child.

I had a dream about the ninth year of my age as follows: I saw the
moon rise near the west and run a regular course eastward, so swift that
in about a quarter of an hour she reached our meridian, when there de-
scended from her a small cloud on a direct line to the earth, which lighted
on a pleasant green about twenty yards from the door of my father's
house (in which I thought I stood) and was immediately turned into a
beautiful green tree. The moon appeared to run on with equal swiftness
and soon set in the east, at which time the sun arose at the place where
it commonly does in the summer, and shining with full radiance in a
serene air, it appeared as pleasant a morning as ever I saw.

All this time I stood still in the door in an awful[5] frame of mind, and
I observed that as heat increased by the rising sun, it wrought so powerfully on the little green tree that the leaves gradually withered; and before noon it appeared dry and dead. There then appeared a being, small
of size, full of strength and resolution, moving swift from the north,
southward, called a sun worm.[6]

Another thing remarkable in my childhood was that once, going to a
neighbour's house, I saw on the way a robin sitting on her nest; and as I
came near she went off, but having young ones, flew about and with
many cries expressed her concern for them. I stood and threw stones at
her, till one striking her, she fell down dead. At first I was pleased with
the exploit, but after a few minutes was seized with horror, as having in
a sportive way killed an innocent creature while she was careful for her
young. I beheld her lying dead and thought those young ones for which
she was so careful must now perish for want of their dam to nourish
them; and after some painful considerations on the subject, I climbed up
the tree, took all the young birds and killed them, supposing that better
than to leave them to pine away and die miserably, and believed in this
case that Scripture proverb was fulfilled, "The tender mercies of the

5. See glossary.
6. The phrase "called a sun worm" has been crossed out, probably by the original
editorial committee, but possibly by Woolman. MS. C adds: "Though I was a child,
this dream was instructive to me." In MS. A the account of this dream has been
crossed out by the original editorial committee. Although the committee neglected to
cross it out in MS B, it is omitted from the first printed edition.

wicked are cruel" [Prov. 12:10]. I then went on my errand, but for some hours could think of little else but the cruelties I had committed, and was much troubled.[7]

Thus he whose tender mercies are over all his works hath placed a principle in the human mind which incites to exercise goodness toward every living creature; and this being singly attended to, people become tender-hearted and sympathizing, but being frequently and totally rejected, the mind shuts itself up in a contrary disposition.

About the twelfth year of my age, my father being abroad, my mother reproved me for some misconduct, to which I made an undutiful reply; and the next First Day as I was with my father returning from meeting, he told me he understood I had behaved amiss to my mother and advised me to be more careful in future. I knew myself blameable, and in shame and confusion remained silent. Being thus awakened to a sense of my wickedness, I felt remorse in my mind, and getting home I retired and prayed to the Lord to forgive me, and do not remember that I ever after that spoke unhandsomely to either of my parents, however foolish in other things.[8]

Having attained the age of sixteen years, I began to love wanton company, and though I was preserved from profane language or scandalous conduct, still I perceived a plant in me which produced much wild grapes. Yet my merciful Father forsook me not utterly, but at times through his grace I was brought seriously to consider my ways, and the sight of my backsliding affected me with sorrow. But for want of rightly attending to the reproofs of instruction, vanity was added to vanity, and repentance to repentance; upon the whole my mind was more and more alienated from the Truth,[9] and I hastened toward destruction. While I meditate on the gulf toward which I travelled and reflect on my youthful disobedience, for these things I weep; mine eye runneth down with water.[10]

Advancing in age the number of my acquaintance increased, and thereby my way grew more difficult. Though I had heretofore found comfort in reading the Holy Scriptures and thinking on heavenly things, I was now estranged therefrom. I knew I was going from the flock of

7. MS. C reads: 'little else but my cruel conduct toward the poor old bird, which thoughts were very afflicting."

8. The original editorial committee inserted "some" between "in" and "other."

9. See glossary.

10. MS. C adds: "The kindness of the Most High is superior to all language. Blessed are they who serve him faithfully."

Christ and had no resolution to return; hence serious reflections were
uneasy to me and youthful vanities and diversions my greatest pleasure.[11]
Running in this road I found many like myself, and we associated in that
which is reverse to true friendship.

But in this swift race it pleased God to visit me with sickness, so that
I doubted of recovering. And then did darkness, horror, and amazement
with full force seize me, even when my pain and distress of body was
very great. I thought it would have been better for me never to have had
a being than to see the day which I now saw. I was filled with confusion,
and in great affliction both of mind and body I lay and bewailed myself.
I had not confidence to lift up my cries to God, whom I had thus offended, but in a deep sense of my great folly I was humbled before him,
and at length that Word which is as a fire and a hammer broke and dissolved my rebellious heart. And then my cries were put up in contrition,
and in the multitude of his mercies I found inward relief,[12] and felt a
close engagement that if he was pleased to restore my health, I might
walk humbly before him.

After my recovery this exercise remained with me a considerable
time;[13] but by degrees giving way to youthful vanities, they gained
strength, and getting with wanton young people I lost ground.[14] The
Lord had been very gracious and spoke peace to me in the time of my
distress, and I now most ungratefully turned again to folly, on which
account at times I felt sharp reproof but did not get low enough to cry
for help.[15] I was not so hardy as to commit things scandalous, but to
exceed in vanity [16] and promote mirth was my chief study. Still I retained
a love and esteem for pious people, and their company brought an awe
upon me.

My dear parents several times admonished me in the fear of the
Lord, and their admonition entered into my heart and had a good
effect for a season, but not getting deep enough to pray rightly, the
tempter when he came found entrance. I remember once, having spent a

11. MS. C reads: "uneasy to me, and I seemed happiest when I thought least about
true virtue."

12. MS. C adds: "My hope was renewed, and I found his favour to be more than
life."

13. MS. C adds: "and I had hopes of standing." See glossary for the meaning of
"exercise."

14. MS. C reads: "I let go my hold of God's covenant."

15. MS. C adds: "For I served folly to that degree that I had no resolution to
leave it."

16. For "vanity" MS. C substitutes "the art of foolish jesting."

part of the day in wantonness, as I went to bed at night there lay in a window near my bed a Bible, which I opened, and first cast my eye on the text, "We lie down in our shame, and our confusion covers us" [Jer. 3:25]. This I knew to be my case, and meeting with so unexpected a reproof, I was somewhat affected with it and went to bed under remorse of conscience, which I soon cast off again.

Thus time passed on; my heart was replenished with mirth and wantonness, while pleasing scenes of vanity were presented to my imagination [17] till I attained the age of eighteen years, near which time I felt the judgments of God in my soul like [18] a consuming fire, and looking over my past life the prospect was moving. I was often sad and longed to be delivered from those vanities; then again my heart was strongly inclined to them, and there was in me a sore conflict. At times I turned to folly, [19] and then again sorrow and confusion took hold of me. In a while I resolved totally to leave off some of my vanities, but there was a secret reserve in my heart of the more refined part of them, and I was not low enough to find true peace. [20] Thus for some months I had great trouble, there remaining in me an unsubjected will which rendered my labours fruitless, till at length through the merciful continuance of heavenly visitations I was made to bow down in spirit before the Lord.

I remember one evening [21] I had spent some time in reading a pious author, and walking out alone I humbly prayed to the Lord for his help, that I might be delivered from all those vanities which so ensnared me. [22] Thus being brought low, he helped me; [23] and as I learned to bear the cross I felt refreshment to come from his presence; but not keeping in

17. MS. C adds: "I most grievously abused the mercies of God, forsaking him who had helped me in my distress. With abasement of mind I mention it; still he cast me not off utterly."

18. MS. C reads: "I felt a fresh visitation and his judgments in my soul were like."

19. MS. C adds: "and though the Lord was near to me as a most righteous judge, yet I rebelled against him."

20. In MS. B the word preceding "I was not" was originally "that." The change was probably made by Woolman, but possibly by the original editorial committee.

In MS. C the latter part of the sentence reads: "some of my follies; yet as to the more refined part of them I said in my heart, 'In this thing the Lord pardon me,' which reserve spoiled all my religion. I was now destitute of all satisfactions, for I felt the wrath of God revealed in me against unrighteousness; nor had I attained to that resignation wherein true peace standeth."

21. MS. C reads: "And now I come to a winter evening which to me is memorable."

22. MS. C adds: "and afflicted my mind."

23. MS. C adds: "and through faith mountains were removed."

that strength which gave victory, I lost ground again, the sense of which greatly affected me; and I sought deserts and lonely places and there with tears did confess my sins to God and humbly craved help of him. And I may say with reverence he was near to me in my troubles, and in those times of humiliation opened my ear to discipline.

I was now led to look seriously at the means by which I was drawn from the pure Truth, and learned this: that if I would live in the life which the faithful servants of God lived in, I must not go into company as heretofore in my own will, but all the cravings of sense must be governed by a divine principle. In times of sorrow and abasement these instructions were sealed upon me, and I felt the power of Christ prevail over selfish desires, so that I was preserved in a good degree of steadiness.[24] And being young and believing at that time that a single life was best for me,[25] I was strengthened to keep from such company as had often been a snare to me.

I kept steady to meetings, spent First Days after noon chiefly in reading the Scriptures and other good books, and was early convinced in my mind that true religion consisted in an inward life, wherein the heart doth love and reverence God the Creator and learn to exercise true justice and goodness, not only toward all men but also toward the brute creatures; that as the mind was moved on an inward principle to love God as an invisible, incomprehensible being, on the same principle it was moved to love him in all his manifestations in the visible world; that as by his breath the flame of life was kindled in all animal and sensitive creatures, to say we love God as unseen and at the same time exercise cruelty toward the least creature moving by his life, or by life derived from him, was a contradiction in itself.

I found no narrowness respecting sects and opinions, but believed that sincere, upright-hearted people in every Society who truly loved God were accepted of him.

As I lived under the cross and simply followed the openings[26] of Truth, my mind from day to day was more enlightened; my former acquaintance was left to judge of me as they would, for I found it safest for me to live in private and keep these things sealed up in my own breast.

24. MS. C adds "all" before "selfish." MS. B originally had "all," which Woolman apparently intended to erase, but which is still legible. After "steadiness" MS. C adds the sentence: "I found it my true interest to serve God in faithfulness."
25. MS. C reads: "believing a single life best for me at present."
26. See glossary.

While I silently ponder on that change wrought in me, I find no language equal to it nor any means to convey to another a clear idea of it.[27] I looked upon the works of God in this visible creation and an awfulness covered me; my heart was tender and often contrite, and a universal love to my fellow creatures increased in me. This will be understood by such who have trodden in the same path. Some glances of real beauty may be seen in their faces who dwell in true meekness. There is a harmony in the sound of that voice to which divine love gives utterance, and some appearance of right order in their temper and conduct whose passions are fully regulated.[28] Yet all these do not fully show forth that inward life to such who have not felt it, but this white stone and new name is known rightly to such only who have it.[29]

Now though I had been thus strengthened to bear the cross, I still found myself in great danger, having many weaknesses attending me and strong temptations to wrestle with, in the feeling whereof I frequently withdrew into private places and often with tears besought the Lord to help me, whose gracious ear was open to my cry.

All this time I lived with my parents[30] and wrought on the plantation, and having had schooling pretty well for a planter, I used to improve in winter evenings and other leisure times. And being now in the twenty-first year of my age, a man in much business shopkeeping and baking asked me if I would hire with him to tend shop and keep books. I acquainted my father with the proposal, and after some deliberation it was agreed for me to go.[31]

At home I had lived retired, and now having a prospect of being much in the way of company, I felt frequent and fervent cries in my heart to God, the Father of Mercies, that he would preserve me from all taint and corruption, that in this more public employ[32] I might serve him, my

27. Between "change" and "wrought" are the words "which was," through part of which Woolman drew a line, apparently intending to cross them out.

28. Instead of "There is a" Woolman originally wrote, "Some tincture of true." He probably made the change, but it may have been made by the original editorial committee.

29. Cf. Revelation 2:17.

30. MS. C reads: "with my father."

31. Additional sentence crossed out by Woolman in MS. A: "I had for a considerable time found my mind less given to husbandry than heretofore, having often in view some other way of living." A similar statement appears in MS. C.

The employer may have been John Ogburn; he seems to have retired prior to 1747, in which year he sold Woolman some property which included a small shop.

32. Revised to "employment," apparently by the original editorial committee. MS. A reads "employ."

gracious Redeemer, in that humility and self-denial with which I had been in a small degree exercised in a very private life.

The man who employed me furnished a shop in Mount Holly, about five miles from my father's house and six from his own, and there I lived alone and tended his shop. Shortly after my settlement here I was visited by several young people, my former acquaintance, who knew not but vanities would be as agreeable to me now as ever; and at these times I cried to the Lord in secret for wisdom and strength, for I felt myself encompassed with difficulties and had fresh occasion to bewail the follies of time past in contracting a familiarity with a libertine people. And as I had now left my father's house outwardly,[33] I found my Heavenly Father to be merciful to me beyond what I can express.

By day I was much amongst people and had many trials to go through, but in evenings I was mostly alone and may with thankfulness acknowledge that in those times the spirit of supplication was often poured upon me, under which I was frequently exercised and felt my strength renewed.

In a few months after I came here, my master bought several Scotch menservants from on board a vessel and brought them to Mount Holly to sell, one of which was taken sick and died. The latter part of his sickness he, being delirious, used to curse and swear most sorrowfully, and after he was buried I was left to sleep alone the next night in the same chamber where he died. I perceived in me a timorousness. I knew, however, I had not injured the man but assisted in taking care of him according to my capacity, and was not free to ask anyone on that occasion to sleep with me. Nature was feeble, but every trial was a fresh incitement to give myself up wholly to the service of God, for I found no helper like him in times of trouble.

After a while my former acquaintance gave over expecting me as one of their company, and I began to be known to some whose conversation was helpful to me. And now, as I had experienced the love of God through Jesus Christ to redeem me from many pollutions and to be a succour to me through a sea of conflicts, with which no person was fully acquainted, and as my heart was often enlarged in this heavenly principle, I felt a tender compassion for the youth who remained entangled in snares like those which had entangled me. From one month to another this love and tenderness increased, and my mind was more strongly engaged for the good of my fellow creatures.[34]

33. See glossary.
34. MS. C reads: "and I found it too strong and forcible to be much longer confined to my own breast."

I went to meetings in an awful frame of mind and endeavoured to be inwardly acquainted with the language of the True Shepherd. And one day being under a strong exercise of spirit,[35] I stood up and said some words in a meeting, but not keeping close to the divine opening, I said more than was required of me; and being soon sensible of my error, I was afflicted in mind some weeks without any light or comfort, even to that degree that I could take satisfaction in nothing. I remembered God and was troubled, and in the depth of my distress he had pity upon me and sent the Comforter. I then felt forgiveness for my offense, and my mind became calm and quiet, being truly thankful to my gracious Redeemer for his mercies. And after this, feeling the spring of divine love opened and a concern to speak, I said a few words in a meeting, in which I found peace. This I believe was about six weeks from the first time, and as I was thus humbled and disciplined under the cross, my understanding became more strengthened to distinguish the language of the pure Spirit which inwardly moves upon the heart[36] and taught [me] to wait in silence sometimes many weeks together, until I felt that rise which prepares the creature to stand like a trumpet through which the Lord speaks to his flock.

From an inward purifying, and steadfast abiding under it, springs a lively operative desire for the good of others. All faithful people are not called to the public ministry, but whoever are, are called to minister of that which they have tasted and handled spiritually. The outward modes of worship are various, but wherever men are true ministers of Jesus Christ it is from the operation of his spirit upon their hearts, first purifying them and thus giving them a feeling sense of the conditions of others. This truth was early fixed in my mind, and I was taught to watch the pure opening and to take heed lest while I was standing to speak, my own will should get uppermost and cause me to utter words from worldly wisdom and depart from the channel of the true gospel ministry.

In the management of my outward affairs I may say with thankfulness I found Truth to be my support,[37] and I was respected in my master's family, who came to live in Mount Holly within two year after my going there.

35. MS. C reads "endeavoured to keep to my exercise, till one day, feeling the word of the Lord in my heart."

36. MS. C reads: "which moves upon the intellectual deep." MS. B originally read the same. It was apparently Woolman who made the change.

The word "me" was inserted after "taught," apparently by the original editorial committee.

37. MS. C reads: "I was preserved in a good degree of steadiness."

About the twenty-third year of my age,[38] I had many fresh and heavenly openings in respect to the care and providence of the Almighty over his creatures in general, and over man as the most noble amongst those which are visible. And being clearly convinced in my judgment that to place my whole trust in God was best for me,[39] I felt renewed engagements that in all things I might act on an inward principle of virtue and pursue worldly business no further than as Truth opened my way therein.

About the time called Christmas I observed many people from the country and dwellers in town who, resorting to the public houses, spent their time in drinking and vain sports, tending to corrupt one another, on which account I was much troubled. At one house in particular there was much disorder,[40] and I believed it was a duty laid on me to go and speak to the master of that house. I considered I was young and that several elderly Friends in town had opportunity to see these things, and though I would gladly have been excused, yet I could not feel my mind clear.

The exercise was heavy, and as I was reading what the Almighty said to Ezekiel respecting his duty as a watchman, the matter was set home more clearly; and then with prayer and tears I besought the Lord for his assistance, who in loving-kindness gave me a resigned heart. Then at a suitable opportunity I went to the public house, and seeing the man amongst a company, I went to him and told him I wanted to speak with him; so we went aside, and there in the fear and dread of the Almighty I expressed to him what rested on my mind, which he took kindly, and afterward showed more regard to me than before. In a few years after, he died middle-aged, and I often thought that had I neglected my duty in that case it would have given me great trouble,[41] and I was humbly thankful to my gracious Father, who had supported me herein.[42]

My employer, having a Negro woman, sold her and directed me to write a bill of sale, the man being waiting who bought her.[43] The thing was sudden, and though the thoughts of writing an instrument of slavery for one of my fellow creatures felt uneasy,[44] yet I remembered I was

38. MS. C adds: "my mind was often inward, meditating on God's providence."
39. MS. C adds: "and not to lean to my own understanding."
40. MS. C reads: "was uncommon reveling."
41. MS. C reads: "great remorse."
42. MS. C reads: "Father, that by his aid I had discharged what he laid upon me."
43. MS. C indicates that this incident occurred within a year after Woolman went to Mount Holly.
44. See "Easy" in glossary.

hired by the year, that it was my master who directed me to do it, and that it was an elderly man, a member of our Society,[45] who bought her; so through weakness I gave way and wrote it, but at the executing it, I was so afflicted in my mind that I said before my master and the Friend that I believed slavekeeping to be a practice inconsistent with the Christian religion. This in some degree abated my uneasiness, yet as often as I reflected seriously upon it I thought I should have been clearer if I had desired to be [46] excused from it as a thing against my conscience, for such it was. And some time after this a young man of our Society spake to me to write an instrument of slavery, he having lately taken a Negro into his house. I told him I was not easy to write it, for though many kept slaves in our Society, as in others,[47] I still believed the practice was not right, and desired to be excused from writing [it]. I spoke to him in good will, and he told me that keeping slaves was not altogether agreeable to his mind, but that the slave being a gift made to his wife, he had accepted of her.[48]

45. See glossary.

46. MS. C reads: "clearer if leaving all consequences I had craved to be."

47. MS. C adds: "and seemed easy in it." The last part of this sentence originally read: "from doing the writing." Woolman crossed off "doing the," and "it" has been added after "writing," probably by the original editorial committee. The present editor has supplied "it" to complete the sentence.

48. MS. C reads: "but that the slave was a gift to his wife from some of her friends, and so we parted."

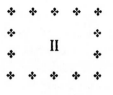

1743–1748

[MS. B, p. 34]

M Y ESTEEMED FRIEND Abraham Farrington * being about to make a visit to Friends on the eastern side of this province and having no companion, he proposed to me to go with him, and after a conference with some elderly Friends I agreed to go; so we set off 25th day, 9th month, 1743. Had an evening meeting at a tavern in Brunswick, a town in which none of our Society dwells. The room was full and the people quiet. Thence to Amboy and had an evening meeting in the courthouse, to which came many people, amongst whom were several members of Assembly, they being in town on the public affairs of the province. In both these meetings my ancient companion was enlarged in the love of the gospel. Thence we were at Woodbridge, Rahway, and Plainfield and had six or seven meetings in places where Friends meetings are not usually held, being made up chiefly of Presbyterians; and my beloved companion was frequently strengthened to hold forth the Word of Life amongst them. As for me, I was frequently silent through the meetings, and when I spake, it was with much care that I might speak only what Truth opened. My mind was often tender and I learned some profitable lessons. We were out about two weeks.

Near this time being on some outward business in which several families were concerned and which was attended with difficulties, some things relating thereto not being clearly stated nor rightly understood by all, there arose some heat in the minds of the parties, and one valuable Friend got off his watch. I had a great regard for him and felt a strong inclination after matters were settled to speak to him concerning his conduct in that case, but I being a youth and he far advanced in age and experience, my way appeared difficult. But after some days deliberation and inward seeking to the Lord for assistance, I was made subject, so that I expressed what lay upon me in a way which became my youth and his years; and though it was a hard task to me, it was well taken, and I believe was useful to us both.

Having now been several years with my employer, and he doing less at merchandise than heretofore, I was thoughtful of some other way of business,[1] perceiving merchandise to be attended with much cumber in the way of trading in these parts. My mind through the power of Truth was in a good degree weaned from the desire of outward greatness, and I was learning to be content with real conveniences that were not costly, so that a way of life free from much entanglements appeared best for me, though the income was small. I had several offers of business that appeared profitable, but did not see my way clear to accept of them, as believing the business proposed would be attended with more outward care and cumber than was required of me to engage in. I saw that a humble man with the blessing of the Lord[2] might live on a little, and that where the heart was set on greatness, success in business did not satisfy the craving, but that in common with an increase of wealth the desire of wealth increased. There was a care on my mind to so pass my time as to things outward[3] that nothing might hinder me from the most steady attention to the voice of the True Shepherd.

My[4] employer, though now a retailer of goods, was by trade a tailor and kept a servant man at that business; and[5] I began to think about learning the trade, expecting that if I should settle, I might by this trade and a little retailing of goods get a living in a plain way without the load of great business.[6] I mentioned it to my employer and we soon agreed on terms, and then when I had leisure from the affairs of merchandise, I worked with his man. I believed the hand of Providence pointed out this business for me and was taught to be content with it, though I felt at times a disposition that would have sought for something greater. But through the revelation of Jesus Christ, I had seen the happiness of humility, and there was an earnest desire in me to enter deep into it; and at times this desire arose to a degree of fervent supplication, wherein my

1. MS. C adds: "in case I should settle," which meant "marry."
2. MS. C reads: "the blessing of Providence."
3. Crossed out, probably by the original editorial committee: "as to things outward."
4. A bracket has been placed before "My," why or by whom is not clear. Woolman may have used it to indicate the beginning of a new paragraph.
5. MS. C adds: "my business in the shop growing slack."
6. MS. C adds: "and have opportunity for retirement and inward recollection."

soul was so environed with heavenly light and consolation that things were made easy to me which had been otherwise.

In the year [blank][7] my employer's wife died. She was a virtuous woman and generally beloved of her neighbours; and soon after this he left shopkeeping and we parted. I then wrought at my trade as a tailor, carefully attended meetings for worship and discipline, and found an enlargement of gospel love in my mind and therein a concern to visit Friends in some of the back settlements of Pennsylvania and Virginia. And being thoughtful about a companion, I expressed it to my beloved friend Isaac Andrews,* who then told me that he had drawings[8] there and also to go through Maryland, Virginia, and Carolina. After considerable time passed and several conferences with him, I felt easy to accompany him throughout, if way opened for it. I opened the case in our Monthly Meeting, and Friends expressing their unity therewith, we obtained certificates to travel as companions—his from Haddonfield and mine from Burlington.

We left our province on the 12th day, 3rd month, 1746, and had several meetings in the upper part of Chester County and near Lancaster, in some of which the love of Christ prevailed, uniting us together in his service. Then we crossed the River Susquehanna and had several meetings in a new settlement called the Red Lands, the oldest of which did not exceed ten years. It is the poorer sort of people that commonly begin to improve remote deserts. With a small stock[9] they have houses to build, lands to clear and fence, corn to raise, clothes to provide, and children to educate, that Friends who visit such may well sympathize with them in their hardships in the wilderness; and though the best entertainment such can give may seem coarse to some who are used to cities or old settled places, it becomes the disciples of Christ to be content with it.[10] Our hearts were sometimes enlarged in the love of our Heavenly Father amongst these people, and the sweet influence of his spirit supported us through some difficulties. To him be the praise.

We passed on to Monocacy, Fairfax, Hopewell, and Shenandoah and had meetings, some of which were comfortable and edifying. From

---

7. Woolman left a space here, apparently intending to fill in the year. MS. C reads: "A few years after." The exact year has not been determined.

8. See glossary.

9. See glossary.

10. Following the semicolon, MS. C reads: "But to express uneasiness at coarse entertainment, when in good will they give us their best, does not become the disciples of Christ."

Shenandoah we set off in the afternoon for the old settlements of Friends in Virginia, and the first night we, with our pilot, lodged in the woods, our horses feeding near us. But he being poorly provided with a horse, and we young and having good horses, [we] were free the next day to part with him and did so.[11] And in two days beside the first afternoon we reached to our friend John Cheagles in Virginia.[12] So we took the meetings in our way through Virginia, were in some degree baptized [13] into a feeling sense of the conditions of the people,[14] and our exercise in general was more painful in these old settlements than it had been amongst the back inhabitants. But through the goodness of our Heavenly Father, the well of living waters was at times opened, to our encouragement and the refreshment of the sincere-hearted.

We went on to Perquimans River in North Carolina, had several meetings which were large, and found some openness in those parts and a hopeful appearance amongst the young people. So we turned again to Virginia and attended most of the meetings which we had not been at before, labouring amongst Friends in the love of Jesus Christ as ability was given, and thence went to the mountains up James River to a new settlement and had several meetings amongst the people, some of whom had lately joined in membership with our Society. In our journeying to and fro, we found some honest-hearted Friends who appeared to be concerned for the cause of Truth among a backsliding people.

We crossed from Virginia over the river Potomac at Hoe's Ferry and made a general visit to the meetings of Friends on the western shore of Maryland [15] and were at their Quarterly Meeting.[16] We had some hard labour amongst them, endeavouring to discharge our duties honestly as way opened in the love of Truth. And thence taking sundry meetings in our way, we passed homeward, where through the favour of divine providence we reached the 16th day, 6th month, 1746; [17] and I may say that through the assistance of the Holy Spirit, which mortifies selfish

11. MS. C adds: "Once in a while we met with a house and inquired, and for our money took such refreshment as the people had."
12. The first part of this sentence has been shortened to read: "In two days we reached . . ." It is not clear who made the change.
13. See glossary.
14. MS. C adds: "the pure lamb-like nature of Jesus Christ being too much departed from by many of them."
15. MS. C adds: "being chiefly old settlements."
16. MS. C adds: "at Herring Creek."
17. MS. C adds: "having been out three months and four days and travelled by estimation fifteen hundred miles."

desires, my companion and I travelled in harmony and parted in the nearness of true brotherly love.

Two things were remarkable to me in this journey. First, in regard to my entertainment: When I eat, drank, and lodged free-cost with people who lived in ease on the hard labour of their slaves, I felt uneasy; and as my mind was inward to the Lord, I found, from place to place, this uneasiness return upon me at times through the whole visit. Where the masters bore a good share of the burden and lived frugal, so that their servants were well provided for and their labour moderate, I felt more easy; but where they lived in a costly way and laid heavy burdens on their slaves, my exercise was often great, and I frequently had conversation with them in private concerning it. Secondly, this trade of importing them from their native country [18] being much encouraged amongst them and the white people and their children so generally living without much labour was frequently the subject of my serious thoughts. And I saw in these southern provinces so many vices and corruptions increased by this trade and this way of life that it appeared to me as a dark gloominess hanging over the land; and though now many willingly run into it, yet in future the consequence will be grievous to posterity! I express it as it hath appeared to me, not at once nor twice, but as a matter fixed on my mind.

Soon after my return home I felt an increasing concern for Friends on our seacoast. And on the 8th day, 8th month, 1746, with the unity of Friends and in company with my beloved friend and neighbour Peter Andrews,* brother to my before-mentioned companion, we set forward and visited the meetings generally about Salem, Cape May, Great and Little Egg Harbor, and had meetings at Barnegat, Manahawkin, and Squan, and so to the Yearly Meeting at Shrewsbury.[19] Through the goodness of the Lord way was opened, and the strength of divine love was sometimes felt in our assemblies, to the comfort and help of those who were rightly concerned before him.[20] We were out 22 days and rode by computation 340 miles. At Shrewsbury Yearly Meeting we met

18. MS. C reads: "from Guinea."

19. Judging by the contexts in which "Squan" and "Manasquan" are mentioned in journals of Woolman's day, they either were different names for the same place or were located close to each other. Woolman mentions Squan again in Chapter 8. Only Manasquan appears on ancient and modern maps. In this sentence someone has inserted "Manes" before "Squan."

20. MS. C reads: "who fear and serve God."

with our dear friends Michael Lightfoot and Abraham Farrington,* who had good service in that Yearly Meeting.[21]

The winter following died my eldest sister, Elizabeth Woolman, Jr.,* of the smallpox, aged 31 years. She was from her youth of a thoughtful disposition and very compassionate to her acquaintance in their sickness or distress, being ready to help as far as she could. She was dutiful to her parents, one instance whereof follows: It happened that she and two of her sisters, being then near the estate of young women, had an inclination one First Day after meeting to go on a visit to some other young women at some distance off, whose company I believe would have done them no good. They expressed their desire to our parents, who were dissatisfied with the proposal and stopped them. The same day, as my sisters and I were together and they talking about their disappointment, Elizabeth expressed her contentment under it, signifying she believed it might be for their good.[22]

A few years after she attained to mature age, through the gracious visitations of God she was strengthened to live a self-denying, exemplary life,[23] giving herself much to reading and meditation. The following letter may show in some degree her disposition.

HADDONFIELD, 1st day, 11th month, 1743.
BELOVED BROTHER, JOHN WOOLMAN:
In that love which desires the welfare of all men I write unto thee. I received thine, dated 2nd day, 10th month last, with which I was comforted. My spirit is bowed with thankfulness that I should be remembered, who am unworthy, but the Lord is full of mercy and his goodness is extended to the meanest of his creation. Therefore, in his infinite love he hath pitied and spared and showed mercy, that I have not been cut off nor quite lost. But at times I am refreshed and comforted as with the glimpse of his presence, which is more to the immortal part than all which this world can afford. So with desires for thy preservation with my own, I remain thy affectionate sister, ELIZABETH WOOLMAN, JR.*

The fore part of her illness she was in great sadness and dejection of mind, of which she told one of her intimate friends and said, "When I was a young girl I was wanton and airy, but I thought I had thoroughly repented for it," and added, "I have of late had great satisfaction in

21. MS. A reads: "that great assembly."
22. MS. C adds: "adding this rhyme: Such as thy companions be, so will people think of thee."
23. MS. C reads: "strengthened to bear the cross, living a sober, self-denying life."

meetings." [24] Though she was thus disconsolate, still she retained a hope which was as an anchor to her; and some time after, the same friend came again to see her, to whom she mentioned her former expressions and said, "It is otherwise now, for the Lord hath rewarded me seven-fold, and I am unable to express the greatness of his love manifested to me.

Her disorder appearing dangerous [25] and our mother being sorrowful, she took notice of it and said, "Dear mother, weep not for me; I go to my God," and many times with an audible voice uttered praise to her Redeemer. A friend, coming some miles to see her the morning before she died, asked her how she did. She answered, "I have had a hard night, but shall not have another such, for I shall die, and it will be well with my soul," and accordingly died the next evening.

The following ejaculations were found amongst her writings, wrote I believe at four times:

1. Oh! that my head were as waters and mine eyes as a fountain of tears that I might weep day and night until acquainted with my God.

2. O Lord that I may enjoy thy presence, or else my time is lost and my life a snare to my soul.

3. O Lord that I may receive bread from thy table and that thy grace may abound in me.

4. O Lord that I may be acquainted with thy presence, that I may be seasoned with thy salt, that thy grace may abound in me.[26]

Of late I found drawings in my mind to visit Friends in New England, and having an opportunity of joining in company with my beloved friend Peter Andrews,* we, having obtained certificates from our Monthly Meeting, set forward 16th day, 3rd month, 1747, and reached the Yearly Meeting on [27] Long Island, at which were our friends Samuel Nottingham from England, John Griffith, Jane Hoskins,* and Elizabeth Hudson from Pennsylvania, and Jacob Andrews* from Chesterfield, several of whom were favoured in their public exercise; and through the goodness of the Lord we had some edifying meetings. After this Samuel,

24. Here the ink becomes darker and the lines narrower, but the writing remains almost certainly that of Woolman. The history of the manuscripts at this point (MS. B, pages 51–55, inclusive) cannot be reconstructed with certainty, but the fact that essentially the same material is in MSS. A and C means that it is a genuine part of Woolman's narrative.

25. MS. C adds: "that her life was despaired of."

26. A line is drawn under this sentence in MS. B, as though to indicate a shift of subject.

27. The word "on" has been written over "at," probably by Woolman.

John, and Jacob went toward Rhode Island, and my companion and I visited Friends on Long Island,[28] and through the mercies of God we were helped in the work.

Besides going to the settled meetings of Friends, we were at a general meeting at Setauket, chiefly made up of other Societies, and had a meeting at Oyster Bay in a dwelling house, at which were many people, at the first of which there was not much said by way of testimony, but was I believe a good meeting. At the latter, through the springing up of living waters, it was a day to be thankfully remembered. Having visited the island, we went over to the main, taking meetings in our way to Oblong, Nine Partners, and New Milford.

In these back settlements we met with several people who, through the immediate workings of the Spirit of Christ on their minds, were drawn from the vanities of the world to an inward acquaintance with him. They were educated in the way of the Presbyterians,[29] and a considerable number of youth,[30] members of that Society, were used to spend their time often together in merriment; and some of the principal young men of that company, being visited by the powerful workings of the Spirit of the Lord, and thereby led humbly to take up the cross of Christ, could no longer join in those vanities.[31] And as these stood steadfast to that inward convincement, they were made a blessing to some of their former companions, so that through the power of Truth, several were brought into a close exercise concerning the eternal well-being of their souls. These young people continued for a time to frequent their public worship, and besides that had meetings of their own, which meet-

28. MS. C reads: "and we continued to visit the meetings of Friends on this island."

Crossed out in MS. B, probably by the original editorial committee: "Samuel, John, and Jacob went towards Rhode Island and."

29. At this point in MS. C is an erasure of four lines (to the end of page 48) over which Woolman has written: "therefore I take this out. I think it is well to take this part of what I have wrote out of this book and." Perhaps MS. C originally contained more pages (later discarded by Woolman or lost), but it now ends here. At this point in MS. B (page 55) the darker, narrower ink lines end (see note 24, above). In the margin of this page Woolman has written "Second" and "1," meaning the first page of the second part. Apparently also by Woolman is the notation, "page 23," referring to MS. A. This and "Second" have been crossed out, by whom is uncertain. The first page of this second section continues where the last page of MS. C leaves off.

30. The word "and" has been crossed off before "a considerable," by whom is not certain; "the" has been inserted before "youth," probably by the original editorial committee.

31. Someone (probably not Woolman) substituted "Christ" for "the Lord" and substituted "his cross" for "the cross of Christ."

ings were a while allowed by their preacher, who sometimes met with
them. But in time their judgement in matters of religion disagreeing with
some of the articles of the Presbyterians, their meetings were disapproved
by that Society; and such who stood firm to their duty, as it was inwardly
manifested, had many difficulties to go through.

Their meetings were in a while dropped, some of them returning to
the Presbyterians, and others of them after a time joined to our Society.
I had conversation with some of the latter to my help and edification and
believe several of them are acquainted with the nature of that worship
which is performed in spirit and in Truth.

From hence accompanied by Amos Powell,* a Friend from Long
Island, we rode through Connecticut, chiefly inhabited by Presbyterians,
who were generally civil to us so far as I saw. And after three days riding
we came amongst Friends in the colony of Rhode Island. We visited
Friends in and about Newport and Dartmouth and generally in those
parts, and then to Boston and proceeded eastward as far as Dover, and
then returned to Newport and not far from thence met our Friend
Thomas Gawthrop, from England, who was on a visit to these parts.
From Newport we sailed to Nantucket, was there near a week, and from
thence came over to Dartmouth; and having finished our visit in these
parts, we crossed the sound from New London to Long Island, and
taking some meetings on the island, proceeded homeward, where we
reached 13th day, 7th month, 1747, having rode about 1500 miles and
sailed about 150.

In this journey I may say in general we were sometimes in much weakness and laboured under discouragements, and at other times, through the
renewed manifestations of divine love, we had seasons of refreshment
wherein the power of Truth prevailed.

We were taught by renewed experience to labour for an inward stillness, at no time to seek for words, but to live in the spirit of Truth and
utter that to the people which Truth opened in us. My beloved companion and I belonged both to one meeting, came forth in the ministry
near together, and were inwardly united in the work. He was about
thirteen years older than I, bore the heaviest burden, and was an instrument of the greatest use.

Finding a concern to visit Friends in the lower counties on Delaware
and on the eastern shore of Maryland, and having an opportunity to join
with my well-beloved and ancient friend John Sykes,* we obtained
certificates and set off the 7th day, 8th month, 1748, were at the meetings

of Friends in the lower counties, attended the Yearly Meeting at Little Creek, and made a visit to chief of the meetings on the eastern shore, and so home by the way of Nottingham; were abroad about six weeks and rode by computation about 550 miles.

Our exercise at times was heavy, but through the goodness of the Lord we were often refreshed, and I may say by experience, "He is a stronghold in the day of trouble" [Nahum 1:7]. Though our Society in these parts appeared to me to be in a declining condition, yet I believe the Lord hath a people amongst them, who labour to serve him uprightly, but have many difficulties to encounter.

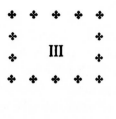

III

1749–1756

[MS. B, p. 61]

[A BOUT THIS TIME believing it good for me to settle, and thinking seriously about a companion, my heart was turned to the Lord with
desires that he would give me wisdom to proceed therein agreeable to his
will; and he was pleased to give me a well-inclined damsel, Sarah Ellis,* to
whom I was married the 18th day, 8th month, 1749.]¹

In the fall of the year 1750 died my father Samuel Woolman * with a
fever, aged about sixty years. In his lifetime he manifested much care for
us his children, that in our youth we might learn to fear the Lord, often
endeavouring to imprint in our minds the true principles of virtue, and
particularly to cherish in us a spirit of tenderness, not only toward poor
people, but also towards all creatures of which we had the command.

After my return from Carolina I made some observations on keeping
slaves, which I had some time before showed him, and he perused the
manuscript, proposed a few alterations, and appeared well satisfied that
I found a concern on that account.² And in his last sickness as I was
watching with him one night, he being so far spent that there was no
expectation of his recovery, but had the perfect use of his understanding,

1. This paragraph about his marriage appears, in Woolman's handwriting, in a
blank space between Chapters 2 and 3 of MS. A. Because of this location and because
the width of line and color of ink differ slightly from that used in most of MS. A, this
paragraph seems to be a later addition. Woolman did not include it in MS. B, but the
original editorial committee copied it in (page 60), with the result that it has been included in the various printed editions.

In the margin of page 61 is written in pencil, not by Woolman: "Chaps. III and
IV."

2. After "Carolina," the original editorial committee added: "in 1746." The essay
mentioned here and a few pages later, entitled *Some Considerations on the Keeping of
Negroes,* is contained in this volume.

he asked me concerning the manuscript, whether I expected soon to offer it to the Overseers of the Press, and after some conversation thereon said, "I have all along been deeply affected with the oppression of the poor Negroes, and now at last my concern for them is as great as ever."

By his direction I had wrote his will in a time of health, and that night he desired me to read it to him, which I did, and he said it was agreeable to his mind. He then made mention of his end, which he believed was now near, and signified that though he was sensible of many imperfections in the course of his life, yet his experience of the power of Truth and of the love and goodness of God from time to time, even till now, was such that he had no doubt but that in leaving this life he should enter into one more happy.

The next day his sister Elizabeth came to see him and told him of the decease of their sister Anne, who died a few days before. He then said, "I reckon sister Anne was free to leave this world." Elizabeth said she was. He then said, "I also am free to leave it," and being in great weakness of body said, "I hope I shall shortly go to rest." He continued in a weighty frame of mind and was sensible till near the last.[3]

2nd day, 9th month, 1751. Feeling drawings in my mind to visit Friends at the Great Meadows, in the upper part of West Jersey, with the unity of our Monthly Meeting I went there and had some searching laborious exercise amongst Friends in those parts, and found inward peace therein.[4]

In the 9th month, 1753, in company with my well-esteemed friend John Sykes * and with the unity of Friends, we travelled about two weeks visiting Friends in Bucks County. We laboured in the love of the gospel according to the measure received, and through the mercies of him who is strength to the poor who trust in him, we found satisfaction in our visit. And in the next winter, way opening to visit Friends' families within the compass of our Monthly Meeting, partly by the labours of two friends from Pennsylvania, I joined some in it, having had a desire some time that it might go forward amongst us.

About this time a person at some distance lying sick, his brother came to me to write his will. I knew he had slaves, and asking his brother, was

3. See glossary for the meaning of "weighty."
4. Added by Woolman in MS. A, and then crossed out, probably by the original editorial committee: "Was out nine days and rode about 170 miles." Originally "so-called" appeared after "Great Meadows" and "this province" appeared instead of "West Jersey." The changes were probably made by Woolman.

told he intended to leave them slaves [5] to his children. As writing is a
profitable employ, as offending sober people is disagreeable to my inclination, I was straitened in my mind; but as I looked to the Lord, he
inclined my heart to his testimony, and I told the man that I believed the
practice of continuing slavery to this people was not right and had a
scruple in mind against doing writings of that kind: that though many in
our Society kept them as slaves, still I was not easy to be concerned in it
and desired to be excused from going to write the will. I spake to him in
the fear of the Lord, and he made no reply to what I said, but went away;
he also had some concerns in the practice, and I thought he was dis-
pleased with me.

In this case I had a fresh confirmation that acting contrary to present
outward interest from a motive of divine love and in regard to truth and
righteousness, and thereby incurring the resentments of people, opens
the way to a treasure better than silver and to a friendship exceeding the
friendship of men.[6]

On the 7th day, 2nd month, 1754, at night, I dreamed that I was walking in an orchard, it appeared to be about the middle of the afternoon;
when on a sudden I saw two lights in the east resembling two suns, but
of a dull and gloomy aspect. The one appeared about the height of the
sun at three hours high, and the other more northward and one-third
lower. In a few minutes the air in the east appeared to be mingled with
fire, and like a terrible storm coming westward the streams of fire reached
the orchard where I stood, but I felt no harm. I then found one of my
acquaintance standing near me, who was greatly distressed in mind at
this unusual appearance. My mind felt calm, and I said to my friend, "We
must all once die, and if it please the Lord that our death be in this way,
it is good for us to be resigned." Then I walked to a house hard by, and
going upstairs, saw people with sad and troubled aspects, amongst whom
I passed into another room where the floor was only some loose boards.
There I sat down alone by a window, and looking out I saw in the south
three great red streams standing at equal distance from each other, the
bottom of which appeared to stand on the earth and the top to reach
above the region of the clouds. Across those three streams went less ones,

5. Woolman originally wrote: "them as slaves." Then he erased "as," but the original editorial committee restored it.

6. The following account of a dream has been crossed out in MSS. A and B,
probably by the original editorial committee, and was omitted from the earliest editions. In MS. B are the words, apparently written by the editorial committee, "Leave
this dream out in printing."

and from each end of such small stream others extended in regular lines to the earth, all red and appeared to extend through the whole southern firmament.[7] There then appeared on a green plain a great multitude of men in a military posture, some of whom I knew. They came near the house, and passing on westward some of them, looking up at me, expressed themselves in a scoffing, taunting way, to which I made no reply; soon after, an old captain of the militia came to me, and I was told these men were assembled to improve in the discipline of war.

The manuscript before-mentioned having lain by me several years, the publication of it rested weightily upon me, and this year I offered it to the Overseers of the Press, who, having examined and made some small alterations in it, ordered a number of copies thereof to be published by the Yearly Meeting stock and dispersed amongst Friends.

In the year 1754 I found my mind drawn to join in a visit to Friends' families belonging to Chesterfield Monthly Meeting, and having the approbation of our own, I went to their Monthly Meeting in order to confer with Friends and see if way opened for it. I had conference with some of their members, the proposal having been opened before in their meeting, and one Friend agreed to join with me as a companion for a beginning; but when meeting was ended, I felt great distress of mind and doubted what way to take or whether to go home and wait for greater clearness. I kept my distress secret, and going with a Friend to his house, my desires were to the great Shepherd for his heavenly instruction; and in the morning I felt easy to proceed on the visit, being very low in my mind. And as mine eye was turned to the Lord, waiting in families in deep reverence before him, he was pleased graciously to afford help, so that we had many comfortable [8] opportunities and it appeared as a fresh visitation to some young people. I spent several weeks this winter in the service, part of which time was employed near home. And again in the following winter I was several weeks in the same service, some part of the time at Shrewsbury in company with my beloved friend John Sykes,* and have cause humbly to acknowledge that through the goodness of the Lord our hearts were at times enlarged in his love, and strength was given to go through the trials which in the course of our visit attended us.

From a disagreement between the powers of England and France, it was now a time of trouble on this continent, and an epistle to Friends

7. In MS. A Woolman drew a diagram here but requested that it not be printed. It is omitted from MS. B.

8. See glossary.

went forth from our General Spring Meeting, which I thought good to give a place in this Journal.[9]

An Epistle from our General Spring Meeting, etc., 1755.
To Friends on the Continent of America

[DEAR FRIENDS,

In an humble sense of divine goodness and the gracious continuation of God's love to his people, we tenderly salute you, and are at this time therein engaged in mind that all of us who profess the Truth as held forth and published by our worthy predecessors in this latter age of the world may keep near to that Life which is the light of men, and be strengthened to hold fast the profession of our faith without wavering—that our trust may not be in man, but in the Lord alone, who ruleth in the army of heaven and in the kingdoms of men, before whom the earth is "as the dust of the balance and her inhabitants as grasshoppers" [Is. 40:15 and 22].

We (being convinced that the gracious design of the Almighty in sending his son into the world was to repair the breach made by disobedience, to finish sin and transgression that his kingdom might come and his will be done on earth as it is in heaven) have found it to be our duty to cease from those national contests productive of misery and bloodshed, and submit our cause to him, the Most High, whose tender love to his children exceeds the most warm affections of natural parents, and who hath promised to his seed throughout the earth, as to one individual, "I will never leave thee nor forsake thee" [Heb. 13:5].

And as we, through the gracious dealings of the Lord our God, have had experience of that work which is carried on "not by earthly might nor power, but by my Spirit, saith the Lord of Hosts" [Zech. 4:6]. By which operation that spiritual kingdom is set up which is to subdue and break in pieces all kingdoms that oppose it, and shall

9. This introductory statement by Woolman appears in MS. B—and in MS. A in slightly different form. It seems clearly to have been substituted by him for the following statement written by Woolman and crossed out, apparently by him: "It came upon me to write an epistle to Friends, the which I took to our General Spring Meeting and proposed to some elderly Friends to have it inspected and signed by a number of brethren in behalf of the meeting, which, with some amendments, was agreed to and is as follows."

This original introductory statement appears in MSS. A and B. The epistle itself appears only in MS. A. In MS. B Woolman originally wrote, "Let it be printed." This was then erased, but he wrote "Here add the epistle" in its stead. It is included in the first printed edition.

The "time of trouble" refers to what is generally known as the French and Indian War, in which the British were pitted against the French and, to some extent, the Indians. This corresponded roughly to the Seven Years War in Europe.

stand for ever. In a deep sense thereof and of the safety, stability, and peace there is in it, we are desirous that all who profess the Truth may be inwardly acquainted with it and thereby be qualified to conduct [ourselves] in all parts of our life as becomes our peaceable profession. And we trust [that] as there is a faithful continuance to depend wholly upon the Almighty arm from one generation to another, the peaceable kingdom will gradually be extended "from sea to sea and from the river to the ends of the earth," to the completion of those prophecies already begun, that "nation shall not lift up sword against nation nor learn war any more." Is. 2:4; Zech. 9:10.[10]

And dearly beloved Friends, seeing we have these promises and believe that God is beginning to fulfil them, let us constantly endeavour to have our minds sufficiently disentangled from the surfeiting cares of this life and redeemed from the love of this world that no earthly possessions nor enjoyments may bias our judgments or turn us from that resignation and entire trust in God to which his blessing is most surely annexed; then may we say, "Our Redeemer is mighty; he will plead our cause for us." Jer. 50:34.

And if for the further promoting his most gracious purposes in the earth, he should give us to taste of that bitter cup which his faithful ones have often partook of—oh, that we may be rightly prepared to receive it!

And now dear Friends, with respect to the commotions and stirrings of the powers of the earth at this time near us, we are desirous that none of us may be moved thereat, but repose ourselves in the munition of that rock that all these shakings shall not move, even in the knowledge and feeling of the eternal power of God keeping us subjectly given up to his heavenly will, and feel it daily to mortify that which remains in any of us which is of this world. For the worldly part in any is the changeable part, and that is up and down, full and empty, joyful and sorrowful, as things go well or ill in this world. For as the Truth is but one and many are made partakers of its spirit, so the world is but one and many are made partakers of the spirit of it; and so many as do partake of it, so many will be straitened and perplexed with it. But they who are single to the Truth, waiting daily to feel the life and virtue of it in their hearts, these shall rejoice in the midst of adversity and have to experience with the prophet that, "though the fig tree shall not blossom neither shall fruit be in the vines, the labour of the olive shall fail and the fields shall yield no meat, the flock shall be cut off from the fold and there shall be no herd in the stall, yet will they rejoice in the Lord and joy in the God of their salvation." Hab. 3:18.

If contrary to this we profess the Truth, and not living under the

10. Woolman inserted these Scripture references. The Zechariah quotation appears first in the sentence.

power and influence of it are producing fruits disagreeable to the purity thereof and trust to the strength of man to support ourselves therein, our confidence will be vain. For he who removed the hedge from his vineyard and gave it to be trodden under foot by reason of the wild grapes it produced remains unchangeable [Is. 5:3–7]. And if for the chastisement of wickedness and the further promoting his own glory, he doth arise even to shake terribly the earth, who then may oppose Him and prosper.

We remain, in the love of the gospel, your friends and brethren.]
SIGNED BY FOURTEEN FRIENDS [11]

Scrupling to do writings relative to keeping slaves having been a means of sundry small trials to me, in which I have so evidently felt my own will set aside that I think it good to mention a few of them. Tradesmen and retailers of goods, who depend on their business for a living, are naturally inclined to keep the good will of their customers; nor is it a pleasant thing for young men to be under a necessity to question the judgment or honesty of elderly men, and more especially of such who have a fair reputation.[12] Deep-rooted customs, though wrong, are not easily altered, but it is the duty of everyone to be firm in that which they certainly know is right for them. A charitable, benevolent man, well acquainted with a Negro, may, I believe, under some certain [13] circumstances keep him in his family as a servant on no other motives than the Negro's good; but man, as man, knows not what shall be after him, nor hath he any assurance that his children will attain to that perfection in wisdom and goodness necessary in every absolute governor. Hence it is clear to me that I ought not to be the scribe where wills are drawn in which some children are made absolute masters over others during life.

About this time an ancient man of good esteem in the neighbourhood came to my house to get his will wrote. He had young Negroes, and I

11. Woolman wrote this phrase in the margin of MS. B and at the bottom of the epistle in MS. A. The signatures in the original epistle were arranged as follows:

Joseph Tomlinson	Jacob Howell	J. W. Evans
Samuel Abbott	James Bartram	Mordecai Yarnall
	Joseph White*	Daniel Stanton*
	John Scarbrough*	John Churchman*
	John Woolman	W. Morris
	Josiah Foster	
	Isaac Andrews*	

12. Woolman originally had "good character" but changed it to "fair reputation" —a notable difference!

13. "Certain" has been crossed out, apparently by the original editorial committee.

asking him privately how he purposed to dispose of them, he told me. I
then said, "I cannot write thy will without breaking my own peace," and
respectfully gave him my reasons for it. He signified that he had a choice
that I should have wrote it, but as I could not consistent with my conscience, he did not desire it, and so he got it wrote by some other person.
And a few years after,[14] there being great alterations in his family, he
came again to get me to write his will. His Negroes were yet young, and
his son, to whom he intended to give them, was since he first spoke to
me, from a libertine become a sober young man; and he supposed that I
would have been free on that account to write it. We had much friendly
talk on the subject and then deferred it, and a few days after, he came
again and directed their freedom, and so I wrote his will.

Near the time the last-mentioned friend first spoke to me, a neighbour
received a bad bruise in his body and sent for me to bleed him, which
being done he desired me to write his will. I took notes, and amongst
other things he told me to which of his children he gave his young Negro.
I considered the pain and distress he was in and knew not how it would
end, so I wrote his will, save only that part concerning his slave, and
carrying it to his bedside read it to him and then told him in a friendly
way that I could not write any instruments by which my fellow creatures
were made slaves, without bringing trouble on my own mind. I let him
know that I charged nothing for what I had done and desired to be excused from doing the other part in the way he proposed. Then we had
a serious conference on the subject, and at length, he agreeing to set her
free, I finished his will.[15]

Having found drawings in my mind to visit Friends on Long Island,
and having got a certificate from our Monthly Meeting, I set off 12th
day, 5th month, 1756. When I reached the island I lodged the first night
at the house of my dear friend Richard Hallett.* The next day being the
first of the week, I was at their meeting,[16] in which we had experience of
the renewed manifestations of the love of Jesus Christ, to the comfort of
the honest-hearted. I went that night to Flushing, and the next day in
company with my beloved friend Matthew Franklin* we crossed the
ferry at White Stone, were at three meetings on that side the water, and

14. Crossed out at this point, apparently by Woolman: "(passing over time to
finish the relation)."
15. The next seven paragraphs, closing with "to his heavenly will," are printed
here in the order in which they appear in MS. B, which is different from the order
in MS. A.
16. Added by the original editorial committee: "at Newton."

then came on to the island, where I spent the remainder of the week in
visiting meetings. The Lord I believe hath a people in those parts who
are honestly concerned to serve him, but many I fear are too much
clogged with the things of this life and do not come forward bearing the
cross in such faithfulness as the Almighty calls for.[17]

My mind was deeply engaged in this visit, both in public and private;
and at several places where I was, on observing that they had slaves, I
found myself under a necessity in a friendly way to labour with them on
that subject, expressing as way opened the inconsistency of that practice
with the purity of the Christian religion and the ill effects of it manifested amongst us.

The latter end of the week their Yearly Meeting began, at which were
our Friends John Scarborough,* Jane Hoskins,* and Susanna Brown from
Pennsylvania. The public meetings were large and measurably favoured
with divine goodness.

The exercise of my mind at this meeting was chiefly on account of
those who were considered as the foremost rank in the Society, and in a
meeting of ministers and elders, way opened that I expressed in some
measure what lay upon me; and at a time when Friends were met for
transacting public business, we sitting a while silent,[18] I felt a weight on
my mind and stood up; and through the gracious regard of our Heavenly
Father,[19] strength was given fully to clear my mind of a burden which
for some days had been increasing upon me.

Through the humbling dispensations of divine providence men are
sometimes fitted for his service. The messages of the prophet Jeremiah
were so disagreeable to the people and so reverse to the spirit they lived
in that he became the object of their reproach and in the weakness of
nature thought to desist from his prophetic office, but saith he: "His
word was in my heart as a burning fire shut up in my bones, and I was
weary with forebearing and could not stay" [Jer. 20:9]. I saw at this
time that if I was honest to declare that which Truth opened in me, I
could not please all men, and laboured to be content in the way of my
duty, however disagreeable to my own inclination. After this I went

17. In MS. A Woolman replaced "the Almighty" with "he." The same change is
made in MS. B, apparently by the original editorial committee.
18. Because of blotting and revision, the words "we sitting" are not clear in MS.
B. Woolman may have intended it to read "we sat" or simply (but awkwardly) "sat."
19. "Regard" is written above "condescension," which has been crossed out. The
change seems clearly to have been made by Woolman.

homeward, taking Woodbridge and Plainfield in my way, in both which meetings the pure influence of divine love was manifested, in a humbling sense whereof I went home, having been out about 24 days and rode about 316 miles.

While I was out on this journey my heart was much affected with a sense of the state of the churches in our southern provinces, and believing the Lord was calling me to some further labour amongst them, I was bowed in reverence before him, with fervent desires that I might find strength to resign myself up to his heavenly will.

Until the year 1756 I continued to retail goods, besides following my trade as a tailor, about which time I grew uneasy on account of my business growing too cumbersome. I began with selling trimmings for garments and from thence proceeded to sell clothes and linens, and at length having got a considerable shop of goods, my trade increased every year and the road to large business appeared open; but I felt a stop in my mind.

Through the mercies of the Almighty I had in a good degree learned to be content with a plain way of living.[20] I had but a small family, that on serious consideration I believed Truth did not require me to engage in much cumbrous affairs.[21] It had been my general practice to buy and sell things really useful. Things that served chiefly to please the vain mind in people I was not easy to trade in, seldom did it, and whenever I did I found it weaken me as a Christian.

The increase of business became my burden, for though my natural inclination was toward merchandise, yet I believed Truth required me to live more free from outward cumbers, and there was now a strife in my mind between the two; and in this exercise my prayers were put up to the Lord, who graciously heard me and gave me a heart resigned to his holy will. Then I lessened my outward business, and as I had opportunity told my customers of my intentions that they might consider what shop to turn to, and so[22] in a while wholly laid down merchandise, following

20. In MS. B the following was erased by Woolman at this point: "my outward affairs had been prosperous and."

21. In this sentence two changes seem clearly to have been made by Woolman: "reflections" has been changed to "consideration," and "that" has been crossed out before "Truth." Two other changes seem clearly to have been made by the original editorial committee: after "family," "that" has been changed to "and," and "cumbrous" has been changed to "cumbering."

22. The word "so" has been crossed out, whether by Woolman or not is uncertain.

my trade as a tailor, myself only, having no apprentice. I also had a
nursery of apple trees, in which I employed some of my time—hoeing,
grafting, trimming, and inoculating.[23]

In merchandise it is the custom where I lived to sell chiefly on credit,
and poor people often get in debt, and when payment is expected, not
having wherewith to pay, their creditors often sue for it at law. Having
often observed occurrences of this kind, I found it good for me to advise
poor people to take such goods as were most useful and not costly.[24]

In the time of trading, I had an opportunity of seeing that too liberal
a use of spirituous liquors and the custom of wearing too costly apparel
lead some people into great inconveniences, and these two things appear
to be often connected one with the other. For by not attending to that
use of things which is consistent with universal righteousness,[25] there is an
increase of labour which extends beyond what our Heavenly Father
intends for us. And by great labour, and often by much sweating in the
heat, there is even amongst such who are not drunkards a craving of some
liquors to revive the spirits: that partly by the wanton, luxurious drinking
of some, and partly by the drinkings of others led to it through immoderate labour, very great quantities of rum are every year expended in our
colonies, the greater part of which we should have no need did we
steadily attend to pure wisdom.

Where men take pleasure in feeling their minds elevated with strong
drink and so indulge their appetite as to disorder their understandings,
neglect their duty as members in a family or civil society, and cast off all
pretense to religion, their case is much to be pitied. And where such
whose lives are for the most part regular, and whose examples have a
strong influence on the minds of others, adhere to some customs which
strongly draw toward the use of more strong liquor than pure wisdom
directs to the use of, this also, as it hinders the spreading of the spirit of
meekness and strengthens the hands of the more excessive drinkers, is a
case to be lamented.

As the least degree of luxury hath some connection with evil, for those
who profess to be disciples of Christ and are looked upon as leaders of
the people, to have that mind in them which was also in him, and so

23. Woolman substituted "some of my" for his original words, "a good deal of."
24. In this sentence and the preceding one, several minor revisions were made,
probably by Woolman, which do not significantly affect the meaning. It may have
been the original editorial committee, however, who changed "sues" to "sue."
25. Woolman may have written "divine" before changing it to "universal."

stand separate from every wrong way, is a means of help to the weaker. As I have sometimes been much spent in the heat and taken spirits to revive me, I have found by experience that in such circumstance the mind is not so calm nor so fitly disposed for divine meditation as when all such extremes are avoided, and have felt an increasing care to attend to that Holy Spirit which sets right bounds to our desires and leads those who faithfully follow it to apply all the gifts of divine providence to the purposes for which they were intended. Did such who have the care of great estates attend with singleness of heart to this Heavenly Instructor, which so opens and enlarges the mind that men love their neighbours as themselves, they would have wisdom given them to manage without finding occasion to employ some people in the luxuries of life or to make it necessary for others to labour too hard. But for want[26] of steadily regarding this principle of divine love, a selfish spirit takes place in the minds of people, which is attended with darkness and manifold confusions in the world.

In the course of my trading being somewhat troubled at the various law suits about collecting money which I saw going forward, on applying to a constable he gave me a list of his proceeding for one year as follows —to wit, served 267 warrants, 103 summonses, and 79 executions. As to writs served by the sheriff, I got no account of them.

I once had a warrant for an idle man who I believed was about to run away, which was the only time I applied to the law to recover money.[27]

Though trading in things useful is an honest employ, yet through the great number of superfluities which are bought and sold and through the corruption of the times, they who apply to merchandise for a living have great need to be well experienced in that precept which the prophet Jeremiah laid down for his scribe: "Seekest thou great things for thyself? Seek them not" [Jer. 45:5].

This winter, 1756, I was several times out with Friends in visiting families, and through the goodness of the Lord we had oftentimes experience of his heart-tendering presence amongst us.[28]

26. A bracket before "want" was apparently placed there by the printer to indicate the beginning of the next printed page.

27. This sentence and the preceding paragraph were crossed out by the original editorial committee.

28. Written in margin: "Copy bound book 43." The letter that follows appears in MS. A, page 43.

A Copy of a Letter Wrote to a Friend [29]

In this thy late affliction I've found a deep fellow-feeling with thee and had a secret hope throughout that it might please the Father of Mercies to raise thee up and sanctify thy troubles to thee: that thou, being more fully acquainted with that way which the world esteems foolish, may feel the clothing of divine fortitude and be strengthened to resist that spirit which leads from the simplicity of the everlasting Truth.

We may see ourselves crippled and halting and from a strong bias to things pleasant and easy find an impossibility to advance forward; but things impossible with men are possible with God, and our wills being made subject to his, all temptations are surmountable.

This work of subjecting the will is compared to the mineral in the furnace which through fervent heat is reduced from its first principle. He refine [sic] them as silver is refined; "he shall sit as a refiner and purifier of silver" [Mal. 3:3]. By these comparisons we are instructed in the necessity of the melting operation of the hand of God upon us to prepare our hearts truly to adore him and manifest that adoration by inwardly turning away from that spirit, in all its workings, which is not of him.

To forward this work the all-wise God is sometimes pleased through outward distress to bring us near the gates of death, that life being painful and afflicting and the prospect of eternity open before us, all earthly bonds may be loosened and the mind prepared for that deep and sacred instruction which otherwise would not be received.

If kind parents love their children and delight in their happiness, then he who is Perfect Goodness, in sending abroad mortal contagions doth assuredly direct their use. Are the righteous removed by it, their change is happy. Are the wicked taken away in their wickedness, the Almighty is clear. Do we pass through it with anguish and great bitterness and yet recover, he intends that we should be purged from dross and our ear opened to discipline.

And now on thy part, after thy sore affliction and doubts of recovery, thou art again restored. Forget not him who hath helped thee, but in humble gratitude hold fast his instructions, thereby to shun those by-paths which leads from the firm foundation. I am sensible of that variety of company to which one in thy business must be exposed. I have painfully felt the force of conversation proceeding from men deeply rooted in an earthly mind, and can sympathize with others in such conflicts, in that much weakness still attends me.

29. "A Copy" is written over the following, which has been partly erased: "13th day, 12th month, 1757."

I find that to be a fool as to worldly wisdom and commit my cause to God, not fearing to offend men who take offense at the simplicity of Truth, is the only way to remain unmoved at the sentiments of others. The fear of man brings a snare; by halting in our duty and giving back in the time of trial, our hands grow weaker, our spirits gets mingled with the people, our ears grows dull as to hearing the language of the True Shepherd, that when we look at the way of the righteous, it seems as though it was not for us to follow them.

There is a love clothes my mind while I write, which is superior to all expressions, and I find my heart open to encourage to a holy emulation to advance forward in Christian firmness. Deep humility is a strong bulwark, and as we enter into it we find safety and true exaltation. The foolishness of God is wiser than man, and the weakness of God is stronger than man. Being unclothed of our own wisdom and knowing the abasement of the creature, therein we find that power to arise which gives health and vigor [to] us.

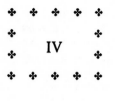

IV

1757

THE 13TH DAY, 2nd month, 1757. Being then in good health and abroad with Friends visiting families, I lodged at a Friend's house in Burlington, and going to bed about the time usual with me, I woke in the night and my meditations as I lay were on the goodness and mercy of the Lord, in a sense whereof my heart was contrite. After this I went to sleep again, and sleeping a short time I awoke. It was yet dark and no appearance of day nor moonshine, and as I opened my eyes I saw a light in my chamber at the apparent distance of five feet, about nine inches diameter, of a clear, easy brightness and near the center the most radiant. As I lay still without any surprise looking upon it, words were spoken to my inward ear which filled my whole inward man. They were not the effect of thought nor any conclusion in relation to the appearance, but as the language of the Holy One spoken in my mind. The words were, "Certain Evidence of Divine Truth," and were again repeated exactly in the same manner, whereupon the light disappeared.

Feeling an exercise in relation to a visit to the southern parts to increase upon me, I acquainted our Monthly Meeting therewith and obtained their certificate. I expecting to go alone, one of my brothers[1] who lived in Philadelphia, having some business in North Carolina, proposed going with me part of the way. But as he had a view of some outward affairs, to accept of him as a companion seemed some difficulty with me, whereupon I had conversation with him at sundry times; and at length feeling easy in my mind, I had conversation with several elderly Friends of Philadelphia on the subject, and he obtaining a certificate suitable to the occasion, we set off [blank] day, 5th month, 1757, and fell in at

1. Uriah Woolman.*

Nottingham Week Day Meeting and lodged at John Churchman's.* [2] Here I met with our friend Benjamin Buffington from New England, who was returning from a visit to the southern provinces.

Thence we crossed the river Susquehanna and lodged at William Cox's * in Maryland; and soon after I entered this province a deep and painful exercise came upon me, which I often had some feeling of since my mind was drawn towards these parts, and with which I had acquainted my brother before we agreed to join as companions.

As the people in this and the southern provinces live much on the labour of slaves, many of whom are used hardly, my concern was that I might attend with singleness of heart to the voice of the True Shepherd and be so supported as to remain unmoved at the faces of men.

As it is common for Friends on a visit to have entertainment free cost, a difficulty arose in my mind with respect to saving my own money by kindness received which to me appeared to be the gain of oppression.[3] Receiving a gift, considered as a gift, brings the receiver under obligations to the benefactor and has a natural tendency to draw the obliged into a party with the giver. To prevent difficulties of this kind and to preserve the minds of judges from any bias was that divine prohibition, "Thou shalt not receive any gift, for a gift blindeth the eyes of the wise, and perverteth the words of the righteous."—Law of Moses [Ex. 23:8].

As the disciples were sent forth without any provision for their journey and our Lord said the workman is worthy of his meat, their labour in the gospel was considered as a reward for their entertainment, and therefore not received as a gift; [4] yet in regard to my present journey I could not see my way clear in that respect. The odds [5] appeared thus: The entertainment the disciples met with was from such whose hearts God had opened to receive them, from a love to them and the Truth they

2. Alterations have been made in this sentence, apparently by both Woolman and the original editorial committee. Woolman may have intended to end the sentence with "Meeting," omitting "and" before "lodged," making the final two sentences of the paragraph: "Lodged . . . provinces."

3. Whether Woolman wrote "which to me appeared" or "which appears" cannot be determined with certainty. This sentence has been revised by someone other than Woolman, apparently—since the revision was printed in the first edition—by a member of the original editorial committee. However, the handwriting is unlike that usually associated with the committee. At several points from here on, modifications are made by the same hand.

4. "Reward" has been written above "compensation," which has been crossed out. The change seems clearly to have been made by Woolman.

5. See glossary.

published; but we, considered as members of the same Society, look upon it as a piece of civility to receive each other in such visits, and such reception at times is partly in regard to reputation, and not from an inward unity of heart and spirit.[6]

Conduct is more convincing than language, and where people by their actions manifest that the slave trade is not so disagreeable to their principles but that it may be encouraged, there is not a sound uniting with some Friends who visit them.

The prospect of so weighty a work, and being so distinguished from many who I esteemed before myself, brought me very low, and such were the conflicts of my soul that I had a near sympathy with the prophet in the time of his weakness, when he said, "If thou deal thus with me, kill me I pray thee out of hand, if I have found favour in thy sight" [Num. 11:15]. But I soon saw that this proceeded from the want of a full resignation to him.

Many were the afflictions which attended me, and in great abasement with many tears, my cries were to the Almighty for his gracious and fatherly assistance; and then after a time of deep trial, I was favoured to understand the state mentioned by the Psalmist more clearly than ever I had before, to wit: "My soul is even as a weaned child" [Ps. 131:2]. Being thus helped to sink down into resignation, I felt a deliverance from that tempest in which I had been sorely exercised, and in calmness of mind went forward, trusting that the Lord, as I faithfully attended to him, would be a counsellor to me in all difficulties, and that by his strength I should be enabled even to leave money with the members of [the] Society where I had entertainment when I found that omitting of it would obstruct that work to which I believed he had called me.[7] And as I copy this after my return, I may here add that oftentimes I did so under a sense of duty.

The way in which I did it was thus: When I expected soon to leave a Friend's house where I had entertainment, if I believed that I should not keep clear from the gain of oppression without leaving money, I spoke to one of the heads of the family privately and desired them to accept of them pieces of silver and give them to such of their Negroes as they believed would make the best use of them; and at other times I gave them to the Negroes myself, as the way looked clearest to me.[8] As I expected

6. Woolman substituted "reputation" for his original "character."
7. After "Lord," Woolman wrote and crossed out "Jesus Christ."
8. Woolman wrote "desired" in place of his original "told."

this before I came out, I had provided a large number of small pieces, and thus offering them to some who appeared to be wealthy people was a trial both to me and them. But the fear of the Lord so covered me at times that way was made easier than I expected, and few if any manifested any resentment at the offer, and most of them after some talk accepted of them.

7th day, 5th month, 1757. Lodged at a Friend's house, and the next day being first day of the week was at Patapsco Meeting, then crossed Patuxent River and lodged at a public house at the head of Severn.

9th. Breakfasted at a Friend's house, who afterward putting us a little on our way, I had conversation with him in the fear of the Lord concerning his slaves, in which my heart was tender; and I used much plainness of speech with him, which he appeared to take kindly. We pursued our journey without appointing meetings, being pressed in my mind to be at the Yearly Meeting in Virginia, and in my travelling on the road I often felt language rise from the center of my mind thus: "Oh Lord, I am a stranger in the earth; hide not thy face from me" [Ps. 119:19].

11th day, 5th month. We crossed the rivers Potomac and Rappahannock and lodged at Port Royal. And on the way, we happening in company with a colonel of the militia who appeared to be a thoughtful man, I took occasion to remark on the odds in general betwixt a people used to labour moderately for their living, training up their children in frugality and business, and those who live on the labour of slaves, the former in my view being the most happy life; with which he concurred and mentioned the trouble arising from the untoward, slothful disposition of the Negroes, adding that one of our labourers would do as much in a day as two of their slaves. I replied that free men whose minds were properly on their business found a satisfaction in improving, cultivating, and providing for their families, but Negroes, labouring to support others who claim them as their property and expecting nothing but slavery during life, had not the like inducement to be industrious.

After some further conversation I said that men having power too often misapplied it; that though we made slaves of the Negroes and the Turks made slaves of the Christians, I, however, believed that liberty was the natural right of all men equally, which he did not deny, but said the lives of the Negroes were so wretched in their own country that many of them lived better here than there. I only said, "There's great odds in regard to us on what principle we act." And so the conversation on that subject ended. And I may here add that another person some time afterward mentioned the wretchedness of the Negroes occasioned by their intestine wars as an argument in favour of our fetching them away for slaves, to which I then replied: "If compassion on the Africans in regard to their domestic troubles were the real motives of our purchasing them, that spirit of tenderness being attended to would incite us to use them kindly, that as strangers brought out of affliction their lives might be happy among us; and as they are human creatures, whose souls are as precious as ours and who may receive the same help and comfort from the Holy Scriptures as we do, we could not omit suitable endeavours to instruct them therein. But while we manifest by our conduct that our views in purchasing them are to advance ourselves, and while our buying captives taken in war animates those parties to push on that war and increase desolations amongst them, to say they live unhappy in Africa is far from being an argument in our favour."

And I further said, "The present circumstances of these provinces to me appears difficult, that the slaves look like a burdensome stone to such who burden themselves with them, and that if the white people retain a resolution to prefer their outward prospects of gain to all other considerations and do not act conscientiously toward them as fellow creatures, I believe that burden will grow heavier and heavier till times change in a way disagreeable to us"—at which the person appeared very serious and owned that in considering their condition and the manner of their treatment in these provinces, he had sometimes thought it might be just in the Almighty to so order it.

Having travelled through Maryland, we came amongst Friends at Cedar Creek in Virginia on 12th day, 5th month, and the next day rode in company with several Friends a day's journey to Camp Creek.[9] And as I was riding along in the morning, my mind was deeply affected in a sense I had of the want of divine aid to support me in the various difficulties which attended me. And in an uncommon distress of mind I cried in secret to the Most High, "Oh Lord be merciful, I beseech thee, to thy poor afflicted creature."

After some time I felt inward relief, and soon after, a Friend in company began to talk in support of the slave trade and said the Negroes were understood to be the offspring of Cain, their blackness being the mark God set upon him after he murdered Abel his brother, that it was

9. After "Having" the word "thus" has been inserted, probably by the original editorial committee. After "Maryland," Woolman wrote and crossed out: "on a direct line."

the design of providence they should be slaves, as a condition proper to the race of so wicked a man as Cain was. Then another spake in support of what had been said. To all which I replied in substance as follows: that Noah and his family were all who survived the flood according to Scripture, and as Noah was of Seth's race, the family of Cain was wholly destroyed. One of them said that after the flood Ham went to the land of Nod and took a wife, that Nod was a land far distant, inhabited by Cain's race, and that the flood did not reach it, and as Ham was sentenced to be a servant of servants to his brethren, these two families being thus joined were undoubtedly fit only for slaves. I replied the flood was a judgment upon the world for their abominations, and it was granted that Cain's stock was the most wicked, and therefore unreasonable to suppose they were spared. As to Ham's going to the land of Nod for a wife, no time being fixed, Nod might be inhabited by some of Noah's family before Ham married a second time. Moreover, the text saith that all flesh died that moved upon the earth. I further reminded them how the prophets repeatedly declare that the son shall not suffer for the iniquity of the father, but every one be answerable for his own sins.

I was troubled to perceive the darkness of their imaginations, and in some pressure of spirit said: "The love of ease and gain are the motives in general of keeping slaves, and men are wont to take hold of weak arguments to support a cause which is unreasonable," and added: "I've no interest on either side save only the interest which I desire to have in the truth, and as I believe liberty is their right and see they are not only deprived of it but treated in other respects with inhumanity in many places, I believe he who is a refuge for the oppressed will in his own time plead their cause, and happy will it be for such who walk in uprightness before him." Thus our conversation ended.

14th day, 5th month. Was at Camp Creek Monthly Meeting and then rode to the mountains up James River and had a meeting at a Friend's house, in both which I felt sorrow of heart, and my tears were poured out before the Lord, who was pleased to afford a degree of strength by which way opened to clear my mind amongst Friends in those places. From thence I went to Fork Creek and so to Cedar Creek again, at which place I now had a meeting. Here I found a tender seed, and as I was preserved in the ministry to keep low with the Truth, the same Truth in their hearts answered it, that it was a time of mutual refreshment from the presence of the Lord. I lodged at James Stanley's, father to William Stanley,* one of the young men who suffered imprisonment at Winchester last summer on account of their testimony against fighting, and I had some satisfactory conversation with him concerning it.[10]

Hence I went to the Swamp Meeting and to Wainoak Meeting,[11] and then crossed James River and lodged near Burleigh. From the time of my entering Maryland I have been much under sorrow, which of late so increased upon me that my mind was almost overwhelmed, and I may say with the Psalmist, "In my distress I called upon the Lord and cried to my God" [Ps. 18:6], who in infinite goodness looked upon my affliction and in my private retirement sent the Comforter for my relief, for which I humbly bless his holy name.

The sense I had of the state of the churches brought a weight of distress upon me. The gold to me appeared dim and the fine gold changed, and though this is the case too generally, yet the sense of it in these parts hath in a particular manner borne heavy upon me. It appeared to me that through the prevailing of the spirit of this world the minds of many were brought to an inward desolation,[12] and instead of the spirit of meekness, gentleness, and heavenly wisdom, which are the necessary companions of the true sheep of Christ, a spirit of fierceness and the love of dominion too generally prevailed.

From small beginnings in error great buildings by degrees are raised and from one age to another are [13] more and more strengthened by the general concurrence of the people; and as men of reputation [depart] from the Truth,[14] their virtues are mentioned as arguments in favour of general error, and those of less note, to justify themselves, say, "Such and such good men did the like." By what other steps could the people of Judah arise to that height in wickedness as to give just ground for the prophet Isaiah to declare in the name of the Lord that *none* called for justice nor pleaded for the Truth? Or for the Almighty to call upon the

10. Twenty-one years later the Pemberton brothers were imprisoned at the same place (Winchester, Virginia) for failing to support the American Revolution.

11. The name of this meeting, in Henrico County, just north of Richmond, Virginia, has been spelled in at least seven ways. The version adopted here is taken from Stephen B. Weeks, *Southern Quakers and Slavery* (Baltimore, 1896), 344ff.

12. The passage: "through . . . desolation" is written over a passage which was revised and then erased.

13. "Are" has been written by the original editorial committee—apparently for the sake of legibility—above Woolman's word, which appears also to have been "are."

14. "Depart," missing in MS. B, is supplied from MS. A. At this point the original editorial committee revised this passage to read: "as men obtain reputation by their profession of the Truth"—a change that obscures Woolman's reasoning and the sharpness of his indictment.

great city Jerusalem, just before the Babylonish captivity, to find *a man* who executed judgment and sought the Truth, and he would pardon it? [Is. 59:4 and Jer. 5:1, respectively].

The prospect of a road lying open to the same degeneracy in some parts of this newly settled land of America, in respect to our conduct towards the Negroes, hath deeply bowed my mind in this journey; and though to briefly relate how these people are treated is no agreeable work, yet after often reading over the notes I made as I travelled, I find my mind engaged to preserve them.

Many of the white people in those provinces take little or no care of Negro marriages, and when Negroes marry after their own way, some make so little account of those marriages that with views of outward interest they often part men from their wives by selling them far asunder, which is common when estates are sold by executors at vendue. Many whose labour is heavy being followed at their business in the field by a man with a whip, hired for that purpose, have in common little else to eat but one peck of Indian corn and salt for one week with some few potatoes. (The potatoes they commonly raise by their labour on the first day of the week.) [15]

The correction ensuing on their disobedience to overseers or slothfulness in business is often very severe and sometimes desperate. Men and women have many times scarce clothes enough to hide their nakedness, and boys and girls ten and twelve years old are often stark naked amongst their master's children.[16]

Some of our Society and some of the Society called New Lights use some endeavours to instruct those they have in reading, but in common this is not only neglected but disapproved.[17]

These are a people by whose labour the other inhabitants are in a great measure supported, and many of them in the luxuries of life. These are a people who have made no agreement to serve us and who have not

15. Woolman wrote this sentence in the margin, apparently as an afterthought.

16. A bracket appears before "dren," and in the margin is "65 F." This corresponds to page 65 in the first edition, which starts with "dren." (Apparently "F" signifies "Folio.")

17. "Some of our Society and" appears to have been added later by Woolman—doubtless in an attempt to be fair to the Quakers. The "New Light" or "New Side" sect of Presbyterians split from the main Presbyterian body in 1741. In contrast to the "Old Side" Presbyterians, they emphasized emotional revivalist methods. Their growth in Virginia was aided by three visits of George Whitefield, powerful evangelistic leader of the great awakenings of the mid-eighteenth century. This division within Presbyterianism ended in 1758.

forfeited their liberty that we know of. These are souls for whom Christ died, and for our conduct toward them we must answer before that Almighty Being who is no respecter of persons.

They who know the only true God and Jesus Christ whom he hath sent, and are thus acquainted with the merciful, benevolent Gospel Spirit, will therein perceive that the indignation of God is kindled against oppression and cruelty, and in beholding the great distress of so numerous a people will find cause for mourning.

From my lodgings I went to Burleigh Meeting, where I felt my mind drawn into a quiet, resigned state, and after long silence I felt an engagement to stand up, and through the powerful operation of divine love we were favoured with an edifying meeting. Next we had a meeting at Black Water, and so on to the Yearly Meeting at the Western Branch.

When business began some queries were produced by some of their members to be now considered, and if approved, to be answered hereafter by their respective Monthly Meetings. They were the Pennsylvania queries, which had been examined by a committee of Virginia Yearly Meeting appointed the last year, who made some alterations in them, one of which alterations was made in favour of a custom which troubled me. The query was: "Are there any concerned in the importation of Negroes or buying them after imported?", which they altered thus: "Are there any concerned in the importation of Negroes or buying them to trade in?"

As one query admitted with unanimity was: "Are any concerned in buying or vending goods unlawfully imported or prize goods?", I found my mind engaged to say that as we professed the Truth and were there assembled to support the testimony of it, it was necessary for us to dwell deep and act in that wisdom which is pure, or otherwise we could not prosper. I then mentioned their alteration, and referring them to the last mentioned query, added [that] as purchasing any merchandise taken by the sword was always allowed to be inconsistent with our principles, Negroes being captives of war or taken by stealth, those circumstances make it inconsistent with our testimony to buy them, and their being our fellow creatures who are sold as slaves adds greatly to the difficulty. Friends appeared attentive to what was said; some expressed a care and concern about their Negroes; none made any objection by way of reply to what I said. But the query was admitted as they had altered it.

As some of their members have heretofore traded in Negroes as in other merchandise, this query being admitted will be one step further than they have heretofore gone, and I did not see it my duty to press for an alteration, but felt easy to leave all to him who alone is able to turn the hearts of the mighty and make way for the spreading of Truth in the earth by means agreeable to his infinite wisdom. But in regard to those they already had, I felt my mind engaged to labour with them and said that as we believe the Scriptures were given forth by holy men as they were moved by the Holy Ghost, and many of us know by experience that they are often helpful and comfortable and believe ourselves bound in duty to teach our children to read them, I believe that if we were divested of all selfish views the same good Spirit that gave them forth would engage us to learn them to read, that they might have the benefit of them. Some I perceived amongst them who at this time manifested a concern in regard to taking more care in the education of their Negroes.[18]

29th day, 5th month. At the house where I lodged was a meeting of ministers and elders at the ninth hour in the morning, at which time I found an engagement to speak freely and plainly to them concerning their slaves, mentioning how they as the first rank in the Society, whose conduct in that case was much noticed by others, were under the stronger obligations to look carefully to themselves, expressing how needful it was for them in that situation to be thoroughly divested of all selfish views, that living in the pure Truth, and acting conscientiously toward those people in their education, and otherwise, they might be instrumental in helping forward a work so exceeding necessary and so much neglected amongst them. At the 12th hour the meeting of worship began, which was a solid meeting.

The 30th, about the 10th hour, Friends met to finish their business, and then the meeting for worship ensued, which to me was a laborious time; but through the goodness of the Lord, Truth I believe gained some ground, and it was a strengthening opportunity to the honest-hearted.

About this time I wrote an epistle to Friends in the back settlements of North Carolina, as follows:

To Friends at Their Monthly Meeting at New Garden and Cane Creek in North Carolina

DEAR FRIENDS,

It having pleased the Lord to draw me forth on a visit to some parts of Virginia and Carolina, you have often been in my mind, and though my way is not clear to come in person to visit you, yet

18. Someone (possibly Woolman) changed "I perceived" to "there were."

I feel it in my heart to communicate a few things as they arise in the love of Truth. First, my dear Friends, dwell in humility and take heed that no views of outward gain get too deep hold of you, that so your eyes being single to the Lord you may be preserved in the way of safety.

Where people let loose their minds after the love of outward things and are more engaged in pursuing the profits and seeking the friendships of this world than to be inwardly acquainted with the way of true peace, such walk in a vain shadow while the true comfort of life is wanting. Their examples are often hurtful to others, and their treasures thus collected do many times prove dangerous snares to their children.

But where people are sincerely devoted to follow Christ and dwell under the influence of his Holy Spirit, their stability and firmness through a divine blessing is at times like dew on the tender plants round about them, and the weightiness of their spirits secretly works on the minds of others; and in this condition, through the spreading influence of divine love they feel a care over the flock and way is opened for maintaining good order in the Society. And though we meet with opposition from another spirit, yet as there is a dwelling in meekness, feeling our spirits subject and moving only in the gentle, peaceable wisdom, the inward reward of quietness will be greater than all our difficulties. Where the pure life is kept to and meetings of discipline are held in the authority of it, we find by experience that they are comfortable and tend to the health of the body.

Awhile I write, the youth comes fresh in my way. Dear young people, choose God for your portion; love his Truth and be not ashamed of it. Choose for your company such who serve him in uprightness, and shun as most dangerous the conversation of those whose lives are of an ill savor; for by frequenting such company some hopeful young people have come to great loss and been drawn from less evils to greater, to their utter ruin. In the bloom of youth no ornament is so lovely as that of virtue, nor any enjoyments equal to those which we partake of in fully resigning ourselves to the divine will. These enjoyments add sweetness to all other comforts and give true satisfaction in company and conversation where people are mutually acquainted with it, and as your minds are thus seasoned with the Truth you will find strength to abide steadfast to the testimony of it and be prepared for services in the church.

And now, dear Friends and brethren, as you are improving a wilderness and may be numbered amongst the first planters in one part of a province, I beseech you in the love of Jesus Christ to wisely consider the force of your examples and think how much your successors may be thereby affected. It is a help in a country, yea, a great favour and a blessing, when customs first settled are agreeable to sound wisdom; so when they are otherwise the effect of them is grievous, and children feel themselves encompassed with difficulties prepared for them by their predecessors.

As moderate care and exercise under the direction of sound wisdom is useful both to mind and body, so by this means in general the real wants of life are easily attained, our gracious Father having so proportioned one to the other that keeping in the true medium we may pass on quietly. Where slaves are purchased to do our labour, numerous difficulties attend it. To rational creatures bondage is uneasy and frequently occasions sourness and discontent in them, which affects the family and such who claim the mastery over them, and thus people and their children are many times encompassed with vexations which arise from their applying to wrong methods to get a living.

I have been informed that there are a large number of Friends in your parts who have no slaves, and in tender and most affectionate love I now beseech you to keep clear from purchasing any.[19] Look, my dear Friends, to divine providence, and follow in simplicity that exercise of body, that plainness and frugality, which true wisdom leads to; so may you be preserved from those dangers which attend such who are aiming at outward ease and greatness.

Treasures, though small, attained on a true principle of virtue are sweet in the possession, and while we walk in the light of the Lord there is true comfort and satisfaction. Here neither the murmurs of an oppressed people, nor throbbing, uneasy conscience, nor anxious thoughts about the event of things hinder the enjoyment of it.

When we look toward the end of life and think on the division of our substance among our successors, if we know that it was collected in the fear of the Lord, in honesty, in equity, and in uprightness of heart before him, we may consider it as his gift to us and with a single eye to his blessing bestow it on those we leave behind us. Such is the happiness in the plain ways of true virtue. "The work of righteousness is peace, and the effect of righteousness is quietness and assurance forever" [Is. 32:17].

Dwell here, my dear friends, and then in remote and solitary deserts you may find true peace and satisfaction. If the Lord be our God in truth and reality, there is safety for us; for he is a "stronghold in the day of trouble and knoweth them that trust in him" [Nahum 1:7].

ISLE OF WIGHT COUNTY IN VIRGINIA
29th day, 5th month, 1757.

19. There is some doubt about the word "are," which has been tampered with considerably, apparently by the original editorial committee. The word "now" has been crossed off, apparently by that committee.

From the Yearly Meeting in Virginia I went to Carolina, and on the 1st day, 6th month, was at Wells Creek Monthly Meeting, where the spring of the gospel ministry was opened and the love of Jesus Christ experienced amongst us. To his name be the praise.

[As the neglected condition of the poor slaves often affects my mind, meetings for discipline hath seemed to me suitable places to express what the Holy Spirit may open on that subject; and though in this meeting they were much in my mind, I found no engagement to speak concerning them and therefore kept silence, finding by experience that to keep pace with the gentle motions of Truth, and never move but as that opens the way, is necessary for the true servants of Christ.] [20]

Here my brother joined with some Friends from New Garden who were going homeward, and I went next to Simons Creek Monthly Meeting. Here I was silent during the meeting for worship, and when business came on, my mind was exercised concerning the poor slaves, but did not feel my way clear to speak. And in this condition I was bowed in spirit before the Lord and with tears and inward supplications besought him to so open my understanding that I might know his will concerning me, and at length my mind was settled in silence. And near the end of their business, a member of their meeting expressed a concern that had some time lain upon him on account of Friends so much neglecting their duty in the education of their slaves, and proposed having meetings sometimes appointed for them on a week day, to be only attended by some Friends to be named in their Monthly Meetings. Many present appeared to unite with the proposal. One said he had often wondered that they, being our fellow creatures and capable of religious understanding, had been so exceedingly neglected. Another expressed the like concern and appeared zealous that Friends in future might more closely consider it. At length a minute was made and the further consideration of it referred to their next Monthly Meeting. The Friend who made this proposal hath Negroes. He told me that he was at New Garden, about 250 miles from home, and came back alone, and that in this solitary journey this exercise in regard to the education of their Negroes was from time to time renewed in his mind.

A Friend of some note in Virginia, who hath slaves, told me that he being far from home on a lonesome journey had many serious thoughts

20. This paragraph is taken from MS. A. In the margin Woolman wrote: "Let this be left out." It is omitted from MS. B.

about them, and that his mind was so impressed therewith that he believed that he saw a time coming when divine providence would alter
the circumstance of these people respecting their condition as slaves.

From hence I went to Newbegun Creek and sat a considerable time in
much weakness. Then I felt Truth open the way to speak a little in much
plainness and simplicity, till at length through the increase of divine love
amongst us we had a seasoning opportunity. From thence to the head
of Little River on a First Day, where was a crowded meeting and I believe was through divine goodness made profitable to some. Thence to
the Old Neck, where I was led into a careful searching out the secret
workings of the mystery of iniquity, which under a cover of religion
exalts itself against that pure spirit which leads in the way of meekness
and self-denial. From thence to Piney Woods; this was the last meeting
I was at in Carolina and was large, and my heart being deeply engaged,
I was drawn forth into a fervent labour amongst them.

When I was at Newbegun Creek, a Friend was there who laboured
for his living, having no Negroes, and had been a minister many years.
He came to me the next day, and as we rode together he signified that
he wanted to talk with me concerning a difficulty he had been under,
and related it near as follows, to wit: That as monies had of late years
been raised by a tax to carry on the wars, he had a scruple in his mind in
regard to paying it and chose rather to suffer distraint of goods than pay
it. And as he was the only person who refused it in them parts and knew
not that anyone else was in the like circumstance, he signified that it had
been a heavy trial upon him, and the more so for that some of his
brethren had been uneasy with his conduct in that case, and added that
from a sympathy he felt with me yesterday in meeting, he found a
freedom thus to open the matter in the way of querying concerning
Friends in our parts; whereupon I told him the state of Friends amongst
us as well as I was able, and also that I had for some time been under the
like scruple.[21] I believed him to be one who was concerned to walk
uprightly before the Lord and esteemed it my duty to preserve this
memorandum.[22]

From hence I went back into Virginia and had a meeting near James
Copeland's; it was a time of inward suffering, but through the goodness

21. After "scruple" Woolman wrote and crossed out: "of mind."
22. In the margin: "Samuel Newby," apparently written by Woolman. Little more
is known of Samuel Newby, except that he was on one of the committees of the
North Carolina Yearly Meeting.

of the Lord I was made content. Then to another meeting where through the renewings of pure love we had a very comfortable meeting.[23]

Travelling up and down of late, I have had renewed evidences that to be faithful to the Lord and content with his will concerning me [24] is a most necessary and useful lesson for me to be learning, looking less at the effects of my labour than at the pure motion and reality of the concern as it arises from heavenly love. In the Lord Jehovah is everlasting strength, and as the mind by a humble resignation is united to him and we utter words from an inward knowledge that they arise from the heavenly spring, though our way may be difficult and require close attention to keep in it, and though the manner in which we may be led may tend to our own abasement, yet if we continue in patience and meekness, heavenly peace is the reward of our labours.

From hence I went to Curles Meeting, which, though small, was reviving to the honest-hearted. Thence to Black Creek and Caroline Meetings, from whence, accompanied by William Stanley * before-mentioned, we rode to Goose Creek, being much through the woods and about one hundred miles. We lodged the first night at a public house, the second in the woods, and the next day we reached a Friend's house at Goose Creek. In the woods we lay under some disadvantage, having no fireworks, nor bells for our horses, but we stopped some before night and let them feed on wild grass, which was plenty, we the meantime cutting with our knives a store against night, and then tied them; and gathering some bushes under an oak we lay down, but the mosquitoes being plenty and the ground damp, I slept but little.

Thus lying in the wilderness and looking at the stars, I was led to contemplate the condition of our first parents when they were sent forth from the garden, and considered that they had no house, no tools for business, no garments but what their Creator gave them, no vessels for use, nor any fire to cook roots or herbs. But the Almighty, though they had been disobedient, was a father to them; way opened in process of time for all the conveniences of life. And he who by the gracious influence of his spirit illuminated their understanding and showed them what was acceptable to him and tended to their felicity as intelligent creatures,

23. Woolman originally wrote "through the goodness." Apparently he intended to write "goodness of the Lord," but then changed it in order to avoid repetition with the preceding sentence.

24. Original reading: "that to keep pace with duty and be content with the allotments of divine providence." The change was almost certainly made by Woolman.

did also provide means for their happy living in this world as they attended to the manifestations of his wisdom.[25]

To provide things relative to our outward living in the way of true wisdom is good, and the gift of improving in things useful is a good gift and comes from the Father of Lights. Many have had this gif[t][26] and from age to age there have been improvements of this kind made in the world. But some, not keeping to the pure gift, have in the creaturely cunning and self-exaltation sought out many inventions, which inventions of men, as distinct from that uprightness in which man was created, as in the first motion it was evil so the effects of it have been, and are, evil. That at this day it is as necessary for us constantly to attend on the heavenly gift to be qualified to use rightly the good things in this life amidst great improvements, as it was for our first parents, when they were without any improvements, without any friend or father but God only.

I was at meeting at Goose Creek and next at a Monthly Meeting at Fairfax, where, through the gracious dealings of the Almighty with us, his power prevailed over many hearts. Thence to Monocacy and Pipe Creek in Maryland, at both which places I had cause humbly to adore him who supported me through sundry exercises, and by whose help I was enabled to reach the true witness in the hearts of others. There were some hopeful young people in those parts. Thence I had meetings at John Everitt's, at Menallen, and at Huntington, and I was made humbly thankful to the Lord, who opened my heart amongst the people in these new settlements, so that it was a time of encouragement to the honest-minded.

At Menallen a Friend gave me some account of a religious Society amongst the Dutch, called Minonists, and amongst other things related a passage in substance as follows: One of the Minonists having acquaintance with a man of another Society at a considerable distance, and being with his wagon on business near the house of his said acquaintance, and night coming on, he had thoughts of putting up with him; but passing by his fields and observing t[he] distressed appearance of his slaves, he kind[led] a fire in the woods hard by and lay th[ere] that night.[27] His said acquaint-

---

25. The passage "and considered . . . of his wisdom" has been revised extensively by the original editorial committee.

26. In MS. B, "t" has been torn off, but it is clear in MS. A.

27. By "Minonists" Woolman doubtless refers to the Mennonites, some of whom had come into Maryland and Virginia from Lancaster County, Pennsylvania, their American center. Although they were mostly Germans, a number were of Dutch descent; their name came from that of Menno Simons (1492-1559), Anabaptist leader

ance [heard] where he lodged, and afterward mee[ting] the Minonist told him of it, adding he should have been heartily welcome at his house, and from their acquaintance beforetime wondered at his conduct in that case.

The Minonist replied: "Ever since I lodged by thy field I've wanted an opportunity to speak with thee. The matter was, I intended to have come to thy house for entertainment, but seeing thy slaves at their work and observing the manner of their dress, I had no liking to come to partake with thee." [He] then admonished him to use them with more humanity, and added: "As I lay by the fire that night, I thought that as I was a man of substance, thou would have received me freely, but if I had been as poor as one of thy slaves, and had no power to help myself, I should have received from th[y] hand no kinder usage than they." [28]

Thence [takin]g three meetings in my way, I went home under a humbling [sense] of the gracious dealings of the Lord with me in preserv[ing m]e through many trials and afflictions in my [journey].[29]

---

of the Dutch Reformation. Like the Quakers, they were pacifists and refused to take oaths.

The lower corner of the sheet comprising pages 137 and 138 of MS. B has been broken off and lost. As a result, the bracketed portions in this paragraph have been supplied from MS. A (page 67) to fill the gaps on page 137 of MS. B.

28. For the sake of clarity, "[He]" has been added by the present editor. With this exception, the items enclosed in brackets in this paragraph and the next have been supplied from MS. A to fill the gaps caused by the absence of a corner of page 138 in MS. B. That members of the original editorial committee made similar additions (writing them in the inner margin of page 138) is evidence that the corner was missing when they worked on the MS. and that they had MS. A at their disposal.

29. The second word in this sentence was almost certainly "taking," although only "g" remains. MS. A reads: "Thence I was at three meetings in my way, and so I went . . ." In copying to MS. B, when Woolman changed "I was at" to "taking," he then omitted "and so."

After "journey" MS. A adds a final sentence, which Woolman omitted from MS. B: "I was out about two months and rode about 1150 miles." The committee copied this onto the bottom of page 138, changing "rode" to "travelled." (See note 28 for explanation of brackets.)

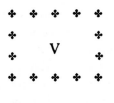

V

1755–1758

A FEW YEARS PAST, money being made current in our province for carrying on wars, and to be sunk [1] by taxes laid on the inhabitants, my mind was often affected with the thoughts of paying such taxes, and I believe it right for me to preserve a memorandum concerning it. I was told that Friends in England frequently paid taxes when the money was applied to such purposes. I had conference with several noted Friends on the subject, who all favoured the payment of such taxes, some of whom I preferred before myself; and this made me easier for a time. Yet there was in the deeps of my mind a scruple which I never could get over, and at certain times [2] I was greatly distressed on that account.

I all along believed that there were some upright-hearted men who paid such taxes, but could not see that their example was a sufficient reason for me to do so, while I believed that the spirit of Truth required of me as an individual to suffer patiently the distress of goods rather than pay actively.

I have been informed that Thomas à Kempis lived and died in the profession of the Roman Catholic religion, and in reading his writings I have believed him to be a man of a true Christian spirit, as fully so as many who died martyrs because they could not join with some superstitions in that church. All true Christians are of the same spirit but their gifts are diverse, Jesus Christ appointing to each one their peculiar office agreeable to his infinite wisdom.

1. See glossary.
2. At some point in his revision of this sentence, Woolman used "intellect" and "intervals," respectively, instead of "mind" and "times." The latter probably represent his final preference, but this is not certain. This paragraph has been revised considerably by Woolman and by the original editorial committee. The words "frequently" and "noted" are probably by Woolman, but they may have been written by the committee to fill in gaps left by Woolman's erasures.

John Huss contended against the errors crept into the church, in
opposition to the Council of Constance, which the historian reports to
have consisted of many thousands people.[3] He modestly vindicated the
cause which he believed was right, and though his language and conduct
toward his judges appear to have been respectful, yet he never could be
moved from the principles settled in his mind. To use his own words,
"This I most humbly require and desire you all, even for his sake who is
the God of us all, that I be not compelled to the thing which my conscience doth repugn or strive against." And again, in his answer to the
Emperor, "I refuse nothing, most noble Emperor, whatsoever the Council
shall decree or determine upon me, this only one thing I except, that I do
not offend God and my conscience."—Foxe's *Acts and Monuments*, p.
233.[4] At length, rather than act contrary to that which he believed the
Lord required of him, [he] chose to suffer death by fire.[5] Thomas à
Kempis, without disputing against the articles then generally agreed to,
appears to have laboured, by a pious example as well as by preaching and
writing, to promote virtue and an inward spiritual religion. And I believe
they were both sincere-hearted followers of Christ.[6]

3. Woolman wrote "many" in place of his original "upwards of twenty." In the
next sentence he may have written "appears" instead of "appear." The MS. is not
clear.

4. John Foxe, *Actes and Monumentes of These Latter and Perillous Days* . . .
(London, 1563). This first English version of 1471 pages was followed by a revised,
enlarged edition of 2314 pages in 1570. Many other editions followed. John Foxe
(1516-1587) through this volume exerted a tremendous influence in England during
the Elizabethan period. From its publication until the close of the seventeenth century, *The Book of Martyrs* (as it is generally called) was probably more widely read
in England than any other book except the Bible, and thus became the generally
accepted interpretation of the history of both church and nation. Of the several
studies of Foxe and his work, probably the most scholarly and up-to-date is William
Haller, *Foxe's Book of Martyrs and the Elect Nation* (London, 1963).

5. In MS. B Woolman wrote "act contrary" above "conform to a thing reverse,"
which he crossed out. In MS. A "act contrary" is written, apparently by Woolman,
in a space left by an erasure. This is one of several instances in which MS. B was
revised by crossing out and MS. A by erasing. The same procedure is followed in the
next sentence, where "disputing against" is written in place of impugning" in MS. B
and to replace an erasure in MS. A. In hardly any of these passages is it possible to
determine the original wording in MS. A, but from the length of the erasures one
may suppose that it was the same as in MS. B. It is certain that Woolman did some
revision of MS. B. Often, but not always, MS. A was changed to correspond to
MS. B. Sometimes the change was made by Woolman, sometimes by the committee;
sometimes who made it cannot be determined.

6. The phrase "I believe . . . Christ" was substituted by Woolman for his earlier

True charity is an excellent virtue, and to sincerely labour for their good whose belief in all points doth not agree [7] with ours is a happy case. To refuse the active payment of a tax which our Society generally paid was exceeding disagreeable, but to do a thing contrary to my conscience appeared yet more dreadful.

When this exercise came upon me, I knew of none under the like difficulty, and in my distress I besought the Lord to enable me to give up all,[8] that so I might follow him wheresoever he was pleased to lead me. And under this exercise I went to our Yearly Meeting at Philadelphia in 1755, at which a committee was appointed, some from each Quarter, to correspond with the Meeting for Sufferings in London, and another to visit our Monthly and Quarterly Meetings. And after their appointment, before the last adjournment of the meeting, it was agreed on in the meeting that these two committees should meet together in Friends' school-house in the city, at a time when the meeting stood adjourned, to consider some things in which the cause of Truth was concerned; and these committees meeting together had a weighty conference in the fear of the Lord, at which time I perceived there were many Friends under a scruple like that before-mentioned.[9]

---

phrase "to me it looks likely that they were both in their proper places." He neglected to cross off "to" before "me"; the original editorial committee did so.

Thomas à Kempis (ca. 1379–1471) was the reputed author of *The Imitation of Christ*, a devotional book of great insight and depth. Whether he actually composed the book is irrelevant; its author was obviously a good Catholic, not in rebellion against the church. John Huss (ca. 1369–1415), a Bohemian precursor of the Protestant Reformation, vigorously criticized and defied the bulls of the pope. He was tried as a heretic and burned at the stake.

7. Before Woolman revised this passage, it read: "whose sentiments in all points do not exactly agree."

8. At this point Woolman erased "outward considerations."

9. Marginal note by Woolman: "Christians refused to pay taxes to support heathen temples. See *Primitive Christianity*, Part III, p. 327."

The reference is to William Cave, *Primitive Christianity: or, The Religion of the Ancient Christians in the First Ages of the Gospel*, 6th ed. (London, 1702). Cave (1637–1713) wrote other books, some in Latin and some in English, the best known being *The Lives ... of the Holy Apostles ...*

The material that follows (enclosed in brackets) is taken from MS. A, where it appears at this point. In the margin Woolman wrote (apparently at a later date): "If this Journal be printed, let all the quotation from J. Churchman's notes be left out." The passage is lacking in MS. B. The earliest extant version of it in Woolman's writing is MS. R1. It consists (with slight modifications) of two passages that were later printed on pages 69–73 and 169–171 of the first edition of John Churchman, *An Ac-*

[Since I had finished my narrative of this affair, having been favoured by my beloved friend John Churchman * with the perusal of some notes which he made concerning some exercise he went through on account of our testimony against wars, as they contain some things relative to facts hereafter spoken of, I thought good by his permission to copy the substance of them in this place:

"In the 4th month, 1748, it was on my mind to join with Friends in the city of Philadelphia on a visit to some families there, and whilst I was on that service the Governor called the Assembly together and [10] laid before them the defenceless state of Pennsylvania in order to prevail with the House to give a sum of money to station a ship of force at our capes, as also to assist in finishing a battery below the city which had been begun by subscriptions.[11]

"One night as I lay in bed, it came very weightily upon me to go to the House of Assembly and lay before the members the danger of departing from that divine arm of power which had hitherto protected the inhabitants of our land and preserved us in peace and safety. The concern rested on me several days and occasioned me with earnest breathings to seek to the Lord that if the motion was from him, he would be pleased to direct my steps therein so that I might be preserved from giving just cause of offence to any, for it appeared to be a difficult time,[12] many even of our Society expressing a willingness that a sum should be given to show our loyalty to the king, though as a peaceable people we had a testimony to bear against outward wars and fighting.[13]

"I made no man privy to this my concern until about a week had passed, when one morning it came so heavy upon me that I went to the house of a particular Friend, and as we sat together he was sensible that something was upon me and asked if I was concerned about the Assembly, upon which I asked him if he ever knew of any Friends going to the

---

count of the Gospel Labours and Christian Experiences of a Faithful Minister of Christ (Philadelphia, 1779). The passage in MS. A (reproduced here) is a condensed version of MS. R1. Unless otherwise indicated, the variant readings in MS. R1, documented in the notes, appear also in the first printed edition of Churchman's book.

10. MS. R1 adds: "in pressing terms."

11. MS. R1 adds: "but likely to be too heavy for the undertakers."

12. MS. R1 reads: "very critical time." The first edition reads: "very difficult time."

13. After "loyalty to the king" MS. R1 adds: "and willingness to impart of our substance for his use." Before "people" Woolman (in MS. A) inserted "peaceable," which is lacking from MS. R1 and from the first edition.

Assembly with a concern to speak to them. He answered, 'No, but I have wondered that they have not, for I have understood,' added he, 'that it was formerly a common practice for them to sit in silence like solemn worship before they proceeded to do business.'

"I told him I had it on my mind to go to the House that morning but should be glad of company. He directed me to a Friend whom he thought suitable, and I went and acquainted him with my concern, and withal told him if he did not feel clear and easy I believed it best for him not to go.[14] He replied, 'Thy way is before thee, but I believe I must not go with thee.' So I returned to my friend before-mentioned, who did not discourage me though I had no company.

"And being pressed in my mind I went directly to the State House just as the Speaker, John Kinsey,* was going in, to whom I beckoned; and he came and met me. I told him that I wanted to be admitted into the House, for I thought I had something to say to them which seemed to me of importance. He said it was a critical time and they had a difficult affair before them, and queried whether I had not better wait till the House parted; and another member being near said he thought it would be best and less liable to give offence, for there were a pretty many members that were not of our Society, but if I would wait until the House broke up, they would inform all the members that were of our Society, not doubting but they would be willing to give me an opportunity to inform them of what I had upon my mind. But I told them that would give me no relief, for I had a particular desire to have those members that were not of our Society present,[15] and I requested the Speaker that he would go in and inform them that there was a countryman waiting who had a desire to be admitted into the House that had something to communicate to them, and if they refused I expected to be clear. He readily and affectionately answered he would and soon brought me word the House was willing.

"There was a great awe over my mind when I went in, which I thought in some measure spread and prevailed over the members, and after a

14. Between "acquainted him" and "He replied," MS. R1 originally read: "of my intention, but as I spoke I felt that I had better go alone, and therefore told him if he did not feel clear and easy to go with me, I advised him to stay, for it was better that one man should perish alone than two should be slain together." The words after "stay" have been crossed out; nor do they appear in the first edition.

15. MS. R1 adds: "believing that it would be better for them to hear and judge for themselves than to have it at second hand, as it might be differently represented, at which they were a little silent."

silence of perhaps ten or twelve minutes, I felt as though all fear of man
was taken away and my mind influenced to speak to them nearly [16] in
substance as follows:

"*My Countrymen and Fellow Subjects, Representatives of the
Inhabitants of this Province*:

"Under an apprehension of the difficulties before you, I feel a
strong sympathy with you and have to remind you of a just and true
saying of a great minister of Christ, to wit: 'The powers that be,
are ordained of God' [Rom. 13:1]. Now if men in power in whatsoever station do seek unto God (who will be a spirit of judgment
to them who sit in judgment) for wisdom and counsel to act singly
for him that ordained the power and permitted them to be stationed
therein, that they should be his ministers, such will be a blessing
under God to their country; but if those in authority do suffer their
own fears and the fears and persuasions of others to prevail with
them to neglect such attention, and so make laws in order to their
own protection and defence by carnal weapons and fortifications
styled 'human prudence,' he who is Superintendent, by withdrawing
the arm of his power, may permit those evils they feared to come
suddenly upon them. May it with gratitude be ever remembered
how remarkably we have been preserved in peace and tranquillity
for more than fifty years: no invasion by foreign enemies, and the
treaties of peace with the natives, wisely began by our proprietor
William Penn, preserved inviolable to this day.[17]

"Though you now represent and act for a mixed people of various
denominations as to religion, yet remember the charter is the same
as at first. Beware therefore of acting to oppress tender consciences,
for there are many of the inhabitants whom you now represent that
still hold forth the same religious principles with their predecessors,
who were some of the first adventurers into this (at that time)
wilderness land, that would be greatly grieved to see warlike prepa-
rations carried on and encouraged by a law consented to by their
brethren in profession, or others, contrary to the charter, still conscientiously concluding that the reverent and pure fear of God with
a humble trust in his ancient arm of power would be our greatest
safety and defence. And those who hold different principles and are
settled in this government can have no just cause of reflection if warlike measures are forborne, because the charter was framed and the
peaceable constitution settled before they ventured themselves
therein.

16. See glossary.

17. William Penn (1644–1718) was the English Quaker who founded Pennsylvania
as a model commonwealth, with a government based on Quaker principles, where
liberty of conscience was guaranteed.

"We may observe by sundry laws enacted in parliament when the reformation was but newly begun in England, there seemed to be wisdom from above to influence their minds. May you be directed rightly to act at this time, many of whom do believe in the immediate influence of the spirit of Christ, the wisdom of God, which is truly profitable to direct.

"It is not with disrespect to the king or government that I speak after this manner, for I am thankful in my heart that the Lord in mercy vouchsafed that the throne of Great Britain should be filled with our present benevolent prince, King George.

"I acknowledged their kindness in hearing me patiently, and withdrew.

"In the 11th month, 1755," continues he, "I being at Shrewsbury Yearly Meeting in company with John Evans and several other Friends, a consideration was in my mind respecting the nature of giving money for the king's use, knowing the same to be for the carrying on of war.[18] John Evans and I took a few meetings in our way, the last of which was Evesham. I told John I felt an engagement to get to Philadelphia and requested him to go that way,[19] to which he consented. And when we came to the city, the Assembly were sitting and a committee of the House appointed to prepare a bill for giving a sum[20] of money for the king's use, to be sunk by a provincial tax.

"And several Friends, being under an exercise on that account, some of whom being providentially together, concluded it was expedient to request a conference with those members that were of our Society; and on applying to the Speaker, who was one himself, an opportunity was obtained with them,[21] after which we believed an address to the Assembly on behalf of the Society would be necessary. But we then, being only five in number, consulted several weighty Friends thereupon, and at length upward of twenty gathered together, who were all of opinion that the Assembly should be addressed on behalf of the Society; and one being drawn was signed by about twenty, who went together to the House and presented the same to the Speaker, which was read while we were present; notwithstanding, the law passed; which said address is as follows:

18. MS. R1 (but not the first edition) adds: "and whether if a sum should be given by our Assembly and a law by them made for raising the same by a tax, Friends would be clear in their testimony against wars if they paid such a tax."

19. MS. R1 (but not the first edition) reads: "and pressed him to that way."

20. MS. R1 (but not the first edition) reads: "large sum."

21. MS. R1 (but not the first edition) adds: "to some satisfaction as we thought, but alas, the same we soon found had little effect." The Speaker was Isaac Norris (1701-1766).

"To the Representatives of the Freemen of the Province of Pennsylvania in General Assembly Met—The Address of Some of the People Called Quakers on behalf of Themselves and Others.

"The consideration of the measures which have lately been pursued and are now proposed having been weightily impressed on our minds, we apprehend that we should fall short of our duty to you, to ourselves, and to our brethren in religious fellowship, if we did not in this manner inform you that although we shall at all times heartily and freely contribute according to our circumstances, either by the payment of taxes or in such other manner as may be judged necessary, toward the exigencies of government, and sincerely desire that due care may be taken and proper funds provided for raising money to cultivate our friendship with our Indian neighbours, and to support such of our fellow subjects who are or may be in distress, and such other like benevolent purposes; yet as the raising sums of money and putting them into the hands of committees who may apply them to purposes inconsistent with the peaceable testimony we profess, and have borne to the world, appears to us in its consequences to be destructive of our religious liberties, we apprehend many among us will be under the necessity of suffering, rather than consenting thereto by the payment of a tax for such purposes. And thus the fundamental part of our constitution may be essentially affected and that free enjoyment of liberty of conscience, for the sake of which our forefathers left their native country and settled in this then a wilderness, by degrees be violated.

"We sincerely assure you we have no temporal motives in thus addressing you; and could we have preserved peace in our own minds and with each other, we should have declined it, being unwilling to give you any unnecessary trouble and deeply sensible of your difficulty in discharging the trust committed to you irreproachably in these perilous times, which hath engaged our fervent desires that the immediate instruction of Supreme Wisdom may influence your minds, and that being preserved in a steady attention thereto you may be enabled to secure peace and tranquillity to yourselves, and those you represent, by pursuing measures consistent with our peaceable principles. And then we trust we may continue humbly to confide in the protection of that Almighty Power whose providence has heretofore been as walls and bulwarks round about us.

SIGNED BY TWENTY FRIENDS

"After the passing of the said Act, some Friends of those committees appointed by the last Yearly Meeting before-mentioned believed it was expedient for the said committees to meet together to deliberate upon the matter, as the payment of the tax was appointed to be before the Yearly Meeting, and I being acquainted therewith went to Philadelphia at the time appointed."][22]

As scrupling to pay a tax on account of the application hath seldom been heard of heretofore, even amongst men of integrity who have steadily borne their testimony against outward wars in their time, I may here note some things which have occurred to my mind as I have been inwardly exercised on that account.

From the steady opposition which faithful Friends in early times made to wrong things then approved of, they were hated and persecuted by men living in the spirit of this world,[23] and suffering with firmness they were made a blessing to the church, and the work prospered. It equally concerns men in every age to take heed to their own spirit, and in comparing their situation with ours, it looks to me there was less danger of their being infected with the spirit of this world, in paying their taxes, than there is of us now. They had little or no share in civil government,[24] and many of them declared they were through the power of God separated from the spirit in which wars were; and being afflicted by the rulers on account of their testimony, there was less likelihood of uniting in spirit with them in things inconsistent with the purity of Truth.[25] We, from the first settlement of this land, have known little or no troubles of that sort. The profession which for a time was accounted reproachful, at length the uprightness of our predecessors being understood by the rulers and their innocent sufferings moving them, the way of worship was tolerated, and many of our members in these colonies became active in civil government. Being thus tried with favour and prosperity, this world hath appeared inviting. Our minds have been turned to the improvement of our country, to merchandise and sciences, amongst which are many things useful, being followed in pure wisdom;[26] but in our present condition, that a carnal mind is gaining upon us I believe will not be denied.

Some of our members who are officers in civil government are in one

22. Here ends the section from Churchman's notes, as transcribed in MS. A. At this point Woolman wrote: "Thus far leave it out." The last paragraph is considerably expanded in the first printed edition of Churchman's volume.

23. In this sentence and the next, Woolman originally wrote "wrong spirit," and then substituted "spirit of this world." His equation of the two phrases is significant.

24. After "civil government" Woolman wrote and crossed out: "neither legislative nor executive."

25. Woolman wrote "purity of Truth" in place of his original "perfection of Christianity."

26. Woolman wrote "pure wisdom" in place of his original "sound wisdom."

case or other called upon in their respective stations to assist in things relative to the wars. Such being in doubt whether to act or crave to be excused from their office, seeing their brethren united in the payment of a tax to carry on the said wars, might think their case not much different and so quench the tender movings of the Holy Spirit in their minds. And thus by small degrees there might be an approach toward that of fighting, till we came so near it as that the distinction would be little else but the name of a peaceable people.

It requires great self-denial and resignation of ourselves to God to attain that state wherein we can freely cease from fighting when wrongfully invaded, if by our fighting there were a probability of overcoming the invaders. Whoever rightly attains to it does in some degree feel that spirit in which our Redeemer gave his life for us, and through divine goodness many of our predecessors and many now living have learned this blessed lesson. But many others, having their religion chiefly by education and not being enough acquainted with that cross which crucifies to the world, do manifest a temper distinguishable from that of an entire trust in God.

In calmly considering these things, it hath not appeared strange to me that an exercise hath now fallen upon some which, as to the outward means of it, is different from what was known to many of those who went before us.

Some time after the Yearly Meeting, a day being appointed and letters wrote to distant members, the said committees met at Philadelphia and by adjournments continued several days. The calamities of war were now increasing. The frontier inhabitants of Pennsylvania were frequently surprised, some slain and many taken captive by the Indians; and while these committees sat, the corpse of one so slain was brought in a wagon and taken through the streets of the city in his bloody garments to alarm the people and rouse them up to war.

Friends thus met were not all of one mind in relation to the tax, which to such who scrupled it made the way more difficult. To refuse an active payment at such a time might be construed an act of disloyalty and appeared likely to displease the rulers, not only here but in England. Still there was a scruple so fastened upon the minds of many Friends that nothing moved it. It was a conference the most weighty that ever I was at, and the hearts of many were bowed in reverence before the Most High. Some Friends of the said committees who appeared easy to pay the tax, after several adjournments withdrew; others of them continued till the last. At length an epistle was drawn by [27] [some Friends concerned on that account, and being read several times and corrected, was then signed by such who were free to sign it, which is as follows:

An Epistle of Tender Love and Caution to Friends in Pennsylvania

PHILADELPHIA, 16th day, 12th month, 1755

DEAR AND WELL BELOVED FRIENDS,

We salute you in a fresh and renewed sense of our Heavenly Father's love, which hath graciously overshadowed us in several weighty and solid conferences we have had together with many other Friends upon the present situation of the affairs of the Society in this province; and in that love we find our spirits engaged to acquaint you that under a solid exercise of mind to seek for counsel and direction from the High Priest of our profession, who is the Prince of Peace, we believe he hath renewedly favoured us with strong and lively evidences that in his due and appointed time, the day which hath dawned in these later ages foretold by the prophets, wherein swords should be beaten into plowshares and spears into pruning hooks [Is. 2:4], shall gloriously rise higher and higher, and the spirit of the gospel which teaches to love enemies prevail to that degree that the art of war shall be no more learned, and that it is his determination to exalt this blessed day in this our age, if in the depth of humility we receive his instruction and obey his voice.

And being painfully apprehensive that the large sum granted by the late Act of Assembly for the king's use is principally intended for purposes inconsistent with our peaceable testimony, we therefore think that as we cannot be concerned in wars and fightings, so neither ought we to contribute thereto by paying the tax directed by the said Act, though suffering be the consequence of our refusal, which we hope to be enabled to bear with patience.

And [we take this position even] though some part of the money to be raised by the said Act is said to be for such benevolent purposes as supporting our friendship with our Indian neighbours and relieving the distresses of our fellow subjects who have suffered in the present calamities, for whom our hearts are deeply pained; and we affectionately and with bowels of tenderness sympathize with

27. The last words at the bottom of page 148 in MS. B are "drawn by." The next page begins: "On the 9th day." Apparently some intervening pages of MS. B were lost. This is confirmed by a sudden break in the continuity of Woolman's page numbers. In the present edition the rest of this paragraph, the epistle that follows, and the ensuing paragraphs up to "On the 9th day" were taken from MS. A, pages 78–81. The original editorial committee drew upon MS. A to conclude the paragraph after "drawn by." The first edition adopts that reading and then omits the epistle and subsequent paragraphs, resuming the account with "On the 9th day."

them therein. And we could most cheerfully contribute to those purposes if they were not so mixed that we cannot in the manner proposed show our hearty concurrence therewith without at the same time assenting to, or allowing ourselves in, practices which we apprehend contrary to the testimony which the Lord hath given us to bear for his name and Truth's sake. And having the health and prosperity of the Society at heart, we earnestly exhort Friends to wait for the appearing of the true Light and stand in the council of God, that we may know him to be the rock of our salvation and place of our refuge forever. And beware of the spirit of this world, that is unstable and often draws into dark and timorous reasonings, lest the God thereof should be suffered to blind the eye of the mind, and such not knowing the sure foundation, the Rock of Ages, may partake of the terrors and fears that are not known to the inhabitants of that place where the sheep and lambs of Christ ever had a quiet habitation, which a remnant have to say, to the praise of his name, they have been blessed with a measure of in this day of distress.

And as our fidelity to the present government and our willingly paying all taxes for purposes which do not interfere with our consciences may justly exempt us from the imputation of disloyalty, so we earnestly desire that all who by a deep and quiet seeking for direction from the Holy Spirit are, or shall be, convinced that he calls us as a people to this testimony may dwell under the guidance of the same divine Spirit, and manifest by the meekness and humility of their conversation that they are really under that influence, and therein may know true fortitude and patience to bear that and every other testimony committed to them faithfully and uniformly, and that all Friends may know their spirits clothed with true charity, the bond of Christian fellowship, wherein we again salute you and remain your friends and brethren.

Signed by ABRAHAM FARRINGTON,* JOHN EVANS, JOHN CHURCHMAN,* MORDECAI YARNALL, SAMUEL FOTHERGILL, SAMUEL EASTBURN,* WILLIAM BROWN, JOHN SCARBOROUGH,* THOMAS CARLETON, JOSHUA ELY, WILLIAM JACKSON, JAMES BARTRAM, THOMAS BROWN, DANIEL STANTON,* JOHN WOOLMAN, ISAAC ZANE, WILLIAM HORNE,* BENJAMIN TROTTER, ANTHONY BENEZET,* JOHN ARMITT, JOHN PEMBERTON.*

Copies of this epistle were sent amongst Friends in the several parts of the Province of Pennsylvania, and as some in the Society who were easy to pay the tax spake openly against it, and as some of those who were concerned in the conference believed themselves rightly exercised in putting forward the epistle, they in the next Yearly Meeting expressed a willingness to have their conduct in that case enquired into, but Friends in the Yearly Meeting did not enter into the consideration of it.

When the tax was gathered, many paid it actively and others scrupled the payment, and in many places (the collectors and constables being Friends) distress was made on their goods by their fellow members. This difficulty was considerable, and at the Yearly Meeting at Philadelphia, 1757, the matter was opened and a committee of about forty Friends were appointed, some from each Quarter, to consider the case and report their judgment on this point: whether or no it would be best at this time publicly to consider it in the Yearly Meeting.

At this meeting were our Friends William Reckitt,* John Hunt, and Christopher Wilson from England, Benjamin Ferris from the Province of New York, and Thomas Nicholson from North Carolina, who at the request of the Yearly Meeting all sat with us. We met and, sitting some hours, adjourned until the next morning. It was a time of deep exercise to many minds, and after some hours spent at our second meeting, the following report was drawn and signed by a Friend in behalf of the committee:

> Agreeable to the appointment of the Yearly Meeting we have met and had several weighty and deliberate conferences on the subject committed to us, and as we find there are diversity of sentiments, we are for that and several other reasons unanimously of the judgment that it is not proper to enter into a public discussion of the matter, and we are one in judgment that it is highly necessary for the Yearly Meeting to recommend that Friends everywhere endeavour earnestly to have their minds covered with fervent charity towards one another.

Which report was entered on the minutes and copies sent in the extracts to the Quarterly and Monthly Meetings.]²⁸

On the 9th day, 8th month, 1757, at night, orders came to the military officers in our county, directing them to draft the militia and prepare a number of men to go off as soldiers to the relief of the English at Fort William Henry in [New] York government.²⁹ And in a few days there was a general review of the militia at Mount Holly, and a number of men chosen and sent off under some officers. Shortly after, there came orders to draft three times as many, to hold themselves in readiness to march when fresh orders came. And on the 17th day, 8th month, there was a meeting of the military officers at Mount Holly, who agreed on a draft,

28. The section taken from MS. A ends here.

29. Written and crossed out here by Woolman: "Then besieged by a number of French and Indians." Earlier in this sentence the original editorial committee inserted "Burlington" after "county" and "N." before "York."

and orders were sent to the men so chosen to meet their respective captains at set times and places, those in our township to meet at Mount Holly, amongst whom were a considerable number of our Society.

My mind being affected herewith, I had fresh opportunity to see and consider the advantage of living in the real substance of religion, where practice doth harmonize with principle. Amongst the officers are men of understanding, who have some regard to sincerity where they see it; and in the execution of their office, when they have men to deal with whom they believe to be upright-hearted men, to put them to trouble on account of scruples of conscience is a painful task and likely to be avoided as much as may be easily. But where men profess to be so meek and heavenly minded and to have their trust so firmly settled in God that they cannot join in wars, and yet by their spirit and conduct in common life manifest a contrary disposition, their difficulties are great at such a time.

Officers in great anxiety endeavouring to get troops to answer the demands of their superiors, seeing men who are insincere pretend scruple of conscience in hopes of being excused from a dangerous employment, they are likely to be roughly handled. In this time of commotion some of our young men left the parts and tarried abroad till it was over. Some came and proposed to go as soldiers. Others appeared to have a real tender scruple in their minds against joining in wars and were much humbled under the apprehension of a trial so near; I had conversation with several of them to my satisfaction.

At the set time when the captain came to town some of those last-mentioned went and told in substance as follows: That they could not bear arms for conscience sake, nor could they hire any to go in their places, being resigned as to the event of it. At length the captain acquainted them all that they might return home for the present and required them to provide themselves as soldiers and to be in readiness to march when called upon.[30] This was such a time as I had not seen before, and yet I may say with thankfulness to the Lord that I believed this trial was intended for our good, and I was favoured with resignation to him. The French army, taking the fort they were besieging, destroyed it and went away. The company of men first drafted, after some days march had orders to return home, and these on the second draft were no more called upon on that occasion.

The 4th day, 4th month, 1758, orders came to some officers in Mount

30. Woolman wrote "themselves as soldiers" in place of his original "soldier-like accoutrements such as he mentioned to them."

Holly to prepare quarters a short time for about one hundred soldiers; and an officer and two other men, all inhabitants of our town, came to my house, and the officer told me that he came to speak with me to provide lodging and entertainment for two soldiers, there being six shillings a week per man allowed as pay for it. The case being new and unexpected, I made no answer suddenly but sat a time silent, my mind being inward. I was fully convinced that the proceedings in wars are inconsistent with the purity of the Christian [31] religion, and to be hired to entertain men who were then under pay as soldiers was a difficulty with me. I expected they had legal authority for what they did, and after a short time I said to the officer, "If the men are sent here for entertainment, I believe I shall not refuse to admit them into my house, but the nature of the case is such that I expect I cannot keep them on hire." One of the men intimated that he thought I might do it consistent with my religious principles, to which I made no reply, as believing silence at that time best for me.

Though they spake of two, there came only one, who tarried at my house about two weeks and behaved himself civilly. And when the officer came to pay me I told him that I could not take pay for it, having admitted him into my house in a passive obedience to authority. I was on horseback when he spake to me,[32] and as I turned from him he said he was obliged to me, to which I said nothing; but thinking on the expression I grew uneasy, and afterwards being near where he lived I went and told him on what grounds I refused pay for keeping the soldier.

Near the beginning of the year 1758 I went one evening in company with a friend to visit a sick person, and before our return we were told of a woman living near who of late had several days been disconsolate, occasioned by a dream wherein death and the judgments of the Almighty after death were represented to her mind in a moving manner. Her sadness on that account being worn off, the friend with whom I was in company went to see her and had some religious conversation with her and her husband. With this visit they were somewhat affected, and the man with many tears expressed his satisfaction; and in a short time after, the poor man being on the river in a storm of wind, he with one more was drowned.

31. Woolman first wrote "of true religion" and then changed it.
32. The section "when the officer . . . horseback when he" is enclosed in brackets, which seem to have been inserted by Woolman. Perhaps he considered omitting this passage and then decided to retain it.

In the 8th month, 1758, having had drawings in my mind to be at the Quarterly Meeting in Chester County and at some meetings in the County of Philadelphia, I went first to said Quarterly Meeting, which was large, and several weighty matters came under consideration and debate, and the Lord was pleased to qualify some of his servants with strength and firmness to bear the burden of the day. Though I said but little my mind was deeply exercised, and under a sense of God's love in the anointing and fitting some young men for his work I was comforted, and my heart was tendered before him.

From hence I went to the youth's meeting at Darby, where my beloved friend and brother Benjamin Jones * met me by an appointment before I left home, to join in the visit. And we were at Radnor, Merion, Richland, North Wales, Plymouth, and Abington, and had cause to bow in reverence before the Lord, our gracious God, by whose help way was opened for us from day to day. I was out about two weeks and rode about two hundred miles.

[One evening a Friend came to our lodgings who was a justice of the peace and in a friendly way introduced the subject of refusing to pay taxes to support wars, and perceiving that I was one who scrupled the payment, said he had wanted an opportunity with some in that circumstance;[33] whereupon we had some conversation in a brotherly way on some texts of Scripture relating thereto, in the conclusion of which he said that according to our way of proceeding it would follow that whenever administration of government was ill, we must suffer distraint of goods rather than pay actively toward supporting it. To which I replied, "Men put in public stations are intended for good purposes, some to make good laws, others to take care that those laws are not broken. Now if those men thus set apart do not answer the design of their institution, our freely contributing to support them in that capaciy when we certainly know that they are wrong is to strengthen them in a wrong way and tends to make them forget that it is so. But when from a clear understanding of the case we are really uneasy with the application of money, and in the spirit of meekness suffer distress to be made on our goods rather than to pay actively, this joined with an upright uniform life may tend to put men athinking about their own public conduct."

33. This conversation with a justice of the peace ("One evening . . . conscience' sake") does not appear in MS. B. It is taken from MS. A, where Woolman suggests in a marginal note: "If this Journal is printed, leave out this conference and begin again at fourth line in page 88."

He said he would propose a medium: that is, where men in authority do not act agreeable to the mind of those who constituted them, he thought the people should rather remonstrate than refuse a voluntary payment of moneys so demanded, and added, "Civil government is an agreement of free men by which they oblige themselves to abide by certain laws as a standard, and to refuse to obey in that case is of like nature as to refuse to do any particular act which we had convenanted to do."

I replied that in making covenants it was agreeable to honesty and uprightness to take care that we do not foreclose ourselves from adhering strictly to true virtue in all occurrences relating thereto. But if I should unwarily promise to obey the orders of a certain man, or number of men, without any proviso, and he or they command me to assist in doing some great wickedness, I may then see my error in making such promise, and an active obedience in that case would be adding one evil to another; that though by such promise I should be liable to punishment for disobedience, yet to suffer rather than act to me appears most virtuous.

The whole of our conversation was in calmness and good will. And here it may be noted that in Pennsylvania, where there are many Friends under that scruple, a petition was presented to the Assembly by a large number of Friends, asking that no law might be passed to enjoin the payment of money for such uses which they as a peaceable people could not pay for conscience' sake.]

The Monthly Meeting of Philadelphia having been under a concern on account of some Friends who this summer, 1758, had bought Negro slaves, the said meeting moved it in their Quarterly Meeting to have the minute reconsidered in the Yearly Meeting which was made last on that subject. And the said Quarterly Meeting appointed a committee to consider it and report to their next, which committee having met once and adjourned, and I, going to Philadelphia to meet a committee of the Yearly Meeting, was in town the evening on which the Quarterly Meeting's committee met the second time, and finding an inclination to sit with them, was admitted; and Friends had a weighty conference on the subject. And soon after their next Quarterly Meeting I heard that the case was coming to our Yearly Meeting, which brought a weighty exercise upon me, and under a sense of my own infirmities and the great danger I felt of turning aside from perfect purity, my mind was often drawn to retire alone and put up my prayers to the Lord that he would be graciously pleased to strengthen me, that setting aside all views of self-interest and the friendship of this world, I might stand fully resigned to his holy will.

In this Yearly Meeting several weighty matters were considered, and toward the last, that in relation to dealing with persons who purchase slaves. During the several sittings of the said meeting, my mind was frequently covered with inward prayer, and I could say with David that tears were my meat day and night [Ps. 42:3]. The case of slavekeeping lay heavy upon me, nor did I find any engagement to speak directly to any other matter before the meeting. Now when this case was opened, several faithful Friends spake weightily thereto, with which I was comforted, and feeling a concern to cast in my mite, I said in substance as follows:

> In the difficulties attending us in this life, nothing is more precious than the mind of Truth inwardly manifested, and it is my earnest desire that in this weighty matter we may be so truly humbled as to be favoured with a clear understanding of the mind of Truth and follow it; this would be of more advantage to the Society than any mediums which are not in the clearness of divine wisdom. The case is difficult to some who have them, but if such set aside all self-interest and come to be weaned from the desire of getting estates, or even from holding them together when Truth requires the contrary, I believe way will open that they will know how to steer through those difficulties.

Many Friends appeared to be deeply bowed under the weight of the work and manifested much firmness in their love to the cause of truth and universal righteousness in the earth. And though none did openly justify the practice of slavekeeping in general, yet some appeared concerned lest the meeting should go into such measures as might give uneasiness to many brethren, alleging that if Friends patiently continued under the exercise, the Lord in time to come might open a way for the deliverance of these people.[34] And I, finding an engagement to speak, said:

> My mind is often led to consider the purity of the Divine Being and the justice of his judgments, and herein my soul is covered with awfulness. I cannot omit to hint of some cases where people have

34. The passage "alleging that . . . these people" was written by Woolman on a slip of paper which has been pasted on the page and keyed to this point. At the bottom of the slip Woolman wrote, "This was occasioned by an omission in copying." This is part of the conclusive evidence that Woolman copied (revising as he did so) from MS. A to MS. B, not vice versa. The wording of this passage in MS. A is exactly the same.

not been treated with the purity of justice, and the event hath been melancholy.

Many slaves on this continent are oppressed, and their cries have reached the ears of the Most High! Such is the purity and certainty of his judgments that he cannot be partial in our favour. In infinite love and goodness he hath opened our understandings from one time to another concerning our duty toward this people, and it is not a time for delay.

Should we now be sensible of what he requires of us, and through a respect to the private interest of some persons or through a regard to some friendships which do not stand on an immutable foundation, neglect to do our duty in firmness and constancy, still waiting for some extraordinary means to bring about their deliverance, it may be that by terrible things in righteousness God may answer us in this matter.

Many faithful brethren laboured with great firmness, and the love of Truth in a good degree prevailed. Several Friends who had Negroes expressed their desire that a rule might be made to deal with such Friends as offenders who bought slaves in future. To this it was answered that the root of this evil would never be effectually struck at until a thorough search was made into the circumstances of such Friends who kept Negroes, in regard to the righteousness of their motives in keeping them, that impartial justice might be administered throughout.

Several Friends expressed their desire that a visit might be made to such Friends who kept slaves, and many Friends declared that they believed liberty was the Negro's right, to which at length no opposition was made publicly, so that a minute was made more full on that subject than any heretofore and the names of several Friends entered who were free to join in a visit to such who kept slaves.[35]

35. The passage, "entered who were free to join in a visit to such who kept slaves," appears at the top of page 165 in MS. B, the rest of the page remaining blank. "Friends" has been crossed out with two lines, probably by Woolman. The whole passage has been crossed out with an additional single line. The original editorial committee then copied the passage (minus "Friends") at the bottom of page 164.

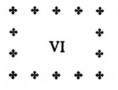

VI

1758–1759

[MS.B, p. 166]

I I TH DAY, 11TH MONTH, 1758. I set out for Concord.[1] That Quarterly Meeting, which heretofore was one, was now divided into two at our last Yearly Meeting by reason of a great increase of members. Here I met with our beloved Friends Samuel Spavold and Mary Kirby from England, and with Joseph White * from Bucks County, who had taken leave of his family in order to go on a religious visit to Friends in England, and through divine goodness we were favoured with a strengthening opportunity together.

After this meeting I joined with my friends Daniel Stanton * and John Scarborough * in visiting Friends who had slaves, and at night we had a family meeting at William Trimble's, there being a good many young people, and it was a precious, reviving opportunity. Next morning we had a comfortable sitting with a sick neighbour, and thence to the burial of the corpse of a Friend at Uwchlan Meeting, at which were many people, and it was a time of divine favour, after which we visited some who had slaves. [The next day we visited several who had slaves][2] and at night had a family meeting at our friend's Aaron Ashbridge's, where the channel of gospel love was opened and my mind was comforted after a hard day's labour.

The next day we were at Goshen Monthly Meeting, and then on the 18th, 11th month, 1758, attended the Quarterly Meeting at London Grove, it being the first held at that place. Here we met again with all the before-mentioned Friends and had some edifying meetings. And near

1. This Concord (as distinguished from one west of Harrisburg) was located about four miles south of West Chester. Uwchlan (next paragraph) was about fifteen miles north of West Chester.
2. This phrase is taken from MS. A. It seems to have been omitted inadvertently in the process of copying from MS. A to MS. B.

the conclusion of the meeting for business, Friends were incited to constancy in supporting the testimony of Truth and reminded of the necessity which the disciples of Christ are under to attend principally to his business,[3] as he is pleased to open it to us, and to be particularly careful to have our minds redeemed from the love of wealth, to have our outward affairs in as little room as may be, that so no temporal concerns may entangle our affections or hinder us from diligently following the dictates of Truth, in labouring to promote the pure spirit of meekness and heavenly-mindedness amongst the children of men in these days of calamity and distress, wherein God is visiting our land with his just judgments.

Each of these Quarterly Meetings were large and sat near eight hours. Here I had occasion to consider that it is a weighty thing to speak much in large meetings for business. First, except our minds are rightly prepared and we clearly understand the case we speak to, instead of forwarding, we hinder business and make more labour for those on whom the burden of the work is laid.

If selfish views or a partial spirit have any room in our minds, we are unfit for the Lord's work. If we have a clear prospect of the business and proper weight on our minds to speak, it behooves us to avoid useless apologies and repetitions. Where people are gathered from far, and adjourning a meeting of business attended with great difficulty, it behooves all to be cautious how they detain a meeting, especially when they have sat six or seven hours and a good way to ride home.

In three hundred minutes are five hours, and he that improperly detains three hundred people one minute, besides other evils that attend it, does an injury like that of imprisoning one man five hours without cause.[4] After this meeting I rode home.

In the beginning of the 12th month, 1758, I joined in company with my friends John Sykes * and Daniel Stanton * in visiting such who had slaves. Some whose hearts were rightly exercised about them[5] appeared

3. A bracket, inserted by someone other than Woolman, appears before "the disciples." These words start a new page (97) in the first edition. Elsewhere such brackets (perhaps inserted by the printer) mark the beginning of a new page in the first edition.

4. The passage "In three hundred . . . without cause" was crossed out by the original editorial committee.

5. At this point "and were concerned to do the thing that was right" has been crossed out in MS. B. This seems clearly to have been done by Woolman. It is likely that these words originally appeared in MS. A, where there is an erasure of approxi-

to be glad of our visit. And in some places our way was more difficult, and I often saw the necessity of keeping down to that root from whence our concern proceeded, and have cause in reverent thankfulness humbly to bow down before the Lord, who was near to me and preserved my mind in calmness under some sharp conflicts and begat a spirit of sympathy and tenderness in me toward some who were grievously entangled in the spirit of this world.

In the 1st month, 1759, having found my mind drawn toward a visit to some of the more active members in our Society at Philadelphia, who had slaves, I met my friend John Churchman * there by an agreement, and we continued about a week in the city. We visited some sick people and some widows and their families, and the other part of our time was mostly employed in visiting such who had slaves. It was a time of deep exercise, looking often to the Lord for his assistance, who in unspeakable kindness favoured with the influence of that spirit which crucifies to the greatness and showy grandeur of this world and enabled us to go through some heavy labours in which we found peace.

24th day, 3rd month, 1759. I was at our General Spring Meeting at Philadelphia,[6] after which I again joined with John Churchman * on a visit to some more who had slaves in Philadelphia, and with thankfulness to our Heavenly Father I may say that divine love and a true sympathizing tenderness of heart prevailed at times in this service.

Having at times perceived a shyness in some Friends of considerable note toward me, I found an engagement in gospel love to pay a visit to one of them, and as I dwelt under the exercise I felt a resignedness in my mind to go; so I went and told him in private I had a desire to have an opportunity with him alone, to which he readily agreed. And then in the fear of the Lord, things relating to that shyness were searched to the bottom, and we had a large conference which I believe was of use to both of us, and am thankful that way was opened for it.

14th day, 6th month, 1759. Having felt drawings in my mind to visit Friends about Salem, and having the agreement of our Monthly Meeting therein, I attended their Quarterly Meeting and was out seven days and at seven meetings, in some of which I was chiefly silent; and in others, through the baptizing power of Truth, my heart was enlarged in

---

mately the same length. It is difficult to reconstruct the exact process of revision, but apparently after copying from MS. A to MS. B, Woolman decided to eliminate this phrase, and then took it out of both versions.

6. MS. A adds: "at which was William Reckitt * and John Storer * from England."

heavenly love and found a near fellowship with the brethren and sisters in the manifold trials attending their Christian progress through this world.

In 7th month, 1759, I found an increasing concern on my mind to visit some active members in our Society who had slaves, and having no opportunity of the company of such who were named on the minutes of the Yearly Meeting, I went alone to their houses and in the fear of the Lord acquainted them with the exercise I was under; and thus, sometimes by a few words, I found myself discharged from a heavy burden. After this, our friend John Churchman * coming into our province with a view to be at some meetings and to join again in the visit to those who had slaves, I bore him company in the said visit to some active members, in which I found inward satisfaction.

At our Yearly Meeting, 1759, we had some weighty meetings where the power of Truth was largely extended to the strengthening of the honest-minded. As Friends read over the epistles to be sent to the Yearly Meetings along this continent, I observed in most of them, both this year and last, it was recommended to Friends to labour against that of buying and keeping slaves, and in some of them closely treated upon. As this practice hath long been a heavy exercise to me, as I have often went[7] through mortifying labours on that account and at times in some meetings been almost alone therein, now observing the increasing concern in the Society and seeing how the Lord was raising up and qualifying servants for his work, not only in this respect but for promoting the cause of Truth in general, I was humbly bowed in thankfulness before him.

This meeting continued near a week, and for several days in the fore part of it my mind was drawn into a deep inward stillness, and being at times covered with the spirit of supplication my heart was secretly poured out before the Lord. And near the conclusion of the meeting for business way opened that in the pure flowings of divine love I expressed what lay upon me, which as it then arose in my mind was first to show how deep answers to deep in the hearts of the sincere and upright, though in their different growths they may not all have attained to the same clearness in some points relating to our testimony,[8] wherein I was led to mention the integrity and constancy of many martyrs who gave their lives

7. In both MS. A and MS. B the words "and" and "waded" have been written over what seems to be "as" and what is definitely "went." This appears to have been done by the original editorial committee.

8. Woolman wrote "in their different . . . to our testimony" in place of his original "their sentiments in all circumstances may not exactly agree."

for the testimony of Jesus and yet in some points held doctrines distinguishable from some which we hold; and how that in all ages where people were faithful to the light and understanding which the Most High afforded them, they found acceptance with him; and that now, though there are different ways of thinking amongst us in some particulars, yet if we mutually kept to that spirit and power which crucifies to the world, which teaches us to be content with things really needful and to avoid all superfluities, giving up our hearts to fear and serve the Lord, true unity may still be preserved amongst us; and that if such who were at times under sufferings on account of some scruples of conscience kept low and humble and in their conduct in life manifested a spirit of true charity, it would be more likely to reach the witness in others, and be of more service in the church, than if their sufferings were attended with a contrary spirit and conduct. In which exercise I was drawn into a sympathizing tenderness with the sheep of Christ, however distinguished one from another in this world, and the like disposition appeared to spread over some others in the meeting. Great is the goodness of the Lord toward his poor creatures.

An epistle went forth from this Yearly Meeting which I thought good to give a place in this Journal, which is as follows: [9]

[*From our Yearly Meeting held at Philadelphia, for Pennsylvania and New Jersey, from the 22nd day of the ninth month to the 28th of the same (inclusive) 1759.*
To the Quarterly and Monthly Meetings of Friends Belonging to the Said Yearly Meeting

DEARLY BELOVED FRIENDS AND BRETHREN,

In an awful sense of the wisdom and goodness of the Lord our God, whose tender mercies have long been continued to us in this land, we affectionately salute you, with sincere and fervent desires that we may reverently regard the dispensations of his providence and improve under them.

The empires and kingdoms of the earth are subject to his almighty power; he is the God of the spirits of all flesh, and deals with his people agreeable to that wisdom the depth whereof is to us unsearchable. We in these provinces may say he hath, as a gracious and tender parent, dealt bountifully with us, even from the days of our fathers: It was he who strengthened them to labour

---

9. This epistle does not appear in MS. B. See Appendix D for evidence of Woolman's authorship, an account of the discovery of his copy of it, and its location.

through the difficulties attending the improvement of a wilderness and made way for them in the hearts of the natives, so that by them they were comforted in times of want and distress. It was by the gracious influences of his Holy Spirit that they were disposed to work righteousness and walk uprightly one towards another and towards the natives, and in life and conversation to manifest the excellency of the principles and doctrines of the Christian religion; and thereby they retained their esteem and friendship. Whilst they were labouring for the necessaries of life, many of them were fervently engaged to promote piety and virtue in the earth and educate their children in the fear of the Lord.

If we carefully consider the peaceable measures pursued in the first settlement of the land, and that freedom from the desolations of war which for a long time we enjoyed, we shall find ourselves under strong obligations to the Almighty, who, when the earth is so generally polluted with wickedness, gave us a being in a part so signally favoured with tranquillity and plenty, and in which the glad tidings of the gospel of Christ are so freely published that we may justly say with the Psalmist, "What shall we render unto the Lord for all his benefits?" [Ps. 116:12].

Our own real good and the good of our posterity in some measure depends on the part we act, and it nearly concerns us to try our foundations impartially. Such are the different rewards of the just and unjust in a future state that to attend diligently to the dictates of the spirit of Christ, to devote ourselves to his service and engage fervently in his cause, during our short stay in this world, is a choice well becoming a free, intelligent creature. We shall thus clearly see and consider that the dealings of God with mankind in a national capacity, as recorded in Holy Writ, do sufficiently evidence the truth of that saying, "It is righteousness which exalteth a nation" [Prov. 14:34]; and though he doth not at all times suddenly execute his judgments on a sinful people in this life, yet we see by many instances that where "men follow lying vanities they forsake their own mercies" [Jon. 2:8]; and as a proud, selfish spirit prevails and spreads among a people, so partial judgment, oppression, discord, envy, and confusions increase, and provinces and kingdoms are made to drink the cup of adversity as a reward of their own doings. Thus the inspired prophet, reasoning with the degenerated Jews, saith, "Thine own wickedness shall correct thee, and thy backslidings shall reprove thee; know, therefore, that it is an evil thing and bitter that thou hast forsaken the Lord thy God, and that my fear is not in thee, saith the Lord of Hosts." Jer. 2nd chap. and 19th verse.

The God of our fathers who hath bestowed on us many benefits, furnished a table for us in the wilderness, and made the deserts and solitary places to rejoice, he doth now mercifully call upon us to serve him more faithfully. We may truly say with the prophet, "It

is his voice which crieth to the city, and men of wisdom see his
name; they regard the rod and him who hath appointed it" [Mic.
6:9]. People who look chiefly at things outward too little consider
the original cause of the present troubles; but such who fear the
Lord and think often upon his name, they see and feel that a wrong
spirit is spreading among the inhabitants of our country, that the
hearts of many are waxed fat and their ears dull of hearing, that the
Most High in his visitations to us, instead of calling, he lifteth up
his voice and crieth; he crieth to our country and his voice waxeth
louder and louder. In former wars between the English and other
nations since the settlement of our provinces, the calamities attending them have fallen chiefly on other places, but now of late they
have reached to our borders; many of our fellow subjects have
suffered on and near our frontiers, some have been slain in battle,
some killed in their houses and some in their fields, some wounded
and left in great misery, and others separated from their wives and
little children, who have been carried captives among the Indians.
We have seen men and women who have been witnesses of these
scenes of sorrow and, being reduced to want, have come to our
houses asking relief. It is not long since it was the case of many
young men in one of these provinces to be drafted, in order to be
taken as soldiers; some were at that time in great distress and had
occasion to consider that their lives had been too little conformable
to the purity and spirituality of that religion which we profess,
and found themselves too little acquainted with that inward humility in which true fortitude to endure hardness for the Truth's sake
is experienced. Many parents were concerned for their children
and in that time of trial were led to consider that their care to get
outward treasure for them had been greater than their care for their
settlement in that religion which crucifieth to the world and en-
ableth to bear a clear testimony to the peaceable government of the
Messiah.—These troubles are removed, and for a time we are released from them.

Let us not forget that the Most High hath his way in the deep,
in clouds, and in thick darkness—that it is his voice which crieth to
the city and to the country, and oh, that these loud and awakening
cries may have a proper effect upon us, that heavier chastisement
may not become necessary! For though things as to the outward
may for a short time afford a pleasing prospect, yet while a selfish
spirit that is not subject to the cross of Christ continueth to spread
and prevail, there can be no long continuance in outward peace and
tranquillity. If we desire an inheritance incorruptible and to be at
rest in that state of peace and happiness which ever continues, if we
desire in this life to dwell under the favour and protection of that
Almighty Being whose habitation is in holiness, whose ways are all
equal, and whose anger is now kindled because of our backslidings,

let us then awfully regard these beginnings of his sore judgments, and with abasement and humiliation turn to him whom we have offended.

Contending with one equal in strength is an uneasy exercise; but if the Lord is become our enemy, if we persist to contend with him who is omnipotent, our overthrow will be unavoidable.

Do we feel an affectionate regard to posterity and are we employed to promote their happiness? Do our minds in things outward look beyond our own dissolution, and are we contriving for the prosperity of our children after us? Let us then like wise builders lay the foundation deep, and by our constant, uniform regard to an inward piety and virtue, let them see that we really value it. Let us labour in the fear of the Lord that their innocent minds, while young and tender, may be preserved from corruptions, that as they advance in age they may rightly understand their true interest, may consider the uncertainty of temporal things, and above all have their hope and confidence firmly settled in the blessing of that Almighty Being who inhabits eternity and preserves and supports the world.

In all our cares about worldly treasures, let us steadily bear in mind that riches possessed by children who do not truly serve God are likely to prove snares that may more grievously entangle them in that spirit of selfishness and exaltation which stands in opposition to real peace and happiness, and renders them enemies to the cross of Christ who submit to the influence of it.

To keep a watchful eye towards real objects of charity, to visit the poor in their lonesome dwelling places, to comfort them who through the dispensations of divine providence are in strait and painful circumstances in this life, and steadily to endeavour to honour God with our substance from a real sense of the love of Christ influencing our minds thereto, is more likely to bring a blessing to our children and will afford more satisfaction to a Christian favoured with plenty than an earnest desire to collect much wealth to leave behind us; for "here we have no continuing city"; may we therefore diligently seek one that is to come, "whose builder and maker is God" [Heb. 13:14 and 11:10].

"Finally, brethren, whatsoever things are true, . . . whatsoever things are just, whatsoever things are pure, whatsoever things are lovely, whatsoever things are of good report; if there be any virtue, if there be any praise, think on these things . . . and do them, and the God of peace shall be with you" [Phil. 4:8, 9].

Signed by appointment and on behalf of our said meeting by MORDECAI YARNALL, THOMAS MASSEY, JOHN CHURCHMAN,* JOHN SCARBOROUGH,* PETER FEARON, THOMAS EVANS, JOSEPH PARKER]

28th day, 11th month, 1759. I was at the Quarterly Meeting in Bucks County, this day being the Meeting of Ministers and Elders. My heart was enlarged in the love of Jesus Christ, and the favour of the Most High was extended to us in that and the ensuing meeting.

I had conversation at my lodging with my beloved friend Samuel Eastburn,* who expressed a concern to join in a visit to some Friends in that county who had Negroes; and as I had felt a draught in my mind to that work in the said county, I came home and put things in order. And on the 11th day, 12th month, I went over the river and on the next day was at Buckingham Meeting, where through the descendings of the heavenly dew my mind was comforted and drawn into a near unity with the flock of Jesus Christ.

Entering upon this visit appeared weighty, and before I left home my mind was often sad, under which exercise I felt at times that Holy Spirit which helps our infirmities, through which in private my prayers at times were put up to God that he would be pleased to so purge me from all selfishness that I might be strengthened to discharge my duty faithfully, how hard soever to the natural part. We proceeded on the visit in a weighty frame of spirit and went to the houses of the most active members through the county who had Negroes, and through the goodness of the Lord my mind was preserved in resignation in times of trial. And though the work was hard to nature, yet through the strength of that love which is stronger than death, tenderness of heart was often felt amongst us in our visits, and we parted with several families with greater satisfaction than we expected.

We visited Joseph White's * family, he being in England, had also a family meeting at the house of an elder who bore us company, and was at Makefield on a First Day, at all which times my heart was truly thankful to the Lord, who was graciously pleased to renew his loving-kindness to us, his poor servants, uniting us together in his work.

In the winter, 1759, the smallpox being in our town and many being inoculated, of which a few died, some things were opened in my mind which I wrote as follows: [10]

The more fully our lives are conformable to the will of God, the better it is for us. I have looked at the smallpox as a messenger sent from the Almighty to be an assistant in the cause of virtue, and to incite us to consider whether we employ our time only in such things as are consistent with perfect wisdom and goodness.

Building houses suitable to dwell in for ourselves and our creatures, preparing clothing suitable for the climate and season, and food con-

10. Woolman wrote "were opened" above his crossed-out "occurred to."

venient, are all duties incumbent on us, and under these general heads are many branches of business in which we may venture health and life as necessity may require.

This disease being in a house and my business calling me to go near it, it incites me to think whether this business is a real indispensable duty, whether it is not in conformity to some custom which would be better laid aside, or whether it does not proceed from too eager a pursuit after some outward treasure. If the business before me springs not from a clear understanding and a regard to that use of things which Perfect Wisdom approves,[11] to be brought to a sense of it and stopped in my pursuit is a kindness; for when I proceed to business without some evidence of duty, I have found by experience that it tends to weakness.

If I am so situated that there appears no probability of missing the infection, it tends to make me think whether my manner of life in things outward has nothing in it which may unfit my body to receive this messenger in a way the most favourable to me. Do I use food and drink in no other sort and in no other degree than was designed by him who gave these creatures for our sustenance? Do I never abuse my body by inordinate labour, striving to accomplish some end which I have unwisely proposed? Do I use action enough in some useful employ? Or do I sit too much idle, while some persons who labour to support me have too great a share of it? If in any of these things I am deficient, to be incited to consider it is a favour to me.[12]

There is employ necessary in social life, and this mortal infection incites me to think whether these social acts of mine are real duties. If I go on a visit to the widows and fatherless, do I go purely on a principle of charity, free from every selfish view? If I go to a religious meeting, it puts [13] me athinking whether I go in sincerity and in a clear sense of duty, or whether it is not partly in conformity to custom, or partly from a sensible delight which my animal spirits feel in the company of other people, and whether to support my reputation as a religious man has no share in it.[14]

11. Woolman may have intended to replace the word "Perfect" with the word "pure." The manuscript is not clear at this point.

12. Before the word "things" in MS. B is a bracket, and opposite it in the margin appears: "113." Not in Woolman's handwriting, these notations were apparently made by the printer, or by someone comparing MS. B with the first edition, page 113 of which begins at this point with the word "things."

13. Or "put." The MS. is not clear.

14. Woolman wrote "reputation" above his crossed-out "character."

Do affairs relating to civil society call me near this infection? If I go, it is at the hazard of my health and life, and becomes me to think seriously whether love to truth and righteousness is the motive of my attending, whether the manner of proceeding is altogether equitable, or whether aught of narrowness, party interest, respect to outward dignities, names, or colours of men do not stain the beauty of those assemblies and render the case doubtful in point of duty, etc., whether a disciple of Christ ought to attend, as a member united to the body, or not.

Whenever there are blemishes which for a series of time remain such, that which is a means of stirring us up to look attentively on those blemishes and to labour, according to our capacities, to have health and soundness restored in our country, we may justly account a kindness from our gracious Father, who appointed that mean.[15]

The care of a wise and good man for his only son is inferior to the regard of the great Parent of the universe for his creatures. He hath the command of all the powers and operations in nature and "doth not afflict willingly, nor grieve the children of men" [Lam. 3:33]. Chastisement is intended for instruction, and instruction being received by gentle chastisement, greater calamities are prevented.

By an earthquake hundreds of houses are sometimes shaken down in a few minutes and multitudes of people perish suddenly, and many more, being crushed and bruised in the ruins of the buildings, pine away and die with great misery.

By the breaking in of enraged, merciless armies, flourishing countries have been laid waste and great numbers of people perished in a short time, and many more pressed with poverty and grief.

By the pestilence people have died so fast in a city that through fear and grief and confusion those in health have found great difficulty in burying the dead, even without coffins.

By a famine great numbers of people in some places have been brought to the utmost distress and pined away for want of the necessaries of life. Thus where the kind invitations and gentle chastisements of a gracious God have not been attended to, his sore judgments have at times been poured out upon people.

While some rules approved in civil society and conformable to human policy, so called, are distinguishable from the purity of truth and righ-

---

15. Woolman seems to have written "mien," in contrast to his correct spelling of "means" a few lines above. (He was often erratic in his spelling.) The original editorial committee changed it to "mean," correcting the spelling but failing to add "s."

teousness, while many professing Truth are declining from that ardent love and heavenly-mindedness which was amongst the primitive followers of Jesus Christ, it is a time for us to attend diligently to the intent of every chastisement and consider the most deep and inward design of them.[16]

The Most High doth not often speak with an outward voice to our outward ears, but if we humbly meditate on his perfections, consider that he is perfect wisdom and goodness and to afflict his creatures to no purpose would be utterly reverse to his nature, we shall hear and understand his language, both in his gentle and more heavy chastisements, and take heed that we do not in the wisdom of this world endeavour to escape his hand by means too powerful for us.

Had he endowed man with understanding to hinder the force of this disease by innocent means, which had never proved mortal nor hurtful to our bodies, such discovery might be considered as the period of chastisement by this distemper where that knowledge extended. But as life and health are his gifts, and not to be disposed of in our own wills, to take upon us when in health a distemper of which some die requires great clearness of knowledge that it is our duty to do so.

Was no business done, no visits made, nor any assembling of people together but such as were consistent with pure wisdom, nor any inoculation, there would be a great alteration in the operation of this disorder amongst men.[17]

16. Woolman crossed out "religious Societies" and replaced it with "many professing Truth." After "Christ," Woolman crossed out "Whilst I and thee as individuals feel ourselves short of that perfection in virtue, which our Heavenly Father hath made possible for us to attain to." Instead of "time for us," Woolman originally wrote: "time for countries, societies, and individuals."

17. This final paragraph was crossed out by the original editorial committee.

VII

1760

HAVING FOR SOME TIME PAST felt a sympathizing in my mind with Friends eastward, I opened my concern in our Monthly Meeting, and obtaining a certificate, set forward 17th day, 4th month, 1760, joining in company by a previous agreement with my beloved friend Samuel Eastburn.* We had meetings at Woodbridge, Rahway, and Plainfield and was at their Monthly Meeting of Ministers and Elders in Rahway. We laboured under some discouragement, but through the invisible power of Truth our visit was made reviving to the lowly-minded, with whom I felt a near unity of spirit, being much reduced in my own mind. We passed on and visited chief of the meetings on Long Island. It was my concern from day to day to say no more nor less than what the spirit of Truth opened in me, being jealous over myself, lest I should speak anything to make my testimony look agreeable to that mind in people which is not in pure obedience to the cross of Christ.

The spring of the ministry was often low, and through the subjecting power of Truth we were kept low with it, and from place to place such whose hearts were truly concerned for the cause of Christ appeared to be comforted in our labours. And though it was in general a time of abasement of the creature, yet through his goodness who is a helper of the poor, we had some truly edifying seasons, both in meetings and in families where we tarried, and sometimes found strength to labour earnestly with the unfaithful, especially with those whose station in families or in the Society was such that their example had a powerful tendency to open the way for others to go aside from the purity and soundness of the blessed Truth.

At Jericho on Long Island I wrote home as follows:

DEARLY BELOVED WIFE,   24th day, 4th month, 1760

We are favoured with health, have been at sundry meetings in East Jersey and on this island. My mind hath been much in an inward watchful frame since I left thee, greatly desiring that our proceedings may be singly in the will of our Heavenly Father.

As the present appearance of things is not joyous, I have been much shut up from outward cheerfulness, remembering that promise, "Then shalt thou delight thyself in the Lord" [Ps. 37:4]. As this from day to day has been revived in my memory, I have considered that his internal presence on our minds is a delight of all others the most pure, and that the honest-hearted not only delight in this but in the effect of it upon them. He who regards the helpless and distressed and reveals his love to his children under affliction, they delight in beholding his benevolence and feeling divine charity moving upon them. Of this I may speak a little, for though since I left you, I have often found an engaging love and affection toward thee and my daughter and friends about home, [so] that going out at this time, when sickness is so great amongst you, is a trial upon me, yet I often remember there are many widows and fatherless, many who have poor tutors, many who have evil examples before them, and many whose minds are in captivity, for whose sake my heart is at times moved with [such] compassion that I feel my mind resigned to leave you for a season, to exercise that gift which the Lord hath bestowed on me, which though small compared with some, yet in this I rejoice: that I feel love unfeigned toward my fellow creatures. I recommend you to the Almighty, who I trust cares for you, and under a sense of his heavenly love remain, thy loving husband.

We crossed from the east end of Long Island to New London, about thirty miles, in a large open boat. While we were out, the wind rising high, the waves several times beat over us, that to me it appeared dangerous, but my mind was at that time turned to him who made and governs the deep, and my life was resigned [to] him; and as he was mercifully pleased to preserve us, I had fresh occasion to consider every day as a day lent to me and felt a renewed engagement to devote my time, and all I had, to him who gave it.

We had five meetings in Narraganset and thence to Newport. Our gracious Father preserved us in a humble dependence on him, through deep exercises that were mortifying to the creaturely will. In several families in the country where we lodged, I felt an engagement on my mind to have a conference with them in private concerning their slaves, and through divine aid I was favoured to give up thereto. Though in this thing I appear singular [1] from many whose service in travelling I believe is greater than mine, I do not think hard of them for omitting it. I do not repine at having so unpleasant a task assigned me, but look with awfulness to him who appoints to his servants their respective employments and is good to all who serve him sincerely.

We got to Newport in the evening, and on the next day visited two sick persons and had comfortable sittings with them, and in the afternoon attended the burial of a Friend. The next day we were at the meeting at Newport, forenoon and after, where the spring of the ministry was opened and strength given to declare the Word of Life to the people.

The next day we went on our journey, but the great number of slaves in these parts and the continuance of that trade from there to Guinea made deep impression on me, and my cries were often put up to my Father in secret that he would enable me to discharge my duty faithfully in such way as he might be pleased to point out to me.

We took Swansea, Freetown, and Taunton in our way to Boston, where also we had a meeting. Our exercise was deep and the love of Truth prevailed, for which I bless the Lord. We went eastward about eighty miles beyond Boston, taking meetings, and were in a good degree preserved in a humble dependence on that arm which drew us out; and though we had some hard labour with the disobedient, laying things home and close to such as were stout against the Truth, yet through the goodness of God we had at times to partake of heavenly comfort with them who were meek, and were often favoured to part with Friends in the nearness of true gospel fellowship. We returned to Boston and had another comfortable opportunity with Friends there, and thence rode a day's journey eastward to Bolton.[2] Our pilot being a heavy man and the weather hot, and my companion and I considering it, [we] expressed our freedom to go on without him, to which he consented, and so we respectfully took our leave of him. This we did as believing the journey would have went hard with him and his horse.

We visited the meetings in those parts and were measurably baptized into a feeling of the state of the Society, and in bowedness of spirit went

1. See glossary.
2. Woolman clearly wrote: "eastward to Bolton." Since Bolton is actually westward from Boston, he obviously erred. The original editorial committee and the printer made several changes, with the result that the first printed edition reads "eastward of Boston," as though Woolman retraced the route he had taken into Boston. It seems to the present editor that Woolman probably meant "westward to Bolton," whence he proceeded to Newport, the next point identified on his itinerary.

to the Yearly Meeting at Newport, where I understood that a large number of slaves were imported from Africa and then on sale by a member of our Society. At this meeting we met with John Storer * from England, Elizabeth Shipley, Ann Gauntt,* Hannah Foster, and Mercy Redman * from our parts, all ministers of the gospel, of whose company I was glad. At this time I had a feeling of the condition of Habakkuk as thus expressed: "When I heard, my belly trembled, my lips quivered, my appetite failed, and I grew outwardly weak. I trembled in myself that I might rest in the day of trouble" [Hab. 3:16]. I had many cogitations and was sorely distressed.

I was desirous that Friends might petition the Legislature to use their endeavours to discourage the future importation of them, for I saw that this trade was a great evil and tended to multiply troubles and bring distresses on the people in those parts, for whose welfare my heart was deeply concerned at this time. But I perceived several difficulties in regard to petitioning, and such was the exercise of my mind that I had thought of endeavouring to get an opportunity to speak a few words in the House of Assembly, they being then sitting in town. This exercise came upon me in the afternoon on the second day of the Yearly Meeting, and going to bed I got no sleep till my mind was wholly resigned therein; and in the morning I inquired of a Friend how long the Assembly were likely to continue sitting, who told me they were expected to be prorogued that day or the next.

As I was desirous to attend the business of the meeting and perceived the Assembly were likely to depart before the business was over, after considerable exercise, humbly seeking to the Lord for instruction, my mind settled to attend on the business of the meeting, on the last day of which I had prepared a short essay of a petition to be presented to the Legislature if way opened. And having understood there were men appointed by that Yearly Meeting to speak with men in authority in cases relating to the Society, I opened my mind to several of them and showed them the essay I had made, and afterward opened the case in the meeting for business, in substance as follows:

I have been under a concern for some time on account of the great number of slaves which are imported into this colony. I am aware that it is a tender point to speak to, but apprehend I am not clear in the sight of heaven without speaking to it. I have prepared an essay of a petition proposed, if way open, to be presented to the Legislature, and what I have to propose to this meeting is that some

Friends may be named to walk aside and look over it, and report whether they believe it suitable to be read in this meeting. If they should think well of reading it, it will remain for the meeting, after hearing it, to consider whether to take any further notice of it as a meeting or not.

After a short conference some Friends went out and, looking over it, expressed their willingness to have it read, which being done, many expressed their unity with the proposal, and some signified that to have the subjects of the petition enlarged upon and to be signed out of meeting by such who were free would be more suitable than to do it there. Though I expected at first that if it was done, it would be in that way, yet such was the exercise of my mind that to move it in the hearing of Friends when assembled appeared to me as a duty, for my heart yearned toward the inhabitants of these parts, believing that by this trade there had been an increase of unquietness amongst them and the way made easy for the spreading of a spirit opposite to that meekness and humility which is a sure resting place for the soul, and that the continuance of this trade would not only render their healing more difficult but increase their malady. Having thus far proceeded, I felt easy to leave the essay amongst Friends, for them to proceed in it as they believed best.

And now an exercise revived on my mind in relation to lotteries, which were common in those parts. I had once moved it in a former sitting of this meeting, when arguments were used in favour of Friends being held excused who were only concerned in such lotteries as were agreeable to law; and now on moving it again, it was opposed as before, but the hearts of some solid Friends appeared to be united to discourage the practice amongst their members, and the matter was zealously handled by some on both sides. In this debate it appeared very clear to me that the spirit of lotteries was a spirit of selfishness, which tended to confusion and darkness of understanding, and that pleading for it in our meetings, set apart for the Lord's work, was not right. And in the heat of zeal, I once made reply to what an ancient Friend said, which when I sat down I saw that my words were not enough seasoned with charity, and after this I spake no more on the subject.

At length a minute was made, a copy of which was agreed to be sent to their several Quarterly Meetings, inciting Friends to labour to discourage the practice amongst all professing with us.[3]

Some time after this minute was made I, remaining uneasy with the

3. Before "inciting" Woolman wrote and crossed out "expressing the concern."

manner of my speaking to an ancient Friend, could not see my way clear to conceal my uneasiness, but was concerned that I might say nothing to weaken the cause in which I had laboured. And then after some close exercise and hearty repentance for that I had not attended closely to the safe guide, I stood up and, reciting the passage, acquainted Friends that though I dare not go from what I had said as to the matter, yet [4] I was uneasy with the manner of my speaking, as believing milder language would have been better. As this was uttered in some degree of creaturely abasement, it appeared to have a good savor amongst us, after a warm debate.[5]

The Yearly Meeting being now over, there yet remained on my mind a secret, though heavy, exercise in regard to some leading active members about Newport being in the practice of slavekeeping. This I mentioned to two ancient Friends who came out of the country, and proposed to them, if way opened, to have some conversation with those Friends; and thereupon one of those country Friends and I consulted one of the most noted elders who had them, and he in a respectful manner encouraged me to proceed to clear myself of what lay upon me. Now I had near the beginning of the Yearly Meeting a private conference with this said elder and his wife concerning theirs, so that the way seemed clear to me to advise with him about the way of proceeding. I told him I was free to have a conference with them all together in a private house, or if he believed they would take it unkind to be asked to come together and to be spoke with one in the hearing of another, I was free to spend some time among them and visit them all in their own houses. He expressed his liking to the first proposal, not doubting their willingness to come together, and as I proposed a visit to only ministers, elders, and overseers, he named some others whom he desired might be present also; and as a careful messenger was wanted to acquaint them in a proper manner, he offered to go to all their houses to open the matter to them, and did so.

About the eighth hour the next morning we met in the meeting house chamber, and the last-mentioned country Friend, also my companion and John Storer * with us. Then after a short time of retirement, I acquainted them with the steps I had taken in procuring that meeting and opened

4. At this point MSS. A and B have an erasure (which seems clearly to have been made by Woolman) of these words: "considering the years of the Friend to whom I made reply."

5. The words "creaturely abasement" have been underlined in red, probably by someone other than Woolman. Mrs. Gummere (236n.) has suggested that the "ancient Friend" was John Casey (see Biographical Notes).

the concern I was under, and so we proceeded to a free conference upon the subject. My exercise was heavy and I was deeply bowed in spirit before the Lord, who was pleased to favour with the seasoning virtue of Truth, which wrought a tenderness amongst us, and the subject was mutually handled in a calm and peaceable spirit. And at length feeling my mind released from that burden which I had been under, I took my leave of them in a good degree of satisfaction, and by the tenderness they manifested in regard to the practice and the concern several of them expressed in relation to disposing of them after their decease, I believed that a good exercise was spreading amongst them; and I am humbly thankful to God, who supported my mind and preserved me in a good degree of resignation through these trials.

Thou who sometimes travels in the work of the ministry and art made very welcome by thy friends seest many tokens of their satisfaction in having thee for their guest. It's good for thee to dwell deep, that thou mayest feel and understand the spirits of people. If we believe Truth points toward a conference on some subjects in a private way, it's needful for us to take heed that their kindness, their freedom, and affability do not hinder us from the Lord's work. I have seen that in the midst of kindness and smooth conduct to speak close and home to them who entertain us, on points that relate to their outward interest, is hard labour; and sometimes when I have felt Truth lead toward it, I have found myself disqualified by a superficial friendship, and as the sense thereof hath abased me and my cries have been to the Lord, so I have been humbled and made content to appear weak or as a fool for his sake, and thus a door hath opened to enter upon it.

To attempt to do the Lord's work in our own way and to speak of that which is the burden of the Word in a way easy to the natural part does not reach the bottom of the disorder.[6] To see the failings of our friends and think hard of them, without opening that which we ought to open, and still carry a face of friendship—this tends to undermine the foundation of true unity. The office of a minister of Christ is weighty, and they who now go forth as watchmen had need to be steadily on their guard against the snares of prosperity and an outside friendship.

After the Yearly Meeting was over, we were at meetings at Newton, Cushnet, Long Plain, Rochester, and Dartmouth, and from thence we

6. After "in a way" Woolman originally wrote and then deleted "of affability and." Someone (probably not Woolman) changed "does" to "doth."

sailed for Nantucket in company with Ann Gauntt * and Mercy Red-man * and several other Friends. The wind being slack, we only reached Tarpawling Cove the first day, where, going on shore, we found room in a public house and beds for a few of us, the rest sleeping on the floor. We went on board again about break of day,[7] and though the wind was small, we were favoured to come within about four miles of Nantucket; and then about ten of us getting in our boat, we rowed to the harbour before dark, whereupon a large boat going off brought in the rest of the passengers about midnight.

The next day but one was their Yearly Meeting, which held four days, on the last of which was also their Monthly Meeting of business. We had a laborious time amongst them, our minds were closely exercised, and I believe it was a time of great searching of heart. The longer I was on the island the more I became sensible that there were a considerable number of valuable Friends there, though an evil spirit, tending to strife, had been at work amongst them. I was cautious of making any visits but as my mind was particularly drawn to them, and in that way we had some sittings in Friends' houses, where the heavenly wing was at times spread over us to our mutual comfort. My beloved companion had very acceptable service on this island.

When meeting was over we all agreed to sail the next day if the weather was suitable and we well, and being called up the latter part of the night, we went on board, being in all about fifty; but the wind changing, the seamen thought best to stay in the harbor till it altered again, so we went on shore. And I, feeling clear as to any further visits, spent my time in our chamber, chiefly alone; and after some hours, my heart being filled with the spirit of supplication, my prayers and tears were poured out before my Heavenly Father for his help and instruction in the manifold difficulties which attended me in life.

And while I was waiting upon the Lord, there came a messenger from the women Friends, who lodged at another house, desiring to confer with us about appointing a meeting, which to me appeared weighty, as we had been at so many before; but after a short conference and advising with some elderly Friends, a meeting was appointed, in which the Friend who first moved it and who had been much shut up before was largely

7. Before "break" the printer or someone else has inserted a line, which somewhat resembles a bracket, to indicate the beginning of a new page (129) in the first edition.

opened in the love of the gospel. And the next morning about break of
day going on board, we reached Falmouth on the main before night,
where, our horses being brought, we proceeded toward Sandwich Quarterly Meeting.

Being two days going to Nantucket and having been once before, I
observed many shoals in their bay, which makes sailing more dangerous,
especially in stormy nights. I observed also a great shoal which encloses
their harbor and prevents their going in with sloops except when the tide
is up. Waiting without this shoal for the rising of the tide is sometimes
hazardous in storms, and waiting within they sometimes miss a fair wind.
I took notice that on that small island are a great number of inhabitants
and the soil not very fertile, the timber so gone that for vessels, fences,
and firewood they depend chiefly on buying from the main, the cost
whereof, with most of their other expenses, they depend principally upon
the whale fishery to answer. I considered that if towns grew larger and
lands near navigable waters more cleared, timber and wood would require more labour to get it. I understood that the whales, being much
hunted, and sometimes wounded and not killed, grew more shy and
difficult to come at.

I considered that the formation of the earth, the seas, the islands, bays,
and rivers, the motions of the winds and great waters, which cause bars
and shoals in particular places, were all the works of him who is perfect
wisdom and goodness; and as people attend to his heavenly instruction
and put their trust in him, he provides for them in all parts where he
gives them a being.

And as in this visit to these people I felt a strong desire for their firm
establishment on the sure foundation, besides what was said more publicly
I was concerned to speak with the women Friends in their Monthly
Meeting of business, many being present, and in the fresh spring of pure
love to open before them the advantage, both inward and outward, of
attending singly to the pure guidance of the Holy Spirit, and therein to
educate their children in true humility and the disuse of all superfluities,
reminding them of the difficulties their husbands and sons were frequently exposed to at sea, and that the more plain and simple their way
of living was, the less need of running great hazards to support them in
it—encouraging the young women in their neat, decent way of attending
themselves on the affairs of the house, showing, as the way opened, that
where people were truly humble, used themselves to business, and were
content with a plain way of life, that it had ever been attended with

more true peace and calmness of mind than those have had who, aspiring to greatness and outward show, have grasped hard for an income to support themselves in it. And as I observed they had few or no slaves amongst them, I had to encourage them to be content without them, making mention of the numerous troubles and vexations which frequently attend the minds of people who depend on slaves to do their labour.

We attended the Quarterly Meeting at Sandwich in company with Ann Gauntt * and Mercy Redman,* which was preceded by a Monthly Meeting, and in the whole held three days. We were various ways exercised amongst them in gospel love, according to the several gifts bestowed on us, and were at times overshadowed with the virtue of Truth, to the comfort of the sincere and stirring up of the negligent. Here we parted with Ann and Mercy and went to Rhode Island, taking one meeting in our way, which was a satisfactory time; and reaching Newport the evening before their Quarterly Meeting, we attended it and after that had a meeting with our young people,[8] separated from other Societies.

We had went through much labour in this town; and now in taking leave of it, though I felt close inward exercise to the last, I found inward peace and was in some degree comforted in a belief that a good number remain in that place who retain a sense of Truth, and that there are some young people attentive to the voice of the Heavenly Shepherd. The last meeting, in which Friends from the several parts of the quarter came together, was a Select Meeting,[9] and through the renewed manifestation of our Father's love, the hearts of the sincere were united together.

That poverty of spirit and inward weakness with which I was much tried the forepart of this journey has of late appeared to me as a dispensation of kindness.[10] Appointing meetings never appeared more weighty to me, and I was led into a deep search whether in all things my mind was resigned to the will of God, often querying with myself what should be the cause of such inward poverty, and greatly desired that no secret reserve in my heart might hinder my access to the Divine Fountain. In these humbling times I was made watchful and excited to attend the secret movings of the Heavenly Principle in my mind, which prepared the way to some duties that in more easy and prosperous times as to the outward I believe I should have been in danger of omitting.

8. What appears to be "our" is practically illegible.
9. A meeting of ministers and elders.
10. MS. A reads: "as a kindness from the Lord."

From Newport we went to Greenwich, Shanticut,[11] and Warwick, and were helped to labour amongst Friends in the love of our gracious Redeemer. And then, accompanied by our friend John Casey * from Newport, we rode through Connecticut to Oblong. We visited the meetings of Friends in those parts and thence proceeded to the Quarterly Meeting at Rye Woods, and through the gracious extendings of divine help had some seasoning opportunities in those places. So we visited Friends at York [12] and Flushing and thence to Rahway, and here our roads parting, I took leave of my beloved companion and true yokemate, Samuel Eastburn,* and reached home the 10th day, 8th month, 1760, where I found my family well. And for the favours and protection of the Lord, both inward and outward, extended to me in this little journey, my heart is humbled in grateful acknowledgments, and [I] find renewed desires to dwell and walk in resignedness before him.

11. Apparently Meshanticut, Rhode Island. It was evidently to this same town that Woolman's contemporary, John Fothergill, referred as Shanticoke.

12. Before "York" the original editorial committee inserted "New."

✢ ✢ ✢ ✢ ✢
✢   ✢
✢   VIII   ✢
✢ ✢ ✢ ✢ ✢

1761–1763

HAVING FELT MY MIND DRAWN TOWARD a visit to a few meetings in Pennsylvania, I was very desirous to be rightly instructed as to the time of setting off, and on 10th day, 5th month, 1761, being the first day of the week, I went to Haddonfield Meeting, concluding in my mind to seek for heavenly instruction and come home or go on, as I might then believe best for me; and there through the springing up of pure love I felt encouragement and so crossed the river. In this visit I was at two Quarterly and three Monthly Meetings and in the love of Truth felt my way open to labour with some noted Friends who kept Negroes. And as I was favoured to keep to the root and endeavoured to discharge what I believed was required of me, I found inward peace therein, from time to time, and thankfulness of heart to the Lord, who was graciously pleased to be a guide to me.

In the 8th month, 1761, having felt drawings in my mind to visit Friends in and about Shrewsbury, I went there and was at their Monthly Meeting and their First Day meeting and had a meeting at Squan and another at Squankum, and as way opened had conversation with some noted Friends concerning their slaves, and returned home in a thankful sense of the goodness of the Lord.

From a care I felt growing in me some years, I wrote *Considerations on Keeping Negroes, Part Second*, which were printed this year, 1762.[1] When the Overseers of the Press had done with it, they offered to get a number printed, to be paid for out of the Yearly Meeting stock and to be given away; but I being most easy to publish them at my own expense, and offering my reasons, they appeared satisfied.

This stock is the contribution of the members of our religious Society in general, amongst whom are some who keep Negroes, and being in-

1. This essay was printed by Benjamin Franklin. It is contained in this volume.

clined to continue them in slavery, are not likely to be satisfied with
those books being spread amongst a people where many of the slaves are
learned to read, and especially not at their expense; and such, often receiving them as a gift, conceal them.[2] But as they who make a purchase
generally buy that which they have a mind for, I believed it best to sell
them, expecting by that means they would more generally be read with
attention. Advertisements being signed by order of the Overseers of the
Press, directed to be read in Monthly Meetings of business within our
own Yearly Meeting, informing where the books were and that the price
was no more than the cost of printing and binding them, many were
taken off in our parts. Some I sent to Virginia, some to York, and some
to Newport to my acquaintance there; and some I kept, expecting to give
part of them away where there appeared a prospect of doing it to advantage.[3]

In my youth I was used to hard labour, and though I was middling
healthy, yet my nature was not fitted to endure so much as many others,
that being often weary, I was prepared to sympathize with those whose
circumstance in life as free men required constant labour to answer the
demands of their creditors, and with others under oppression. In the
uneasiness of body which I have many times felt by too much labour,
not as a forced but a voluntary oppression, I have often been excited to
think on the original cause of that oppression which is imposed on many
in the world. And the latter part of the time wherein I laboured on our
plantation, my heart through the fresh visitations of heavenly love being
often tender and my leisure time frequently spent in reading the life and
doctrines of our blessed Redeemer, the account of the sufferings of
martyrs, and the history of the first rise of our Society, a belief was
gradually settled in my mind that if such who had great estates generally
lived in that humility and plainness which belongs to a Christian life, and
laid much easier rents and interests on their lands and moneys and thus
led the way to a right use of things, so great a number of people might
be employed in things useful that labour both for men and other creatures would need to be no more than an agreeable employ, and divers

2. This sentence has been revised in MS. B. The revision seems definitely to have
been made by Woolman. The final result (reproduced here) treats the Society of
Friends a little more kindly than the earlier version in MS. A, where Woolman wrote:
"many who keep Negroes" and "resolved to continue."

3. "N" was inserted before "York" by the original editorial committee. Woolman
probably meant "New York." The original editorial committee substituted "service"
for "doing it to advantage."

branches of business which serves chiefly to please the natural inclinations of our minds, and which at present seems necessary to circulate that wealth which some gather, might in this way of pure wisdom be discontinued. And as I have thus considered these things, a query at times hath arisen: Do I in all my proceedings keep to that use of things which is agreeable to universal righteousness? And then there hath some degree of sadness at times come over me, for that I accustomed myself to some things which occasioned more labour than I believed divine wisdom intends for us.

From my early acquaintance with Truth I have often felt an inward distress [4] occasioned by the striving of a spirit in me against the operation of the Heavenly Principle, and in this circumstance have been affected with a sense of my own wretchedness, and in a mourning condition felt earnest longings for that divine help which brings the soul into true liberty. And sometimes in this state, retiring into private places, the spirit of supplication hath been given me, and under a heavenly covering have asked my gracious Father to give me a heart in all things resigned to the direction of his wisdom; and in uttering language like this, the thoughts of my wearing hats and garments dyed with a dye hurtful to them has made lasting impressions on me.

In visiting people of note in the Society who had slaves and labouring with them in brotherly love on that account, I have seen, and the sight has affected me, that a conformity to some customs distinguishable from pure wisdom has entangled many, and the desire of gain to support these customs greatly opposed the work of Truth. [5] And sometimes when the prospect of the work before me has been such that in bowedness of spirit I have been drawn into retired places, and besought the Lord with tears that he would take me wholly under his direction and show me the way in which I ought to walk, it hath revived with strength of conviction that if I would be his faithful servant I must in all things attend to his wisdom and be teachable, and so cease from all customs contrary thereto, however used amongst religious people.

4. Woolman wrote "distress" in place of his original "sadness."

5. "In visiting . . . of Truth" has been pasted to page 121 of MS. A and keyed to this point. On the pasted slip "and the sight has affected me" has been inserted with a caret. In MS. B (page 230) this double insertion is incorporated smoothly into the text, as would be expected in copying from MS. A to MS. B. At several other points before and after this paragraph, MS. A has been considerably revised, the final result being copied smoothly and verbatim into MS. B. A study of both MSS. makes it evident that Woolman copied from MS. A to MS. B, not vice versa.

As he is the perfection of power, of wisdom, and of goodness, so I believe he hath provided that so much labour shall be necessary for men's support in this world as would, being rightly divided, be a suitable employment of their time, and that we cannot go into superfluities, or grasp after wealth in a way contrary to his wisdom, without having connection with some degree of oppression and with that spirit which leads to self-exaltation and strife, and which frequently brings calamities on countries by parties contending about their claims.[6]

Being thus fully convinced and feeling an increasing desire to live in the spirit of peace, being often sorrowfully affected in thinking on the unquiet spirit in which wars are generally carried on, and with the miseries of many of my fellow creatures engaged therein—some suddenly destroyed, some wounded and after much pain remain cripples, some deprived of all their outward substance and reduced to want, and some carried into captivity—thinking often on these things, the use of hats and garments dyed with a dye hurtful to them and wearing more clothes in summer than are useful grew more uneasy to me, believing them to be customs which have not their foundation in pure wisdom. The apprehension of being singular from my beloved friends was a strait upon me, and thus I remained in the use of some things contrary to my judgment.

And on the 31st day, fifth month, 1761, I was taken ill of a fever, and after having it near a week I was in great distress of body. And one day there was a cry raised in me that I might understand the cause why I was afflicted and improve under it, and my conformity to some customs which I believed were not right were brought to my remembrance. And in the continuation of the exercise I felt all the powers in me yield themselves up into the hands of him who gave me being and was made thankful that he had taken hold of me by his chastisement, feeling the necessity of further purifying. There was now no desire in me for health until the design of my correction was answered, and thus I lay in abasement and brokenness of spirit. And as I felt a sinking down into a calm resignation, so I felt, as in an instant, an inward healing in my nature, and from that time forward I grew better.

Though I was thus settled in mind in relation to hurtful dyes, I felt easy to wear my garments heretofore made, and so continued about nine months. Then I thought of getting a hat the natural colour of the fur, but

6. There is evidence that Woolman did considerable revision of the next paragraph; several lines were erased and replaced by others, words were inserted with carets, etc.

the apprehension of being looked upon as one affecting singularity felt uneasy to me. And here I had occasion to consider that things, though small in themselves, being clearly enjoined by divine authority became great things to us, and I trusted the Lord would support me in the trials that might attend singularity while that singularity was only for his sake. On this account I was under close exercise of mind in the time of our General Spring Meeting, 1762, greatly desiring to be rightly directed. And at a time when one of my dear brethren was concerned in humble supplication, I, being then deeply bowed in spirit before the Lord, was made willing, in case I got safe home, to speak for a hat the natural colour of the fur, and did so.[7]

In attending meetings this singularity was a trial upon me, and more especially at this time, as being in use among some who were fond of following the changeable modes of dress;[8] and as some Friends who knew not on what motives I wore it carried shy of me, I felt my way for a time shut up in the ministry. And in this condition, my mind being turned toward my Heavenly Father with fervent cries that I might be preserved to walk before him in the meekness of wisdom, my heart was often tender in meetings, and I felt an inward consolation, which to me was very precious under those difficulties.

I had several dyed garments fit for use, which I believed it best to wear till I had occasion of new ones, and some Friends were apprehensive that my wearing such a hat savored of an affected singularity, and such who spoke with me in a friendly way I generally informed in a few words that I believed my wearing it was not in my own will. I had at times been sensible that a superficial friendship had been dangerous to me, and many Friends being now uneasy with me I found to be a providential kindness. And though[9] I had an inclination to acquaint some valuable Friends with the manner of my being led into these things, yet upon a deeper thought I was for a time most easy to omit it, believing the present dispensation was profitable and trusting that if I kept my place the Lord

7. In place of this sentence the original editorial committee substituted: "when being deeply bowed in spirit before the Lord I was made willing to submit to what I apprehended was required of me, and when I returned home got a hat of the natural colour of the fur."

8. In place of "as being in use among some" the original editorial committee substituted: "white hats being used by some." Some of Woolman's associates were apparently perplexed and offended by what seemed to be submission to the latest fashion.

9. The words "I found . . . though" were struck out by the original editorial committee.

in his own time would open the hearts of Friends toward me, since which I've had cause to admire his goodness and loving-kindness in leading about and instructing, and opening and enlarging my heart in some of our meetings.

11th [month], 176[2. Fe]eling an engagement of mind to visit some families in Mansfield, I joined my beloved friend Benjamin Jones,* and we spent a few days together in that service.[10] And in 2nd month, 1763, I joined in company with Elizabeth Smith * and Mary Noble on a visit to the families of Friends at Rancocas, in both which visits, through the baptizing power of Truth, the sincere labourers were often comforted and the hearts of Friends opened to receive us. And in the fourth month following I bore some Friends company on a visit to the families of Friends in Mount Holly, in which visit my mind was often drawn into an inward awfulness wherein strong desires were raised for the everlasting welfare of my fellow creatures; and through the kindness of our Heavenly Father our hearts were at times enlarged, and Friends invited in the flowings of divine love to attend to that which would settle them on the sure foundation.[11]

Having many years felt love in my heart toward the natives of this land who dwell far back in the wilderness, whose ancestors were the owners and possessors of the land where we dwell, and who for a very small consideration assigned their inheritance to us, and being at Philadelphia in the 8th month, 1761, on a visit to some Friends who had slaves, I fell in company with some of those natives who lived on the east branch of the river Susquehanna at an Indian town called Wyalusing, about two hundred miles from Philadelphia. And in conversation with them by an interpreter, as also by observations on their countenance and conduct, I believed some of them were measurably acquainted with that

10. The bracketed portions have been torn off of the top of page 239 of MS. B. They have been supplied from the parallel passage in MS. A.

11. At this point in MS. A (at the bottom of page 124) is an interesting note: "manuscript [illeg.] 239 ends here d.d. J. Crukshank 20.4 month. 1774." Page 239 of MS. B does end at this point. The handwriting is the same as that in most of the revisions made by the original editorial committee. The note apparently means that MS. B up to that point had been delivered to Crukshank, the printer of the first edition.

At this point in MS. B a page is left blank. In the margin of the following page (240) Woolman wrote the figure "1," starting a new numbering system, as he did with each new section. Also in the margin, the original editorial committee wrote: "(third part) containing 118 pages." The whole manuscript, as we have it, ends 108 pages further on—at page 348. Perhaps ten pages were lost.

divine power which subjects the rough and froward will of the creature; and at times I felt inward drawings toward a visit to that place, of which I told none except my dear wife until it came to some ripeness.

And then in the winter, 1762, I laid it before Friends at our Monthly and Quarterly and then at our General Spring Meeting, and having the unity of Friends and being thoughtful about an Indian pilot, there came a man and three women from a little beyond that town to Philadelphia on business; and I, being informed thereof by letter, met them in town on the 5th month, 1763. And after some conversation finding they were sober people, I, by the concurrence of Friends in that place, agreed to join with them as companions in their return; and the 7th day, 6th month, following we appointed to meet at Samuel Foulke's * at Richland.¹² Now as this visit felt weighty and was performed at a time when travelling appeared perilous, so the dispensations of divine providence in preparing my mind for it have been memorable, and I believe it good for me to give some hints thereof.¹³

After I had given up to go, the thoughts of the journey were often attended with an unusual sadness, in which times my heart was frequently turned to the Lord with inward breathings for his heavenly support, that I might not fail to follow him wheresoever he might lead me. And being at our youths' meeting at Chesterfield about a week before the time I expected to set off, was there led to speak on that prayer of our Redeemer to his Father: "I pray not that thou shouldest take them out of the world, but that thou shouldest keep them from evil" [Jn. 17:9]. And in attending to the pure openings of Truth, [I] had to mention what he elsewhere said to his Father: "I know that thou hearest me at all times" [Jn. 11:42], so that as some of his followers kept their places, and as his prayer was granted, it followed necessarily that they were kept from evil. And as some of those met with great hardships and afflictions in this world and at last suffered death by cruel men, it appears that whatever befalls men while they live in pure obedience to God, as it certainly works for their good, so it may not be considered an evil as it relates to them. As I spake on this subject my heart was much tendered and great awfulness came over me.

And then on the first day of the next week, being at our own afternoon meeting and my heart being enlarged in love, I was led to speak on the

12. After "Richland" the original editorial committee added "in Bucks County."

13. A bracket has been inserted before "time" by someone other than Woolman. This marks a new page (145) in the first edition.

care and protection of the Lord over his people and to make mention of that passage where a band of Assyrians, endeavouring to take captive the prophet, were disappointed, and how the Psalmist said, "The angel of the Lord encampeth round about them that fear him" [Ps. 34:7]. And thus in true love and tenderness I parted from Friends, expecting the next morning to proceed on my journey, and being weary went early to bed.

And after I had been asleep a short time, I was awaked by a man calling at my door, and arising was invited to meet some Friends at a public house in our town who came from Philadelphia so late that Friends were generally gone to bed. These Friends informed me that an express arrived the last morning from Pittsburgh and brought news that the Indians had taken a fort from the English westward and slain and scalped English people in divers places, some near the said Pittsburgh, and that some elderly Friends in Philadelphia, knowing the time of my expecting to set off, had conferred together and thought good to inform me of these things before I left home, that I might consider them and proceed as I believed best. So I, going again to bed, told not my wife till morning. My heart was turned to the Lord for his heavenly instruction, and it was a humbling time to me.

When I told my dear wife she appeared to be deeply concerned about it, but in a few hours time my mind became settled in a belief that it was my duty to proceed on my journey, and she bore it with a good degree of resignation. In this conflict of spirit there were great searchings of heart and strong cries to the Lord that no motion might be in the least degree attended to but that of the pure spirit of Truth.

The subjects before-mentioned, on which I had so lately spake in public, were now very fresh before me, and I was brought inwardly to commit myself to the Lord to be disposed of as he saw good. So I took leave of my family and neighbours in much bowedness of spirit and went to our Monthly Meeting at Burlington. And after taking leave of Friends there I crossed the river, accompanied by my friends Israel and John Pemberton; * and parting the next morning with Israel, John bore me company to Samuel Foulke's,* where I met the before-mentioned Indians, and we were glad to see each other.

Here my friend Benjamin Parvin * met me and proposed joining as a companion, we having passed some letters before on the subject. And now on his account I had a sharp trial, for as the journey appeared perilous, I thought if he went chiefly to bear me company and we should be taken captive, my having been the means of drawing him into these difficulties would add to my own afflictions. So I told him my mind freely and let him know that I was resigned to go alone, but after all, if he really believed it to be his duty to go on, I believed his company would be very comfortable to me. It was indeed a time of deep exercise, and Benjamin appeared to be so fastened to the visit that he could not be easy to leave me; so we went on, accompanied by our friends John Pemberton, and William Lightfoot of Pikeland, and lodged at Bethlehem.

And there parting with John, William and we went forward on the 9th day, 6th month, and got lodging on the floor at a house about five mile from Fort Allen. Here we parted with William, and at this place we met with an Indian trader lately come from Wyoming, and in conversation with him I perceived that many white people do often sell rum to the Indians, which I believe is a great evil. First, they being thereby deprived of the use of their reason and their spirits violently agitated, quarrels often arise which ends in mischief, and the bitterness and resentments occasioned hereby are frequently of long continuance. Again, their skins and furs, gotten through much fatigue and hard travels in hunting, with which they intended to buy clothing, these when they begin to be intoxicated they often sell at a low rate for more rum; and afterward when they suffer for want of the necessaries of life, [they] are angry with those who for the sake of gain took the advantage of their weakness. Of this their chiefs have often complained at their treaties with the English.

Where cunning people pass counterfeits and impose that on others which is only good for nothing, it is considered as a wickedness, but to sell that to people which we know does them harm and which often works their ruin, for the sake of gain, manifests a hardened and corrupt heart and is an evil which demands the care of all true lovers of virtue to suppress. And while my mind this evening was thus employed, I also remembered that the people on the frontier, among whom this evil is too common, are often poor people, who venture to the outside of a colony that they may live more independent on such who are wealthy, who often set high rents on their land, being renewedly confirmed in a belief that if all our inhabitants lived according to sound wisdom, labouring to promote universal love and righteousness, and ceased from every inordinate desire after wealth and from all customs which are tinctured with luxury, the way would be easy for our inhabitants, though much more numerous than at present, to live comfortably on honest employments, without having that temptation they are often under of being drawn into schemes to make settlements on lands which have not been purchased of the Indians, or of applying to that wicked practice of selling rum to them.[14]

10th day, 6th month. Set out early in the morning and crossed the western branch of Delaware, called the Great Lehigh, near Fort Allen; the water being high we went over in a canoe. Here we met an Indian and had some friendly conversation with him and gave him some biscuit, and he, having killed a deer, gave the Indians with us some of it. Then after travelling some miles we met several Indian men and women with a cow and horse and some household goods, who were lately come from their dwelling at Wyoming and going to settle at another place. We made them some small presents, and some of them understanding English, I told them my motive in coming into their country, with which they appeared satisfied. And one of our guides talking awhile with an ancient woman concerning us, the poor old woman came to my companion and me and took her leave of us with an appearance of sincere affection. So going on we pitched our tent near the banks of the same river, having laboured hard in crossing some of those mountains called the Blue Ridge. And by the roughness of the stones and the cavities between them and the steepness of the hills, it appeared dangerous, but we were preserved in safety, through the kindness of him whose works in those mountainous deserts appeared awful, toward whom my heart was turned during this day's travel.

Near our tent, on the sides of large trees peeled for that purpose were various representations of men going to and returning from the wars, and of some killed in battle, this being a path heretofore used by warriors. And as I walked about viewing those Indian histories,[15] which were painted mostly in red but some with black, and thinking on the innumerable afflictions which the proud, fierce spirit produceth in the world—thinking on the toils and fatigues of warriors travelling over mountains and deserts, thinking on their miseries and distresses when wounded far from home by their enemies, and of their bruises and great weariness in chasing one another over the rocks and mountains, and of their restless, unquiet state of mind who live in this spirit, and of the hatred which mutually grows up in the minds of the children of those nations engaged in war with each other—during these meditations the desire to cherish the spirit of love and peace amongst these people arose very fresh in me.

14. Crossed out before "purchased": "honestly," probably by Woolman.
15. Woolman wrote "Indian histories" in place of his original "Hierogliphicks."

This was the first night that we lodged in the woods, and being wet with travelling in the rain, the ground and our tent wet, and the bushes wet which we purposed [to] lay under our blankets, all looked discouraging. But I believed that it was the Lord who had thus far brought me forward and that he would dispose of me as he saw good, and therein I felt easy. So we kindled a fire with our tent door open to it; and with some bushes next the ground, and then our blankets, we made our bed, and lying down got some sleep. And in the morning feeling a little unwell, I went into the river all over. The water was cold, and soon after I felt fresh and well.

11th day, 6th month. The bushes being wet we tarried in our tent till about eight o'clock, then going on crossed a high mountain supposed to be upward of four miles wide, and the steepness on the north side exceeded all the others. We also crossed two swamps, and it raining near night, we pitched our tent and lodged.

About noon on our way we were overtaken by one of the Moravian brethren going to Wyalusing, and an Indian man with him who could talk English; and we, being together while our horses eat grass, had some friendly conversation; then they, travelling faster than we, soon left us.[16] This Moravian, I understood, had spent some time this spring at Wyalusing and was by some of them invited to come again.

12th day, 6th month, and first of the week. It being a rainy day we continued in our tent, and here I was led to think on the nature of the exercise which hath attended me. Love was the first motion, and then a concern arose to spend some time with the Indians, that I might feel and understand their life and the spirit they live in, if haply I might receive some instruction from them, or they be in any degree helped forward by my following the leadings of Truth amongst them. And as it pleased the Lord to make way for my going at a time when the troubles of war were increasing, and when by reason of much wet weather travelling was more difficult than usual at that season, I looked upon it as a more favourable

16. The Moravian was David Zeisberger (1721-1808), the well-known missionary who spent most of his adult years, despite great hazards, ministering to the Indians of the Pennsylvania wilderness. The Moravians trace their origin to the evangelical movement in Bohemia led by John Huss, who suffered martyrdom in 1415. The sect grew rapidly in Bohemia and Moravia, and was severely persecuted. In 1722, Moravian refugees settled on the estate of Count Zinzendorf in the town of Herrnhut in Saxony. In 1727 a communal religious experience by members of the group inspired them to several evangelistic efforts, of which the mission to the American Indians was one.

opportunity to season my mind and bring me into a nearer sympathy
with them. And as mine eye was to the great Father of Mercies, humbly
desiring to learn what his will was concerning me, I was made quiet and
content.

Our pilot's horse, though hoppled, went away in the night, and after
finding our own and searching some time for him, his footsteps were
discovered in the path going back again, whereupon my kind companion
went off in the rain, and after about seven hours returned with him, and
here we lodged again, tying up our horses before we went to bed and
loosing them to feed about break of day.

13th day, 6th month. The sun appearing, we set forward, and as I rode
over the barren hills my meditations were on the alterations of the circumstances of the natives of this land since the coming in of the English.
The lands near the sea are conveniently situated for fishing. The lands
near the rivers, where the tides flow, and some above, are in many places
fertile and not mountainous, while the running of the tides makes passing
up and down easy with any kind of traffic. Those natives have in some
places, for trifling considerations, sold their inheritance so favourably
situated, and in other places been driven back by superior force, so that
in many places, as their way of clothing themselves is now altered from
what it was and they far remote from us, [they] have to pass over mountains, swamps, and barren deserts, where travelling is very troublesome,
in bringing their skins and furs to trade with us.

By the extending of English settlements and partly by English hunters,
those wild beasts they chiefly depend on for a subsistence are not so
plenty as they were, and people too often, for the sake of gain, open a
door for them to waste their skins and furs in purchasing a liquor which
tends to the ruin of them and their families.

My own will and desires being now very much broken and my heart
with much earnestness turned to the Lord, to whom alone I looked for
help in the dangers before me, I had a prospect of the English along the
coast for upward of nine hundred miles where I have travelled. And the
favourable situation of the English and the difficulties attending the
natives in many places, and the Negroes, were open before me.[17] And a
weighty and heavenly care came over my mind, and love filled my heart
toward all mankind, in which I felt a strong engagement that we might
be obedient to the Lord while in tender mercies he is yet calling to us,
and so attend to pure universal righteousness as to give no just cause of

17. In place of "and the Negroes," MS. A reads: "and the slaves amongst us."

offense to the Gentiles, who do not profess Christianity, whether the blacks from Africa or the native inhabitants of this continent.[18] And here I was led into a close, laborious inquiry whether I, as an individual, kept clear from all things which tended to stir up or were connected with wars, either in this land or Africa, and my heart was deeply concerned that in future I might in all things keep steadily to the pure Truth and live and walk in the plainness and simplicity of a sincere follower of Christ.

And in this lonely journey I did this day greatly bewail the spreading of a wrong spirit, believing that the prosperous, convenient situation of the English requires a constant attention to divine love and wisdom, to guide and support us in a way answerable to the will of that good, gracious, and almighty Being who hath an equal regard to all mankind. And here luxury and covetousness, with the numerous oppressions and other evils attending them, appeared very afflicting to me, and I felt in that which is immutable that the seeds of great calamity and desolation are sown and growing fast on this continent. Nor have I words sufficient to set forth that longing I then felt that we who are placed along coast, and have tasted the love and goodness of God, might arise in his strength and like faithful messengers labour to check the growth of these seeds, that they may not ripen to the ruin of our posterity.

We reached the Indian settlement at Wyoming, and here we were told that an Indian runner had been at that place a day or two before us and brought news of the Indians taking an English fort westward and destroying the people, and that they were endeavouring to take another— and also that another Indian runner came there about midnight the night next before we got there, who came from a town about ten miles above Wyalusing and brought news that some Indian warriors from distant parts came to that town with two English scalps and told the people that it was war with the English.

Our pilots took us to the house of a very ancient man, and soon after we had put in our baggage, there came a man from another Indian house some distance off. And I, perceiving there was a man near the door, went out; and he having a tomahawk wrapped under his match-coat out of sight, as I approached him he took it in his hand. I, however, went for-

18. Erasures and variant renderings indicate that Woolman labored over the passage "we might . . . to us." The revised version in MS. A reads: "might be faithful to the Lord while his mercies are yet extended to us." Woolman changed it in MS. B to: "might be wise while the voice of wisdom is yet calling to us." Further revision produced the rendering given here.

ward, and speaking to him in a friendly way perceived he understood some English. My companion then coming out, we had some talk with him concerning the nature of our visit in these parts; and then he, going into the house with us and talking with our pilots, soon appeared friendly and sat down and smoked his pipe. Though his taking his hatchet in his hand at the instant I drew near him had a disagreeable appearance, I believe he had no other intent than to be in readiness in case any violence was offered to him.

Hearing the news brought by these Indian runners, and being told by the Indians where we lodged that what Indians were about Wyoming expected in a few days to move to some larger towns, I thought that to all outward appearance it was dangerous travelling at this time, and was after a hard day's journey brought into a painful exercise at night, in which I had to trace back and feel over the steps I had taken from my first moving in the visit. And though I had to bewail some weakness which at times had attended me, yet I could not find that I had ever given way to a wilful disobedience. And then as I believed I had under a sense of duty come thus far, I was now earnest in spirit beseeching the Lord to show me what I ought to do.

In this great distress I grew jealous of myself, lest the desire of reputation as a man firmly settled to persevere through dangers, or the fear of disgrace arising on my returning without performing the visit, might have some place in me. Thus I lay full of thoughts great part of the night, while my beloved companion lay and slept by me, till the Lord my gracious Father, who saw the conflicts of my soul, was pleased to give quietness. Then was I again strengthened to commit my life and all things relating thereto into his heavenly hands; and getting a little sleep toward day, when morning came we arose.

And then on the 14th day, 6th month, we sought out and visited all the Indians hereabouts that we could meet with, they being chiefly in one place about a mile from where we lodged, in all perhaps twenty. Here I expressed the care I had on my mind for their good and told them that true love had made me willing thus to leave my family to come and see the Indians and speak with them in their houses. Some of them appeared kind and friendly. So we took our leave of these Indians and went up the river Susquehanna about three miles to the house of an Indian called Jacob January, who had killed his hog, and the women were making store of bread and preparing to move up the river. Here our pilots left their canoe when they came down in the spring, which lying dry was leaky, so that we, being detained some hours, had a good deal of friendly conversation with the family; and eating dinner with them we made them some small presents. Then putting our baggage in the canoe, some of them pushed slowly up the stream, and the rest of us rode our horses; and swimming them over a creek called Lahawahamunk [19] we pitched our tent a little above it, [there] being a shower in the evening. And in a sense of God's goodness in helping me in my distress, sustaining me under trials, and inclining my heart to trust in him, I lay down in a humble, bowed frame of mind and had a comfortable night's lodging.

15th day, 6th month.[20] Proceeded forward till afternoon, when, a storm appearing, we met our canoe at an appointed place; and the rain continuing, we stayed all night, which was so heavy that it beat through our tent and wet us and our baggage. 16th day. We found on our way abundance of trees blown down with the storm yesterday and had occasion reverently to consider the kind dealings of the Lord, who provided a safe place for us in a valley while this storm continued.[21] By the falling of abundance of trees across our path we were much hindered, and in some swamps our way was so stopped that we got through with extreme difficulty.

I had this day often to consider myself as a sojourner in this world, and a belief in the all-sufficiency of God to support his people in their pilgrimage felt comfortable to me, and I was industriously employed to get to a state of perfect resignation.

We seldom saw our canoe but at appointed places, by reason of the path going off from the river; and this afternoon Job Chilaway,* an Indian from Wyalusing, who talks good English and is acquainted with several people in and about Philadelphia, he met our people on the river, and understanding where we expected to lodge, pushed back about six miles and came to us after night. And in a while our own canoe came, it being hard work pushing up stream. Job told us that an Indian came in haste to their town yesterday and told them that three warriors, coming from some distance, lodged in a town above Wyalusing a few nights past and that these three men were going against the English at Juniata. Job was going down the river to the province store at Shamokin. Though I was so far favoured with health as to continue travelling, yet through the various difficulties in our journey and the different way of living from

19. The Lackawanna River.
20. A pin is stuck in the margin here (MS. B, p. 267), for no apparent reason.
21. Woolman wrote "the Lord" in place of his original "kind Providence."

what I had been used to, I grew weak. And the news of these warriors being on their march so near us, and not knowing whether we might not fall in with them, it was a fresh trial of my faith; and though through the strength of divine love I had several times been enabled to commit myself to the divine disposal, I still found the want of my strength to be renewed, that I might persevere therein.[22] And my cries for help were put up to the Lord, who in great mercy gave me a resigned heart, in which I found quietness.

17th day, 6th month. Parting from Job Chilaway,* we went on and reached Wyalusing about the middle of the afternoon, and the first Indian that we saw was a woman of a modest countenance, with a babe,[23] who first spake to our pilot and then with a harmonious voice expressed her gladness at seeing us, having before heard of our coming. Then by the direction of our pilot we sat down on a log, and he went to the town to tell the people that we were come. My companion and I sitting thus together in a deep inward stillness, the poor woman came and sat near us; and great awfulness coming over us, we rejoiced in a sense of God's love manifested to our poor souls.

After a while we heard a conch shell blow several times, and then came John Curtis and another Indian man who kindly invited us into a house near the town, where we found I suppose about sixty people sitting in silence. And after sitting a short time, I stood up and in some tenderness of spirit acquainted them with the nature of my visit and that a concern for their good had made me willing to come thus far to see them —all in a few short sentences, which some of them, understanding, interpreted to the others; and there appeared gladness amongst them. Then I showed them my certificate, which was explained to them; and the Moravian who overtook us on the way, being now here, bid me welcome.

18th day, 6th month. We rested ourselves this forenoon, and the Indians, knowing that the Moravian and I were of different religious Societies, and as some of their people had encouraged him to come and stay awhile with them, were, I believe, concerned that no jarring or discord might be in their meetings; and they, I suppose having conferred together, acquainted me that the people at my request would at any time come together and hold meetings, and also told me that they expected the

---

22. By "found the want of" Woolman means "had the desire for."
23. MS. A clearly reads "babe." MS. B reads "bable," which the original editorial committee revised to read "bible." The first and many subsequent editions render it "bible"; those of Gummere and Whitney both render it "babe."

Moravian would speak in their settled meetings, which are commonly held morning and near evening. So I found liberty in my heart [24] to speak to the Moravian and told him of the care I felt on my mind for the good of these people, and that I believed no ill effects would follow it if I sometimes spake in their meetings when love engaged me thereto, without calling them together at times when they did not meet of course; whereupon he expressed his good will toward my speaking at any time all that I found in my heart to say.

So near evening I was at their meeting, where the pure gospel love was felt, to the tendering some of our hearts. And the interpreters, endeavouring to acquaint the people with what I said, in short sentences, found some difficulty, as none of them were quite perfect in the English and Delaware tongue. So they helped one another and we laboured along, divine love attending. And afterwards feeling my mind covered with the spirit of prayer, I told the interpreters that I found it in my heart to pray to God and believed if I prayed right he would hear me, and expressed my willingness for them to omit interpreting; so our meeting ended with a degree of divine love. And before the people went out I observed Papunehang * (the man who had been zealous in labouring for a reformation in that town, being then very tender) spoke to one of the interpreters, and I was afterward told that he said in substance as follows: "I love to feel where words come from." [25]

19th day, 6th month, and first of the week. This morning in the meeting the Indian who came with the Moravian, being also a member of that Society, prayed, and then the Moravian spake a short time to the people. And in the afternoon, they coming together and my heart being filled with a heavenly care for their good, I spake to them awhile by interpreters, but none of them being perfect in the work. And I, feeling the current of love run strong, told the interpreters that I believed some of the people would understand me, and so proceeded, in which exercise I believe the Holy Ghost wrought on some hearts to edification, where all the words were not understood. I looked upon it as a time of divine favour, and my heart was tendered and truly thankful before the Lord. And after I sat down one of the interpreters seemed spirited up to give the Indians the substance of what I said.

Before our first meeting this morning, I was led to meditate on the

24. "Heart" is underlined in MS. B, probably by the original editorial committee.
25. "Papunehang" is underlined here and also where it appears in the following pages, probably by the original editorial committee.

manifold difficulties of these Indians, who by the permission of the Six Nations dwell in these parts, and a near sympathy with them was raised in me; and my heart being enlarged in the love of Christ, I thought that the affectionate care of a good man for his only brother in affliction does not exceed what I then felt for that people.

I came to this place through much trouble, and though through the mercies of God I believed that if I died in the journey it would be well with me, yet the thoughts of falling into the hands of Indian warriors was in times of weakness afflicting to me; and being of a tender constitution of body, the thoughts of captivity amongst them was at times grievous, as supposing that they, being strong and hardy, might demand service of me beyond what I could well bear. But the Lord alone was my helper, and I believed if I went into captivity it would be for some good end. And thus from time to time my mind was centered in resignation, in which I always found quietness. And now this day, though I had the same dangerous wilderness between me and home, I was inwardly joyful that the Lord had strengthened me to come on this visit and manifested a fatherly care over me in my poor lowly condition, when in mine own eyes I appeared inferior to many amongst the Indians.

When the last-mentioned meeting was ended, it being night, Papune-hang * went to bed; and one of the interpreters sitting by me, I observed Papunehang spoke with a harmonious voice, I suppose a minute or two, and asking the interpreter, was told that he was expressing his thankful-ness to God for the favours he had received that day, and prayed that he would continue to favour him with that same which he had experienced in that meeting—that though Papunehang had before agreed to receive the Moravian and join with them, he still appeared kind and loving to us.

20th day, 6th month. Was at two meetings and silent in them. 21st day. This morning in meeting my heart was enlarged in pure love amongst them, and in short plain sentences expressed several things that rested upon me, which one of the interpreters gave the people pretty readily, after which the meeting ended in supplication. And I had cause humbly to acknowledge the loving-kindness of the Lord toward us, and then I believed that a door remained open for the faithful disciples of Jesus Christ to labour amongst these people.[26]

26. In MS. A a marginal note was written at this point by John Woolman: "At our Yearly Meeting, 1767, information was given in our meeting of ministers and elders that some Indians far back had sent a message in which they desired that some of the Quakers would come and pay them a religious visit. And in the year 1771 a

I now, feeling my mind at liberty to return, took my leave of them in general at the conclusion of what I said in meeting, and so we prepared to go homeward. But some of their most active men told us that when we were ready to move, the people would choose to come and shake hands with us, which those who usually came to meeting did. And from a secret draught in my mind, I went amongst some who did not use to go to meeting and took my leave of them also. And the Moravian and his Indian interpreter appeared respectful to us at parting. This town stands on the bank of Susquehanna and consists, I believe, of about forty houses, mostly compact together: some about thirty foot long and eighteen wide (some bigger, some less), mostly built of split plank, one end set in the ground and the other pinned to a plate, and then rafters and covered with bark. I understand a great flood last winter overflowed the chief part of the ground where the town stands, and some were now about moving their houses to higher ground.

We expected only two Indians to be our company, but when we were ready to go, we found many of them were going to Bethlehem with skins and furs, who chose to go in company with us. So they loaded two canoes which they desired us to go in, telling us that the waters were so raised with the rains that the horses should be taken by such who were better acquainted with the fording places. So we, with several Indians, went in the canoes, and others went on horses, there being seven besides ours. And we meeting with the horseman once on the way by appointment, and then near night a little below a branch called Tunkhannock, we lodged there; and some of the young men, going out a little before dusk with their guns, brought in a deer.

22nd day, 6th month. Through diligence we reached Wyoming before night and understood the Indians were mostly gone from this place. Here we went up a small creek into the woods with our canoes and, pitching our tent, carried out our baggage; and before dark our horses came to us.

23rd day, 6th month. In the morning their horses were loaded, and we prepared our baggage and so set forward, being in all fourteen, and with diligent travelling were favoured to get near half way to Fort Allen. The land on this road from Wyoming to our frontier being mostly poor, and good grass scarce, they chose a piece of low ground to lodge on, as the

message came to the Governor of Pennsylvania part to that import." The second sentence appears to have been added at a later time than the first. These notes are ignored in MS. B.

best for grazing. And I, having sweat much in travelling and being weary, slept sound. I perceived in the night that I had taken cold, of which I was favoured to get better soon.

24th day, 6th month. We passed Fort Allen and lodged near it in the woods, having forded the westerly branch of Delaware three times, and thereby had a shorter way and missed going over the top of the Blue Mountains, called the Second Ridge. In the second time, fording where the river cuts through the mountain, the waters being rapid and pretty deep and my companion's mare being a tall, tractable animal, he sundry times drove her back through the river, and they loaded her with the burdens of some small horses which they thought not sufficient to come through with their loads. The troubles westward, and the difficulty for Indians to pass through our frontier, I apprehend was one reason why so many came, as expecting that our being in company would prevent the outside inhabitants from being surprised.

25th day, 6th month. We reached Bethlehem, taking care on the way to keep foremost and to acquaint people on and near the road who these Indians were. This we found very needful, for that the frontier inhabitants were often alarmed at the report of English being killed by Indians westward.

Amongst our company were some who I did not remember to have seen at meeting, and some of these at first were very reserved, but we being several days together and behaving friendly toward them and making them suitable returns for the services they did us, they became more free and sociable.

26th day, 6th month, and first of the week. Having carefully endeavoured to settle all affairs with the Indians relative to our journey, we took leave of them, and I thought they generally parted with us affectionately. So we, getting to Richland, had a very comfortable meeting amongst our friends. Here I parted with my kind friend and companion Benjamin Parvin,* and accompanied by my friend Samuel Foulke * we rode to John Cadwalader's, from whence I reached home the next day, where I found my family middling well. And they and my friends all along appeared glad to see me return from a journey which they apprehended dangerous. But my mind while I was out had been so employed in striving for a perfect resignation, and I had so often been confirmed in a belief that whatever the Lord might be pleased to allot for me would work for good, [that] I was careful lest I should admit any degree of selfishness in being glad overmuch, and laboured to improve by those trials in such a manner as my gracious Father and Protector intends for me.

Between the English inhabitants and Wyalusing we had only a narrow path, which in many places is much grown up with bushes and interrupted by abundance of trees lying across it, which together with the mountains, swamps, and rough stones, it is a difficult road to travel, and the more so for that rattlesnakes abound there, of which we killed four—that people who have never been in such places have but an imperfect idea of them. But I was not only taught patience but also made thankful to God, who thus led me about and instructed me that I might have a quick and lively feeling of the afflictions of my fellow creatures whose situation in life is difficult.

1763–1769

[T]HE LATTER PART OF SUMMER, 1763, there came a man to Mount Holly who had before published by a printed advertisement that at such a certain public house he would on such a certain night show many wonderful operations, which he therein enumerated.[1] This man at the time appointed did by sleight of hand sundry things which to those gathered appeared strange.

The next day I, hearing of it and understanding that the show was to be continued the next night and the people to meet about sunset, felt an exercise on that account. So I went to the public house in the evening and told the man of the house that I had an inclination to spend a part of the evening there, with which he signified that he was content. Then sitting down on a long seat by the door, I spake to the people as they came together, concerning this show; and more coming and sitting down with us, the seats by the door were mostly filled. And I had conversation with them in the fear of the Lord and laboured to convince them that thus assembling to see those tricks or sleights-of-hand, and bestowing their money to support men who in that capacity were of no use in the world, was contrary to the nature of the Christian religion.

There was one of the company who for a time endeavoured by arguments to show the reasonableness of their proceedings herein, but after

1. This incident of the magician, or juggler, does not appear in MS. B. However, it is included in the preliminary chapter summary prepared by the original editorial committee, and it appears in the first printed edition. Perhaps the printer took it directly from MS. A (pp. 146–147), as the present editor has done. No note regarding it appears in MS. B. It could easily have been omitted inadvertently by Woolman in copying from MS. A to MS. B, since it is on a sheet by itself just preceding another essay (*A Plea for the Poor*), which Woolman wrote into the volume at this point. In passing over the other essay, he might easily have passed over this also. On the other hand, the pages in MS. B have been re-numbered from this point on, perhaps to close the gap occasioned by the loss of a page or more.

considering some texts of Scripture and calmly debating the matter, he gave up the point. So I, having spent I believe about an hour amongst them and feeling my mind easy, departed.]

[MS. B, p. 288]

Notes at our Yearly Meeting at Philadelphia, 9th month, 1764.[2] First John Smith * of Marlborough,[3] aged upward of eighty years, a faithful minister though not eloquent, in our meeting of ministers and elders on the 25th stood up and, appearing to be under a great exercise of spirit, informed Friends in substance as follows, to wit:[4] that he had been a member of the Society upward of sixty years and well remembered that in those early times Friends were a plain, lowly-minded people, and that there was much tenderness and contrition in their meetings; that at the end of twenty years from that time, the Society increasing in wealth[5] and in some degree conforming to the fashions of the world, true humility was less apparent and their meetings in general not so lively and edifying; that at the end of forty years many of them were grown very rich—that wearing of fine costly garments and using of silver (and other) watches became customary with them, their sons, and their daughters,[6] and many of the Society made a spacious appearance in the world, which marks of outward wealth and greatness appeared on many[7] in our meetings of

2. A dream described by Woolman but not included in the *Journal* belongs chronologically before this paragraph. It is printed in Appendix E of this volume.

Section 7 of MS. B begins with this paragraph and continues through "man he calls master" (at note 16, below). Since MS. A (as revised) is a later version of this section, the most significant variant readings of MS. A are indicated in the following notes and the entire parallel passage is reproduced in Appendix C.

3. MS. A reads "Chester County" instead of "Marlborough."

4. The phrase "in substance as follows, to wit" is lacking in MS. A, and has been inserted with a caret in MS. B.

5. Changed by Woolman from his original wording "had increased in wealth." In MS. A the phrase reads smoothly, "increasing in wealth"; very probably it was copied from MS. B after the latter was revised. Later in this sentence, MS. A has "decreased" instead of "was less apparent."

6. In the preceding part of this sentence, MS. A reads "in the Society" instead of "of them," has erasures in the place of "very" and "using of," lacks "(and other)," inserts with a caret "with fashionable furniture" after "watches," and reads "with many" instead of "with them." The words erased in MS. A seem to be the words found at the same points in MS. B. This fact, plus the insertion with a caret in MS. A of words lacking in MS. B, is consistent with the explanation that this section of MS. B was copied from MS. A before MS. A was revised by erasures and additions.

7. The original editorial committee toned down Woolman's indictment by changing "many" to "some."

ministers and elders, and as these things became more prevalent, so the powerful overshadowings of the Holy Ghost were less manifest in the Society; [8] that there had been a continued increase of these ways of life even until now, and that the weakness which hath now overspread the Society and the barrenness manifest amongst us is matter of much sorrow.[9]

He then mentioned the uncertainty of his attending [10] these meetings in future, expecting his dissolution was now near, and signified that he had seen in the true light that the Lord would bring back his people from these things into which they were thus degenerated but that his faithful servants must first go through great and heavy exercises therein.

29th day, 9th month, 1764. The committee appointed by the Yearly Meeting some time since now made report in writing of their proceedings in that service, in which they signified that in the course of their proceedings they had been apprehensive that some persons holding offices in government inconsistent with our principles and others who kept slaves —these remaining active members in our meetings of discipline—had been one means of weakness more and more prevailing in the management thereof in some places.[11]

8. From "daughters" to this point, MS. A was extensively revised, to read as follows: "and as these things prevailed in the Society and appeared in our meetings of ministers and elders [erasure], so the powerful overshadowings of the Holy Spirit were less manifested amongst us."

9. In MS. A, "continued" has been erased and "a" has been changed to "an," so as to read "an increase." As in the preceding sentence, this is an erasure of material found in MS. B. This confirms the theory that at one time the two MSS. at this point were essentially alike, that MS. A was later changed, and that MS. B was not changed accordingly.

From "increase" through "much sorrow," MS. A reads: "of outward greatness till now, and that the weakness amongst us in not living up to our principles and supporting the testimony of Truth in faithfulness was matter of much sorrow."

10. Starting with "attending," Woolman revised the rest of this paragraph and pasted the revised version into MS. A. It reads: "attending Yearly Meetings in future, expecting his dissolution was near. And as pious parents, finally departing from their families, express their last and fervent desires for their good, so did he most tenderly express his concern for us, and signified that he had seen in the true light that the Lord would bring forth his people from that worldly spirit into which too many were thus degenerated, and that his faithful servants must go through great and heavy exercises before this work was brought about." Woolman added this footnote, keyed to "future": "It was the last Yearly Meeting he attended."

Woolman did not copy this revised paragraph into MS. B. However, the original editorial committee (following MS. B here as elsewhere), noted Woolman's phrase (in MS. A) about the pious parents, and inserted these words between "near" and "signified": "and having tenderly expressed his concern for us."

11. Woolman may have meant to cross out "some time since" in MS. B; the manuscript is not clear. In MS. A he improved the style, after "in writing," by

After this report was read, an exercise revived on my mind which at times had attended me several years, and inward cries to the Lord were raised in me that the fear of man might not prevent me from doing what he required of me; and standing up [12] I spake in substance as follows: "I've felt a tenderness in my mind toward persons in two circumstances mentioned in that report—that is, toward such active members who keep slaves and such who hold offices in civil government [13]—and have desired that Friends in all their conduct may be kindly affectioned one toward another. Many Friends who keep slaves are under some exercise on that account and at times think about trying them with freedom, but find many things in their way. And the way of living and annual expenses of some of them are such that it is impracticable for them to set their slaves free without changing their own way of life. It has been my lot to be often abroad,[14] and I have observed in some places, at Quarterly and Yearly Meetings and at some stages where travelling Friends and their horses are often entertained, that the yearly expense of individuals therein is very considerable. And Friends in some places crowding much on persons in these circumstances for entertainment hath often rested as a burden on my mind for some years past, and I now express it in the fear of the Lord, greatly desiring that Friends now present may duly consider it."

In fifty pounds are four hundred half crowns. If a slave be valued at fifty pounds and I with my horse put his owner to half a crown expense, and I with many others for a course of years repeat these expense [*sic*] four hundred times,[15] then on a fair computation this slave may be accounted a slave to the public under the direction of the man he calls master.[16]

---

omitting "of their proceedings in that service." He omitted most of the remainder of the sentence, intending to insert in MS. A the report which he summarized here in MS. B (cf. Appendix C).

12. MS. A adds: "in his dread."

13. MS. A reads: "slaves, and them who are in those offices in government."

14. "Often" is written over an erasure in MS. B. MS. A reads the same way, with no erasure, as though copied from MS. B.

15. MS. A adds: "without any compensation."

16. In MS. B this paragraph appears on a half page, the recto of which contains the end of the preceding paragraph, from "that the yearly expense" to "consider it." As with several of Woolman's mathematical calculations, the margin of this paragraph carries a note by the original editorial committee: "May be spared." The passage is omitted from the first printed edition. In MS. A an additional clause appears at the beginning of the paragraph: "And I may here add what then occurred to me though I did not mention it, to wit." This paragraph brings section 7 of MS. B to a close.

[9th day, 10th] month, 1764.[17] I, having hired a man to work, perceived in conversation that he had been a soldier in the late war on this continent. And in the evening, giving a narrative of his captivity amongst the Indians, he informed me that he saw two of his fellow captives tortured to death,[18] one of which, being tied to a tree, had abundance of pine splinters run into his body and then set on fire, and that this was continued by intervals near two days before he expired;[19] that they opened the belly of the other and fastened a part of his bowels to a tree, and then whipped the poor creature till by his running round the tree his bowels were drawn out of his body.

This relation affected me with sadness, under which I went to bed, and the next morning soon after I awoke a fresh and living sense of divine love was spread over my mind, in which I had a renewed prospect of the nature of that wisdom from above which leads to a right use of all gifts both spiritual and temporal, and gives content therein. Under a feeling thereof I wrote as follows:

Hath he who gave me a being attended with many wants unknown to brute creatures given me a capacity superior to theirs? —and shown me that a moderate application to business is proper to my present condition, and that this, attended with his blessing, may supply all outward wants while they remain within the bounds he hath fixed, and no imaginary wants proceeding from an evil spirit have any place in me? Attend then—O my soul!—to this pure wisdom, as thy sure conductor through the manifold dangers in this world.

Does pride lead to vanity? Does vanity form imaginary wants? Do these wants prompt men to exert their power in requiring that of others which themselves would rather be excused from, was the same required of them?

17. This date is according to MS. A, the earliest extant record. MS. B at this point has "19th day, 6th month, 1764"—a date that seems clearly out of accord with the preceding dates. The earliest editors solved this problem by substituting "in the fall of the year" for the date.

Section 8 of MS. B starts with this paragraph and continues through "love amongst them" (at note 29, below). All points at which MS. A differs in wording are indicated in the following footnotes. MS. A also lacks the question marks (after "to theirs" and "in me") in the paragraph below beginning "Hath he." See Appendix C for further editorial comment on sections 7–9.

18. In MS. B the conclusion of this account, starting with "one of which," has been crossed out by the original editorial committee. Hence it does not appear in the earliest printed editions.

19. MS. A, having apparently first read the same as MS. B, was revised to read: "continued at times near two days before he died."

Do those proceedings beget hard thoughts? Does hard thoughts when ripe become malice? Does malice when ripe become revengeful, and in the end inflict terrible pains on their fellow creatures and spread desolations in the world? [20]

Does mankind walking in uprightness delight in each other's happiness? And do these creatures, capable of this attainment, by giving way to an evil spirit employ their wit and strength to afflict and destroy one another? [21] Remember then—O my soul!—the quietude of those in whom Christ governs, and in all thy proceedings feel after it.

Does he condescend to bless thee with his presence? To move and influence to action? To dwell in thee and walk in thee? [22] Remember then thy station as a being sacred to God, accept of the strength freely offered thee, and take heed that no weakness in conforming to expensive, unwise, and hard-hearted customs, gendering to discord and strife, be given way to. Does he claim my body as his temple and graciously grant that I may be sacred to him? Oh! that I may prize this favour and that my whole life may be conformable to this character. [23]

Remember, O my soul, that the Prince of Peace is thy Lord, that he communicates his unmixed wisdom to his family, that they, living in perfect simplicity, may give no just cause of offense to any creature, but may walk as he walked. [24]

Having felt an openness in my heart toward visiting families in our own meeting, and especially in the town of Mount Holly, the place of

20. In MS. B, brackets appear around "become malice? Does malice when ripe." They were probably inserted by Woolman, who may have considered omitting these words.

In MS. A, "terrible" is written over an erasure of what appears to have been the word "excruciating." In the next sentence (in MS. A) "while" appeared between "mankind" and "walking," but has been erased. In both of these passages the wording of MS. B is identical with the final wording of MS. A, but with no signs of alteration—an indication that MS. B was probably copied from MS. A at this point.

21. The phrase "by giving way to an evil spirit" is inserted with a caret in MS. B. In MS. A the final reading is the same, but "by giving way to an" is written over an erasure. Which MS. was last at this point cannot be determined.

22. MS. A reads "walk thee."

23. Lacking from MS. A: "Does he claim my body . . . to this character." In this and the preceding paragraphs, where the word "Does" appears at the beginning of a sentence it has been changed, in MS. B, to "Doth," except immediately preceding "hard thoughts," where it has been changed to "Do." At all these points in MS. A, "does" has been changed to "doth." Since these changes appear to have been made by the original editorial committee rather than by Woolman, "Does" has been retained here.

24. In MS. A, "pure" appears before "wisdom," having been written over an erasure of what appears to have been the word "unmixed." In MS. B, the "he" before "walked" has been inserted with a caret. MS. A is later at this point.

my abode,[25] I mentioned it in our Monthly Meeting the forepart of the winter, 1764, which being agreed to and several Friends of our meeting being united in the exercise, we proceeded therein and through divine favour were helped in the work, so that it appeared to me as a fresh reviving of godly care amongst Friends. And the latter part of the same winter I joined my friend William Jones in a visit to Friends' families in Mansfield, in which labour I had cause to admire the goodness of the Lord toward his poor creatures.[26]

Having felt my mind drawn toward a visit to Friends along the seacoast from Cape May to near Squan, and also to visit some people in those parts amongst whom there is no settled worship, I joined with my beloved friend Benjamin Jones * in a visit there, having Friends' unity therein.[27] And setting off the 24th day, 10th month, 1765, we had a prosperous and very satisfactory journey, feeling at times, through the goodness of the Heavenly Shepherd, the gospel to flow freely toward a poor people scattered in those places.[28] And soon after our return, I joined my friends John Sleeper * and Elizabeth Smith * in visiting Friends' families at Burlington, there being at this time about fifty families of our Society in that city; and we had cause humbly to adore our Heavenly Father, who baptized us into a feeling of the state of the people and strengthened us to labour in true gospel love amongst them.[29]

25. Original reading in MS. A: "Mount Holly, where I dwell." Original reading in MS. B: "Mount Holly, where I lived." Revised reading in both MS. A and MS. B: "Mount Holly, the place of my abode." The revisions were probably made in this order. Further along in this sentence MS. A reads, "Friends of our own meeting." MS. B is later at this point.

26. The original editorial committee changed "his poor creatures" to "us."

27. The sentence "Having felt . . . unity therein" has been revised considerably in MS. A. A crossed-out section states that Benjamin Jones was "drawn the same way, so having informed Friends at our Monthly Meeting therewith, they expressed their unity by a few lines and we set . . ." In MS. B, although some revision occurs, for the most part the copy is smooth, as though having been transcribed from MS. A after the latter was revised. The final wording is the same in each.

28. Crossed out at this point in MS. A: "We were out about two weeks." In MS B, "And soon" is written over "we wer," as though Woolman had started to copy from MS. A and then decided to leave out the passage. If so, it may have been then that he crossed it out of MS. A. In the preceding sentence MS. A lacks "we" after "1765" and includes "about" between "scattered" and "in."

29. MS. A (the earlier version at this point) reads, "Elisabeth Smith and John Sleeper" and "conditions of the people." Section 8 of MS. B ends with this sentence. This portion of MS. A contains a final sentence that is lacking from MS. B: "And near the same time my friend John Sleeper and I performed a visit to Friends' families belonging to Rancocas Meeting in which I found true satisfaction."

An exercise having at times for several years attended me in regard to paying a religious visit to Friends on the eastern shore of Maryland, such was the nature of this exercise that I believed the Lord moved me [30] to travel on foot amongst them, that by so travelling I might have a more lively feeling of the condition of the oppressed slaves, set an example of lowliness before the eyes of their masters, and be more out of the way of temptation to unprofitable familiarities.[31] The time now drawing near in which I believed it my duty to lay my concern before our Monthly Meeting,[32] I perceived in conversation with my beloved friend John Sleeper * that he was under a concern to travel the same way, and also to travel on foot in the form of a servant amongst them, as he expressed it. This he told me before he knew aught of my exercise.

We, being thus drawn the same way,[33] laid our exercise and the nature of it before Friends, and obtaining certificates we set off the 6th day, 5th month, 1766, and were at meetings with Friends at Wilmington, Duck Creek, Little Creek, and Motherkills, my heart being sundry times tendered under the divine influence and enlarged in love toward the people amongst whom we travelled.[34] From Motherkills we crossed the country about thirty-five miles to Friends at Tuckahoe, in Maryland, and had a meeting there and at Marshy Creek.[35]

At these our three last meetings were a considerable number of people, followers of one Joseph Nichols,* a preacher who I understand is not in outward fellowship with any religious Society of people, but professeth nearly the same principles as our Society doth and often travels up and

30. It would appear that MS. A originally read "required me." The wording was changed so as to read "called me." Section 9 of MS. B starts with this paragraph and continues through "strength given me" (at note 46, below). The MS. A parallel is later than this section (see Appendix C). All nine variant readings are given in the following footnotes.

31. In MS. B "temptation to" has been inserted with a caret; in MS. A it is incorporated smoothly into the text.

After "familiarities" MS. A adds (running into the margin and between the lines) "and be less expense amongst them." This addition does not appear in MS. B.

32. In MS. B, the word "our" is written over "the." In MS. A this change has been incorporated smoothly.

33. After "way," MS. B originally read: "in the same manner." Woolman then crossed this out. It is simply omitted from MS. A.

34. In MS. B, "divine" has been written over "pure." MS. A reads "divine," with no evidence of alteration.

35. In MS. B, "Choptank and Third Haven" has been crossed out after "Marshy Creek." After "At" in the next sentence, "our meeting at the Motherkills, Tuckahoe, and Marshy Creek" has been crossed out and replaced by "these . . . meetings." In MS. A the final wording has been transcribed with no signs of alteration.

down appointing meetings, to which many people come. I heard some Friends speaking of some of their neighbours who had been irreligious people that were now his followers and were become sober, well-behaved men and women.[36] Some irregularities, I hear, have been amongst the people at several of his meetings, but from the whole of what I have perceived I believe the man and some of his followers are honestly disposed, but believe skilful fathers are wanting among them.[37]

From hence we went to Choptank, Third Haven, and thence to Queen Anne's. The weather having some days past been hot and dry and we, to attend meetings pursuant to [38] appointment, having travelled pretty steadily and had hard labour in meetings, I grew weakly, at which I was for a time discouraged. But looking over our journey and thinking how the Lord [39] had supported our minds and bodies, so that we got forward much faster than I expected before we came out, I now saw that I had been in danger of too strongly desiring to get soon through the journey, and that this bodily weakness now attending me was a kindness to me. And then in contrition of spirit I became very thankful to my gracious Father for this manifestation of his love, and in humble submission to his will my trust was renewed in him.

On this part of our journey I had many thoughts on the different circumstances of Friends who inhabit Pennsylvania and Jersey, from those who dwell in Maryland, Virginia, and Carolina. Pennsylvania and New Jersey were settled by many Friends who were convinced of our principles in England in times of suffering, and coming over, bought lands of the natives and applied themselves to husbandry in a peaceable way, and many of their children were taught to labour for their living.[40]

36. In MS. B, "profligate" has been crossed out after "irreligious," "and" has been erased before "that," and "become" has been written over "sober." In MS. A the final copy of MS. B has been transcribed without alteration.

37. Woolman originally wrote in MS. B: "but on the whole I entertain a charitable opinion of the man and of some of his followers, but believe." He later changed this and transcribed the final form into MS. A, writing "among" in place of "amongst."

38. MS. A reads "according to," written over an erasure, and omits "having" before "travelled."

39. In both MSS., Woolman substituted "the Lord" for "divine providence." Later in the sentence Woolman, in MS. B, crossed out "had" between "we" and "got," and inserted "bodily" before "weakness"; both of these revisions are transcribed smoothly into MS. A. At the end of the sentence, instead of "kindness to me," MS. A reads: "kindness from above."

40. In MS. B, "way" is inserted with a caret after "peaceable," and "were" is inserted with a caret after "children." Both changes were transcribed smoothly into MS. A.

Few Friends, I believe, came from England to settle in any of these southern provinces, but by the faithful labours of travelling Friends in early times there was considerable convincements amongst the inhabitants of these parts. Here I remembered reading of the warlike disposition of many of the first settlers in those provinces and of their numerous engagements with the natives, in which much blood was shed, even in the infancy of those colonies. These people inhabiting those places, being grounded in customs contrary to the pure Truth, when some of them were affected with the powerful preaching of the Word of Life and joined in fellowship with our Society, they had a great work to go through.

It is observable in the history of the reformation from popery that it had a gradual progress from age to age. The uprightness of the first reformers to the light and understanding given them opened the way for sincere-hearted people to proceed further afterward, and thus each one truly fearing God and labouring in those works of righteousness appointed for them in their day findeth acceptance with him.[41] And though [42] through the darkness of the times and the corruption of manners and customs, some upright men may have had little more for their day's work than to attend to the righteous principle in their minds as it related to their own conduct in life, without pointing out to others the whole extent of that which the same principle would lead succeeding ages into.

Thus, for instance, amongst an imperious warlike people supported by oppressed slaves, some of these masters I suppose are awakened to feel and see their error and through sincere repentance cease from oppression and become like fathers to their servants, showing by their example a pattern of humility in living and moderation in governing, for the instruction and admonition of their oppressing neighbors. Those,[43] without carrying the reformation further, I believe have found acceptance with the Lord. Such was the beginning, and those who have faithfully attended to the nature and spirit of the reformation have seen the necessity of proceeding forward, and not only to instruct others by their example in

41. In MS. B, "them in their" has been substituted for "him in his," and "with him" has been inserted with a caret. The final wording has been transcribed into MS. A. Variant readings in MS. A: "tended to open" (replacing "open") and "find acceptance."

42. This important sentence can be made grammatical, and thus clearer, by omitting "though." Later in the sentence MS. A reads: "in their own minds."

43. MS. A reads: "Some of those."

governing well, but also to use means to prevent their successors from having so much power to oppress others.[44]

Here I was renewedly confirmed in my mind that the Lord, whose tender mercies are over all his works and whose ear is open to the cries and groans of the oppressed, is graciously moving on the hearts of people to draw them off from the desire of wealth and bring them into such a humble, lowly way of living that they may see their way clearly to repair to the standard of true righteousness, and not only break the yoke of oppression, but know him to be their strength and support in a time of outward affliction.

We (passing on) crossed Chester River and had a meeting there and at Cecil and Sassafras. Through my bodily weakness, joined with a heavy exercise of mind, it was to me a humbling dispensation, and I had a very lively feeling of the state of the oppressed; yet I often thought that what I suffered was little compared with the sufferings of the blessed Jesus and many of his faithful followers, and may say with thankfulness I was made content under them.[45]

From Sassafras we went pretty directly home, where we found our families well. And for several weeks after our return I had often to look over our journey, and though to me it appeared as a small service and that some faithful messengers will yet have more bitter cups to drink in those southern provinces for Christ's sake than we had, yet I found peace in that I had been helped to walk in sincerity according to the understanding and strength given me.[46]

13th, 11th, 1766. With the unity of Friends of our Monthly Meeting, in company with my beloved friend Benjamin Jones,* I set off on a visit to Friends in the upper part of this province, having had drawings of love in my heart that way a considerable time. We travelled as far as Hardwick, and I had inward peace in my labours of love amongst them.[47]

Through the humbling dispensations of divine providence, my mind

44. In MS. B, "so much" and "others" have been inserted in darker ink, of the same kind that Woolman used in the next paragraph. Here as elsewhere he seems to have gone back over his material and revised it.

45. Woolman started to write: "my mind was made" and then revised it to read, "I was made."

He definitely wrote: "content under them." The last two words were later crossed out, probably not by Woolman. They appear in MS. A.

46. Section 9 of MS. B ends here.

47. At this point (halfway down p. 311 in MS. B), a line has been drawn horizontally across the page, apparently by Woolman. This is where the parallel passage in MS. R₃ begins.

hath been brought into a further feeling of the difficulties of Friends and their servants southwestward, and being often engaged in spirit on their account, I believed it my duty to walk into some parts of the western shore of Maryland on a religious visit. And having obtained a certificate from Friends of our Monthly Meeting, I took leave of my family under the heart-tendering operation of Truth, and on the 20th day, 4th month, 1767, rode to the ferry opposite to Philadelphia and from thence walked to William Horne's * at Derby that evening, and so pursued my journey alone and fell in at Concord Week Day Meeting.

Discouragements and a weight of distress had at times attended me in this lonesome walk, through which afflictions I was mercifully preserved. And now sitting down with Friends, my mind was turned toward the Lord to wait for his holy leadings, who in infinite love was pleased to soften my heart into a humble contrition and did renewedly strengthen me to go forward, that to me it was a time of heavenly refreshment in a silent meeting.[48]

The next day I fell in at New Garden Week Day Meeting, in which I sat with bowedness of spirit, and being baptized into a feeling of the state of some present,[49] the Lord gave us a heart-tendering season; to his name be the praise. I passed on and was at Nottingham Monthly Meeting and at a meeting at Little Britain on First Day, and in the afternoon several Friends came to the house where I lodged and we had a little afternoon meeting, and through the humbling power of Truth I had to admire the loving-kindness of the Lord manifested to us.

26th, 4th month. I crossed Susquehanna, and coming amongst people who lived in outward ease and greatness, chiefly on the labour of slaves, my heart was much affected, and in awful retiredness my mind was gathered inward to the Lord, being humbly engaged that in true resignation I

48. MS. R3 reads "that though we had a silent meeting, it was to me a time of heavenly refreshment."

49. At this point MS. R3 adds: "and as I humbly attended to the exercise." In MS. A is an erasure just long enough for this phrase. At twelve other points MS. A has an erasure the same length as a phrase in MS. R3. In some cases parts of the erased portion in MS. A are still sufficiently visible to show that the original reading in MS. A was the same as that found in MS. R3. MS. B, on the other hand, invariably lacks the erased material; the gap is simply closed. MS. B was copied from MS. A after the latter was revised. The relation between MSS. A and R3 is clearly either that MS. A was copied from MS. R3 and later revised, or that MS. R3 was copied from MS. A before its revision. The latter alternative is indicated by the several instances where a correction, insertion, or erasure in MS. A is incorporated smoothly into MS. R3.

might receive instruction from him respecting my duty amongst this people.[50]

Though travelling on foot was wearisome to my body, yet thus travelling was agreeable to the state of my mind. I went gently on, being weakly, and was covered with sorrow and heaviness on account of the spreading, prevailing spirit of this world, introducing customs grievous and oppressive on one hand, and cherishing pride and wantonness on the other. In this lonely walk and state of abasement and humiliation, the state of the church in these parts was opened before me, and I may truly say with the prophet, "I was bowed down at the hearing of it; I was dismayed at the seeing of it" [Is. 21:3]. Under this exercise I attended the Quarterly Meeting at Gunpowder, and in bowedness of spirit I had to open with much plainness what I felt respecting Friends living in fullness on the labours of the poor oppressed Negroes.[51] And that promise of the Most High was now revived, "I will gather all nations and tongues, and they shall come and see my glory" [Is. 66:18].

Here the sufferings of Christ and his tasting death for every man, and the travels, sufferings, and martyrdoms of the apostles and primitive Christians in labouring for the conversion of the Gentiles, was livingly revived in me; and according to the measure of strength afforded, I laboured in some tenderness of spirit, being deeply affected amongst them. And thus the present treatment which these Gentiles, the Negroes, receive at our hands being set side by side with the labours of the primitive Christians for the conversion of the Gentiles, things were pressed home and the power of Truth came over us, under the feeling of which my mind was united to a tender-hearted people in those parts; and the meeting concluded in a sense of God's goodness toward his humble, dependent children.

The next day was a general meeting for worship, much crowded, in which I was deeply engaged in inward cries to the Lord for help, that I might stand wholly resigned and move only as he might be pleased to lead me. And I was mercifully helped to labour honestly and fervently amongst them, in which I found inward peace, and the sincere were comforted.

50. The word "chiefly" in this sentence is found in MSS. A and B but not R3. This is one of several instances showing that MS. R3 is a revised, not an exact, copy of MS. A.

51. After "plainness" the phrase "of speech" appears in MS. R3. It has been erased in MS. A; this is one of several instances where an erased phrase is faintly visible.

From hence I turned toward Pipe Creek and passed on to the Red Lands and had several meetings amongst Friends in those parts.[52] My heart was often tenderly affected under a sense of the Lord's goodness in sanctifying my troubles and exercises, turning them to my comfort and, I believe, to the benefit of many others, for I may say with thankfulness that in this visit it appeared like a fresh, tendering visitation in most places.[53]

I passed on to the Western Quarterly Meeting in Pennsylvania. During the several days of this meeting, I was mercifully preserved in an inward feeling after the mind of Truth, and my public labours tended to my humiliation, with which I was content. And after the Quarterly Meeting of worship ended, I felt drawings to go to the women's meeting of business, which was very full; and here the humility of Jesus Christ as a pattern for us to walk by was livingly opened before me, and in treating on it my heart was enlarged, and it was a baptizing time. From thence I went on and was at meetings at Concord, Middletown, Providence, and Haddonfield, and so home, where I found my family well. A sense of the Lord's merciful preservation in this my journey incite reverent thankfulness to him.[54]

2nd day, 9th month, 1767. With the unity of Friends I set off on a visit to Friends in the upper part of Berks and Philadelphia Counties; was at eleven meetings in about two weeks and have renewed cause to bow in reverence before the Lord, who by the powerful extendings of his humbling goodness, opened my way amongst Friends and made the meetings, I trust, profitable to us. And the winter following I joined Friends on a visit to Friends' families in some part of our meeting, in which exercise the pure influence of divine love made our visits reviving.

On the 5th, 5th month, 1768, I left home under the humbling hand of the Lord, having obtained a certificate in order to visit some meetings in

52. Additional details are provided in MSS. A and R3. They refer to going through the upper part of Maryland before reaching the Red Lands, which are identified as being on the west side of the Susquehanna River.

53. "I may say with thankfulness that" has been inserted with a caret in MS. A, but is integrated into the sentence in MS. B. It is lacking in MS. R3. This tends to confirm the belief that MS. R3 was copied from MS. A before the latter was revised (in this instance by an addition). It is evident that MS. B was copied from MS. A (not from MS. R3) after the revision had been made.

In other ways MS. R3 appears to be more like MS. A than MS. B: MSS. A and R3 have more capital letters, and they fail to drop the final "e" before "ing." They both have "loveing," for example, whereas MS. B has "loving."

54. MS. R3 ends here (MS. B, p. 319). Nothing in MS. B indicates this point.

Maryland; and to proceed without a horse looked clearest to me. I was at
Quarterly Meetings at Philadelphia and Concord and then went on to
Chester River, and crossing the bay with Friends, was at the Yearly Meeting at West River. Thence back to Chester River and, taking a few meetings in my way, proceeded home.[55]

It was a journey of much inward waiting, and as my eye was to the
Lord, way was several times opened to my humbling admiration when
things had appeared very difficult. In my return I felt a relief of mind
very comfortable to me, having through divine help laboured in much
plainness, both with Friends selected and in the more public meetings, so
that I trust the pure witness in many minds was reached.

11th day, 6th month, 1769. Sundry cases have happened of late years
within the limits of our Monthly Meeting respecting that of exercising
pure righteousness toward the Negroes, in which I have lived under a
labour of heart that equity might be steadily kept to. On this account I
have had some close exercises amongst Friends, in which I may thankfully say I find peace. And as my meditations have been on universal
love, my own conduct in time past became of late very grievous to me.[56]

As persons setting Negroes free in our province are bound by law to
maintain them in case they have need of relief, some who scrupled keeping slaves term of life (in the time of my youth) were wont to detain
their young Negroes in their service till thirty years of age, without
wages, on that account. And with this custom I so far agreed that I, as
companion to another Friend in executing the will of a deceased Friend,
once sold a Negro lad till he might attain the age of thirty years and applied the money to the use of the estate.[57]

---

55. MS. A adds: "where I reached 10th day, 6th month, 1768."
56. The parallel passage in MS. P starts with this paragraph, beginning "11th day,"
and continuing to the end of the chapter. Between "grievous to me" and "As persons,"
MS. P has two lines that appeared originally in MS. A but were later erased, probably because they rephrase ideas expressed in the preceding lines. This is one of
several instances showing that MS. P bears the same relation to MS. A as does MS. R3.
It was copied (with some changes) from MS. A before the latter was revised by
erasures and insertions. Other evidence is found in the first sentence of the next
paragraph, where MS. P omits "in our province" and "term of life." Woolman used
carets to insert both of these phrases in MS. A, obviously after MS. P had been
copied from MS. A.
57. Between "estate" and "With abasement," MS. P adds the following passage,
which appears to have been erased from MS. A: "which lad at dating this note is
upward of twenty-four years of age and now a servant and frequently attends the
meeting I belong to."
In the next sentence, between "sat" and "in," the following appears in MS. P
(erased from MS. A): "in the uppermost seat."

With abasement of heart I may now say that sometimes as I have sat in a meeting with my heart exercised toward that awful Being who respecteth not persons nor colours, and have looked upon this lad, I have felt that all was not clear in my mind respecting him. And as I have attended to this exercise and fervently sought the Lord, it hath appeared to me that I should make some restitution, but in what way I saw not till lately, when being under some concern that I may be resigned to go on a visit to some part of the West Indies,[58] and was under close engagement of spirit, seeking to the Lord for counsel herein, that of joining in the sale aforesaid came heavily upon me, and my mind for a time was covered with darkness and sorrow. And under this sore affliction my heart was softened to receive instruction, and here I first saw that as I had been one of the two executors who had sold this lad nine years longer than is common for our own children to serve, so I should now offer a part of my substance to redeem the last half of that nine years; [59] but as the time was not yet come, I executed a bond, binding me and my executors to pay [60] to the man he was sold to what to candid men might appear equitable for the last four years and a half of his time, in case the said youth was then living and in a condition likely to provide comfortably for himself.

[9th day, 10th month, 1769.[61] My heart hath often been deeply affected under a feeling I have had that the standard of pure righteousness is not lifted up to the people by us, as a Society, in that clearness which

58. Between "Indies" and "and was," MS. P (duplicating an erased portion in MS. A) adds: "and have obtained a certificate from Friends, but the time of leaving my family hath not appeared clear to me." This important addition helps explain why Woolman did not make the trip to the West Indies.

59. After "substance to," MS. P, instead of "redeem," reads as follows (corresponding to an erasure in MS. A): "undo what I then did in redeeming."

60. Between "to pay" and "for the last," MS. P has this variant reading (which apparently follows the pre-revision form of MS. A): "what to candid men might appear an equitable compensation to the man he was sold to." The revised copy in MS. A, while changing a few words, retains the same order of phrases. MS. B, however, reverses the order. A study of the variations at this point, as elsewhere, confirms the conclusion that MS. B was copied not from MS. P but from the revised version of MS. A, additional revisions having been made in the process.

61. Woolman omitted this paragraph from MS. B, perhaps inadvertently. The original editorial committee copied it from page 212 of MS. A into MS. B (page 324), and prefaced it with this note: "A paragraph dated 9.10 mo. 1769 in bound book folio [page] 212 should come in here." This note was crossed out, apparently after the copying had been completed. The paragraph was included in the first printed edition.

This page is one piece of evidence that the original committee prepared MS. B for the printer but had access to MS. A.

it might have been had we been so faithful to the teachings of Christ as we ought to have been. And as my mind hath been inward to the Lord, the purity of Christ's government hath often been opened in my understanding, and under this exercise that of Friends being active in civil society in putting laws in force which are not agreeable to the purity of righteousness hath for several years past been an increasing burden upon me, having felt in the openings of universal love that where a people, convinced of the inward teachings of Christ, are active in putting laws in execution which they see are not consistent with pure wisdom, it hath a necessary tendency to bring dimness over their minds. And as my heart hath been thus exercised and a tender sympathy in me towards my fellow members, I have within [a] few months past, in several meetings for discipline, expressed my concern on this subject.] [62]

62. In MS. P, "they see" is omitted from the preceding sentence, as it apparently was from MS. A before that version was revised. In MS. P the final sentence has "begotten" after "sympathy," as it apparently did in MS. A before revision. Between "in me" and "I have," MS. P reads "toward my fellow creatures in general and my fellow members in particular." This seems never to have appeared in MS. A. Apparently Woolman made some revisions as he wrote MS. P, but in producing MS. B he bypassed MS. P and went directly back to MS. A.

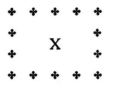

X

1769–1770

[MS. B, p. 325]

12TH, 3RD MONTH, 1770. Having for some years past dieted myself on account of a lump gathering on my nose, and under this diet grew weak in body and not of ability to travel by land as heretofore, I was at times favoured to look with awfulness toward the Lord, before whom are all my ways, who alone hath the power of life and death, and to feel thankfulness incited in me for this his fatherly chastisement, believing if I was truly humbled under it, all would work for good.

While I was under this bodily weakness, my mind being at times exercised for the good of my fellow creatures in the West Indies, I grew jealous over myself lest the disagreeableness of the prospect should hinder me from obediently attending thereto; for though I knew not that the Lord required me to go there, yet I believed that resignation was now called for in that respect, and feeling a danger of not being wholly devoted to him, I was frequently engaged to watch unto prayer that I might be preserved. And upward of a year having passed, I walked one day in a solitary wood; my mind being covered with awfulness, cries were raised in me to my merciful Father that he would graciously keep me in faithfulness, and it then settled on my mind as a duty to open my condition to Friends at our Monthly Meeting, which I did soon after as follows: "An exercise hath attended me for some time past and of late been more weighty upon me, under which I believe it is required of me to be resigned to go on a visit to some part of the West Indies." And in the Quarterly and General Spring Meeting [I] found no clearness to express anything further than that I believed resignation herein was required of me. And having obtained certificates from all said meetings, I felt like a sojourner at my outward habitation, kept free from worldly encumbrance, and was often bowed in spirit before the Lord, with inward breathings to him that I might be rightly directed.

And I may here note that being, when young, joined as executor with another Friend, we two, in executing the will of the deceased, sold a Negro lad till he might attain the age of thirty, on which account I had now great sorrow, as before related; and having settled matters relating to this youth, I soon after provided a sea-store and bed and things fitting for a voyage. And hearing of a vessel likely to sail from Philadelphia for Barbados, I spake with one of the owners at Burlington, and soon after went on purpose to Philadelphia and spake with him again, at which time he told me there was a Friend in town who was part owner of the said vessel.[1] But I felt no inclination at that time to speak with him, but returned home. And awhile after, I took leave of my family, and going to Philadelphia, had some weighty conversation with the first-mentioned owner and showed him a writing as follows:

25th day, 11th month, 1769. As an exercise with respect to a visit to Barbados hath been weighty on my mind, I may express some of the trials which have attended me. Under these trials I have at times rejoiced, in that I have felt my own self-will subjected.

I once, some years ago, retailed rum, sugar, and molasses, the fruits of the labour of slaves, but then had not much concern about them save only that the rum might be used in moderation; nor was this concern so weightily attended to as I now believe it ought to have been. But of late years being further informed respecting the oppressions too generally exercised in these islands, and thinking often on the degrees that there are in connections of interest and fellowship with the works of darkness (Eph. 5:11), and feeling an increasing concern to be wholly given up to the leadings of the Holy Spirit, it hath appeared that the small gain I got by this branch of trade should be applied in promoting righteousness in the earth. And near the first motion toward a visit to Barbados, I believed the outward substance I possess should be applied in paying my passage, if I go, and providing things in a lowly way for my subsistence. But when the time drew near in which I believed it required of me to be in readiness, a difficulty arose which hath been a continued trial for some months past, under which I have with abasement of mind from day to day sought the Lord for instruction, and often had a feeling of the condition of one formerly who bewailed himself for that the Lord hid his face from him.

During these exercises my heart hath been often contrite, and I have had a tender feeling of the temptations of my fellow creatures labouring under those expensive customs distinguishable from "the simplicity that there is in Christ" (2 Cor. 11:3), and sometimes in the renewings of gospel love have been helped to minister to others.

1. Mrs. Gummere (284n.) has identified the owners as John Smith (1722-1771) • and James Pemberton.•

That which hath so closely engaged my mind in seeking to the Lord for instruction is whether, after so full information of the oppression the slaves in the West Indies lie under who raise the West India produce, as I had in reading *A Caution and Warning to Great Britain and Her Colonies*, wrote by Anthony Benezet,* it is right for me to take a passage in a vessel employed in the West India trade.

To trade freely with oppressors and, without labouring to dissuade from such unkind treatment, seek for gain by such traffic tends, I believe, to make them more easy respecting their conduct than they would be if the cause of universal righteousness was humbly and firmly attended to by those in general with whom they have commerce; and that complaint of the Lord by his prophet, "They have strengthened the hands of the wicked" [Ezek. 13:22], hath very often revived in my mind, and I may here add some circumstances preceding any prospect of a visit there.

The case of David hath often been before me of late years. He longed for some water in a well beyond an army of Philistines at war with Israel, and some of his men, to please him, ventured their lives in passing through this army and brought that water. It doth not appear that the Israelites were then scarce of water, but rather that David gave way to delicacy of taste; but having thought on the danger these men were exposed to, he considered this water as their blood, and his heart smote him, [so] that he could not drink it but poured it out to the Lord. And the oppression of the slaves which I have seen in several journeys southward on this continent and the report of their treatment in the West Indies hath deeply affected me, and a care to live in the spirit of peace and minister just cause of offense to none of my fellow creatures hath from time to time livingly revived on my mind, and under this exercise I for some years past declined to gratify my palate with those sugars.

I do not censure my brethren in these things, but believe the Father of Mercies, to whom all mankind by creation are equally related, hath heard the groans of these oppressed people and is preparing some to have a tender feeling of their condition. And the trading in, or frequent use of, any produce known to be raised under such lamentable oppression hath appeared to be a subject which may yet more require the serious consideration of the humble followers of Christ, the Prince of Peace. After long and mournful exercise I am now free to mention how things have opened in my mind, with desires that if it may please the Lord to further open his will to any of his children in this matter, they may faithfully follow him in such further manifestation.

The number of those who decline the use of the West India produce on account of the hard usage of the slaves who raise it appears small, even amongst people truly pious, and the labours in Christian love on that subject of those who do, not very extensive. Was the trade from this continent to the West Indies to be quite stopped at once, I believe many there would suffer for want of bread.

Did we on this continent and the inhabitants of the West Indies generally dwell in pure righteousness, I believe a small trade between us might be right—that under these considerations, when the thoughts of wholly declining the use of trading vessels and of trying to hire a vessel to go under ballast have arose in my mind, I have believed that the labours in gospel love yet bestowed in the cause of universal righteousness are not arrived to that height.

If the trade to the West Indies was no more than was consistent with pure wisdom, I believe the passage money would for good reasons be higher than it is now; and here under deep exercise of mind, I have believed that I should not take the advantage of this great trade and small passage money, but as a testimony in favour of less trading should pay more than is common for others to pay, if I go at this time.

The first-mentioned owner, having read the paper, expressed a willingness to go with me to the other owner; and we going, the said other owner read over the paper, and we had some solid conversation, under which I felt my soul bowed in reverence before the Most High. And at length one of them asked me if I would go and see the vessel, but I had not clearness in my mind to go, but went to my lodgings and retired in private.

I was now under great exercise of mind, and my tears were poured out before the Lord with inward cries that he would graciously help me under these trials. In this case I believe my mind was resigned, but did not feel clearness to proceed; and my own weakness and the necessity of divine instruction was impressed upon me.

I was for a time as one who knew not what to do and was tossed as in a tempest, under which affliction the doctrine of Christ, "Take no thought for the morrow" [Mt. 6:34], arose livingly before me. I remembered it was some days before they expected the vessel to sail and was favoured to get into a good degree of stillness, and having been near two days in town, I believed my obedience to my Heavenly Father consisted in returning homeward. And then I went over amongst Friends on the Jersey shore and tarried till the morning on which they had appointed to sail. And as I lay in bed the latter part of that night my mind was comforted and I felt what I esteemed a fresh confirmation that it was the Lord's will that I should pass through some further exercises near home.[2]

2. The passage, "I believed . . . near home" appears in MS. B on page 341. Woolman wrote it again on page 343. He crossed out the latter and wrote in the margin

So I went home and still felt like a sojourner with my family, and in the fresh spring of pure love had some labours in a private way amongst Friends on a subject relating to Truth's testimony, under which I had frequently been exercised in heart for some years. I remember as I walked on the road under this exercise, that passage in Ezekiel came fresh before me, "Whithersoever their faces were turned, thither they went." [3] And I was graciously helped to discharge my duty in the fear and dread of the Almighty.

And after a few weeks it pleased the Lord to visit me with a pleurisy, and after I had lain a few days and felt the disorder very grievous, I was thoughtful how it might end.[4] I had of late through various exercises been much weaned from the pleasant things of this life, and I now thought if it was the Lord's will to put an end to my labours and graciously receive me into the arms of his mercy, death would be acceptable to me; but if it was his will to further refine me under affliction and make me in any degree useful in his church, I desired not to die. I may with thankfulness say that in this case I felt resignedness wrought in me and had no inclination to send for a doctor, believing if it was the Lord's will through outward means to raise me up, some sympathizing friends would be sent to minister to me, which were accordingly. But though I was carefully attended, yet the disorder was at times so heavy that I had no thoughts of recovery.

One night in particular my bodily distress was great: my feet grew cold, and cold increased up my legs toward my body, and at that time I had no inclination to ask my nurse to apply anything warm to my feet, expecting my end was near. And after I had lain, I believe, near ten hours in this condition, I closed my eyes, thinking whether I might now be delivered out of the body; but in these awful moments my mind was livingly opened to behold the church, and strong engagements were begotten in me for the everlasting well-being of my fellow creatures. And

---

"Entered in 4th Book." He also wrote "5" in the margin, indicating that this was the fifth folded sheet in this section. Later, "4th" was changed to "3rd," and "C" was written in the margin; these alterations were apparently made by the original editorial committee.

3. This is not an exact quotation, but the idea is expressed in Ezekiel 1 verses 9, 12, and 17.

4. The first word in this sentence, "And," has been underlined and crossed out. In the margin is written: "a new par." This all seems to have been done by the original editorial committee. In the first edition, "And" is omitted and a new paragraph begins here.

This is the illness during which Woolman had the vision described in Chapter 12.

I felt in the spring of pure love that I might remain some time longer in the body, in filling up according to my measure that which remains of the afflictions of Christ and in labouring for the good of the church, after which I requested my nurse to apply warmth to my feet, and I revived. And the next night, feeling a weighty exercise of spirit and having a solid Friend sitting up with me, I requested him to write what I said, which he did as follows:

4th day, 1st month, 1770, about five in the morning. I have seen in the light of the Lord that the day is approaching when the man that is the most wise in human policies shall be the greatest fool, and the arm that is mighty to support injustice shall be broken to pieces. The enemies of righteousness shall make a terrible rattle and shall mightily torment one another. For he that is omnipotent is rising up to judgment and will plead the cause of the oppressed. And he commanded me to open the vision.

Near a week after this, feeling my mind livingly opened, I sent for a neighbour, who at my request wrote as follows: [5]

[The place of prayer is a precious habitation, for I now saw [6] that the prayers of the saints was precious incense. And a trumpet was given me that I might sound forth this language, that the children might hear it and be invited to gather to this precious habitation, where the prayers of saints, as precious incense, ariseth up before the throne of God and the Lamb. I saw this habitation to be safe, to be inwardly quiet, when there was great stirrings and commotions in the world.

Prayer at this day in pure resignation is a precious place. The trumpet is sounded; the call goes forth to the church that she gather to the place of pure inward prayer, and her habitation is safe.[7]

5. MS. B, as it now stands, ends here—at the bottom of page 348, as numbered by the original editorial committee. Probably MS. B originally had additional pages that have since been lost. What follows in Chapter 10 of the present edition is taken from MS. A.

6. Between "saw" and "that" the following paraphrase of Revelation 8:1-4 was written by Woolman and then crossed out, also apparently by Woolman: "and the seventh seal was opened, and for a certain time there was silence in heaven; and I saw an angel with a golden censer, and he offered with it incense with the prayers of the saints, and it rose up before the throne. I saw."

7. In the first printed edition, Chapter 10 comes to a close here. At this point in MS. A (pages 223-224), however, is the following account of a dream, which concludes the main body of the Journal—covering events before the sea voyage and the

On the night between the 28th and 29th, 5th month, 1770, I dreamed a man had been hunting and brought a living creature to Mount Holly of a mixed breed, part fox and part cat. It appeared active in various motions, especially with its claws and teeth. I beheld and lo! many people gathering in the house where it was talked one to another, and after some time I perceived by their talk that an old Negro man was just now dead, and that his death was on this wise: They wanted flesh to feed this creature, and they wanted to be quit of the expense of keeping a man who through great age was unable to labour; so raising a long ladder against the house, they hanged the old man.

One woman spake lightly of it and signified she was sitting at the tea table when they hung him up, and though neither she nor any present said anything against their proceedings, yet she said at the sight of the old man a dying, she could not go on with tea drinking.

I stood silent all this time and was filled with extreme sorrow at so horrible an action and now began to lament bitterly, like as some lament at the decease of a friend, at which lamentation some smiled, but none mourned with me.

One man spake in justification of what was done and said the flesh of the old Negro was wanted, not only that this creature might have plenty, but some other creatures also wanted his flesh, which I apprehended from what he said were some hounds kept for hunting. I felt matter on my mind and would have spake to the man, but utterance was taken from me and I could not speak to him. And being in great distress I continued wailing till I began to wake, and opening my eyes I perceived it was morning.

And when I got up, I told this dream to my beloved friend Thomas Middleton, at whose house I lodged, who then told me that this same night he dreamed that being with his wife on the further side of a run of water which is on his plantation, they were coming toward the house, and the run had overflowed its banks, but they came over on a log; and there he saw a ruinous old house which he had not seen before. He observed some iron hinges on the door, which, as it stood on his land, he thought of getting, but on an examination found they would not answer his purpose, and left them. And looking into the house, he saw a great

---

English journey. Originally MS. B may have contained this account. It may have been lost before the first edition was printed, or the original editorial committee may have ignored it, as it ignored all of Woolman's dreams.

quantity of bacon and understood this house was a smoke house, built by a merchant since dead, and that the bacon belonged to some persons now living. He observed one whole creature with its hair all taken off, and though it had some resemblance of bacon, yet it appeared to stand upon its feet, and there was in it some resemblance of a living creature. He said he examined the bacon and found it was tainted.] [8]

8. In the margin Woolman has written his interpretation of some of the symbolism of the dream: "A fox is cunning; a cat is often idle; hunting represents vain delights; tea drinking with which there is sugar points out the slavery of the Negroes, with which many are oppressed to the shortening of their days."

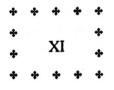

XI

1772

[p. 349] [1]

Memorandum of My Proceedings to Take a Passage
for England on a Religious Visit

My beloved friend Samuel Emlen, Jr.,* having taken a passage for himself in the cabin of the ship called Mary and Elizabeth, James Sparks master, and John Head of the city of Philadelphia the owner, and I feeling a draft in my mind toward the steerage of the same ship, went first of all and opened to Samuel the feeling I had concerning it.[2]

My beloved friend wept when I spake to him and appeared glad that I had thoughts of going in the vessel with him, though my prospect was toward the steerage;[3] and he offering to go with me, we two went on board, first into the cabin, a commodious room, and then into the steerage, where we sat down on a chest, the sailors being busy about us. Then the owner of the ship, a member of our Society, came and sat down with us.

Here my mind was turned toward Christ the heavenly Counsellor, and I feeling at this time my own will subjected, my heart was contrite before him.

1. Here and in the following chapter, the marginal reference in brackets is to MS. S, which is described in the list of major extant manuscripts in the Appendix. The pages were numbered, apparently by the original editorial committee, to continue where MS. B leaves off. The last page in MS. B is 348.

See Appendix F concerning a passage sometimes printed at the beginning of this chapter.

2. Several minor changes in wording have been made in the holograph of this section of MS. S (Chapter 11). Concerning some of them, it is extremely difficult to to be certain whether they were made by Woolman or by the original editorial committee. Concluding that they were probably made by the latter, the present editor has retained the original wording.

3. MS. T1 reads: "with him, and appeared easy as to my prospect of being in the steerage."

A motion was made by the owner to go and sit in the cabin as a place more retired; but I felt easy to leave the ship and made no agreement as to a passage in her, but told the owner if I took a passage in the ship I believed it would be in the steerage, but did not say much as to my exercise in that case.

After I went to my lodgings and the case was a little known in town, a friend laid before me the great inconvenience attending that steerage, which for a time appeared very discouraging to me. I soon after went to bed, and my mind was under a deep exercise before the Lord, whose helping hand was manifested to me as I slept that night, and his love strengthened my heart.[4] And in the morning I went with two friends on board the vessel again; and after a short time spent therein, I went with Samuel Emlen to the house of the owner, to whom in the hearing of Samuel only I opened my exercise in substance as follows, in relation to a scruple I felt with regard to a passage in the steerage.[5]

I told the owner that on the outside of that part of the ship where the cabin was I observed sundry sorts of carved work and imagery, and that in the cabin I observed some superfluity of workmanship of several sorts, and that[6] according to the way of men's reckoning, the sum of money to be paid for a passage in that apartment hath some relation to the expense in furnishing the room to please the minds of such who give way to a conformity[7] to this world, and that in this case, as in other cases, the moneys received from the passengers are calculated to answer every expense relating to their passage, and amongst the rest, the expense of these superfluities;[8] and that in this case I felt a scruple with regard to paying my money to defray such expenses.

As my mind was now opened,[9] I told the owner that I had at several times in my travels seen great oppressions on this continent, at which my heart had been much affected and brought often into a feeling of the

4. MS. T1 omits "and his love strengthened my heart."

5. MS. T1 reads: "with regard to taking a passage in the cabin." In MS. S, Woolman first wrote "in the steerage." The word "cabin" is written over "steerage," whether by Woolman or the editorial committee is uncertain.

6. In MS. T1 between "that" and "according" is the phrase, "on a reasonable computation."

7. MS. T1 reads: "who choose to be conformable."

8. MS. T1 reads simply: "calculated to pay of all the expense of these superfluities."

9. MS. T1 reads: "My mind being in some degree opened to enlarge on the subject." Also at other points Woolman eliminated "in some degree" as he revised his manuscript.

state of the sufferers. And having many times been engaged, in the fear and love of God, to labour with those under whom the oppressed have been borne down and afflicted, I have often perceived that a view to get riches and provide estates for children, to live conformable to customs which stand in that spirit wherein men have regard to the honours of this world—that in the pursuit of these things I had seen many entangled in the spirit of oppression, and the exercise of my soul been such that I could not find peace in joying [10] in anything which I saw was against that wisdom which is pure.

After this I agreed for a passage in the steerage, and hearing in town that Joseph White * had a mind to see me, I felt the reviving of a desire to see him [11] and went then to his house and next day home, where I tarried two nights. And then early in the morning I parted with my family [12] under a sense of the humbling hand of God upon me, and going to Philadelphia had opportunity with several of my beloved friends, who appeared to be concerned for me on account of the unpleasant situation of that part of the vessel where I was likely to lodge.

In these opportunities my mind through the mercies of the Lord was kept low, in an inward waiting for his help; and friends, having expressed [13] their desire that I might have a place more convenient than the steerage, did not urge but appeared disposed to leave me to the Lord.

Having stayed two nights in Philadelphia, I went the next day to Darby Monthly Meeting, where through the strength of divine love my heart was enlarged toward the youth then present, under which I was helped to labour in some tenderness of spirit.[14]

Then lodging at William Horne's,* I with one friend went to Chester, where meeting with Samuel Emlen * we went on board 1st day, 5th month, 1772; and as I sat down alone on a seat on the deck, I felt a satisfactory evidence [15] that my proceedings were not in my own will but under the power of the cross of Christ.

10. In both MS. T1 and MS. S, Woolman wrote "joying." This is probably what he intended, in the sense of "enjoying." In MS. S it has been changed to "joyning"; but this would appear to be the work of the original editorial committee, since it is doubtful that Woolman would have made the same error in both MSS.

11. After "I felt the reviving of a desire to see him" MS. T1 adds: "which I had felt before I heard of his to see me."

12. MS. T1 reads: "I took leave of my family."

13. MS. T1 originally read: "and such friends who came to see me, having spoke." Woolman later revised this in MS. T1 and further revised it in MS. S.

14. MS. T1 adds: "amongst them."

15. MS. T1 adds: "in my mind."

7th day, 5th month. Have had rough weather mostly since I came on board, and the passengers James Reynolds, John Till Adams, Sarah Logan and hired maid, and John Bispham all seasick more or less at times, from which sickness [16] through the tender mercies of my Heavenly Father I have been preserved, my afflictions now being of another kind.

There appeared an openness in the minds of the master of the ship and in the cabin passengers toward me. We were often together on the deck and sometimes in the cabin.

My mind through the merciful help of the Lord hath been preserved in a good degree watchful and inward, and have this day great cause to be thankful in that I remain to feel quietness of mind.[17]

As my lodgings in the steerage, now near a week, hath afforded me sundry opportunities of seeing, hearing, and feeling with respect to the life and spirit of many poor sailors, an inward exercise [18] of soul hath attended me in regard to placing out children and youth where they may be likely to be exampled and instructed in the pure fear of the Lord. And I, being much amongst the seamen, have from a motion of love sundry times taken opportunities with one alone and in a free conversation laboured to turn their minds toward the fear of the Lord; and this day we had a meeting in the cabin,[19] where my heart was contrite under a feeling of divine love.

Now concerning lads being trained up as seamen: I believe a communication from one part of the world to some other parts of it by sea is at times consistent with the will of our Heavenly Father, and to educate some youth in the practice of sailing I believe may be right; but how

16. "Sickness" is inserted with a caret in MS. S, whether by Woolman or the original editorial committee is not certain.

17. Much of the content of the three paragraphs ending at this point is not found in MS. T1, which reads as follows:

7th day, 5th month, 1772. Have had for the most part rough weather since I came on board, and the passengers mostly seasick more or less, except me, who as yet have not felt sick.

My mind through the merciful help of my Heavenly Father hath been preserved in a good degree watchful and inward.

The only prospect which hath been clearly open before me is this: that I came on board in resignedness of mind to my Heavenly Father, and have great cause to be thankful in that I feel inward quietness.

18. Instead of "spirit of many poor sailors, an inward exercise," MS. T1 reads: "spirit of sundry therein, an inward concern and exercise." Elsewhere, in the revising process Woolman also inserted "poor" before "sailors" or "lads."

19. MS. T1 reads: "a friendly free conversation laboured to turn their minds toward virtue. And this day we had a meeting in the cabin with cabin passengers."

lamentable is the present corruption of the world! How impure are the channels through which trade hath a conveyance! How great is that danger to which poor lads are now exposed [20] when placed on shipboard to learn the art of sailing?

Five lads training up for the seas were now on board this ship, two of them brought up amongst our Society, one of which hath a right amongst Friends, by name James Nayler, to whom James Nayler * mentioned in Sewel's history appears to have been uncle to his father. I often feel a tenderness of heart toward these poor lads and at times look at them as though they were my children according to the flesh.[21]

Oh, that all may take heed and beware of covetousness! Oh, that all may learn of Christ who is meek and low of heart! Then in faithfully following him, he will teach us to be content with food and raiment without respect to the customs or honours of this world. Men thus redeemed will feel a tender concern for their fellow creatures and a desire that those in the lowest stations may be encouraged. And where owners of ships attain to the perfect law [22] of liberty and are doers of the word, these will be blessed in their deeds.

A ship at sea commonly sails all night, and the seamen take their watches four hours at a time. Rising to work in the night is not commonly pleasant in any case, but in dark rainy nights it is very disagreeable, even though each man were furnished with all convenience; but if men must go out at midnight to help manage the ship in the rain, and having small room to sleep and lay their garments in, are often beset to furnish themselves for the watch, their garments or something relating to their business being wanting and not easily found, when from the urgency occasioned by high winds they are hastened and called up suddenly, here is a trial of patience on the poor sailors and the poor lads their companions.[23]

20. MS. T1 reads: "to which youth are exposed." The exclamation points at the end of the two preceding sentences, and the question mark at the end of this one, are all Woolman's.

21. This paragraph does not appear in MS. T1. The passage dealing with the Naylers has been revised, apparently by both Woolman and the original editorial committee, in an effort at succinctness. The word "right" apparently means "birthright."

22. MS. T1 reads: "true law." In the revising process it was natural for Woolman to change "true" to "perfect," the word used in the King James version of the Bible (James 1:25), which is paraphrased here.

23. The phrases referring to being summoned hastily and to "the poor sailors and the poor lads" are lacking in MS. T1.

If after they have been on deck several [24] hours in the night and come down into the steerage [25] soaking wet, and are so close stowed that proper convenience for change of garments is not easily come at, but for want of proper room their wet garments thrown in heaps, and sometimes through much crowding are trodden under foot in going to their lodgings and getting out of them, and great difficulties at times each one to find his own—here are trials on the poor sailors.[26]

Now as I have been with them in my lodge, my heart hath often yearned for them and tender desires been raised in me that all owners and masters of vessels [27] may dwell in the love of God and therein act uprightly, and by seeking less for gain and looking carefully to their ways may earnestly labour to remove all cause of provocation from the poor seamen [28] either to fret or use excess of strong drink; for indeed the poor creatures at times in the wet and cold seem to apply to strong drink to supply the want of other convenience.

Great reformation in the world is wanting! [29] and the necessity of it amongst these who do business in great waters hath at this time been abundantly opened before me.

8th day, 5th month. This morning the clouds gathered, the wind blew strong from southeastward, and before noon increased to that degree that sailing appeared dangerous. The seamen then bound up some of their sails, took some down, and the storm increasing, they put the dead lights, so called, into the cabin windows and lighted a lamp as at night.

The wind now blew vehemently, and the sea wrought to that degree

24. Instead of "several," MS. T1 has "four."

25. MS. T1 omits "into the steerage," "of garments," and "for want of proper room."

26. Instead of "and sometimes through . . . poor sailors," MS. T1 reads: "and often walked upon in some getting to their lodge and hard sometimes in the night each to find his own—here are difficulties for the poor sailors." In MS. S, "trials on" is written over an erasure, where the original wording appears to have been "difficulties for."

27. In MS. T1 Woolman first wrote "owners of vessels and masters of," which he then changed to "owners and masters of vessels." In MS. S Woolman incorporated the revised form smoothly into the text.

The word "been" between "desires" and "raised" was added after the rest of the phrase was written—whether by Woolman or by the original editorial committee is not certain.

28. MS. T1 reads: "from sailors." After "sailors," MS. T1 omits reference to drinking and closes the paragraph as follows: "and where lads are bound apprentice to the trade of mariners that nothing may be wanting on their part toward training them up in the fear of the Lord."

29. In MS. T1, Woolman first wrote: "Great reformation in the business of the," later crossing out the last five words and writing simply, "is wanting" (with no mention of "the world").

that an awful seriousness prevailed in the cabin, in which I spent I believe about seventeen hours; for I believed the poor wet toiling seamen had need of all the room in the crowded steerage, and the cabin passengers had given me frequent invitations.[30] They ceased now from sailing and put the vessel in the posture called lying-to.[31]

My mind in this tempest, through the gracious assistance of the Lord, was preserved in a good degree of resignation, and I felt at times a few words in his love to my shipmates in regard to the all-sufficiency of him who formed the great deep, and whose care is so extensive that a sparrow falls not without his notice, and thus in a tender frame of mind spake to them of the necessity of our yielding in true obedience to the instructions of our Heavenly Father, who sometimes through adversities intendeth our refinement.[32]

About eleven at night I went out on the deck, when the sea wrought exceedingly and the high foaming waves all round about had in some sort the appearance of fire, but did not give much if any light.[33] The sailor then at the helm said he lately saw a corposant at the head of the mast.

About this time I observed the master of the ship ordered the carpenter to keep on the deck, and though he said little, I apprehended his care was that the carpenter with his axe might be in readiness in case of any extremity.[34] Soon after this the vehemency of the wind abated, and before morning they again put the ship under sail.

[Blank] day, 5th month, and first of the week.[35] It being fine weather, we had a meeting in the cabin, at which most of the seamen were present. This meeting to me was a strengthening time.

13th day, 5th month. As I continue to lodge in the steerage, I feel an

---

30. In MS. T1, Woolman wrote and then crossed out three words between "wrought" and "to." In MS. S, there is no gap between "wrought" and "to."
   In MS. T1, "17 hours" is followed by "which thus fell out—that is, I left my lodging very early to walk the deck, and the storm coming on, I believed the poor toiling wet seamen had need of all the room in the steerage; and I, having been invited to the cabin before by a general invitation from those in it, now went there." As one notes carefully the differences between MS. T1 and MS. S, it becomes clear that MS. T1 is the preliminary copy and MS. S the final one.
31. MS. T1 omits this sentence.
32. MS. T1 reads: "who at times through distress as to the outward aimeth at our refinement."
33. MS. T1 originally read: "waves of the sea appeared like fire." Woolman crossed out "appeared like fire," to make the passage read: "waves of the sea had in some sort the appearance of fire." After further revision in MS. S, he reverted to this reading, so that the two MSS. ended up alike from "had" through "fire."
34. MS. T1 omits the sentence about the carpenter.
35. In MS. T1, both day and month are left blank.

openness this morning to express some further the state of my mind in respect to poor lads bound apprentice to learn the art of sailing. As I believe sailing is of some use in the world, a labour of soul attends me that the pure counsel of Truth may be humbly waited for in this case by all concerned in the business of the seas.[36]

A pious father whose mind is exercised for the everlasting welfare of his child may not with a peaceful mind place him out to an employment amongst a people whose common course of life is manifestly corrupt and profane. So great is the present defect amongst seafaring men in regard to piety and virtue, and through an abundant traffic and many ships of war, so many people are employed on the sea, that this subject of placing lads to the employment appears very weighty.

Profane examples are very corrupting and very forcible. And as my mind, day after day and night after night, hath been affected with a sympathizing tenderness toward poor children put to the employment of sailors, I have sometimes had weighty conversation with the sailors in the steerage, who were mostly respectful to me, and more and more so the longer I was with them.[37] They mostly appeared to take kindly what I said to them, but their minds have appeared to be so deeply impressed with that almost universal depravity amongst sailors that the poor creatures, in their answers to me on this subject, have revived in my remembrance that of the degenerate Jews a little before the captivity, as repeated by Jeremiah the prophet, "There is no hope" [Jer. 18:12].[38]

Now under this exercise a sense of the desire of outward gain prevailing amongst us hath felt grievous, and a strong call to the professed followers of Christ *hath* been raised in me that all may take heed, lest through loving this present world they be found in a continued neglect of duty with respect to a faithful labour for a reformation.[39]

Silence as to every motion proceeding from the love of money, and an humble waiting upon God to know his will concerning us, hath now appeared necessary. He alone is able to strengthen us to dig deep, to

---

36. MS. T1 reads: "all concerned herein."

37. MS. T1 omits "and more and more so the longer I was with them." Retrospective comment of this sort would be more likely to appear in the later manuscript.

38. In MS. S at this point the original editorial committee has written: "Mention chapter and verse." In the section, "So great is the present defect . . . no hope," MS. T1 contains many deletions and insertions. These have been incorporated smoothly into MS. S.

39. It is hard to understand why "hath" is underlined, but it seems to have been done by Woolman. The line is clearly drawn though narrow and inconspicuous.

remove all which lies between us and the safe foundation, and so direct us in our outward employments that pure universal love may shine forth in our proceedings.[40]

Desires arising from the spirit of Truth are pure desires; and when a mind divinely opened toward a young generation is made sensible of corrupting examples powerfully working and extensively spreading amongst them, how moving is the prospect.

A great trade to the coast of Africa for slaves, of which I now heard frequent conversation amongst the sailors!

A great trade in that which is raised and prepared through grievous oppression!

A great trade in superfluity of workmanship, formed to please the pride and vanity of peoples' mind!

Great and extensive is that depravity which prevails amongst the poor sailors!

When I remember that saying of the Most High through his prophet, "This people have I formed for myself: they shall show forth my praise" [Is. 43:21], and think of placing children amongst them to learn the practice of sailing joined with a pious education, as to me, my condition hath been like that mentioned by the prophet, "There is no answer from God" [Mic. 3:7].[41]

In a world of dangers and difficulties like a thorny, desolate wilderness, how precious! how comfortable! how safe! are the leadings of Christ the good Shepherd, who said, "I know my sheep and am known of mine" [Jn. 10:14].[42]

40. "Safe" has been written over "firm," and "our outward" is a revision of "all outward." It is probable, though not certain, that these changes were made by Woolman. MS. T1 reads: "firm foundation, and in that wisdom which is pure, direct our proceedings in all the employments required of us in this world."

41. The text between "learn the" and "like that" has been considerably revised, first by Woolman and then (apparently) by the original editorial committee. The process seems to have been as follows: Woolman first wrote, "learn the art of sailing, joined with a pious education." He then revised and completed the phrasing to read: "learn the practice of sailing, joined with a pious education, as to me, my condition hath been like that . . ." The committee changed it still further to "learn the practice of sailing, the consistency of it with a pious education seems to me like that . . ."

42. Beside the quotations from Isaiah 43:21 and from the words of Jesus, the original editorial committee has noted: "Get chapter." But the first edition does not in fact include the Scripture references.

From "moving is the prospect" up to this point, MS. T1 reads:
    A great trade to the coast of Africa for slaves! A great trade in that which

16th day, 5th month, 1772.[43] Wind for several days past often high, what the sailors call squally, rough sea and frequent rains. This last night a very trying night to the poor seamen, the water chief part of the night running over the main deck, and sometimes breaking waves come on the quarter deck. The latter part of the night as I lay in bed, my mind was humbled under the power of divine love,[44] and resignedness to the great Creator of the earth and the seas renewedly wrought in me, whose fatherly care over his children felt precious to my soul; and desires were now renewed in me [45] to embrace every opportunity of being inwardly acquainted with the hardships and difficulties of my fellow creatures and to labour in his love for the spreading of pure universal righteousness in the earth.[46]

The frequent opportunities of hearing conversation amongst the sailors in respect to the voyages to Africa and the manner of bringing the deeply oppressed slaves into our islands, the thoughts of their condition, frequently in chains and fetters, on board the vessels, with hearts loaded with grief under the apprehension of miserable slavery—as my mind was frequently opened to meditate on these things, my own lodging, now in the steerage, with the advantage of walking the deck when I would, appeared a commodious situation compared with theirs.[47]

17th day, 5th month, and first of the week. Had a meeting in the cabin, to which the seamen generally came. My spirit was contrite before the Lord, whose love at this time affected my heart.

---

is brought forth through grievous oppression! A great trade in superfluity of workmanship, formed to please the vanity of people's minds! And great is the danger before us!

How safe are his leadings, who is the Good Shepherd! How desirable the spreading of his kingdom on earth, where truth and equity are always prevalent! where the lowest and meanest as to outward descent are treated in such sort that the pure witness in their minds is reached.

43. In MS. T1, Woolman wrote simply, "Seventh Day morning." In the final version, MS. S, he made the date more precise.

44. MS. T1 reads: "under the seasoning virtue of Truth."

45. At this point MS. T1 adds: "to walk before him in faithfulness and."

46. MS. T1 reads: "to labour diligently according to the strength given me for the coming of the kingdom of Christ on earth as it is in heaven." The next two sentences, consisting of Woolman's reflections on the slave trade and on his lodging in the steerage, are lacking from MS. T1. As he revised and copied the manuscript, he would be more likely to add the reflections than to subtract them. This is another indication that MS. S was his final copy.

47. The word "As" before "my mind" and the passage, "my own lodging . . . with theirs," have been crossed out in MS. S, probably by the original editorial committee.

This afternoon felt a tender sympathy of soul with my poor wife and family left behind, in which state my heart was enlarged in desires that they may walk in that humble obedience wherein the everlasting Father may be their guide and support through all the difficulties in this world; and a sense of that gracious assistance through which my mind hath been strengthened to take up the cross and leave them, to travel in the love of Truth, hath begotten thankfulness in my heart to our great Helper.[48]

24th day, 5th month, and first of the week. A clear, pleasant morning, and as I sat on deck I felt a reviving in my nature, which through much rainy weather and high winds, being shut up in a close, unhealthy air, was weakened. Several nights of late I felt breathing difficult,[49] that a little after the rising of the second watch (which is about midnight) I got up and stood, I believe, near an hour with my face near the hatchway, to get the fresh air at the small vacancy under the hatch door, which was commonly shut down, partly to keep out rain and sometimes to keep the breaking waves from dashing into the steerage.[50]

I may with thankfulness to the Father of Mercies acknowledge that in my present weak state my mind hath been supported to bear the affliction with patience,[51] and have looked at the present dispensation as a kindness from the great Father of mankind, who in this my floating pilgrimage is in some degree bringing me to feel that which many thousands of my fellow creatures often suffer.[52]

My appetite failing, the trial hath been the heavier, and I have felt tender breathing in my soul after God, the fountain of comfort, whose inward help hath supplied at times the want of outward convenience; and strong desires have attended me that his family, who are acquainted with the movings of his Holy Spirit, may be so redeemed from the love of money and from that spirit in which men seek honour one of another [53]

48. MS. T1 reads: "to travel under a prospect of various difficulties, hath begotton thankfulness in my heart at this time." These are the closing words of the first part of MS. T, which is now located at the Mount School in York, England. The second part, now in the Friends Reference Library, Friends House, London, begins at this point. The two parts are distinguished in this edition as T1 and T2.

49. MS. T2 reads: "breathing so very much interrupted by the closeness and disagreeableness of the air." In MS. S, "so" may have been written before "difficult." A blot obscures the word at this point.

50. MS T2 adds: "This I did to get a little fresh air."

51. MS. T2 adds: "which affliction at present is but small."

52. At this point "in a greater degree" has been added, probably by the original editorial committee.

53. Instead of "from that spirit in which men seek honour one of another," MS. T2 reads: "from corrupt customs." Later in this sentence, before "show forth," "may"

that in all business by sea or land we may constantly keep in view the
coming of his kingdom on earth as it is in heaven, and by faithfully following this safe guide, may show forth examples tending to lead out of
that under which the creation groans! This day we had a meeting in the
cabin, in which I was favoured in some degree to experience the fulfilling
of that saying of the prophet, "The Lord hath been a strength to the poor,
a strength to the needy in their distress" [Is. 25:4], for which my heart is
bowed in thankfulness before Him.

28th day, 5th month.[54] Wet weather of late, small winds, inclining to
calms. Our seamen have cast a lead, I suppose about one hundred fathoms,
but find no bottom. Foggy weather this morning. Through the kindness
of the great Preserver of men my mind remains quiet, and a degree of
exercise from day to day attends me that the pure peaceable government
of Christ may spread and prevail amongst mankind.[55]

The leading on of a young generation in that pure way in which the
wisdom of this world hath no place—where parents and tutors, humbly
waiting for the heavenly Counsellor, may example them in the Truth as
it is in Jesus—this for several days hath been the exercise of my mind.[56]
Oh, how safe, how quiet is that state where the soul stands in pure
obedience to the voice of Christ!—and a watchful care maintained not to
follow the voice of the stranger.[57] Here Christ is felt to be our Shepherd,

---

has been crossed out, whether by Woolman or the original editorial committee cannot be determined.

54. MS. T2 has the year "1752," which is obviously wrong. After "winds" in this
line MS. T2 adds: "dull sailing."

55. MS. T2 reads: "attends me for the increase of the government of the Prince
of Peace."

56. Referring to the parents and tutors, MS. T2 adds: "where an inward awfulness
of soul . . . may be so evident . . . and as helps in the church, labour faithfully
against those corrupt customs which so grievously entangle the present age." After
"of my mind," MS. T2 adds: "That prophecy of Moses hath been now opened before me: Israel shall dwell in safety alone!"

57. From here to the word "Esau," MS. T2 contains a good deal of material not
in MS. S. The whole passage in MS T2 reads as follows (three dots are used to
indicate sections not included here because they are essentially the same as in MS. S.):

In the love of money the voice of the stranger finds entrance. In the love of
money the eye is not single to God. In the love of money the understanding is
closed up against the pure counsel of Truth, and thus becomes darkened.

We read that the spirit of God came upon Balaam when he said, "The
people shall dwell alone and shall not be mixed amongst the nations."

Now in the pure counsel of Truth, the people are brought to a stability, and
where . . . concerning us.

Business may be proposed in the will of man, and in carrying on this busi-

and under his leading people are brought to a stability. And where he doth not lead forward, we are bound in the bonds of pure love to stand still and wait upon him.

In the love of money and in the wisdom of this world, business is proposed, then the urgency of affairs push forward, nor can the mind in this state discern the good and perfect will of God concerning us. The love of God is manifested in graciously calling us to come out of that which stands in confusion; but if we bow not in the name of Jesus, if we give not up those prospects of gain which in the wisdom of this world are open before us, but say in our hearts, "I must needs go on, and in going on I hope to keep as near to the purity of Truth as the business before me will admit of," here the mind remains entangled and the shining of the light of life into the soul is obstructed.

This query opens in my mind in the love of Christ: Where shall a pious father place his son apprentice to be instructed in the practice of crossing the seas, and have faith to believe that Christ our holy Shepherd leads him to place his son there?

Surely the Lord calls to mourning and deep humiliation that in his fear we may be instructed and led safely on through the great difficulties and perplexities in this present age. In an entire subjection of our wills the Lord graciously opens a way for his people, where all their wants are bounded by his wisdom; and here we experience the substance of what Moses *the prophet* figured out in the water of separation as a purification from sin.

Esau is mentioned as a child red all over like a hairy garment. In Esau is represented the natural will of man. In preparing the water of separation a red heifer without blemish, on which there had been no yoke, was

---

ness men may find themselves entangled in that in which Israel may not dwell in safety alone.

Thus the love of God . . . Here the mind goes forth into the mixture. Here the pure light of life is not followed. To depart from the counsel of Truth is evil. To take counsel and not of God is exceeding dangerous. To do business because the urgency of our affairs demands it, when we feel it is against the purity of Truth, is to go on in that which like Ephraim mixeth amongst the nations.

This query . . . in this present age.

There is a safe, precious way, in which the soul feels the substance of what the prophet Moses . . . sin. The earthly mind, in which men receive honour one of another, leads into entangling mixtures; but this water of separation cleanseth the soul from the love of money and brings to a humble contentment even in a low estate, where we learn to trust in God that he in his own way will provide for us that which he knows to be best.

to be slain and her blood sprinkled by the priest seven times toward the tabernacle of the congregation. Then her skin, her flesh, and all pertaining to her was to be burnt without the camp, and of her ashes the water was prepared. Thus the crucifying the old man, or natural will, is represented, and hence comes a separation from that carnal mind which is death. "He who toucheth the dead body of a man and purifieth not himself with the water of separation, he defileth the tabernacle of the Lord; he is unclean." Numbers 19:13.

If one through the love of gain go forth into business wherein they dwell amongst the tombs (Isaiah c.v.),[58] and touch the bodies of those who are dead, if these through the infinite love of God feel the power of the cross of Christ to crucify them to the world, and therein learn humbly to follow the divine leader, here is the judgment of this world—here the prince of this world is cast out. The water of separation is felt; and though we have been amongst the slain and through the desire of gain have touched the dead body of a man, yet in the purifying love of Christ we are washed in the water of separation, are brought off from that business, from that gain, and from that fellowship which was not agreeable to his holy will. And I have felt a renewed confirmation in the time of this voyage that the Lord in infinite love is calling to his visited children to so give up all outward possessions and means of getting treasures that his Holy Spirit may have free course in their hearts and direct them in all their proceedings.[59] To feel the substance pointed at in this figure, man must know death as to his own will.

"No man can see God and live" [Ex. 33:20]. This was spoken by the Almighty to Moses the prophet and opened by our blessed Redeemer. As death comes on our own wills and a new life is formed in us, the heart is purified and prepared to understand clearly. "Blessed are the pure in heart, for they shall see God" [Mt. 5:8]. In purity of heart the mind is divinely opened to behold the nature of universal righteousness, or the righteousness of the kingdom of God. "No man hath seen the Father save he that is of God; he hath seen the Father" [Jn. 6:46].[60]

---

58. Here, as elsewhere, "c.v." means "chapter and verse," which Woolman probably intended to look up and insert.

59. This sentence does not appear in MS. T2, in which more emphasis is placed on the Old Testament account and less on its application to Woolman's day. The phrase "in the time" bears the marks of considerable revision. That it represents Woolman's final intention is probable though not certain.

60. At this point the editorial committee wrote: "Chapt. and Verse." The intention was apparently to document the scriptural quotation, but this was not done.

The natural mind is active about the things of this life, and in this natural activity business is proposed and a will in us to go forward in it. And as long as this natural will remains unsubjected, so long there remains an obstruction against the clearness of divine light operating in us; but when we love God with all our heart and with all our strength, then in this love we love our neighbours as ourselves, and a tenderness of heart is felt toward all people,[61] even such who as to outward circumstances may be to us as the Jews were to the Samaritans. "Who is my neighbour?" See this question answered by our Saviour [Lk. 10:25–37].[62] In this love we can say that Jesus is the Lord, and the reformation in our souls, manifested in a full reformation of our lives, wherein all things are new and all things are of God [2 Cor. 5:17–18]—in this the desire of gain is subjected. And employment is honestly followed in the light of Truth, and people become diligent in business, "fervent in spirit serving the Lord" [Rom. 12:11]—here the name is opened. "This is the name by which he shall be called: the Lord our Righteousness" [Jer. 23:6].

Oh, how precious is this name! It is like ointment poured out. The chaste virgin is in love with the Redeemer, and for the promoting his peaceable kingdom in the world are [sic] content to endure hardness like good soldiers, and are so separated in spirit from the desire of riches that in their employments they become extensively careful to give none offense—neither to Jews nor heathens nor the church of Christ.[63]

61. Crossed out after "people," apparently by Woolman: "for whom Christ died."
62. At this point and after "all things are of God" in the next sentence, and after "serving the Lord" in the following sentence, Woolman wrote abbreviations for "chapter" and "verse." Evidently he intended to document these allusions to Scripture. He did not do so.
In the next sentence, "and the reformation" originally read "and in the reformation." Then "in" was crossed off, apparently by Woolman.
63. This paragraph is lacking in MS. T2. The following appears in its place:
Some having large possessions and not dwelling in the pure fear of the Lord, but going on in arraying themselves in purple and fine linen and faring sumptuously every day—these open a channel for business which serves to please that mind which wanders, and the pursuit hath a tendency to a great increase of labour like that mentioned by the prophet, where people labour as in the fire and weary themselves with very vanity.
And many poor people, not abiding under the inward teaching of Christ, where the mind learns contentment in the will of God—these often watch the opportunities of getting gain in gratifying the wrong desires of the wealthy; and the wealthy, to support their expensive customs, lay heavy burdens on those through whose hands their wealth is gathered. Thus business goes on in the spirit of error, and youth are trained up in that which tends to harden their hearts against the pure inward leadings of Christ. And as my mind hath been

31st, 5th month, and first of the week. Had a meeting in the cabin with near all the ship's company, the whole being near thirty. In this meeting the Lord in mercy favoured us with the extendings of his love.

2nd day, 6th month, 1772. Last evening the seamen found bottom at about seventy fathom. This morning fair wind and pleasant, and as I sat on deck, my heart was overcome with the love of Christ and melted into contrition before him. And in this state the prospect of that work to which I have felt my mind drawn when in my native land being in some degree opened before me, I felt like a little child; and my cries were put up to my Heavenly Father for preservation,[64] that in a humble dependence on him my soul may be strengthened in his love and kept inwardly waiting for his counsel.

This afternoon, saw that part of England called the Lizard.[65] Some dunghill fowls yet remained of those the passengers took for eating. I believe about fourteen perished in the storms at sea by the waves breaking over the quarter deck, and a considerable number with sickness at different times. I observed the cocks crew coming down [the] Delaware and while we were near the land, but afterward I think I did not hear one of them crow till we came near the land in England, when they again crowed a few times.[66]

In observing their dull appearance at sea and the pining sickness of some of them, I often remembered the Fountain of Goodness, who gave being to all creatures,[67] and whose love extends to that of caring for the sparrows; and [I] believe where the love of God is verily perfected and the true spirit of government watchfully attended to,[68] a tenderness

---

bowed down under a concern for the coming of the kingdom of God on earth as it is in heaven, I have felt a renewed confirmation that the Lord is calling his visited children to so give up outward substance which they possess that he in hin infinite love may have free course in our minds in directed [sic] the uses and application of it.

64. MS. T2 reads: "my prayers were put up to my gracious Redeemer, that he, by the help of his Holy Spirit, may preserve me."

65. MS. T2 adds: "and with a pleasant breeze of wind stood our course and sailed along in plain sight of the green fields before night." These observations would impress one strongly at the time, but it is not surprising that Woolman did not consider them significant enough to preserve in the final copy (MS. S).

66. MS. T2 reads: "till we came along shore now in England." The word "now," omitted from MS. S, rather clearly identifies MS. T2 as the first draft, written at the scene.

67. MS. T2 adds: "whose tender mercies are over all his works."

68. MS. T2 reads: "I believe as the hearts of mankind are more and more humbled and brought into subjection to the spirit of Christ."

toward all creatures made subject to us will be experienced, and a care felt in us that we do not lessen that sweetness of life in the animal creation which the great Creator intends for them under our government,[69] and believe a less number carried off to eat at sea may be more agreeable to this pure wisdom.

4th day, 6th month, 1772. Wet weather, high winds, and so dark that we could see but a little way. I perceived our seamen were apprehensive of danger of missing the channel, which I understood was narrow. In a while it grew lighter, and they saw the land and knew where we were.[70] Thus the Father of Mercies was pleased to try us with the sight of dangers and then graciously from time to time deliver from them, thus sparing our lives that in humility and reverence we may walk before him and put our trust in him. About noon a pilot came off from Dover, where my beloved friend Samuel Emlen [71] went on shore—and to London, about seventy-two miles by land; but I felt easy in staying in the ship.

7th day, 6th month, and first of the week. Clear morning. Lay at anchor for the tide and had a parting meeting with the ship's company, in which my heart was enlarged in a fervent concern for them, that they may come to experience salvation through Christ.[72] Had a head wind up the Thames; lay sometimes at anchor; saw many ships passing and some at anchor near; and had large opportunity of feeling the spirit in which

69. MS. T2 reads: "that we do not lay them under unnecessary pain." The words "and believe . . . this pure wisdom" have been crossed out, probably by the original editorial committee.

70. At this point three words have been erased and several more crossed out with a pen—apparently, although not certainly, by Woolman. The obliterated words seem to be: "at which sight I discerned a visible alteration in the countenances of several, who appeared very thoughtful." The last word is not very clear. Perhaps it is "thankful."

71. At this point "and Sarah Logan" has been erased. Before "to London," MS. T2 adds, "to go in a stagecoach." Woolman's reluctance to use a stagecoach (as explained in the next chapter) is the probable reason for his staying aboard the ship. MS. T2 adds further: "Parting with Samuel at this time was a trial upon me. To go on shore felt most agreeable to my own will. The Yearly Meeting at London was now near, and though the passage by water is in some places a narrow channel in a wide water in which are many shoals, yet to stay longer in the ship felt most to my inward peace."

72. Instead of "my heart . . . through Christ," MS. T2 reads: "my mind was deeply engaged in fervent labour, and way opened in the love of the gospel to express in the hearing of my poor shipmates the sailors some of the precious effects of divine love operating on our minds, and to encourage them to feel after that which preserves from sin and gives that peace which is superior to the terrors of death." In MS. S, "a fervent" is written over "love."

the poor bewildered sailors too generally live. That lamentable degeneracy which so much prevails on the people employed on the seas so affected my heart that I may not easily convey the feeling I have had to another.

The present state of the seafaring life in general appears so opposite to that of a pious education,[73] so full of corruption and extreme alienation from God, so full of examples the most dangerous to *young people* that in looking [74] toward a young generation I feel a care for them, that they may have an education different from the present education of lads at sea, and that all of us who are acquainted with the pure gospel spirit may lay this case to heart, may remember the lamentable corruptions which attends the conveyance of merchandise across the seas, and so abide in the love of Christ that being delivered from the love of money, from the entangling expenses of a curious, delicate, and luxurious life—that we may learn contentment with a little and promote the seafaring life no further than that spirit which leads into all Truth attends us in our proceedings.[75]

73. MS. T2 reads: "so foreign from the meekness and piety of a soul devoted to God." In the next line, the phrase "most dangerous" is Woolman's final rendering; in MS. T2 he at first wrote simply "dangerous" and then "extremely dangerous."

74. The narration on page 394 of MS. S breaks off in the middle of the word "looking." This is followed by Woolman's note: "See beginning leaf." The narrative is concluded on the extra page which precedes the first page.

At the bottom of page 394 appears this note: "13th day, 6th month, 1772. I commit these notes to the care and keeping of Sophia Hume, and if she hath a mind to revise them, and place them in better order, I am free to it; but I desire she may not show them to anyone, but with a very weighty consideration. John Woolman."

75. Between "delicate" and "luxurious" Woolman first wrote "life," over which he then wrote "and." A horizontal line may have been intended to eliminate "and" as well as "life." Instead of "learn contentment with a little," MS. T2 reads: "stand firmly and walk carefully in the Truth as it is in Jesus."

1772

8TH DAY, 6TH MONTH, 1772.[1] Landed at London and went straightway to the Yearly Meeting of Ministers and Elders which had been gathered about (I suppose) half an hour. In this meeting my mind was humbly contrite. Afternoon meeting of business opened, which by adjournments held near a week. In these meetings I often felt a living concern for the establishment of Friends in the pure life of Truth, and my heart was enlarged in the meeting of ministers, meeting of business, and in several meetings for public worship, and I felt my mind united in true love to the faithful labourers now gathered from the several parts of this Yearly Meeting.

15th, 6th month. Left London and went to Quarterly Meeting at Hertford.

1st day, 7th month, 1772. Have been at Quarterly Meetings at Sherrington, at Northampton, at Banbury, at Shipston, and had sundry meetings

---

1. Across the top of this first page appears a line written by Woolman and crossed out, apparently by him: "P. Charran on Gold, Wm. Penn's works 83 page." The pages on which Woolman wrote this part of his *Journal* occasionally contained such miscellaneous notes.

Although the page number is wrong, Woolman apparently referred to William Penn: *Select Works* (London, 1771), 85, where Chapter 13, paragraph 21 of *No Cross No Crown* contains a long quotation by Peter Charron, described by Penn as "a famous Frenchman (and in particular for the book he wrote of wisdom)." The passage, a strong indictment of covetousness, includes the following: "For what greater folly can there be than to adore that which nature itself hath put under our feet and hidden in the bowels of the earth, as unworthy to be seen . . . ?" This may well have reminded Woolman of his earlier dream about the oppressed silver miners in Africa, recalled during his stay in England and described in this final chapter.

Also on this page, a note has been written in the margin and then crossed out, by whom is uncertain. It reads: "35 pages wrote, 62 [*illeg.*]."

between.[2] My mind hath been bowed under a sense of divine goodness manifested amongst us. My heart hath often been enlarged in true love amongst ministers and elders and in public meetings, that through the Lord's goodness I believe it hath been a fresh visitation to many, in particular to the youth.

17th day, 7th month. Was this day at Birmingham. Have been at Coventry, at Warwick, and have been at meetings in Oxfordshire and sundry places. Have felt the humbling hand of the Lord upon me and through his tender mercies find peace in the labours I have went through.

26th day, 7th month, 1772. Have continued travelling northward, visiting meetings. Was this day at Nottingham, which in the forenoon especially was through divine love a heart-tendering season. Next day had a meeting in a Friend's house with Friends' children and some Friends. This through the strengthening arm of the Lord was a time to be thankfully remembered.[3]

2nd day, 8th month, first of week. Was this day at Sheffield, a large inland town. Have been at sundry meetings last week and feel inward thankfulness for that divine support which hath been graciously extended to me.

9th day, 8th month, first of week. Was at Rushworth.[4] Have lately passed through some painful labour but have been comforted under a sense of that divine visitation which I feel extended toward many young people.

16th, 8th month, and first of week. Was at Settle. It hath of late been a time of inward poverty, under which my mind hath been preserved in a watchful, tender state, feeling for the mind of the Holy Leader, and find peace in the labours I have passed through.

On inquiry in many places I find the price of rye about 5 shillings; wheat about 8 shillings; oatmeal 12 shillings for 120 pound; mutton from 3 pence to 5 pence per pound; bacon from 7 pence to 9 pence; cheese from 4 pence to 6 pence; butter from 8 pence to 10 pence; house rent for a poor man from 25 shillings to 40 shillings per year, to be paid weekly;

2. In the margin opposite "Sherrington, at Northampton" is a question mark, probably inserted by Woolman. Perhaps he intended to verify a location or date.

3. In the margin opposite this paragraph is an apparently irrelevant note by Woolman: "27:4:55. Nati Meeting dublin."

4. In the margin opposite "9th day . . . Rushworth," is a question mark, probably inserted by Woolman.

wood for fire very scarce and dear; coal in some places 2 shillings 6 pence per hundredweight, but near the pits not a quarter so much. Oh, may the wealthy consider the poor! [5]

The wages of labouring men in several counties toward London, 10 pence per day in common business; the employer finds small beer and the labourer finds his own food; but in harvest and hay time, wages about 1 shilling and the labourer have all his diet. In some parts of the north of England poor labouring men have their food where they work and appear in common to do rather better than nearer London. Industrious women who spin in the factories get some 4 pence, some 5 pence, and so on: 6, 7, 8, 9 pence, or 10 pence, and find their own house-room and diet. Great numbers of poor people live chiefly on bread and water in the southern parts of England and some in the northern parts, and many poor children learn not to read.[6] May those who have plenty lay these things to heart!

Stagecoaches frequently go upwards of a hundred miles in 24 hours, and I have heard Friends say in several places that it is common for horses to be killed with hard driving, and many others driven till they grow blind. These coaches running chief part of the night do often run over foot people in the dark.[7]

Postboys pursue their business, each one to his stage, all night through the winter. Some boys who ride long stages suffer greatly in winter nights, and at several places I have heard of their being froze to death. So great is the hurry in the spirit of this world that in aiming to do business quick and to gain wealth the creation at this day doth loudly groan!

As my journey hath been without a horse, I have had several offers of being assisted on my way in these stages, but have not been in them, nor have I had freedom to send letters by these posts in the present way of their riding, the stages being so fixed and one boy dependent on another as to time, that they commonly go upward of 100 mile in 24 hours, and in the cold long winter nights the poor boys suffer much.

I heard in America of the way of these posts and cautioned Friends in

5. This sentence appears in the margin.
6. Woolman inserted with a caret (probably after he visited the north and observed these conditions there also) "of England . . . northern parts." The section, "northern parts . . . to read" has been heavily revised by Woolman and others; this appears to be Woolman's final version.
7. This sentence has been crossed out, probably by the original editorial committee—a deletion that has the effect of toning down Woolman's indictment.

the General Meeting of Ministers and Elders at Philadelphia and in the Yearly Meeting of Ministers and Elders at London not to send letters to me on any common occasion by post. And though on this account I may be likely to hear seldomer from the family I left behind, yet for righteousness sake I am through divine favour made content.

I have felt great distress of mind since I came on this island, on account of the members of our Society being mixed with the world in various sorts of business and traffic carried on in impure channels. Great is the trade to Africa for slaves! And in loading these ships abundance of people are employed in the factories, amongst whom are many of our Society! Friends in early times refused on a religious principle to make or trade in superfluities, of which we have many large testimonies on record, but for want of faithfulness some gave way, even some whose examples were of note in Society, and from thence others took more liberty.[8] Members of our Society worked in superfluities and bought and sold them, and thus dimness of sight came over many. At length Friends got into the use of some superfluities in dress and in the furniture of their houses, and this hath spread from less to more, till superfluity of some kinds is common amongst us.

In this declining state many look at the example one of another and too much neglect the pure feeling of Truth. Of late years a deep exercise hath attended my mind that Friends may dig deep, may carefully cast forth the loose matter and get down to the rock, the sure foundation, and there hearken to that divine voice which gives a clear and certain sound; and I have felt in that which doth not deceive that if Friends who have known the Truth keep in that tenderness of heart where all views of outward gain are given up, and their trust is only on the Lord, he will graciously lead some to be patterns of deep self-denial in things relating to trade and handicraft labour, and that some who have plenty of the treasures of this world will example in a plain frugal life and pay wages to such whom they may hire, more liberally than is now customary in some places.[9]

23rd, 8th month. Was this day at Preston Patrick. Here I dreamed of

8. "Society" probably refers to the Society of Friends.
9. In the margin opposite this paragraph appear these aphorisms: "Seal words with silence. Flatter no man. Choose well and hold fast. Use time well. Virtue maketh bold. Learn to forgive injuries." This is one of several pages that had previously been used for miscellaneous notes.

mother.[10] Had a comfortable meeting. I have several times been entertained at the houses of Friends who had sundry things about them which
had the appearance of outward greatness, and as I have kept inward, way
hath opened for conversation in private, in which divine goodness hath
favoured us together with heart-tendering times.[11]

A deviation amongst us as a Society from that simplicity that there is
in Christ becoming so general, and the trade from this island to Africa for
slaves, and other trades carried on through oppressive channels, and
abundance of the inhabitants being employed in factories to support a
trade in which there is unrighteousness, and some growing outwardly
great by gain of this sort: the weight of this degeneracy hath lain so
heavy upon me, the depth of this revolt been so evident, and desires in
my heart been so ardent for a reformation, so ardent that we might come
to that right use of things where, living on a little, we might inhabit that
holy mountain on which they neither *hurt nor destroy*! and may not only
stand clear from oppressing our fellow creatures, but may be so disentangled from connections in interest with known oppressors, that in us
may be fulfilled that prophecy: "Thou shalt be far from oppression"
[Is. 54:14]. Under the weight of this exercise the sight of innocent birds
in the branches and sheep in the pastures, who act according to the will
of their Creator, hath at times tended to mitigate my trouble.

26th day, 8th month, 1772. Being now at George Crosfield's, in West-
moreland County in England, I feel a concern to commit to writing that
which to me hath been a case uncommon. In a time of sickness with the
pleurisy a little upward of two years and a half ago, I was brought so near
the gates of death that I forgot my name.[12] Being then desirous to know
who I was, I saw a mass of matter of a dull gloomy colour, between the
south and the east, and was informed that this mass was human beings in
as great misery as they could be and live, and that I was mixed in with
them and henceforth might not consider myself as a distinct or separate
being. In this state I remained several hours. I then heard a soft, melodious

10. This sentence was inserted with a caret by Woolman. It has been crossed out,
probably by the original editorial committee. Although it does not appear in MS. Y,
it could easily have been missed in the copying process.

11. In the original the following paragraph ("A deviation . . . my trouble") has
been crossed out, probably by Woolman. These portions were written in the margin:
"the depth of this revolt been so evident" and "of their Creator . . . trouble." The
paragraph does not appear in MS. Y.

12. This is the illness described in the latter part of Chapter 10.

voice, more pure and harmonious than any voice I had heard with my ears before, and I believed it was the voice of an angel who spake to other angels. The words were, "*John Woolman is dead.*" I soon remembered that I once was John Woolman, and being assured that I was alive in the body, I greatly wondered what that heavenly voice could mean. I believed beyond doubting that it was the voice of an holy angel, but as yet it was a mystery to me.

I was then carried in spirit to the mines, where poor oppressed people were digging rich treasures for those called Christians, and heard them blaspheme the name of Christ, at which I was grieved, for his name to me was precious. Then I was informed that these heathens were told that those who oppressed them were the followers of Christ, and they said amongst themselves: "If Christ directed them to use us in this sort, then Christ is a cruel tyrant."

All this time the song of the angel remained a mystery, and in the morning my dear wife and some others coming to my bedside, I asked them if they knew who I was; and they, telling me I was John Woolman, thought I was only light-headed, for I told them not what the angel said, nor was I disposed to talk much to anyone, but was very desirous to get so deep that I might understand this mystery.

My tongue was often so dry that I could not speak till I had moved it about and gathered some moisture, and as I lay still for a time, at length I felt divine power prepare my mouth that I could speak, and then I said: "I am crucified with Christ, nevertheless I live; yet not I, but Christ that liveth in me, and the life I now live in the flesh is by faith in the Son of God, who loved me and gave himself for me" [Gal. 2:20]. Then the mystery was opened, and I perceived there was joy in heaven over a sinner who had repented and that that language *John Woolman is dead* meant no more than the death of my own will.

Soon after this I coughed and raised much bloody matter, which I had not during this vision, and now my natural understanding returned as before. Here I saw that people getting silver vessels to set off their tables at entertainments was often stained with worldly glory, and that in the present state of things, I should take heed how I fed myself from out of silver vessels.

Soon after my recovery I, going to our Monthly Meeting, dined at a Friend's house, where drink was brought in silver vessels and not in any other. And I, wanting some drink, told him my case with weeping, and he ordered some drink for me in another vessel.

The like I went through in several Friends' houses in America and have also in England since I came here, and have cause with humble reverence to acknowledge the loving-kindness of my Heavenly Father, who hath preserved me in such a tender frame of mind that none, I believe, have ever been offended at what I have said on that occasion. John Woolman.[13]

After this sickness I spake not in public meetings for worship for near one year, but my mind was very often in company with the oppressed slaves as I sat in meetings, and though under this dispensation I was shut up from speaking, yet the spring of the gospel ministry was many times livingly opened in me and the divine gift operated by abundance of weeping in feeling the oppression of this people.[14]

It being now so long since I passed through this dispensation and the matter remaining fresh and livingly on my mind, I believe it safest for me to write it.

30th day, 8th month, 1772. This morning wrote a letter in substance as follow [sic]:

BELOVED FRIEND,
    My mind is often affected as I pass along under a sense of the state of many poor people who sit under that sort of ministry which requires much outward labour to support it, and the loving-kindness

13. The signature "John Woolman" has been crossed out, probably by the original editorial committee.
    The Friend mentioned in the preceding paragraph (to whom he told his case with weeping) is identified by Mrs. Whitney (*John Woolman: Quaker*, 341) as John Smith (1722–1771).*
    14. This paragraph is followed by a note that reads: "By J. W.'s order in his illness the above to stand instead of that wrote in the margin on the other side of this page." The paragraph and note are in a handwriting identified by Mrs. Gummere as that of William Tuke * (Gummere, 310, note 2)
    Apparently Woolman, during his last illness, went back to this section and decided to add to the marginal passage, which had been written in his usual clear, firm hand, and which reads: "After this sickness I spake not in public meetings for worship for near one year, but my mind was very often in company with the oppressed slaves as I sat in meetings, and it was to me a time of abundance of weeping."
    The addition he now made, written in an uneven hand across the lines on the main body of the page, is as follows: "and though I think I never felt the spring of the min[istry] opened in me more powerfully, yet feeling a [illeg.] and in the live [illeg.] to speak, yet the gift had a way in my heart in contrition." (At each illegible point no more than 3 or 4 letters are involved.) It was apparently after making this rather incoherent attempt that he enlisted the help of Tuke. The paragraphs are probably printed here in the proper order, but Woolman, Tuke,* and the original editorial committee made so many changes that Woolman's final intention cannot be certain.

of our Heavenly Father in opening a pure gospel ministry in this nation hath often raised thankfulness in my heart toward him.

I often remember the conflicts of the faithful under persecution and now look at the free exercise of the pure gift, uninterrupted by outward laws, as a trust committed to us, which requires our deepest gratitude and most careful attention. I feel a tender concern that the work of reformation so prosperously carried on in this land within a few ages past may go forward and spread amongst the nations, and may not go backward through dust gathering on our garments, who have been called to a work so great and so precious.

Last evening I had a little opportunity at thy house with some of thy family, in thy absence, in which I rejoiced; and feeling a sweetness on my mind toward thee, I now endeavour to open a little of the feeling I had there.

I have heard that you in these parts have at certain seasons meetings of conference in relation to Friends living up to our principles, in which several meetings unite in one, with which I feel unity, I having in some measure felt Truth lead that way amongst Friends in America, and have found, my dear friend, that in these labours all superfluities in our own living are against us. I feel that pure love toward thee in which there is freedom.

I look at that precious gift bestowed on thee, with awfulness before him who gave it, and feel a care that we may be so separated to the gospel of Christ that those things which proceed from the spirit of this world may have no place amongst us. Thy friend, JOHN WOOLMAN [15]

I rested a few days in body and mind with our friend Jane Crosfield, who was once in America. Was on sixth day of the week at Kendal in Westmorland, and at Greyrigg Meeting the 30th, 8th month, and first of the week.

I have known poverty of late and been graciously supported to keep in the patience, and am thankful under a sense of the goodness of the Lord toward those that are of a contrite spirit.

6th day, 9th month, first of week. Was this day at Counterside, a large

15. This letter was written to Rachel Wilson.*The original is in the Friends Reference Library, London, England. It contains a postscript, which Woolman did not include in the *Journal*. It has been reprinted in *The Journal of the Friends Historical Society*, XXII (1925), 18, as follows:

I commit this letter to the hands of our ancient friend at Greyrigg Meeting, at whose house I write, with desire for him not to send it to thee, but keep it laid by till he hath opportunity to give it to thee.

I have sent no letter by post in England, and if thou feels a concern to write to me and art easy to wait an opportunity of conveyance some other way than post or flying coaches, I believe it would be most acceptable. J. W.

Flying coaches, I mean those coaches which run so fast as oft to oppress the horses.

meeting house and very full, and through the opening of pure love it was a strengthening time to me, and I believe to many more.

13th day, 9th month. Was this day at Richmond,[16] a small meeting, but the townspeople coming in, the house was crowded. It was a time of heavy labour and I believe was a profitable meeting.

At this place I heard that my kinsman William Hunt * from Carolina, who was on a religious visit to Friends in England, departed this life the 9th day, 9th month, 1772, at Newcastle, of the smallpox. He appeared in public testimony when he was a youth. His ministry was in the pure love and life of Truth, and his conduct in general agreeable thereto. He travelled much in the work of the gospel in America, and I remember to have heard say in public testimony in America that he had sought to the Lord for his . . .[17]

16. Originally a space appears to have been left at this point, in which the word "Richmond" was added later. The addition may not have been made by Woolman. The first printed edition has "Richmond," as does MS. Y; but some early printed editions (and later ones based upon them) have the name "Leyburn" instead of Richmond. The best explanation of this discrepancy (which still leaves some questions unanswered) is one offered by Henry J. Cadbury, who suggests that before the name of the town was inserted in the original, a copy may have been made in which "Leyburn" was inserted, and from which others adopted that reading.

17. In MS. S this sentence breaks off at the bottom of a page (48 as numbered by Woolman and 415 as numbered, apparently, by the original editorial committee). It may have been continued on another page that has since been lost. Since Woolman crossed off this paragraph and put a note next to it "turn a leaf forward," it appears likely that he composed a substitute paragraph (also later lost). MS. Y, which was apparently copied from MS. S by William Tuke * (in England) shortly after Woolman's death, contains such a substitute paragraph. With three minor deviations, this same paragraph was copied into MS. S on a separate page by the original editorial committee—from what source can only be a matter of conjecture.

It may be noted that on the margin of page 48 the original editorial committee has written "see page 54"; but there is no page 54, the next sheet containing pages 55 and 56. The committee's substitute paragraph appears (following various unrelated items) some 25 pages further on in MS. S, on a page numbered 416 to show that it followed the committee's "p. 415" (Woolman's page 48).

Because the pages were stitched together after the committee worked on them, and because some pages appear to be lost, it is impossible to be certain that the latter part of this chapter is reproduced exactly as Woolman left it.

MS. Y renders the substitute paragraph as follows: "I being now in Yorkshire heard that my kinsman William Hunt * from North Carolina, who was on a religious visit to Friends in England, departed this life the 9th day of 9th month, 1772, of the smallpox at Newcastle. He appeared in the ministry when a youth, and his labours therein were of a good savor. He travelled much in that work in America. I once heard him say in public testimony that his concern was in that visit to be devoted to the service of Christ so fully that he might not spend one minute in pleasing himself, which words, joined with his example, was a means of stirring up the pure mind in me."

Having of late travelled often in wet weather through narrow streets in towns and villages, where dirtiness under foot and the scent arising from that filth which more or less infects the air of all thick settled towns, and I, being but weakly, have felt distress both in body and mind with that which is impure. In these journeys I have been where much cloth hath been dyed and sundry times walked over ground where much of their dye-stuffs have drained away.

Here I have felt a longing in my mind that people might come into cleanness of spirit, cleanness of person, cleanness about their houses and garments. Some who are great carry delicacy to a great height themselves, and yet the real cleanliness is not generally promoted. Dyes being invented partly to please the eye and partly to hide dirt, I have felt in this weak state, travelling in dirtiness and affected with unwholesome scents, a strong desire that the nature of dyeing cloth to hide dirt may be more fully considered.

To hide dirt in our garments appears opposite to real cleanliness. To wash garments and keep them sweet, this appears cleanly. Through giving way to hiding dirt in our garments, a spirit which would cover that which is disagreeable is strengthened. Real cleanness becometh a holy people, but hiding that which is not clean by colouring our garments appears contrary to the sweetness of sincerity.

Through some sorts of dyes cloth is less useful. And if the value of dye-stuffs, the expense of dyeing, and the damage done to cloth were all added together and that expense applied to keep all sweet and clean, how much more cleanly would people be.

Near large towns there are many beasts slain to supply the market, and from their blood, etc., ariseth that which mixeth in the air. This, with the cleaning of many stables and other scents, the air in cities in a calm, wettish time is so opposite to the clear pure country air that I believe even the minds of people are in some degree hindered from the pure operation of the Holy Spirit, where they breathe a great deal in it.[18] *With God* all things are possible, and the sincere in heart find help under the greatest difficulties, but I believe if Truth be singly attended to, way may open for some to live a country life who now are in cities.[19]

18. It is not certain whether Woolman meant the first word in this sentence to be "Thus" or "This," or whether his final choice later in the sentence was "wettish" or "damp."

19. Written in the margin alongside this paragraph, apparently by the original editorial committee, are the words: "This may be left out." The paragraph has been omitted from the first edition. It appears on page 419 of MS. S. The previous para-

Copy of a Letter

YORK, 22nd day, 9th month, 1772

BELOVED FRIEND,[20]

When I followed the trade of a tailor, I had a feeling of that which pleased the proud mind in people, and growing uneasy, was strengthened to leave off that which was superfluous in my trade.

When I was at your house, I believe I had a sense of the pride of people being gratified in some part of the business thou followest and feel a concern in pure love to endeavour thus to inform thee of it.

Christ our leader is worthy of being followed in his leadings at all times. The enemy gets many on his side. Oh, that we may not be divided between the two, but may be wholly on the side of Christ.

In true love to you all I remain thy friend, JOHN WOOLMAN

9th month, 28, '72. Being now at the house of my friend Thomas Priestman * in the city of York, so weak in body that I know not how my sickness may end, I am concerned to leave in writing a case the remembrance whereof hath often affected me. An honest-hearted Friend in America, who departed this life a little less than a year ago, some months before his departure, he told me in substance as follows:

That he saw in a dream or night vision a great pond of blood from which a fog rose up. Some distance from him he saw this fog spread round about and great numbers of people walking backwards and forward in it, the garments of whom had a tincture of blood in 'em. I perceived he apprehended that by the pool of blood was represented the state of those hardhearted men through whose means much blood is shed in Africa and many lives destroyed through insupportable stench and other hardships in crossing the sea, and through extreme oppression bring many slaves to an untimely end, and that the fog in which the people were walking represented the gain arising on merchandise or traffic which many were taking hold of and, at the same time, knew that the gain was the gain of oppression.

This Friend, in his last sickness having several days had an inclination to see me, at length sent a messenger and I without delay went. He asked to be with me in private, which was granted; he then told me some matters in particular in regard to the gain of oppression, which he

---

graph appears on page 418. Between the two pages are many others without numbers, containing miscellaneous notes, copies of letters, etc.

20. The "Friend" was probably John Wilson, son of Rachel Wilson * (Gummere, 141–142, 321).

felt not easy to leave the world without [opening to me. All this time] he appeared calm [and quiet], and the family coming in by his consent, death in about one hour appeared evidently upon him, and I believe in about five hours from my going in he quietly breathed his last; and as I believe he left no memorandum in writing of that dream or vision of the night, at this time I believe it seasonable for me to do it.[21] JOHN WOOLMAN.

21. This entry for September 28 appears to have been dictated by Woolman and written by someone else, probably Thomas Priestman.* Some revisions have been made in the manuscript; since it cannot be determined which of them may have been suggested by Woolman at the time, the present editor has had to decide rather arbitrarily which readings to transcribe. The problem involves only minor changes of phrase, which do not materially affect the meaning. The signature, in very shaky handwriting, appears to be Woolman's own.

The "honest-hearted Friend" who had this dream has been identified by H. J. Cadbury (*John Woolman in England*, 112) as a cousin of Woolman, Peter Harvey, who died October 9, 1771. Woolman spoke at his funeral service and drafted a testimony to him, in which he wrote, "I was twice with him in his last illness."

The words "opening to me. All this time" are taken from MS. Y, since the bottom line of the page in MS. S has been worn away. The words "and quiet" are taken from a microfilm of MS. S in the Swarthmore College Library, made before 1960. They appear in Woolman's handwriting under "and calm," which are the last words in the final line on the page. By 1966, when the present editor first examined critically the holograph of MS. S, they were no longer there, the bottom of the page having been broken off. Traces of the tops of some of the letters are still discernible, however. The words "and quiet" do not appear in a copy of MS. S made by Samuel Comfort in 1839. The explanation for this may be that since they appear by themselves under the line, Comfort did not consider them an integral part of the manuscript. They are included in MS. Y.

Some editorial directions have been written on these pages. Along the right margin of one of them, upside down, is a double column of numbers listing the days of the week (1-7) opposite the thirty-one numbers representing the days in October.

PART TWO

❖

Major Essays of John Woolman

Introduction To The Essays

THE USE of these essays in history—who read them and to what effect —has already been discussed in the general introduction to this volume. Focusing on race relations and the deep pockets of poverty in the midst of affluence, they are especially relevant to the closing years of the twentieth century.

Some Considerations on the Keeping of Negroes was written in 1746, shortly after Woolman's first major journey into parts of the South—Maryland, Virginia, and North Carolina—where slavery was more pervasive than in the North. His father, as he lay dying in 1750, asked John whether he "expected soon to take the advice of friends in publishing" the manuscript. In 1753 Woolman presented it for examination to some personal friends and to the Publications Committee of the Philadelphia Yearly Meeting. In 1754, after some revision, it was printed by James Chattin of Church Alley in Philadelphia.

The first draft of *Considerations on Keeping Negroes, Part Second* was completed by November, 1761. Woolman submitted it for criticism to such leading Friends as John Churchman, Israel Pemberton, and Anthony Benezet, as well as to the Publications Committee. In a letter to Pemberton he wrote:

> I remain well satisfied with what thou proposed relating to the preface, and though I have looked over the piece with some care and done according to the best of my understanding, I have all along been apprehensive that if it be made public there was a further labour for some other person necessary; and if thou can feel liberty from thy other concerns and freedom to spend some time in a deliberate reviewing and correcting of it, and make such alterations or additions as thou believes may be useful, the prospect of it is agreeable to me.[1]

Woolman revised it in the light of the suggestions he received. It was then accepted by the committee and printed in Philadelphia in 1762 by Ben Franklin and D. Hall. A revealing account of how it was financed and distributed is given by Woolman in the first two pages of Chapter 8 of

1. *Pemberton Papers*, XV, 111, Historical Society of Pennsylvania.

the *Journal*. Incidentally, the care with which Woolman worked through proper Quaker channels was in marked contrast to the practice of certain earlier Friends, who published their antislavery tracts without regard to, or in opposition to, customary denominational procedures.

Both of the essays on Negroes were reprinted in 1774 (two years after Woolman's death) in the *Works* of Woolman, which were published in the same volume as the first edition of the *Journal*. Both have been reprinted with the *Journal* and other essays. The versions included in the *Works* of Woolman published in 1837 are worthy of note because they may have been based on the holographs; they were reprinted alone as a small book in 1839. Edited by John Comly and printed by T. E. Chapman in Philadelphia, these versions depart at several points from the first editions. Whether the essays in Comly's edition adhere to the holographs more closely than do the first editions cannot be ascertained; but there is no real reason to think so, since Comly's edition of the *Journal*, printed in the same volume (1837), deviates at many important points from MSS. A and B.

Mrs. Gummere stated (334) that the originals of both essays on Negroes "are in John Woolman's manuscript in the folio A." But they are neither there nor elsewhere in the archives of the Historical Society of Pennsylvania. The present editor studied the Gummere papers in the Quaker Collection of the Haverford College Library for a clue to the location of the holographs, but to no avail. Nor have any of the leading Quaker scholars consulted in the United States and England been able to furnish a fruitful lead. Accordingly, in this volume the two essays have been based on the first printed editions.

The first known printed edition of the essay here entitled *A Plea for the Poor* was published in Dublin, Ireland, in late 1793, under the title, *A Word of Remembrance and Caution to the Rich*. The present edition was based upon the only known holograph of this work, MS. *Plea*, plus MS. M (see Appendix B). However, after the pages of the present edition were set in type, a significant document was discovered and placed on deposit in the Haverford College Library. Designated by the present editor MS. W, it is without question a holograph of Chapters 1–13. The cover bears the title (apparently in Woolman's hand) *A Word of Remembrance and Caution to the Rich etc.* Of an original total of 76 pages, the first half sheet, comprising two pages, has been torn out. The remaining folded sheets, each consisting of four pages, have been lettered consecutively from B through U in Woolman's characteristic fashion. The pages measure approximately 7½ x 5½ inches and are of a size and texture similar to those of MS. B and other Woolman holographs. The manuscript is strongly bound in a cover of heavy blue paper, to all appearances a unit in itself—not part of a larger volume.

MS. W helps clarify several textual problems encountered in MS. *Plea.* It also provides modern scholars with the first evidence that the title *A Word . . . Rich etc.* probably originated with Woolman, and that at one time he apparently considered Chapters 1–13 a complete work. The pages contain many editorial emendations, apparently by the same hand that made similar revisions in MS. B. This adds to the mystery of why it was not published with the *Journal* and *Works* in 1774.

MSS. G and H, and the 1793 printed edition, are all closer to MS. W than to MS. *Plea*; they share the same title and omit Chapters 14–16. Yet they all differ markedly from both Woolman holographs. Since the versions of Comly, Gummere, and others are replete with deviations, this means that no previous edition has been faithful to either of Woolman's holographs. In pursuing our primary aim—to reflect Woolman's final intentions—we need not explore further the complex relationships of these documents produced after his death. The crucial issue is the relationship between MSS. *Plea* and W.

With the assistance of Henry J. Cadbury and the cooperation of Edwin Bronner and Mrs. Tritle of the Haverford College Library, the present editor has carefully examined the available documents. This study reveals that MS. W is a fair copy of MS. *Plea* (or conceivably of a lost holograph similar to MS. *Plea*), with essentially the same wording, but that MS. *Plea* is more complete and contains several later revisions not copied into MS. W. At numerous points Woolman's final intention is not certain. Lacking a clear contrary mandate, and since the pages were already set in type, the editor decided to retain MS. *Plea* as the manuscript printed herewith. Unless otherwise specified, footnote references are to MS. *Plea*, where changes made in the process of composition can be noted. The bracketed MS. page numbers appearing at the head of each chapter also refer to MS. *Plea*. In an addendum to this volume the editor has explored more thoroughly the relation of MS. *Plea* to MS. W, and recorded every substantive variant reading in MS. W, giving the basis (where such exists) for judging Woolman's final intention.

Incidentally, Chapter 16 (usually omitted, along with Chapters 14 and 15) deals specifically with the issue of reparations, which was raised forcibly in the Black Manifesto two hundred years later.

Some Considerations on the Keeping of Negroes

Recommended to the Professors of Christianity of Every Denomination

Introduction

CUSTOMS GENERALLY APPROVED and opinions received by youth from their superiors become like the natural produce of a soil, especially when they are suited to favourite inclinations. But as the judgments of God are without partiality, by which the state of the soul must be tried, it would be the highest wisdom to forego customs and popular opinions, and try the treasures of the soul by the infallible standard: Truth.

Natural affection needs a careful examination. Operating upon us in a soft manner, it kindles desires of love and tenderness, and there is danger of taking it for something higher. To me it appears an instinct like that which inferior creatures have; each of them, we see, by the ties of nature love self best. That which is a part of self they love by the same tie or instinct. In them it in some measure does the offices of reason, by which, among other things, they watchfully keep and orderly feed their helpless offspring. Thus natural affection appears to be a branch of self-love, good in the animal race, in us likewise with proper limitations, but otherwise is productive of evil by exciting desires to promote some by means prejudicial to others.

Our blessed Saviour seems to give a check to this irregular fondness in nature and, at the same time, a precedent for us: "Who is my mother, and who are my brethren?"—thereby intimating that the earthly ties of relationship are, comparatively, inconsiderable to such who, through a steady course of obedience, have come to the happy experience of the Spirit of God bearing witness with their spirits that they are his children: "And he stretched forth his hands towards his disciples and said, 'Behold my mother and my brethren; for whosoever shall do the will of my Father which is in heaven (arrives at the more noble part of true relationship)[1] the same is my brother, and sister, and mother.'" Mt. 12:48[-50].

This doctrine agrees well with a state truly complete, where love necessarily operates according to the agreeableness of things on principles unalterable and in themselves perfect. If endeavouring to have my children eminent amongst men after my death be that which no reasons grounded on those principles can be brought to support, then to be temperate in my pursuit after gain and to keep always within the bounds of those principles is an indispensable duty, and to depart from it a dark unfruitful toil.

In our present condition, to love our children is needful; but except this love proceeds from the true heavenly principle which sees beyond earthly treasures, it will rather be injurious than of any real advantage to them. Where the fountain is corrupt, the streams must necessarily be impure.

That important injunction of our Saviour (Mt. 6:33), with the promise annexed, contains a short but comprehensive view of our duty and happiness. If then the business of mankind in this life is to first seek another, if this cannot be done but by attending to the means, if a summary of the means is not to do that to another which (in like circumstances) we would not have done unto us, then these are points of moment and worthy of our most serious consideration.

What I write on this subject is with reluctance, and the hints given are in as general terms as my concern would allow. I know it is a point about which in all its branches men that appear to aim well are not generally agreed, and for that reason I chose to avoid being very particular.[2] If

1. Parenthetical phrase inserted by Woolman.

2. On September 2, 1762, Woolman wrote a letter to Israel Pemberton,* with which he enclosed a list of three alterations he wished made in this Introduction if the essay were reprinted to accompany Part 2. In place of the biblical allusion in the preceding paragraph, "not to do . . . done unto us," Woolman asked that the following be substituted: "to love the Lord our God with all our hearts, and our neighbors as ourselves." He requested that the following be omitted: "What I write on this subject is with reluctance and." Finally, he asked for the omission of "I know it is a point . . . avoid being very particular." The essay was not reprinted with Part 2 in 1762; and in 1774, when it was reprinted, the alterations were not made. The holographs of the letter and suggested alterations are in Pemberton Papers, XV, 112, Historical Society of Pennsylvania.

Instead of "chose to avoid," which appears in the first edition, some of the later editions, including that of Mrs. Gummere, read "choose to avoid." Further deviations of this sort will not be documented here.

I may happily have let drop anything that may excite such as are concerned in the practice to a close thinking on the subject treated of, the
candid amongst them may easily do the subject such further justice as,
on an impartial enquiry, it may appear to deserve; and such an enquiry I
would earnestly recommend.

Some Considerations on the Keeping of Negroes

"Forasmuch as ye did it to the least of these my brethren, ye did it
unto me." Mt. 25:40.

As many times there are different motives to the same actions, and one
does that from a generous heart which another does for selfish ends, the
like may be said in this case.

There are various circumstances amongst them that keep Negroes,
and different ways by which they fall under their care; and, I doubt not,
there are many well-disposed persons amongst them who desire rather to
manage wisely and justly in this difficult matter than to make gain of it.
But the general disadvantage which these poor Africans lie under in an
enlightened Christian country having often filled me with real sadness,
and been like undigested matter on my mind, I now think it my duty,
through divine aid, to offer some thoughts thereon to the consideration
of others.

When we remember that all nations are of one blood (Gen. 3:20);
that in this world we are but sojourners; that we are subject to the like
afflictions and infirmities of body, the like disorders and frailties in mind,
the like temptations, the same death and the same judgment; and that the
All-wise Being is judge and Lord over us all, it seems to raise an idea of a
general brotherhood and a disposition easy to be touched with a feeling
of each other's afflictions. But when we forget those things and look
chiefly at our outward circumstances, in this and some ages past, constantly retaining in our minds the distinction betwixt us and them with
respect to our knowledge and improvement in things divine, natural,
and artificial, our breasts being apt to be filled with fond notions of
superiority, there is danger of erring in our conduct toward them.

We allow them to be of the same species with ourselves; the odds is
we are in a higher station and enjoy greater favours than they. And when
it is thus that our Heavenly Father endoweth some of his children with
distinguished gifts, they are intended for good ends. But if those thus
gifted are thereby lifted up above their brethren, not considering them-

selves as debtors to the weak nor behaving themselves as faithful stewards, none who judge impartially can suppose them free from ingratitude. When a people dwell under the liberal distribution of favours from heaven, it behooves them carefully to inspect their ways and consider the purposes for which those favours were bestowed, lest through forgetfulness of God and misusing his gifts they incur his heavy displeasure, whose judgments are just and equal, who exalteth and humbleth to the dust as he seeth meet.

It appears by Holy Record that men under high favours have been apt to err in their opinions concerning others. Thus Israel, according to the description of the prophet (Is. 65:5), when exceedingly corrupted and degenerated, yet remembered they were the chosen people of God and could say, "Stand by thyself, come not near me, for I am holier than thou." That this was no chance language, but their common opinion of other people, more fully appears by considering the circumstances which attended when God was beginning to fulfil his precious promises concerning the gathering of the Gentiles.

The Most High, in a vision, undeceived Peter, first prepared his heart to believe, and at the house of Cornelius showed him of a certainty that God was no respecter of persons. The effusion of the Holy Ghost upon a people with whom they, the Jewish Christians, would not so much as eat was strange to them. All they of the circumcision were astonished to see it, and the apostles and brethren of Judea contended with Peter about it, till he having rehearsed the whole matter and fully shown that the Father's love was unlimited, they are thereat struck with admiration and cry out, "Then hath God also to the Gentiles granted repentance unto life!" [Acts 11:18]

The opinion of peculiar favours being confined to them was deeply rooted, or else the above instance had been less strange to them, for these reasons: First, they were generally acquainted with the writings of the prophets, by whom this time was repeatedly spoken of and pointed at. Secondly, our blessed Lord shortly before expressly said, "I have other sheep, not of this fold; them also must I bring," etc. [Jn. 10:16] Lastly, his words to them after his resurrection, at the very time of his ascension, "Ye shall be witnesses to me not only in Jerusalem, Judea, and Samaria, but to the uttermost parts of the earth" [Acts 1:8].

Those concurring circumstances, one would think, might have raised a strong expectation of seeing such a time. Yet when it came, it proved matter of offense and astonishment.

To consider mankind otherwise than brethren, to think favours are peculiar to one nation and exclude others, plainly supposes a darkness in the understanding. For as God's love is universal, so where the mind is sufficiently influenced by it, it begets a likeness of itself and the heart is enlarged towards all men. Again, to conclude a people froward, perverse, and worse by nature than others (who ungratefully receive favours and apply them to bad ends), this will excite a behavior toward them unbecoming the excellence of true religion.

To prevent such error let us calmly consider their circumstance, and, the better to do it, make their case ours. Suppose, then, that our ancestors and we have been exposed to constant servitude in the more servile and inferior employments of life; that we had been destitute of the help of reading and good company; that amongst ourselves we had had few wise and pious instructors; that the religious amongst our superiors seldom took notice of us; that while others in ease have plentifully heaped up the fruit of our labour, we had received barely enough to relieve nature, and being wholly at the command of others had generally been treated as a contemptible, ignorant part of mankind. Should we, in that case, be less abject than they now are? Again, if oppression be so hard to bear that a wise man is made mad by it (Eccles. 7:7), then a series of those things altering the behaviour and manners of a people is what may reasonably be expected.

When our property is taken contrary to our mind by means appearing to us unjust, it is only through divine influence and the enlargement of heart from thence proceeding that we can love our reputed oppressors. If the Negroes fall short in this, an uneasy, if not a disconsolate, disposition will be awakened and remain like seeds in their minds, producing sloth and many other habits appearing odious to us, with which being free men they perhaps had not been chargeable. These and other circumstances, rightly considered, will lessen that too great disparity which some make between us and them.

Integrity of heart hath appeared in some of them, so that if we continue in the word of Christ (previous to discipleship, Jn. 8:31) and our conduct towards them be seasoned with his love, we may hope to see the good effect of it, the which, in a good degree, is the case with some into whose hands they have fallen. But that too many treat them otherwise, not seeming conscious of any neglect, is, alas! too evident.

When self-love presides in our minds our opinions are biased in our own favour. In this condition, being concerned with a people so situated that they have no voice to plead their own cause, there's danger of using ourselves to an undisturbed partiality till, by long custom, the mind becomes reconciled with it and the judgment itself infected.

To humbly apply to God for wisdom, that we may thereby be enabled to see things as they are and ought to be, is very needful; hereby the hidden things of darkness may be brought to light and the judgment made clear. We shall then consider mankind as brethren. Though different degrees and a variety of qualifications and abilities, one dependent on another, be admitted, yet high thoughts will be laid aside, and all men treated as becometh the sons of one Father, agreeable to the doctrine of Christ Jesus.

> He hath laid down the best criterion by which mankind ought to judge of their own conduct, and others judge for them of theirs, one towards another—viz., "Whatsoever ye would that men should do unto you, do ye even so to them." I take it that all men by nature are equally entitled to the equity of this rule and under the indispensable obligations of it. One man ought not to look upon another man or society of men as so far beneath him but that he should put himself in their place in all his actions towards them, and bring all to this test—viz., How should I approve of this conduct were I in their circumstance and they in mine?—Arscott's *Considerations*, Part III, Fol. 107.[3]

This doctrine, being of a moral unchangeable nature, hath been likewise inculcated in the former dispensation: "If a stranger sojourn with thee in your land, ye shall not vex him; but the stranger that dwelleth with you shall be as one born amongst you, and thou shalt love him as thyself." Lev. 19:33, 34. Had these people come voluntarily and dwelt amongst us, to have called them strangers would be proper. And their being brought by force, with regret and a languishing mind, may well raise compassion in a heart rightly disposed. But there is nothing in such treatment which upon a wise and judicious consideration will any ways

3. This quotation, slightly altered, is found in Alexander Arscott, *Some Considerations Relating to the Present State of the Christian Religion, wherein the Nature, End, and Design of Christianity, as well as the Principle Evidence of the Truth of it, are Explained and Recommended out of the Holy Scriptures; with a General Appeal to the Experience of all Men for Confirmation thereof*, Part III (London, 1734), 78. Arscott (1676–1737), an Oxford graduate, was a schoolmaster. About 1700, to the great dismay of his parents, he became a Quaker. He served many years as clerk of the London Yearly Meeting. He intended this volume as an apologetic for Christianity based on both Scripture and reason, apart from the special point of view of the Friends. All three parts were reprinted in Philadelphia, the first two by Benjamin Franklin in 1732, the third by A. Bradford in 1738.

lessen their right of being treated as strangers. If the treatment which many of them meet with be rightly examined and compared with those precepts, "Thou shalt not vex him nor oppress him; he shall be as one born amongst you, and thou shalt love him as thyself" (Lev. 19:33; Deut. 27:19), there will appear an important difference betwixt them.

It may be objected there is cost of purchase and risk of their lives to them who possess 'em, and therefore needful that they make the best use of their time. In a practice just and reasonable such objections may have weight; but if the work be wrong from the beginning, there's little or no force in them. If I purchase a man who hath never forfeited his liberty, the natural right of freedom is in him. And shall I keep him and his posterity in servitude and ignorance? How should I approve of this conduct were I in his circumstances and he is mine? It may be thought that to treat them as we would willingly be treated, our gain by them would be inconsiderable; and it were, in diverse respects, better that there were none in our country.

We may further consider that they are now amongst us, and those of our nation the cause of their being here, that whatsoever difficulty accrues thereon we are justly chargeable with, and to bear all inconveniences attending it with a serious and weighty concern of mind to do our duty by them is the best we can do. To seek a remedy by continuing the oppression because we have power to do it and see others do it, will, I apprehend, not be doing as we would be done by.

How deeply soever men are involved in the most exquisite difficulties, sincerity of heart and upright walking before God, freely submitting to his providence, is the most sure remedy. He only is able to relieve not only persons but nations in their greatest calamities. David, in a great strait when the sense of his past error and the full expectation of an impending calamity as the reward of it were united to the aggravating his distress, after some deliberation saith, "Let me fall now into the hands of the Lord, for very great are his mercies; let me not fall into the hand of man." 1 Chron. 21:13.

To act continually with integrity of heart above all narrow or selfish motives is a sure token of our being partakers of that salvation which God hath appointed for walls and bulwarks (Is. 5:26; Rom. 15:8), and is, beyond all contradiction, a more happy situation than can ever be promised by the utmost reach of art and power united, not proceeding from heavenly wisdom.

A supply to nature's lawful wants, joined with a peaceful, humble mind, is the truest happiness in this life. And if here we arrive to this and remain to walk in the path of the just, our case will be truly happy. And though herein we may part with or miss of some glaring shows of riches and leave our children little else but wise instructions, a good example, and the knowledge of some honest employment, these, with the blessing of providence, are sufficient for their happiness, and are more likely to prove so than laying up treasures for them which are often rather a snare than any real benefit, especially to them who, instead of being exampled to temperance, are in all things taught to prefer the getting of riches and to eye the temporal distinctions they give as the principal business of this life. These readily overlook the true happiness of man as it results from the enjoyment of all things in the fear of God, and miserably substituting an inferior good, dangerous in the acquiring and uncertain in the fruition, they are subject to many disappointments; and every sweet carries its sting.

It is the conclusion of our blessed Lord and his apostles, as appears by their lives and doctrines, that the highest delights of sense or most pleasing objects visible ought ever to be accounted infinitely inferior to that real intellectual happiness suited to man in his primitive innocence and now to be found in true renovation of mind, and that the comforts of our present life, the things most grateful to us, ought always to be received with temperance and never made the chief objects of our desire, hope, or love, but that our whole heart and affections be principally looking to that city "which hath foundations, whose maker and builder is God" [Heb. 11:10].

Did we so improve the gifts bestowed on us that our children might have an education suited to these doctrines, and our example to confirm it, we might rejoice in hopes of their being heirs of an inheritance incorruptible. This inheritance, as Christians, we esteem the most valuable; and how then can we fail to desire it for our children? Oh, that we were consistent with ourselves in pursuing means necessary to obtain it!

It appears by experience that where children are educated in fullness, ease, and idleness, evil habits are more prevalent than is common amongst such who are prudently employed in the necessary affairs of life.[4] And if children are not only educated in the way of so great temptation, but have also the opportunity of lording it over their fellow creatures and being masters of men in their childhood, how can we hope otherwise

---

4. The first edition reads "in common," as do subsequent editions. The present editor assumes that Woolman meant (and probably wrote) "is common."

than that their tender minds will be possessed with thoughts too high for them?—which by continuance, gaining strength, will prove like a slow current, gradually separating them from (or keeping from acquaintance with) that humility and meekness in which alone lasting happiness can be enjoyed.

Man is born to labour, and experience abundantly showeth that it is for our good. But where the powerful lay the burden on the inferior, without affording a Christian education and suitable opportunity of improving the mind, and a treatment which we in their case should approve —that themselves may live at ease and fare sumptuously and lay up riches for their posterity—this seems to contradict the design of Providence and, I doubt, is sometimes the effect of a perverted mind. For while the life of one is made grievous by the rigour of another, it entails misery on both.

Amongst the manifold works of Providence displayed in the different ages of the world, these which follow (with many others) may afford instruction:

Abraham was called of God to leave his country and kindred, to sojourn amongst strangers. Through famine and danger of death he was forced to flee from one kingdom to another. He at length not only had assurance of being the father of many nations, but became a mighty prince. Gen. 23:6.

Remarkable was the dealings of God with Jacob in a low estate. The just sense he retained of them after his advancement appears by his words: "I am not worthy of the least of all thy mercies." Gen. 32:10; 48:15.

The numerous afflictions of Joseph are very singular, the particular providence of God therein no less manifest. He at length became governor of Egypt and famous for wisdom and virtue.

The series of troubles David passed through, few amongst us are ignorant of; and yet he afterwards became as one of the great men of the earth.

Some evidences of the divine wisdom appears in those things, in that such who are intended for high stations have first been very low and dejected, that Truth might be sealed on their hearts, and that the characters there imprinted by bitterness and adversity might in after years remain, suggesting compassionate ideas and, in their prosperity, quicken their regard to those in the like condition, which yet further appears in the case of Israel. They were well acquainted with grievous sufferings, a long and rigorous servitude, then through many notable events were made chief amongst the nations. To them we find a repetition of precepts to the purpose above-said. Though for ends agreeable to infinite wisdom they were chose as a peculiar people for a time, yet the Most High acquaints them that his love is not confined, but extends to the stranger, and to excite their compassion, reminds them of times past: "Ye were strangers in the land of Egypt." Deut. 10:19. Again, "Thou shalt not oppress a stranger, for ye know the heart of a stranger, seeing ye were strangers in the land of Egypt." Ex. 23:9.

If we call to mind our beginning, some of us may find a time wherein our fathers were under afflictions, reproaches, and manifold sufferings. Respecting our progress in this land, the time is short since our beginning was small and number few, compared with the native inhabitants. He that sleeps not by day nor night hath watched over us and kept us as the apple of his eye. His almighty arm hath been round about us and saved us from dangers.

The wilderness and solitary deserts in which our fathers passed the days of their pilgrimage are now turned into pleasant fields. The natives are gone from before us, and we establish peaceably in the possession of the land, enjoying our civil and religious liberties. And while many parts of the world have groaned under the heavy calamities of war, our habitation remains quiet and our land fruitful.

When we trace back the steps we have trodden and see how the Lord hath opened a way in the wilderness for us, to the wise it will easily appear that all this was not done to be buried in oblivion, but to prepare a people for more fruitful returns, and the remembrance thereof ought to humble us in prosperity and excite in us a Christian benevolence towards our inferiors.

If we do not consider these things aright, but through a stupid indolence conceive views of interest separate from the general good of the great brotherhood, and in pursuance thereof treat our inferiors with rigour, to increase our wealth and gain riches for our children, what then shall we do when God riseth up; and when he visiteth, what shall we answer him? Did not he that made us make them, and "did not one fashion us in the womb?" Job 31:14[-15].

To our great Master we stand or fall; to judge or condemn is most suitable to his wisdom and authority. My inclination is to persuade and entreat, and simply give hints of my way of thinking.

If the Christian religion be considered, both respecting its doctrines and the happy influence which it hath on the minds and manners of all real Christians, it looks reasonable to think that the miraculous manifestation thereof to the world is a kindness beyond expression. Are we the people thus favoured? Are we they whose minds are opened, influenced, and governed by the spirit of Christ and thereby made sons of God? Is it not a fair conclusion that we, like our Heavenly Father, ought in our degree to be active in the same great cause—of the eternal happiness of at least our whole families, and more, if thereto capacitated?

If we, by the operation of the Spirit of Christ, become heirs with him in the kingdom of his Father, and are redeemed from the alluring counterfeit joys of this world, and the joy of Christ remain in us; to suppose that one remaining in this happy condition can, for the sake of earthly riches, not only deprive his fellow creatures of the sweetness of freedom (which, rightly used, is one of the greatest temporal blessings), but therewith neglect using proper means for their acquaintance with the Holy Scriptures and the advantage of true religion, seems, at least, a contradiction to reason.

Whoever rightly advocates the cause of some thereby promotes the good of all. The state of mankind was harmonious in the beginning; and though sin hath introduced discord, yet through the wonderful love of God in Christ Jesus our Lord, the way is open for our redemption, and means appointed to restore us to primitive harmony.

That if one suffer by the unfaithfulness of another, the mind, the most noble part of him that occasions the discord, is thereby alienated from its true and real happiness. Our duty and interest is inseparably united, and when we neglect or misuse our talents we necessarily depart from the heavenly fellowship and are in the way to the greatest of evils. Therefore, to examine and prove ourselves, to find what harmony the power presiding in us bears with the divine nature, is a duty not more incumbent and necessary than it would be beneficial.

In Holy Writ the Divine Being saith of himself, " 'I am the Lord, which exercise loving-kindness, judgment, and righteousness in the earth; for in these things I delight,' saith the Lord." Jer. 9:24. Again, speaking in the way of man to show his compassion to Israel, whose wickedness had occasioned a calamity, and then being humbled under it, it is said, "His soul was grieved for their miseries." Judg. 10:16.

If we consider the life of our blessed Saviour when on earth, as it is recorded by his followers, we shall find that one uniform desire for the eternal and temporal good of mankind discovered itself in all his actions. If we observe men, both apostles and others in many different ages, who have really come to the unity of the spirit and the fellowship of the saints, there still appears the like disposition; and in them the desire of the real happiness of mankind has out-balanced the desire of ease, liberty, and many times life itself.

If upon a true search we find that our natures are so far renewed that to exercise righteousness and loving-kindness (according to our ability) towards all men, without respect of persons, is easy to us or is our delight; if our love be so orderly and regular that he who doth the will of our Father who is in heaven appears in our view to be our nearest relation, our brother and sister and mother; if this be our case, there is a good foundation to hope that the blessing of God will sweeten our treasures during our stay in this life, and our memory be savory when we are entered into rest.

To conclude, 'tis a truth most certain that a life guided by wisdom from above, agreeable with justice, equity, and mercy, is throughout consistent and amiable, and truly beneficial to society. The serenity and calmness of mind in it affords an unparalleled comfort in this life, and the end of it is blessed. And, no less true, that they who in the midst of high favours remain ungrateful, and under all the advantages that a Christian can desire are selfish, earthly, and sensual, do miss the true fountain of happiness and wander in a maze of dark anxiety, where all their treasures are insufficient to quiet their minds. Hence, from an insatiable craving they neglect doing good with what they have acquired, and too often add oppression to vanity, that they may compass more.

"Oh, that they were wise, that they understood this, that they would consider their latter end!" Deut. 32:29.

Considerations on Keeping Negroes

Recommended to the Professors of Christianity of Every Denomination

PART SECOND

"Ye shall not respect persons in judgment, but you shall hear the small as well as the great. You shall not be afraid of the face of man, for the judgment is God's." Deut. 1:17.

Preface

All our actions are of like nature with their root, and the Most High weigheth them more skillfully than men can weigh them one for another.

I believe that one Supreme Being made and supports the world, nor can I worship any other deity without being an idolater and guilty of wickedness. Many nations have believed in and worshipped a plurality of deities, but I do not believe they were therefore all wicked. Idolatry indeed is wickedness; but it is the thing, not the name, which is so. Real idolatry is to pay that adoration to a creature which is known to be due only to the true God.

He who professeth to believe in one Almighty Creator and in his son Jesus Christ, and is yet more intent on the honours, profits, and friendships of the world than he is in singleless of heart to stand faithful to the Christian religion, is in the channel of idolatry, while the Gentile who under some mistaken opinions is notwithstanding established in the true principle of virtue, and humbly adores an Almighty Power, may be of that number who fear God and work righteousness.

I believe the Bishop of Rome assumes a power that does not belong to any officer in the church of Christ; and if I should knowingly do anything tending to strengthen him in that capacity, it would be great iniquity. There are many thousands of people who by their profession acknowledge him to be the representative of Jesus Christ on earth; and to say that none of them are upright in heart would be contrary to my sentiments.

Men who sincerely apply their minds to true virtue and find an inward support from above by which all vicious inclinations are made subject, that they love God sincerely and prefer the real good of mankind universally to their own private interest, though these through the strength of education and tradition may remain under some speculative and great errors, it would be uncharitable to say that therefore God rejects them. He who creates, supports, and gives understanding to all men—his knowledge and goodness is superior to the various cases and circumstances of his creatures which to us appear the most difficult.

The apostles and primitive Christians did not censure all the Gentiles as wicked men (Rom. 2:14; Col. 3:2), but as they were favoured with a gift to discern things more clearly respecting the worship of the true God, they with much firmness declared against the worshiping of idols and with true patience endured many sufferings on that account.

Great numbers of faithful Protestants have contended for the Truth in opposition to papal errors and with true fortitude laid down their lives in the conflict, without saying that no man was saved who made profession of that religion.

While we have no right to keep men as servants for term of life but that of superior power, to do this with design by their labour to profit ourselves and our families I believe is wrong. But I do not believe that all who have kept slaves have therefore been chargeable with guilt. If their motives thereto were free from selfishness and their slaves content, they were a sort of freemen, which I believe hath sometimes been the case.

Whatever a man does in the spirit of charity, to him it is not sin; and while he lives and acts in this spirit, he learns all things essential to his happiness as an individual. And if he doth not see that any injury or injustice to any other person is necessarily promoted by any part of his form of government, I believe the merciful Judge will not lay iniquity to his charge. Yet others who live in the same spirit of charity from a clear convincement may see the relation of one thing to another and the necessary tendency of each; and hence it may be absolutely binding on them to desist from some parts of conduct which some good men have been in.

Considerations on Keeping Negroes, Etc.

As some in most religious Societies amongst the English are concerned in importing or purchasing the inhabitants of Africa as slaves, and as the professors of Christianity of several other nations do the like, these circumstances tend to make people less apt to examine the practice so closely as they would if such a thing had not been, but was now proposed to be entered upon. It is, however, our duty and what concerns us individually, as creatures accountable to our Creator, to employ rightly the understanding which he hath given us, in humbly endeavouring to be acquainted with his will concerning us and with the nature and tendency of those things which we practice. For as justice remains to be justice, so many people of reputation in the world joining with wrong things do not excuse others in joining with them nor make the consequence of their proceedings less dreadful in the final issue than it would be otherwise.

Where unrighteousness is justified from one age to another, it is like dark matter gathering into clouds over us. We may know that this gloom will remain till the cause be removed by a reformation or change of times and may feel a desire, from a love of equity, to speak on the occasion; yet where error is so strong that it may not be spoken against without some prospect of inconvenience to the speaker, this difficulty is likely to operate on our weakness and quench the good desires in us, except we dwell so steadily under the weight of it as to be made willing to endure hardness on that account.

Where men exert their talents against vices generally accounted such, the ill effects whereof are presently perceived in a government, all men who regard their own temporal good are likely to approve the work. But when that which is inconsistent with perfect equity hath the law or countenance of the great in its favour, though the tendency thereof be quite contrary to the true happiness of mankind in an equal, if not greater, degree than many things accounted reproachful to Christians, yet as these ill effects are not generally perceived, they who labour to dissuade from such things which people believe accord with their interest have many difficulties to encounter.

The repeated charges which God gave to his prophets imply the danger they were in of erring on this hand: "Be not afraid of their faces; for I am with thee to deliver thee, saith the Lord." Jer. 1:8. "Speak . . . all the words that I command thee to speak to them; diminish not a word." Jer. 26:2. "And thou son of man, be not afraid of them . . . nor dismayed at their looks. Speak my words to them, whether they will bear or forebear." Ezek. 2:6[-7].

Under an apprehension of duty, I offer some further considerations on this subject, having endeavoured some years to consider it candidly. I have observed people of our own colour whose abilities have been inferior of the affairs which relate to their convenient subsistence, who have been taken care of by others, and the profit of such work as they could do applied toward their support. I believe there are such amongst Negroes and that some people in whose hands they are keep them with no view of outward profit, do not consider them as black men who, as such, ought to serve white men, but account them persons who have need of guardians, and as such take care of them. Yet where equal care is taken in all parts of education, I do not apprehend cases of this sort are likely to occur more frequently amongst one sort of people than another.

It looks to me that the slave trade was founded and hath generally been carried on in a wrong spirit, that the effects of it are detrimental to the real prosperity of our country, and will be more so except we cease from the common motives of keeping them and treat them in future agreeable to Truth and pure justice.

Negroes may be imported who, for their cruelty to their countrymen and the evil disposition of their minds, may be unfit to be at liberty; and if we, as lovers of righteousness, undertake the management of them, we should have a full and clear knowledge of their crimes and of those circumstances which might operate in their favour; but the difficulty of obtaining this is so great that we have great reason to be cautious therein. But should it plainly appear that absolute subjection were a condition the most proper for the person who is purchased, yet the innocent children ought not to be made slaves because their parents sinned.

We have account in Holy Scripture of some families suffering where mention is only made of the heads of the family committing wickedness; and it is likely that the degenerate Jews, misunderstanding some occurrences of this kind, took occasion to charge God with being unequal, so that a saying became common: "The fathers have eaten sour grapes, and the children's teeth are set on edge" [Ezek. 18:2]. Jeremiah and Ezekiel, two of the inspired prophets who lived near the same time, were concerned to correct this error. Ezekiel is large on the subject. First, he reproves them for their error: "What mean ye, that ye do so?" Chap. 18, verse 1 [2–3]. " 'As I live,' saith the Lord God, 'ye shall not have occasion any more to use this proverb in Israel.' " The words "any more" have reference to time past, intimating that though they had not rightly understood some things they had heard or seen, and thence supposed the proverb to be well grounded, yet henceforth they might know of a certainty that the ways of God are all equal—that as sure as the Most High liveth, so sure men are only answerable for their own sins. He thus sums up the matter: "The soul that sinneth, it shall die. The son shall not bear the iniquity of the father; neither shall the father bear the iniquity of the son. The righteousness of the righteous shall be upon him, and the wickedness of the wicked shall be upon him" [Ezek. 18:20].

Where men are wicked they commonly are a means of corrupting the succeeding age and thereby hasten those outward calamities which fall on nations when their iniquities are full.

Men may pursue means which are not agreeable to perfect purity, with a view to increase the wealth and happiness of their offspring, and thereby make the way of virtue more difficult to them. And though the ill example of a parent or a multitude does not excuse a man in doing evil, yet the mind being early impressed with vicious notions and practices and nurtured up in ways of getting treasure which are not the ways of Truth, this wrong spirit getting first possession and being thus strengthened frequently prevents due attention to the true spirit of wisdom, so that they exceed in wickedness those before them. And in this channel, though parents labour as they think to forward the happiness of their children, it proves a means of forwarding their calamity. This being the case in the age next before the grievous calamity in the siege of Jerusalem, and carrying Judah captive to Babylon, they might say with propriety: "This came upon us because our fathers forsook God and because we did worse than our fathers."

As the generation next before them inwardly turned away from God, who yet waited to be gracious, and as they in that age continued in those things which necessarily separated from perfect goodness, growing more stubborn till the judgments of God were poured out upon them, they might properly say, "Our fathers have sinned and we have borne their iniquities." And yet, wicked as their fathers were, had they not succeeded them in their wickedness, they had not borne their iniquities.

To suppose it right that an innocent man shall at this day be excluded from the common rules of justice, be deprived of that liberty which is the natural right of human creatures, and be a slave to others during life on account of a sin committed by his immediate parents or a sin committed by Ham, the son of Noah, is a supposition too gross to be admitted into the mind of any person who sincerely desires to be governed by solid principles.

It is alleged in favour of the practice that Joshua made slaves of the Gibeonites. What men do by the command of God and what comes to pass as a consequence of their neglect are different, such as the latter case now mentioned was.

It was the express command of the Almighty to Israel concerning the inhabitants of the promised land: "Thou shalt make no covenant with them, nor with their gods. They shall not dwell in thy land." Ex. 23:32. Those Gibeonites came craftily, telling Joshua that they were come from a far country, that their elders had sent them to make a league with the people of Israel, and as an evidence of their being foreigners showed their old clothes, etc. "And the men took of their victuals and asked not counsel at the mouth of the Lord; and Joshua made peace with them and made a league with them to let them live; and the princes swore to them" [Josh. 9:14, 15].

When the imposition was discovered, the congregation murmured against the princes. But all the princes said to all the congregation: "We have sworn to them by the Lord God of Israel; now therefore, we may not touch them; . . . we will even let them live, lest wrath be upon us; . . . but let them be hewers of wood and drawers of water unto the congregation" [Josh. 9:19–21].

Omitting to ask counsel involved them in great difficulty. The Gibeonites were of those cities of which the Lord said: "Thou shalt save alive nothing that breatheth" [Deut. 20:16], and of the stock of the Hivites, concerning whom he commanded by name: "Thou shalt smite them and utterly destroy them. Thou shalt make no covenant with them, nor show mercy unto them." Deut. 7:1[2]. Thus Joshua and the princes, not knowing them, had made a league with them to let them live, and in this strait they resolve to make them servants. Joshua and the princes suspected them to be deceivers: "Peradventure you dwell amongst us; and how shall we make a league with you?" [Josh. 9:7], which words show that they remembered the command beforementioned, and yet did not enquire at the mouth of the Lord, as Moses directed Joshua when he gave him a charge respecting his duty as chief man among that people. Num. 27:21. By this omission things became so situated that Joshua and the princes could not execute the judgments of God on them without violating the oath which they had made.

Moses did amiss at the waters of Meribah and doubtless he soon repented, for the Lord was with him. And it is likely that Joshua was deeply humbled under a sense of his omission, for it appears that God continued him in his office and spared the lives of those people for the sake of the league and oath made in his name.

The wickedness of these people was great, and they worthy to die, or perfect justice had not passed sentence of death upon them; and as their execution was prevented by this league and oath, they appear content to be servants: "As it seemeth good and right unto thee to do unto us, do" [Josh. 9:25]. These criminals, instead of death, had the sentence of servitude pronounced on them in these words: "Now therefore ye are cursed; and there shall none of you be freed from being bondmen and hewers of food and drawers of water for the house of my God" [Josh. 9:23].

We find (Deut. 20:10) that there were cities far distant from Canaan against which Israel went to battle, unto whom they were to proclaim peace; and if the inhabitants made answer of peace and opened their gates, they were not to destroy them but make them tributaries.

The children of Israel were then the Lord's host and executioners of his judgments on people hardened in wickedness. They were not to go to battle but by his appointment. The men who were chief in his army had their instructions from the Almighty, sometimes immediately and sometimes by the ministry of angels. Of these, amongst others, were Moses, Joshua, Othniel, and Gideon (see Ex. 3:2 and 18:19, Josh. 5:13). These people far off from Canaan against whom Israel was sent to battle were so corrupt that the Creator of the universe saw it good to change their situation; and in case of their opening their gates and coming under tribute, this their subjection, though probably more mild than absolute slavery, was to last little or no longer than while Israel remained in the true spirit of government. ⏐

It was pronounced by Moses the prophet as a consequence of their wickedness: "The stranger that is within thee shall get above thee very high; and thou shalt come down very low. He shall be the head and thou the tail [Deut. 28:43–44]. This we find in some measure verified in their being made tributaries to the Moabites, Midianites, Amorites, and Philistines.

It is alleged in favour of the practice of slavekeeping that the Jews by their law made slaves of the heathen. Lev. 25:45: "Moreover, of the children of the stranger that do sojourn amongst you, of them shall ye buy and of their children which are with you which they beget in your land. And they shall be your possession; and you shall take them as an inheritance for your children after you, to inherit them as a possession; they shall be your bondmen forever." It is difficult for us to have any certain knowledge of the mind of Moses in regard to keeping slaves, any other way than by looking upon him as a true servant of God, whose mind and conduct were regulated by an inward principle of justice and equity. To admit a supposition that he in that case was drawn from perfect equity by the alliance of outward kindred would be to disown his authority.

Abraham had servants born in his house and bought with his money. And the Almighty said of Abraham: "I know him, that he will order his house after him" [Gen. 18:19], which implies that he was as a father, an instructor, and a good governor over his people. And Moses, considered as a man of God, must necessarily have had a prospect of some real advantage in the strangers and heathens being servants to the Israelites for a time.

As mankind had received and established many erroneous opinions and hurtful customs, their living and conversing with the Jews while the Jews stood faithful to their principles might be helpful to remove those errors and reform their manners. But for men with private views to assume an absolute power over the persons and properties of others and continue it from age to age in the line of natural generation, without regard to the virtues and vices of their successors, as it is manifestly contrary to true universal love and attended with great evils, there requires the clearest evidence to beget a belief in us that Moses intended that the strangers should as such be slaves to the Jews.

He directed them to buy strangers and sojourners. It appears that there were strangers in Israel who were free men, and considering with what tenderness and humanity the Jews by their Law were obliged to use their servants and what care was to be taken to instruct them in the true religion, it is not unlikely that some strangers in poverty and distress were willing to enter into bonds to serve the Jews as long as they lived; and in such case the Jews by their Law had a right to their service during life.

When the awl was bored through the ear of the Hebrew servant, the text saith: "He shall serve forever" [Ex. 21:6]. Yet we do not suppose that by the word "forever" it was intended that none of his posterity should afterwards be free. When it is said in regard to the strangers which they bought: "They shall be your possession" [Lev. 25:45], it may be well understood to mean only the persons so purchased. All preceding relates to buying them, and what follows to the continuance of their service: "You shall take them as an inheritance to your children after you; they shall be your bondmen forever" [Lev. 25:46]. It may be well understood to stand limited to those they purchased.

Moses, directing Aaron and his sons to wash their hands and feet when they went into the tabernacle of the congregation, saith: "It shall be a statute forever to them, even to him and his seed throughout all generations" [see Ex. 40:12, 15]. And to express the continuance of the Law, it was his common language: "It shall be a statute forever throughout your generations" [see Lev. 3:17]; so that had he intended the posterity of the strangers so purchased to continue in slavery to the Jews it looks likely that he would have used some terms clearly to express it. The Jews undoubtedly had slaves whom they kept as such from one age to another. But that this was agreeable to the genuine design of their inspired Lawgiver is far from being a clear case.

Making constructions of the Law contrary to the true meaning of it was common amongst that people. Samuel's sons took bribes and perverted judgment. Isaiah complained that they justified the wicked for reward. Zephaniah, contemporary with Jeremiah, on account of the injustice of the civil magistrates declared that those judges were evening wolves, and that the priests did violence to the law.

Jeremiah acquaints us that the priests cried, "Peace, peace," when there was no peace, by which means the people grew bold in their wickedness —and having committed abominations were not ashamed, but through wrong constructions of the Law they justified themselves and boastingly said: "We are wise; and the law of the Lord is with us" [Jer. 8:8]. These corruptions continued till the days of our Saviour, who told the Pharisees: "You have made the commandment of God of none effect through your tradition" [Mt. 15:6].

Thus it appears that they corrupted the law of Moses. Nor is it unlikely that among many others this was one; for oppressing the strangers was a heavy charge against the Jews and very often strongly represented by the Lord's faithful prophets.

That the liberty of man was by the inspired Lawgiver esteemed precious appears in this: that such who unjustly deprived men of it were to be punished in like manner as if they had murdered them. "He that stealeth a man and selleth him, or if he be found in his hand, shall surely be put to death" [Ex. 21:16]. This part of the Law was so considerable that Paul, the learned Jew, giving a brief account of the uses of the Law, adds this: "It was made for men-stealers." 1 Tim. 1:10.

The great men amongst that people were exceeding oppressive and, it is likely, exerted their whole strength and influence to have the law construed to suit their turns [terms?]. The honest servants of the Lord had heavy work with them in regard to their oppression. A few instances follow: "Thus saith the Lord of hosts, the God of Israel: 'Amend your ways and your doings, and I will cause you to dwell in this place. . . . If you throughly execute judgment between a man and his neighbour, if you oppress not the stranger, the fatherless, and the widow, and shed not innocent blood in this place, neither walk after other gods to your hurt, then will I cause you to dwell in this place.'" Jer. 7: [3–7].[1] Again, a message was sent not only to the inferior ministers of justice, but also to the chief ruler: "Thus saith the Lord: 'Go down to the house of the king of Judah and speak there this word; . . . execute ye judgment and righteousness and deliver the spoiled out of the hand of the oppressor; and do no wrong. Do no violence to the stranger, the fatherless, and the widow; neither shed innocent blood in this place,'" then adds that in so doing they should prosper. "'But if ye will not hear these words, I swear by myself,' saith the Lord, 'that this house shall become a desolation.'" Jer. 22: [1–5].

The king, the princes, and rulers were agreed in oppression before the Babylonish captivity; for whatever courts of justice were retained amongst them or however they decided matters betwixt men of estates, it is plain that the cause of the poor was not judged in equity.

It appears that the great men amongst the Jews were fully resolved to have slaves, even of their own brethren. Jer. 34. Notwithstanding the promises and threatenings of the Lord, by the prophet, and their solemn covenant to set them free, confirmed by the imprecation of passing between the parts of a calf cut in twain (intimating by that ceremony that on breach of the covenant it were just for their bodies to be so cut in pieces), yet after all, they held fast to their old custom and called home the servants whom they had set free: "'And ye were now turned, and had done right in my sight in proclaiming liberty every man to his neighbour; and ye had made a covenant before me in the house which is called by my name; but ye turned and polluted my name, and caused every man his servant—whom he had set at liberty at their pleasure—to return, and brought them into subjection, to be unto you for servants and for handmaids.' Therefore, thus saith the Lord: 'Ye have not hearkened unto me in proclaiming liberty every one to his neighbour and every

1. The word spelled "throughly" in this sentence appears twice in the King James Version of Jeremiah 7:5. In some printings of that version it is spelled "throughly" and in others it is spelled "thoroughly." The spelling here was probably following Woolman's holograph. The Revised Standard Version reads "truly," and other twentieth century versions use synonyms for "truly." See note 1 to Chapter 14 of *A Plea for the Poor*.

one to his brother. Behold, I proclaim liberty to you,' saith the Lord, 'to the sword, to the pestilence, and to the famine; and I will make you to be removed into all the kingdoms of the earth. The men who transgressed my covenant which they made and passed between the parts of the calf I will give into the hands of their enemies, and their dead bodies shall be for meat unto the fowls of the heaven and the beasts of the earth'" [Jer. 34:15–20].

Soon after this their city was taken and burnt, the king's sons and the princes slain, and the king, with the chief men of his kingdom, carried captive to Babylon. Ezekiel, prophesying the return of that people to their own land, directs: "Ye shall divide the land by lot for an inheritance unto you and to the strangers that sojourn amongst you. In what tribe the stranger sojourns, there shall ye give him his inheritance, saith the Lord God" [Ezek. 47:22–23]. Nor is this particular direction and the authority with which it is enforced without a tacit implication—that their ancestors had erred in their conduct towards the stranger.

Some who keep slaves have doubted as to the equity of the practice; but as they knew men noted for their piety who were in it, this, they say, has made their minds easy. To lean on the example of men in doubtful cases is difficult. For only admit that those men were not faithful and upright to the highest degree, but that in some particular case they erred, and it may follow that this one case was the same about which we are in doubt; and to quiet our minds by their example may be dangerous to ourselves, and continuing in it prove a stumbling-block to tender-minded people who succeed us, in like manner as their examples are to us.

But supposing charity was their only motive and they, not foreseeing the tendency of paying robbers for their booty, were not justly under the imputation of being partners with a thief (Prov. 29:24), but were really innocent in what they did, are we assured that we keep them with the same views they kept them? If we keep them from no other motive than a real sense of duty, and true charity governs us in all our proceedings toward them, we are so far safe. But if another spirit which inclines our minds to the ways of this world prevail upon us, and we are concerned for our own outward gain more than for their real happiness, it will avail us nothing that some good men have had the care and management of Negroes.

Since mankind spread upon the earth, many have been the revolutions attending the several families, and their customs and ways of life different from each other. This diversity of manners, though some are preferable to others, operates not in favour of any so far as to justify them to do violence to innocent men, to bring them from their own to another way of life. The mind, when moved by a principle of true love, may feel a warmth of gratitude to the universal Father and a lively sympathy with those nations where divine light has been less manifest.

This desire for their real good may beget a willingness to undergo hardships for their sakes, that the true knowledge of God may be spread amongst them. But to take them from their own land with views of profit to ourselves by means inconsistent with pure justice is foreign to that principle which seeks the happiness of the whole creation. Forced subjection, on innocent persons of full age, is inconsistent with right reason: on one side, the human mind is not naturally fortified with that firmness in wisdom and goodness necessary to an independent ruler; on the other side, to be subject to the uncontrollable will of a man liable to err, is most painful and afflicting to a conscientious creature.

It is our happiness faithfully to serve the Divine Being who made us. His perfection makes our service reasonable; but so long as men are biased by narrow self-love, so long an absolute power over other men is unfit for them. Men taking on them the government of others may intend to govern reasonably and make their subjects more happy than they would be otherwise. But as absolute command belongs only to him who is perfect, where frail men in their own wills assume such command it hath a direct tendency to vitiate their minds and make them more unfit for government.

Placing on men the ignominious title SLAVE, dressing them in uncomely garments, keeping them to servile labour in which they are often dirty, tends gradually to fix a notion in the mind that they are a sort of people below us in nature, and leads us to consider them as such in all our conclusions about them. And, moreover, a person which in our esteem is mean and contemptible, if their language or behaviour toward us is unseemly or disrespectful, it excites wrath more powerfully than the like conduct in one we accounted our equal or superior, and where this happens to be the case it disqualifies for candid judgment; for it is unfit for a person to sit as judge in a case where his own personal resentments are stirred up, and as members of society in a well-framed government we are mutually dependent. Present interest incites to duty and makes each man attentive to the convenience of others; but he whose will is a law to others and can enforce obedience by punishment, he whose wants are supplied without feeling any obligation to make equal returns to his benefactor, his irregular appetites find an open field for motion, and he is in danger of growing hard and inattentive to their convenience who labour for his support, and so loses that disposition in which alone men are fit to govern.

The English government hath been commended by candid foreigners for the disuse of racks and tortures, so much practiced in some states; but this multiplying slaves now leads to it. For where people exact hard labour of others without a suitable reward and are resolved to continue in that way, severity to such who oppose them becomes the consequence; and several Negro criminals among the English in America have been executed in a lingering, painful way, very terrifying to others.

It is a happy case to set out right and persevere in the same way. A wrong beginning leads into many difficulties, for to support one evil, another becomes customary. Two produces more, and the further men proceed in this way the greater their dangers, their doubts and fears, and the more painful and perplexing are their circumstances, so that such who are true friends to the real and lasting interest of our country and candidly consider the tendency of things cannot but feel some concern on this account.

There is that superiority in men over the brute creatures, and some of them so manifestly dependent on men for a living, that for them to serve us in moderation so far as relates to the right use of things looks consonant to the design of our Creator. There is nothing in their frame, nothing relative to the propagating their species, which argues the contrary; but in men there is. The frame of men's bodies and the disposition of their minds are different. Some who are tough and strong and their minds active choose ways of life requiring much labour to support them. Others are soon weary, and though use makes labour more tolerable, yet some are less apt for toil than others and their minds less sprightly. These latter, labouring for their subsistence, commonly choose a life easy to support, being content with a little. When they are weary they may rest, take the most advantageous part of the day for labour, and in all cases proportion one thing to another that their bodies be not oppressed.

Now while each is at liberty the latter may be as happy and live as comfortably as the former; but where men of the first sort have the latter under absolute command, not considering the odds in strength and firmness, do sometimes in their eager pursuit lay on burdens grievous to be borne, by degrees grow rigorous, and aspiring to greatness they increase oppression; and the true order of kind Providence is subverted. There are weaknesses sometimes attending us which make little or no alteration in our countenances, nor much lessen our appetite for food, and yet so effect us as to make labour very uneasy. In such case masters intent on putting forward business and jealous of the sincerity of their slaves may disbelieve what they say and grievously afflict them.

Action is necessary for all men, and our exhausting frame requires a support which is the fruit of action. The earth must be laboured to keep us alive: labour is a proper part of our life; to make one answer the other in some useful motion looks agreeable to the design of our Creator. Motion rightly managed tends to our satisfaction, health, and support. Those who quit all useful business and live wholly on the labour of others have their exercise to seek; some such use less than their health requires; others choose that which by the circumstances attending it proves utterly reverse to true happiness. Thus while some are divers ways distressed for want of an open channel of useful action, those who support them sigh and are exhausted in a stream too powerful for nature, spending their days with too little cessation from labour.

Seed sown with the tears of a confined oppressed people, harvest cut down by an overborne discontented reaper, makes bread less sweet to the taste of an honest man, than that which is the produce or just reward of such voluntary action which is one proper part of the business of human creatures.

Again, the weak state of the human species in bearing and bringing forth their young, and the helpless condition of their young beyond that of other creatures, clearly show that Perfect Goodness designs a tender care and regard should be exercised toward them, and that no imperfect, arbitrary power should prevent the cordial effects of that sympathy which is in the minds of well-met pairs to each other and toward their offspring.

In our species the mutual ties of affection are more rational and durable than in others below us, the care and labour of raising our offspring much greater. The satisfaction arising to us in their innocent company and in their advances from one rational improvement to another is considerable when two are thus joined and their affections sincere. It however happens among slaves that they are often situated in different places, and their seeing each other depends on the will of men liable to human passions and a bias in judgment, who with views of self-interest may keep them apart more than is right. Being absent from each other and often with other company, there is a danger of their affections being alienated, jealousies arising, the happiness otherwise resulting from their offspring frustrated, and the comforts of marriage destroyed. These things being considered closely as happening to a near friend will appear to be hard and painful.

He who reverently observes that goodness manifested by our gracious Creator toward the various species of beings in this world, will see that in our frame and constitution is clearly shown that innocent men capable to manage for themselves were not intended to be slaves.

A person lately travelling amongst the Negroes near Senegal hath this remark: "Which way soever I turned my eyes on this pleasant spot, I beheld a perfect image of pure nature: an agreeable solitude bounded on every side by charming landscapes, the rural situation of cottages in the midst of trees, the ease and indolence of the Negroes reclined under the shade of their spreading foliage, the simplicity of their dress and manners —the whole revived in my mind the idea of our first parents, and I seemed to contemplate the world in its primitive state."—M. Adanson, page 55.[2]

Some Negroes in these parts who have had an agreeable education have manifested a brightness of understanding equal to many of us. A remark of this kind we find in Bosman, page 328: "The Negroes of Fida," saith he, "are so accurately quick in their merchandise accounts that they easily reckon as justly and quickly in their heads only, as we with the assistance of pen and ink, though the sum amounts to several thousands." [3]

Through the force of long custom it appears needful to speak in relation to colour. Suppose a white child born of parents of the meanest sort who died and left him an infant falls into the hands of a person who endeavours to keep him a slave. Some men would account him an unjust man in doing so, who yet appear easy while many black people of honest

2. Michel Adanson, *Voyage to Senegal, the Isle of Goree and the River Gambia*, "translated from the French, with notes by an English gentleman who resided some time in that country" (London, 1759). Adanson (1727-1806) was a noted French botanist, who commented on the customs of the people among whom he travelled. Of the several published studies about him, probably the most comprehensive is A. Chevalier, *Michel Adanson, voyageur, naturaliste et philosophe* (Paris, 1934).

3. Willem Bosman, *A New and Accurate Description of the Coast of Guinea . . . Containing a . . . History of the . . . Countries: with a Particular Account of the . . . Condition of all the European Settlements upon that Coast; and the just Measures for Improving the Several Branches of the Guinea Trade*, 2d ed., "written originally in Dutch . . . and faithfully done into English" (London, 1721). See additional quotations from Bosman in the next several pages. According to Forrest Altman (see Bibliography), Bosman served fourteen (not sixteen) years as Dutch factor at Delmina, on the Gold Coast. His book contains twenty letters written by Bosman and two by persons from parts of the coast where he had not been.

lives and good abilities are enslaved in a manner more shocking than the case here supposed. This is owing chiefly to the idea of slavery being connected with the black colour and liberty with the white. And where false ideas are twisted into our minds, it is with difficulty we get fairly disentangled.

A traveller in cloudy weather misseth his way, makes many turns while he is lost, still forms in his mind the bearing and situation of places; and though the ideas are wrong, they fix as fast as if they were right. Finding how things are, we see our mistake. Yet the force of reason with repeated observations on places and things do not soon remove those false notions so fastened upon us, but it will seem in the imagination as if the annual course of the sun was altered; and though by recollection we are assured it is not, yet those ideas do not suddenly leave us.

Selfishness being indulged clouds the understanding; and where selfish men for a long time proceed on their way without opposition, the deceivableness of unrighteousness gets so rooted in their intellects that a candid examination of things relating to self-interest is prevented; and in this circumstance some who would not agree to make a slave of a person whose colour is like their own, appear easy in making slaves of others of a different colour, though their understandings and morals are equal to the generality of men of their own colour.

The colour of a man avails nothing in matters of right and equity. Consider colour in relation to treaties. By such, disputes betwixt nations are sometimes settled. And should the Father of us all so dispose things that treaties with black men should sometimes be necessary, how then would it appear amongst the princes and ambassadors to insist on the prerogative of the white colour? Whence is it that men who believe in a righteous Omnipotent Being, to whom all nations stand equally related and are equally accountable, remain so easy in it, but for that the ideas of Negroes and slaves are so interwoven in the mind that they do not discuss this matter with that candour and freedom of thought which the case justly calls for?

To come at a right feeling of their condition requires humble serious thinking, for in their present situation they have but little to engage our natural affection in their favour. Had we a son or a daughter involved in the same case in which many of them are, it would alarm us and make us feel their condition without seeking for it. The adversity of an intimate friend will incite our compassion, while others equally good in the like trouble will but little affect us.

Again, the man in worldly honour whom we consider as our superior, treating us with kindness and generosity, begets a return of gratitude and friendship toward him. We may receive as great benefits from men a degree lower than ourselves, in the common way of reckoning, and feel ourselves less engaged in favour of them. Such is our condition by nature, and these things, being narrowly watched and examined, will be found to center in self-love.

The blacks seem far from being our kinsfolks; and did we find an agreeable disposition and sound understanding in some of them, which appeared as a good foundation for a true friendship between us, the disgrace arising from an open friendship with a person of so vile a stock in the common esteem would naturally tend to hinder it. They have neither honours, riches, outward magnificence nor power, their dress coarse and often ragged, their employ drudgery and much in the dirt. They have little or nothing at command, but must wait upon and work for others to obtain the necessaries of life, so that in their present situation there is not much to engage the friendship or move the affection of selfish men. But such who live in the spirit of true charity, to sympathize with the afflicted in the lowest stations of life is a thing familiar to them.

Such is the kindness of our Creator that people applying their minds to sound wisdom may, in general, with moderate exercise, live comfortably where no misapplied power hinders it. We in these parts have cause gratefully to acknowledge it. But men leaving the true use of things, their lives are less calm and have less of real happiness in them.

Many are desirous of purchasing and keeping slaves that they may live in some measure conformable to those customs of the times which have in them a tincture of luxury; for when we in the least degree depart from that use of the creatures which the Creator of all things intended for them, there luxury begins.

And if we consider this way of life seriously, we shall see there is nothing in it sufficient to induce a wise man to choose it before a plain, simple way of living. If we examine stately buildings and equipage, delicious foods, superfine clothes, silks, and linens; if we consider the splendor of choice metal fastened upon raiment, and the most showy inventions of men; it will yet appear that the humble-minded man who is contented with the true use of houses, food, and garments, and cheerfully exerciseth himself agreeable to his station in civil society to earn them, acts more reasonably and discovers more soundness of understand-

ing in his conduct than such who lay heavy burdens on others to support
themselves in a luxurious way of living.

George Buchanan, in his *History of Scotland*, page 62, tells of some
ancient inhabitants of Britain who were derived from a people that "had
a way of marking their bodies, as some said, with instruments of iron,
with variety of pictures, and with animals of all shapes, and wear no
garments—that they should not hide their pictures—and were therefore
called Picts." [4] Did we see those people shrink with pain for a considerable
time together under the point or edge of this iron instrument and their
bodies all bloody with the operation, did we see them sometimes naked,
suffering with cold, and refuse to put on garments that those imaginary
ensigns of grandeur might not be concealed, it is likely we should pity
their folly and fondness for those things. But if we candidly compare
their conduct in that case with some conduct amongst ourselves, will it
not appear that our folly is the greatest?

In true gospel simplicity free from all wrong use of things, a spirit
which breathes peace and good will is cherished; but when we aspire
after imaginary grandeur and apply to selfish means to attain our end,
this desire in its original is the same with the Picts in cutting figures on
their bodies; but the evil consequences attending our proceedings are the
greatest.

A covetous mind which seeks opportunity to exalt itself is a great
enemy to true harmony in a country. Envy and grudging usually accompany this disposition, and it tends to stir up its likeness in others. And
where this disposition ariseth so high as to embolden us to look upon
honest, industrious men as our own property during life, and to keep them
to hard labour to support us in those customs which have not their
foundation in right reason, or to use any means of oppression, a haughty
spirit is cherished on one side and the desire of revenge frequently on the
other, till the inhabitants of the land are ripe for great commotion and

4. 3d ed. (London, 1733), I. This edition, which is probably the one Woolman
used, is a translation from the original Latin of Buchanan (1506–1582). The passage
quoted appears on page 66. (It appears on page 53 of the 1960 edition.) Woolman
apparently erred in writing "page 62." Born in Scotland and educated at the University of Paris and St. Andrews University, Buchanan was a college teacher of
Latin in France, Portugal, and Scotland, and was noted as a political writer and poet.
Montaigne was one of his pupils, and he served (in Scotland) as tutor to members
of royalty. Originally a Catholic, he was attacked as a heretic and eventually became
a Protestant.

trouble; and thus luxury and oppression have the seeds of war and desolation in them.

Some Account of the Slave Trade From the Writings of Persons Who Have Been at the Places Where They Are First Purchased, Viz.

Bosman on Guinea, who was a factor for the Dutch about sixteen years in that country (page 339), thus remarks:

But since I have so often mentioned that commerce, I shall decribe how it is managed by our factors. The first business of one of our factors when he comes to Fida is to satisfy the customs of the king and the great men, which amounts to about one hundred pounds in Guinea value, as the goods must sell there, after which we have free license to trade, which is published throughout the whole land by the crier. And yet before we can deal with any person, we are obliged to buy the king's whole stock of slaves at a set price, which is commonly one-third or fourth higher than ordinary, after which we have free leave to deal with all his subjects of what rank soever. But if there happen to be no stock of slaves, the factor must resolve to run the risk of trusting the inhabitants with goods to the value of one or two hundred slaves, which commodities they send into the inland country in order to buy with them slaves at all markets—and that sometimes two hundred miles deep in the country. For you ought to be informed that markets of men are here kept in the same manner as they of beasts are with us.

Most of the slaves which are offered to us are prisoners of war, which are sold by the victors as their booty. When these slaves come to Fida, they are put in prisons all together; and when we treat concerning them, they are all brought out in a large plain where, by our surgeons whose province it is, they are thoroughly examined, even to the smallest member—and that naked, both men and women, without the least distinction or modesty. Those which are approved as good are set on one side. The invalids and maimed being thrown out, the remainder are numbered and it is entered who delivered them. In the meanwhile a burning iron with the arms or name of the company lies in the fire, with which ours are marked on the breast. This is done that we may distinguish them from the slaves of the English, French, or others. When we have agreed with the owners of the slaves, they are returned to their prisons, where from that time forward they are kept at our charge, cost us two pence a day a slave, which serves to subsist them like our criminals on bread and water; so that, to save charges, we send them on board our ships the first opportunity, before which their masters strip them of all they have on their backs, so that they come aboard stark naked—as well women as men—in which condition they are obliged to continue if the master of the ship is not so charitable (which he commonly is) as to bestow something on them to cover their nakedness.

The inhabitants of Popo, as well as those of Coto, depend on plunder and the slave trade, in both which they very much exceed the latter; for being endowed with more courage, they rob more successfully and by that means increase their trade, notwithstanding which, to freight a vessel with slaves requires some months attendance. In the year 1697, in three days time I could get but three slaves; but they assured me that if I would have patience for other three days only, they should be able to deliver me one or two hundred. — Same author, page 310.

We cast anchor at Cape Mizurada, but not one Negro coming on board I went on shore; and being desirous to be informed why they did not come on board, was answered that about two months before, the English had been there with two vessels and had ravaged the country, destroyed all their canoes, plundered their houses, and carried off some of their people for slaves, upon which the remainder fled to the inland country. They tell us they live in peace with all their neighbours and have no notion of any other enemy than the English, of which nation they had taken some then, and publicly declared that they would endeavour to get as many of them as the two mentioned ships had carried off of their natives. These unhappy English were in danger of being sacrificed to the memory of their friends, which some of their nation carried off.—Bosman, page 440.[5]

Extracts from a Collection of Voyages, Vol. 1

The author, a popish missionary, speaking of his departing from the Negro country to Brazil, saith:

I remember the Duke of Bambay (a Negro chief) one day sent me several blacks to be my slaves, which I would not accept of, but sent them back to him. I afterwards told him I came not into his country to make slaves, but rather to deliver those from the slavery of the devil, whom he kept in miserable thralldom. The ship I went aboard was loaded with elephants' teeth and slaves, to the number of 680 men, women, and children. It was a pitiful sight to behold how all these people were bestowed. The men were standing in the hold, fastened one to another with stakes for fear they should rise and kill the whites. The women were between the decks, and those that were with child in the great cabin, the children in the steerage pressed together like herrings in a barrel, which caused an intolerable heat and stench (page 507).

5. See note 3, above.

It is now time (saith the same author) to speak of a brutish custom these people have amongst them in making slaves, which I take
not to be lawful for any person of a good conscience to buy.

He then describes how women betray men into slavery, and adds:
"There are others going up into the inland country, and through pretense of jurisdiction seize men upon any trifling offense and sell them for
slaves" (page 537).

The author of this treatise, conversing with a person of good credit,
was informed by him that in his youth while in England he was minded
to come to America, and happening on a vessel bound for Guinea and
from thence into America, he, with a view to see Africa, went on board
her and continued with them in their voyage and so came into this
country. Among other circumstances he related these:

They purchased on the coast about three hundred slaves. Some
of them he understood were captives of war, some stolen by other
Negroes privately. When they had got many slaves on board but
were still on that coast, a plot was laid by an old Negro, notwithstanding the men had irons on their hands and feet, to kill the English
and take the vessel, which being discovered the man was hanged
and many of the slaves made to shoot at him as he hung up.
Another slave was charged with having a design to kill the English; and the captain spoke to him in relation to the charge brought
against him, as he stood on deck, whereupon he immediately threw
himself into the sea and was drowned.
Several Negroes confined on board were (he said) so extremely
uneasy with their condition that after many endeavours used, they
could never make them eat nor drink after they came in the vessel,
but in a desperate resolution starved themselves to death, behaving
toward the last like madmen.[6]

In Randall's *Geography*, printed 1744, we are informed that "in a time
of full peace nothing is more common than for the Negroes of one
nation to steal those of another and sell them to the Europeans. It is
thought that the English transmit annually near fifty thousand of these

6. These quotations apparently come from John Lockman, ed., *The Travels of the
Jesuits in Various Parts of the World, Particularly China and the East Indies* (London,
1743). This book contains selections from *Lettres Edifiantes et Curieuses* . . . , a collection of reports by Jesuits to their superiors, written between 1717 and 1741. Altman,
in his bibliography of Woolman's sources, lists the second edition of Lockman's
volume, which was published in England in 1762. Woolman's correspondence indicates
that although his essay was not published until 1762, it was already being scrutinized
by the Friends Publications Committee in late 1761. Hence it is more likely that he
used the 1743 edition.

unhappy creatures, and the other European nations together about two hundred thousand more." [7]

It is through the goodness of God that the reformation from gross idolatry and barbarity hath been thus far effected. If we consider our conditions as Christians and the benefits we enjoy and compare them with the condition of those people, and consider that our nation trading with them for their country produce have had an opportunity of imparting useful instructions to them, and remember that but little pains have been taken therein, it must look like an indifference in us. But when we reflect on a custom the most shocking of any amongst them, and remember that with a view to outward gain we have joined as parties in it, that our concurrence with them in their barbarous proceedings has tended to harden them in cruelty and been a means of increasing calamities in their country, we must own that herein we have acted contrary to those worthies whose lives and substance were spent in propagating truth and righteousness amongst the heathen. When Saul, by the hand of Doeg, slew four score priests at once, he had a jealousy that one of them at least was confederate with David, whom he considered as his enemy. Herod slaying all the male children in Bethlehem of two years old and under was an act of uncommon cruelty, but he supposed there was a male child there within that age who was likely to be king of the Jews, and finding no way to destroy him but by destroying them all, thought this the most effectual means to secure the kingdom to his own family.

When the sentence against the Protestants of Marindol, etc., in France, was put in execution, great numbers of people fled to the wilderness, amongst whom were ancient people, women great with child, and others with babes in their arms, who endured calamities grievous to relate; and in the end some perished with hunger, and many were destroyed by fire and sword. But they had this objection against them—that they obstinately persisted in opposition to Holy Mother Church, and being heretics, it was right to work their ruin and extirpation and raze out their memory from among men. — Foxe's *Acts and Monuments*, page 646.[8]

In favour of those cruelties, every one had what they deemed a plea. These scenes of blood and cruelty among the barbarous inhabitants of Guinea are not less terrible than those now mentioned. They are continued from one age to another, and we make ourselves parties and fellow-

7. Joseph Randall, *System of Geography* (London, 1744).
8. For a discussion of Foxe's *Actes and Monumentes* . . . , see note 4 to Chapter 5 of the *Journal* (above).

helpers in them. Nor do I see that we have any plea in our favour more plausible than the plea of Saul, of Herod, or the French in those slaughters.

Many who are parties in this trade by keeping slaves with views of self-interest, were they to go as soldiers in one of these inland expeditions to catch slaves, they must necessarily grow dissatisfied with such employ or cease to profess their religious principles. And though the first and most striking part of the scene is done at a great distance and by other hands, yet every one who is acquainted with the circumstances, and notwithstanding joins in it for the sake of gain only, must in the nature of things be chargeable with the others.

Should we consider ourselves present as spectators when cruel Negroes privately catch innocent children who are employed in the fields, hear their lamentable cries under the most terrifying apprehensions, or should we look upon it as happening in our own families—having our children carried off by savages—we must needs own that such proceedings are contrary to the nature of Christianity. Should we meditate on the wars which are greatly increased by this trade and on that affliction which many thousands live in, through apprehensions of being taken or slain; on the terror and amazement that villages are in when surrounded by these troops of enterprisers; on the great pain and misery of groaning, dying men who get wounded in those skirmishes; we shall necessarily see that it is impossible to be parties in such a trade on the motives of gain and retain our innocence.

Should we consider the case of multitudes of those people who in a fruitful soil and hot climate with a little labour raise grain, roots, and pulse to eat, spin and weave cotton, and fasten together the large feathers of fowls to cover their nakedness, many of whom in much simplicity live inoffensive in their cottages and take great comfort in raising up children; should we contemplate on their circumstances when suddenly attacked and labour to understand their inexpressible anguish of soul who survive the conflict; should we think on inoffensive women who fled at the alarm and at their return saw that village, in which they and their acquaintance were raised up and had pleasantly spent their youthful days, now lying in a gloomy desolation, some shocked at finding the mangled bodies of their near friends amongst the slain, others bemoaning the absence of a brother, a sister, a child, or a whole family of children, who by cruel men are bound and carried to market, to be sold without the least hopes of seeing them again; add to this the afflicted condition of these poor captives who are separated from family connections and all the comforts arising from friendship and acquaintance, carried amongst a people of a strange language, to be parted from their fellow captives, put to labour in a manner more servile and wearisome than what they were used to, with many sorrowful circumstances attending their slavery—and we must necessarily see that it belongs not to the followers of Christ to be parties in such a trade on the motives of outward gain.

Though there were wars and desolations among the Negroes before the Europeans began to trade there for slaves, yet now the calamities are greatly increased, so many thousands being annually brought from thence; and we by purchasing them with views of self-interest are become parties with them and accessory to that increase.

In this case, we are not joining against an enemy who is fomenting discords on our continent and using all possible means to make slaves of us and our children, but against a people who have not injured us. If those who were spoiled and wronged should at length make slaves of their oppressors and continue slavery to their posterity, it would look rigorous to candid men. But to act that part toward a people when neither they nor their fathers have injured us, hath something in it extraordinary, and requires our serious attention.

Our children breaking a bone, getting so bruised that a leg or an arm must be taken off, lost for a few hours, so that we despair of their being found again, a friend hurt so that he dieth in a day or two—these move us with grief. And did we attend to these scenes in Africa in like manner as if they were transacted in our presence, and sympathize with the Negroes in all their afflictions and miseries as we do with our children or friends, we should be more careful to do nothing in any degree helping forward a trade productive of so many and so great calamities. Great distance makes nothing in our favour. To willingly join with unrighteousness to the injury of men who live some thousand miles off is the same in substance as joining with it to the injury of our neighbours.

In the eye of pure justice actions are regarded according to the spirit and disposition they arise from. Some evils are accounted scandalous, and the desire of reputation may keep selfish men from appearing openly in them. But he who is shy on that account and yet by indirect means promotes that evil and shares in the profit of it cannot be innocent. He who with view to self-interest buys a slave made so by violence, and only on the strength of such purchase holds him a slave, thereby joins hands with those who committed that violence and in the nature of things becomes chargeable with the guilt.

Suppose a man wants a slave, and being in Guinea goes and hides by the path where boys pass from one little town to another, and there catches one the day he expects to sail, and taking him on board, brings him home without any aggravating circumstances. Suppose another buys a man taken by them who live by plunder and the slave trade—they often steal them privately and often shed much blood in getting them. He who buys the slave thus taken pays those men for their wickedness and makes himself party with them.

Whatever nicety of distinction there may be betwixt going in person on expeditions to catch slaves, and buying those with a view to self-interest which others have taken, it is clear and plain to an upright mind that such distinction is in words, not in substance; for the parties are concerned in the same work and have a necessary connection with and dependence on each other. For were there none to purchase slaves, they who live by stealing and selling them would of consequence do less at it.

Some would buy a Negro brought from Guinea with a view to self-interest and keep him a slave, who yet would seem to scruple to take arms and join with men employed in taking slaves. Others have civil Negroes who were born in our country, capable and likely to manage well for themselves, whom they keep as slaves without ever trying them with freedom, and take the profit of their labour as a part of their estates, and yet disapprove bringing them from their own country.

If those Negroes had come here as merchants with their ivory and gold dust in order to trade with us, and some powerful person had took their effects to himself and then put them to hard labour and ever after considered them as slaves, the action would be looked upon as unrighteous. Those Negro merchants having children after their being among us, whose endowments and conduct were like other peoples' in common, who attaining to mature age and requesting to have their liberty, should be told they were born in slavery and were lawful slaves, and therefore their request denied—the conduct of such persons toward them would be looked upon as unfair and oppressive.

In the present case relating to home-born Negroes, whose understandings and behaviour are as good as common among other people, if we have any claim to them as slaves, that claim is grounded on their being the children or offspring of slaves who in general were made such through means as unrighteous and attended with more terrible circumstances than the case here supposed, so that when we trace our claim to the bottom, these home-born Negroes having paid for their education and given reasonable security to those who owned them in case of their becoming chargeable, we have no more equitable right to their service than we should if they were the children of honest merchants who came from Guinea in an English vessel to trade with us.

If we claim any right to them as the children of slaves, we build on the foundation laid by them who made slaves of their ancestors, so that of necessity we must either justify the trade or relinquish our right to them as being the children of slaves.

Why should it seem right to honest men to make advantage by these people more than by others? Others enjoy freedom, receive wages equal to their work at, or near, such time as they have discharged these equitable obligations they are under to those who educated them. These have made no contract to serve, been no more expensive in raising up than others, and many of them appear as likely to make a right use of freedom as other people. Which way then can an honest man withhold from them that liberty which is the free gift of the Most High to his rational creatures?

The upright in heart cannot succeed the wicked in their wickedness, nor is it consonant to the life they live to hold fast an advantage unjustly gained. The Negroes who live by plunder and the slave trade steal poor innocent children, invade their neighbours' territories, and spill much blood to get these slaves. And can it be possible for an honest man to think that with view to self-interest we may continue slavery to the off-spring of these unhappy sufferers, merely because they are the children of slaves—and not have a share of this guilt?

It is granted by many that the means used in getting them are un-righteous and that buying them when brought here is wrong; yet as setting them free is attended with some difficulty, they do not comply with it, but seem to be of the opinion that to give them food and raiment and keep them servants without any other wages is the best way to manage them that they know of, and hoping that their children after them will not be cruel to the Negroes, conclude to leave them as slaves to their children.

While present outward interest is the chief object of our attention, we shall feel many objections in our minds against renouncing our claim to them as the children of slaves; for being prepossessed with wrong opin-ions prevents our seeing things clearly which to indifferent persons are easy to be seen.

Suppose a person seventy years past, in low circumstances, bought a Negro man and woman, and that the children of such person are now wealthy and have the children of such slaves. Admit that the first Negro man and his wife did as much business as their master and mistress and that the children of the slaves have done some more than their young masters. Suppose on the whole that the expense of living has been less on the Negroes' side than on the other (all which are no improbable suppositions), it follows that in equity these Negroes have a right to a part of this increase—that should some difficulties arise on their being set free, there is reason for us patiently to labour through them.

As the conduct of men varies relating to civil society, so different treatment is justly due to them. Indiscreet men occasion trouble in the world, and it remains to be the care of such who seek the good of mankind to admonish as they find occasion. The slothfulness of some of them in providing for themselves and families, it is likely, would require the notice of their neighbours. Nor is it unlikely that some would with justice be made servants, and others punished for their crimes. Pure justice points out to each individual their due. But to deny a people the privilege of human creatures on a supposition that being free many of them would be troublesome to us, is to mix the condition of good and bad men together and treat the whole as the worst of them deserve.

If we seriously consider that liberty is the right of innocent men, that the Mighty God is a refuge for the oppressed, that in reality we are indebted to them, that they being set free are still liable to the penalties of our laws and as likely to have punishment for their crimes as other people, this may answer all our objections. And to retain them in perpetual servitude without just cause for it, will produce effects in the event more grievous than setting them free would do when a real love to truth and equity was the motive to it.

Our authority over them stands originally in a purchase made from those who, as to the general, obtained theirs by unrighteousness. Whenever we have recourse to such authority, it tends more or less to obstruct the channels through which the perfect plant in us receives nourishment.

There is a principle which is pure, placed in the human mind, which in different places and ages hath had different names. It is, however, pure and proceeds from God. It is deep and inward, confined to no forms of religion nor excluded from any, where the heart stands in perfect sincerity. In whomsoever this takes root and grows, of what nation soever, they become brethren in the best sense of the expression. Using ourselves to take ways which appear most easy to us, when inconsistent with that purity which is without beginning, we thereby set up a government of our own and deny obedience to him whose service is true liberty.

He that has a servant made so wrongfully, and knows it to be so, when he treats him otherwise than a free man, when he reaps the benefit of his labour without paying him such wages as are reasonably due to free men for the like service (clothes excepted), these things, tho' done in calmness without any show of disorder, do yet deprave the mind in like manner and with as great certainty as prevailing cold congeals water. These steps taken by masters, and their conduct striking the minds of their children whilst young, leave less room for that which is good to work upon them. The customs of their parents, their neighbours, and the people with whom they converse working upon their minds, and they from thence conceiving ideas of things and modes of conduct, the entrance into their hearts becomes in a great measure shut up against the gentle movings of uncreated Purity.

From one age to another the gloom grows thicker and darker, till error gets established by general opinion; that whoever attends to Perfect Goodness and remains under the melting influence of it finds a path unknown to many, and sees the necessity to lean upon the arm of divine strength and dwell alone, or with a few in the right, committing their cause to him who is a refuge for his people in all their troubles.

Where through the agreement of a multitude some channels of justice are stopped, and men may support their characters as just men by being just to a party, there is great danger of contracting an alliance with that spirit which stands in opposition to the God of love and spreads discord, trouble, and vexation among such who give up to the influence of it.

Negroes are our fellow creatures and their present condition amongst us requires our serious consideration. We know not the time when those scales in which mountains are weighed may turn. The parent of mankind is gracious. His care is over his smallest creatures, and a multitude of men escape not his notice; and though many of them are trodden down and despised, yet he remembers them. He seeth their affliction and looketh upon the spreading, increasing exaltation of the oppressor. He turns the channels of power, humbles the most haughty people, and gives deliverance to the oppressed at such periods as are consistent with his infinite justice and goodness. And wherever gain is preferred to equity, and wrong things publicly encouraged, to that degree that wickedness takes root and spreads wide amongst the inhabitants of a country, there is real cause for sorrow to all such whose love to mankind stands on a true principle and wisely consider the end and event of things.

A Plea for the Poor

or

A Word of Remembrance and Caution to the Rich

Chapter One

[MS., p. 148]

WEALTH DESIRED for its own sake obstructs the increase of virtue, and large possessions in the hands of selfish men have a bad tendency, for by their means too small a number of people are employed in things useful; and therefore they, or some of them, are necessitated to labour too hard, while others would want business to earn their bread were not employments invented which, having no real use, serve only to please the vain mind.

Rents set on lands are often so high that persons who have but small substance are straitened in hiring a plantation; and while tenants are healthy and prosperous in business, they often find occasion to labour harder than was intended by our gracious Creator.

Oxen and horses are often seen at work when, through heat and too much labour, their eyes and the emotion of their bodies manifest that they are oppressed. Their loads in wagons are frequently so heavy that when weary with hauling it far, their drivers find occasion in going up hills or through mire to raise their spirits by whipping to get forward. Many poor people are so thronged in their business that it is difficult for them to provide shelter suitable for their animals in great storms.

These things are common when in health, but through sickness and inability to labour, through loss of creatures and miscarriage in business, many are straitened; and so much of their increase goes annually to pay rent or interest that they have not wherewith to hire so much as their case requires. Hence one poor woman, in attending on her children, providing for her family, and helping the sick, does as much business as would for the time be suitable employment for two or three; and honest persons are often straitened to give their children suitable learning. The money which the wealthy receive from the poor, who do more than a proper share of business in raising it, is frequently paid to other poor people for doing business which is foreign to the true use of things.

238

Men who have large possessions and live in the spirit of charity, who carefully inspect the circumstance of those who occupy their estates, and regardless of the customs of the times regulate their demands agreeable to universal love—these, by being righteous on a principle, do good to the poor without placing it as an act of bounty. Their example in avoiding superfluities tends to incite others to moderation. Their goodness in not exacting what the laws or customs would support them in tends to open the channel to moderate labour in useful affairs and to discourage those branches of business which have not their foundation in true wisdom.

To be busied in that which is but vanity and serves only to please the unstable mind tends to an alliance with them who promote that vanity, and is a snare in which many poor tradesmen are entangled.[1] To be employed in things connected with virtue is most agreeable to the character and inclination of an honest man.

While industrious, frugal people are borne down with poverty and oppressed with too much labour in useful things, the way to apply money without promoting pride and vanity remains open to such who truly sympathize with them in their various difficulties.

Chapter Two

[MS., p. 150]

The Creator of the earth is the owner of it. He gave us being thereon, and our nature requires nourishment which is the produce of it. As he is kind and merciful, we as his creatures, while we live answerable to the design of our creation, we are so far entitled to a convenient subsistence that no man may justly deprive us of it. By the agreements and contracts of our fathers and predecessors, and by doings and proceedings of our own, some claim a much greater share of this world than others; and whilst those possessions are faithfully improved to the good of the whole, it consists with equity.[2] But he who with a view to self-exaltation causeth some with their domestic animals to labour immoderately, and with the moneys arising to him therefrom employs others in the luxuries of life, acts contrary to the gracious design of him who is the true owner

1. Woolman wrote "tradesmen" in place of his original phrase, which appears to have been: "people who labour for their living."

2. Between "it" and "consists" Woolman erased a phrase, which included the word "integrity." In the preceding sentence, the passage "while we . . . it" was considerably revised and finally written in the margin.

of the earth; nor can any possessions, either acquired or derived from ancestors, justify such conduct.

Goodness remains to be goodness, and the direction of pure wisdom is obligatory on all reasonable creatures—that laws and customs are no further a standard for our proceedings than as their foundation is on universal righteousness.

Though the poor occupy our estates by a bargain to which they in their poor circumstance agreed, and we ask even less than a punctual fulfilling of their agreement, yet if our views are to lay up riches or to live in conformity to customs which have not their foundation in the Truth, and our demands are such as requires greater toil or application to business in them than is consistent with pure love, we invade their rights as inhabitants of that world of which a good and gracious God is proprietor, under whom we are tenants.[3]

Were all superfluities and the desire of outward greatness laid aside and the right use of things universally attended to, such a number of people might be employed in things useful that moderate labour with the blessing of heaven would answer all good purposes relating to people and their animals, and a sufficient number have leisure to attend on proper affairs of civil society.[4]

Chapter Three

[MS., p. 151]

While our strength and spirits are lively, we go cheerfully through business. Either too much or too little action is tiresome, but a right portion is healthful to our bodies and agreeable to an honest mind.

Where men have great estates they stand in a place of trust. To have it in their power without difficulty to live in that fashion which occasions much labour, and at the same time confine themselves to that use of things prescribed by our Redeemer, and confirmed by his example and the example of many who lived in the early ages of the Christian church, that they may more extensively relieve objects of charity—for men possessed of great estates to live thus—requires close attention to divine love.[5]

3. Woolman wrote "is consistent with pure love" in place of his original phrase, which appears to have been "that God intends for us."

4. In this paragraph, the words "outward" and "proper" were added by Woolman in the process of revision.

5. In the margin opposite the passage, "by his example . . . lived in the," Woolman wrote "look." Perhaps this was a reminder to himself to revise the next line, which he changed by adding "Christian" and "that they may more extensively relieve objects of charity."

Our gracious Creator cares and provides for all his creatures. His tender mercies are over all his works; and so far as his love influences our minds, so far we become interested in his workmanship and feel a desire to take hold of every opportunity to lessen the distresses of the afflicted and increase the happiness of the creation. Here we have a prospect of one common interest from which our own is inseparable— that to turn all the treasures we possess into the channel of universal love becomes the business of our lives.[6] Men of large estates whose hearts are thus enlarged are like fathers to the poor, and in looking over their brethren in distressed circumstances and considering their own more easy condition, find a field for humble meditation and feel the strength of those obligations they are under to be kind and tender-hearted to-ward them.

Poor men eased of their burdens and released from too close an ap-plication to business are at liberty to hire others to their assistance, to provide well for their animals, and find time to perform those visits amongst their acquaintance which belongs to a well-guided social life.

When these reflect on the opportunity those had to oppress them, and consider the goodness of their conduct, they behold it lovely and con-sistent with brotherhood; and as the man whose mind is conformed to universal love hath his trust settled in God and finds a firm foundation to stand on in any changes or revolutions that happen amongst men, so also the goodness of his conduct tends to spread a kind, benevolent dis-position in the world.

Chapter Four

[MS., p. 152]

Our blessed Redeemer, in directing us how to conduct one towards another, appeals to our own feeling: "Whatsoever ye would that other men should do to you, do ye even so to them" [Mt. 7:12]. Now where such live in fullness on the labour of others, who have never had ex-perience of hard labour themselves, there is often a danger of their not having a right feeling of the labourer's condition, and therefore of being disqualified to judge candidly in their case, not knowing what they

6. Woolman changed "our business" to "the business of our lives," thus indicating the primary importance of the imperative to which he referred. Also, "all the trea-sures we possess" replaces an earlier phrase which cannot be deciphered. Perhaps this change had the same intent.

themselves would desire were they to labour hard from one year to another to raise the necessaries of life and to pay large rents beside—that it's good for those who live in fullness to labour for tenderness of heart, to improve every opportunity of being acquainted with the hardships and fatigues of those who labour for their living, and [to] think seriously with themselves: Am I influenced with true charity in fixing all my demands? [7] Have I no desire to support myself in expensive customs because my acquaintance live in those customs? Were I to labour as they do toward supporting them and their children in a station like mine, in such sort as they and their children labour for us, could I not on such a change, before I entered into agreements of rents or interest, name some costly articles now used by me or in my family which have no real use in them, the expense whereof might be lessened? And should I not in such case strongly desire the disuse of those needless expenses, that less answering their way of life the terms might be the easier to me?

If a wealthy man, on serious reflection, finds a witness in his own conscience that there are some expenses which he indulgeth himself in that are in conformity to custom, which might be omitted consistent with the true design of living, and which was he to change places with those who occupy his estate he would desire to be discontinued by them —whoever are thus awakened to their feeling will necessarily find the injunction binding on them: "Do thou even so to them."

Divine love imposeth no rigorous or unreasonable commands, but graciously points out the spirit of brotherhood and way to happiness, in the attaining to which it is necessary that we go forth out of all that is selfish.[8]

Chapter Five

[MS., p. 154]

To pass through a series of hardships and to languish under oppression brings people to a certain knowledge of these things. To enforce the duty

---

7. During the process of revision, "true" was added before "charity."

8. Under the line ending in "selfish," Woolman drew a horizontal line across the page. Below it (repeating himself) he wrote and then crossed out: "go forth out of all that is selfish.—the end." He also wrote and crossed out: " 'Beloved, now are we the sons of God, and it doth not yet appear what we shall be, but we know that when he shall appear, we shall be like him; for we shall see him as he is [1 Jn. 3:2].' He, our Redeemer, is the perfection of pure love, and when by the operation of his Spirit upon us we are cleansed throughout, and our souls so united to him that we love our fellow creatures as he loveth us, we there see evidently that in this inward conformity to divine goodness stands the true happiness of intelligent creatures."

of tenderness to the poor, the inspired Lawgiver referred the children of Israel to their own past experience: "Ye know the heart of a stranger, seeing ye were strangers in the land of Egypt" [Ex. 23:9]. He who hath been a stranger amongst unkind people or under their government who were hard-hearted, knows how it feels; but a person who hath never felt the weight of misapplied power comes not to this knowledge but by an inward tenderness, in which the heart is prepared to sympathy with others.[9]

We may reflect on the condition of a poor, innocent man, who by his labour contributes toward supporting one of his own species more wealthy than himself, on whom the rich man from a desire after wealth and luxuries lays heavy burdens.[10] When this labourer looks over the means of his heavy load, and considers that this great toil and fatigue is laid on him to support that which hath no foundation in pure wisdom, we may well suppose that there ariseth an uneasiness in his mind toward those who might without any inconvenience deal more favourably with him. When he considers that by his industry his fellow creature is benefited, and sees that this man who hath much wealth is not satisfied with being supported in a plain way—but to gratify a wrong desire and conform to wrong customs, increaseth to an extreme the labours of those who occupy his estate—we may reasonably judge that he will think himself unkindly used.

When he considers that the proceedings of the wealthy are agreeable to the customs of the times, and sees no means of redress in this world, how would the inward sighing of an innocent person ascend to the throne of that great, good Being, who created us all and hath a constant care over his creatures. By candidly considering these things, we may have some sense of the condition of innocent people overloaded by the wealthy. But he who toils one year after another to furnish others with wealth and superfluities, who labours and thinks, and thinks and labours, till by overmuch labour he is wearied and oppressed, such an one understands the meaning of that language: "Ye know the heart of a stranger, seeing ye were strangers in the land of Egypt."

As many at this day who know not the heart of a stranger indulge themselves in ways of life which occasions more labour in the world than Infinite Goodness intends for man, and yet are compassionate to-

9. The passage, "by an inward tenderness in which the heart is prepared to sympathy" replaces an earlier version, which cannot be entirely deciphered but which ended, "by a sympathy." When Woolman replaced "by a" with "to," he neglected to make the corresponding change of "sympathy" to "sympathize."

10. The words "wealth and" were inserted with a caret.

ward such in distress who comes directly under their observation,[11] were these to change circumstances a while with some who labour for them, were they to pass regularly through the means of knowing the heart of a stranger and come to a feeling knowledge of the straits and hardships · which many poor, innocent people pass through in a hidden obscure life, were these who now fare sumptuously every day to act the other part of the scene till seven times had passed over them, and return again to their former estate, I believe many of them would embrace a way of life less expensive and lighten the heavy burdens of some who now labour out of their sight to support them and pass through straits with which they are but little acquainted.

To see our fellow creatures under difficulties to which we are in no degree accessory tends to awaken tenderness in the minds of all reasonable people, but if we consider the condition of such who are depressed in answering our demands, who labour out of our sight and are often toiling for us while we pass our time in fullness, if we consider that much less than we demand would supply us with all things really needful,[12] what heart will not relent, or what reasonable man can refrain from mitigating that grief which he himself is the cause of, when he may do it without inconvenience? I shall conclude with the words of Ezekiel the prophet (Chap. 34, verse 18), "Seemeth it a small . . ." etc. ["thing unto you to have eaten up the poor pasture, but ye must tread down with your feet the residue of your pastures?"]

Chapter Six

[MS., p. 156]

People much spent with labour often take strong drink to revive them.[13] Were there more men usefully employed and fewer who eat bread as a reward for doing that which is not useful, then food or raiment would, on a reasonable estimate, be more in proportion to labour than it is at present. In proceeding agreeable to sound wisdom, a small portion of daily labour might suffice to keep a proper stream gently cir-

11. The "s" in "comes", obscure in MS. *Plea*, is clear in MS. W.
12. Woolman had apparently started to write, "all things useful."
13. Woolman first wrote: "Where people are much spent with labour, strong drink is often taken"; then, before finishing the sentence, he erased it and wrote the sentence as it now stands, thus producing a more direct and effective statement, three words shorter than the original would have been. This is a typical example of the way Woolman improved his style as he wrote.

culating through all the channels of society; and this portion of labour might be so divided and taken in the most advantageous parts of the day that people would not have that plea for the use of strong liquors which they have at present.

Question: If 4 men, each working 8 hours in a day, raise 200 bushel of rye in 60 days, how many hours must 5 men work to do the same business in the same time? [14]

```
    m.    h.    m.
    4     8     5
          4                    Answer  h.   m.
    5 | 32 | 6                         6    24
       30
        2
       60
      120 | 24
       10 |
       20
       20
       ··
```

The quantity of rum and spirits imported and made in these colonies is great! [15] Nor may we suppose that so many thousand hogsheads of this liquor can be drank every year in our country without having a powerful effect on our manners. When people are spent with action and take these liquors not only as a refreshment from past labours but to support them to go on without nature having sufficient time to recruit by resting, it gradually turns them from that calmness of thought which attends those who steadily apply their hearts to true wisdom. The spirits scattered by too much bodily motion in the heat and again revived by strong drink—that this makes a person unfit for serious thinking and divine meditation I expect will not be denied; and as multitudes of people are in this practice who do not take so much as to hinder them from managing their outward affairs, this custom requires our serious thoughts.[16] But as

14. Woolman wrote this query and calculation in the margin alongside the preceding paragraph. See Appendix G for Woolman's own further explanation.

15. MS. W: also "rum and spirits." Printed edition of 1793 and Comly edition of 1837: "spiritous liquors."

16. Woolman originally wrote: "custom is strongly supported." Then he started to draw a line through "is strongly supported" and keyed "custom" to a note in the margin, "requires our serious thoughts"; this would appear to be his final version. The

through divine goodness I have found that there is a more quiet, calm, and happy way intended for us to walk in, I am engaged to express what I feel in my heart concerning it.

As cherishing the spirit of love and meekness is our duty, so to avoid those things which they know works against it is a duty also.[17] Every degree of luxury of what kind soever and every demand for money inconsistent with divine order hath some connection with unnecessary labour.[18] By too much labour the spirits are exhausted and people crave help from strong drink;[19] and the frequent use of strong drink works in opposition to the Holy Spirit on the mind. This is plain when men take so much as to suspend the use of their reason, and though there are degrees of this opposition, and a man quite drunk may be furthest removed from that frame of mind in which God is acceptably worshiped, yet a person being often near spent with too much action and revived by spirituous liquors without being quite drunk inures himself to that which is a less degree of the same thing, and which by long continuance does necessarily hurt both mind and body.[20] There is in the nature of people some degree of likeness with that food and air to which they from their youth have been accustomed. This frequently appears in such

---

first and Whittier editions both read "is strongly supported" and ignore the marginal note. The Gummere edition includes both versions without comment.

17. Woolman first wrote, "meekness belongs to the family of Jesus Christ." Then after "meekness" he added "is our duty" and drew a line connecting "duty" with "so to avoid." Thus he bypassed "belongs . . . Christ," but neglected to cross it out, as he normally would have done. Such lack of clarity tends to imply he did not prepare MS. *Plea* for the printer.

In MS. *Plea* a later hand has changed "they know" to "we know." The ink here is darker than elsewhere, and the formation of the "w" is unlike Woolman's.

Woolman originally ended this sentence: "is an indispensible duty." Then he made it read "is a duty also," but failed to cross out the original reading. MS. W retains Woolman's original version: "meekness belongs to the family of Jesus Christ, so to avoid those things which they know works against it is an indispensible duty." MS. *Plea* was apparently changed after MS. W was written.

18. Added later with a caret: "and every demand . . . order." Between "order" and "hath" has been added "we know," apparently by a later hand, but perhaps by Woolman. MS. W reads the same as MS. *Plea* except that it lacks "we know."

19. Original reading: "By too much labour nature craves help from strong drink." In the next clause, "Holy Spirit" is written above the crossed-out phrase "celestial influence." The change seems to have been made by Woolman.

20. The word "strong" has been erased before "spirituous." Later in this sentence the first printed edition reads, "and by long continuance thereof must necessarily." No justification for this version appears in the MS. In the next sentence Woolman improved the style by removing "to" from the end of the sentence to its present location.

who by a separation from their native air and usual diet grow weak and unhealthy for want of them. Nor is it reasonable to suppose that so many thousand hogsheads of this fiery liquor can be drank by us every year and the practice continued from age to age without altering in some degree the natures of men and rendering their minds less apt to receive the pure Truth in the love of it.

As many who manifest some regard to piety do yet in some degree conform to those ways of living and of collecting wealth which increaseth labour beyond the bounds fixed by divine wisdom,[21] my desire is that they may so consider the connection of things as to take heed, lest by exacting of poor men more than is consistent with universal righteousness they promote that by their conduct which in words they speak against.

To treasure up wealth for another generation by means of the immoderate labour of such who in some measure depend upon us is doing evil at present, without knowing but that our wealth, thus gathered, may be applied to evil purposes when we are gone. To labour too hard or cause others to do so, that we may live conformable to customs which Christ our Redeemer contradicted by his example in the days of his flesh, and which are contrary to divine order, is to manure a soil for the propagating an evil seed in the earth.

Such who enter deep into these considerations and live under the weight of them will feel these things so heavy and their ill effects so extensive that the necessity of attending singly to divine wisdom will be evident, thereby to be directed in the right use of things, in opposition to the customs of the times, and supported to bear patiently the reproaches attending singularity.[22] To conform a little to a wrong way strengthens the hands of such who carry wrong customs to their utmost extent; and the more a person appears to be virtuous and heavenly-minded, the more powerfully does his conformity operate in favour of evil doers. Lay aside the profession of a pious life and people expect little or no instruction from the example.[23] But while we profess in all cases to live in constant opposition to that which is contrary to universal righteousness, what expressions are equal to the subject, or what language is

21. Woolman made his indictment specific by the addition, with a caret, of "and of collecting wealth."

22. Woolman first wrote "thereby to be supported," then "to be directed and supported," after which he crossed out "and supported," thus making it possible to use "supported" later in the sentence without repetition.

23. Instead of "pious," Woolman originally wrote "godly," and instead of "life" he seems to have written "person."

sufficient to set forth the strength of those obligations we are under to beware lest by our example we lead others wrong.

Chapter Seven

[MS., p. 159]

"This kind goeth not out but by prayer" [Mt. 17:21].

In our care for our children, should we give way to partiality in things relating to what may be when we are gone, yet after death we cannot look at partiality with pleasure. If by our wealth we make them great without a full persuasion that we could not bestow it better, and thus give them power to deal hardly with others more virtuous than they, it can, after death, give us no more satisfaction than if by this treasure we had raised these others above our own and given them power to oppress ours.

Did a man possess as much good land as would well suffice twenty industrious, frugal people, and expect that he was lawful heir to it and intend to give this great estate to his children, but found on a research into the title that one-half this estate was the undoubted property of a number of poor orphans who, as to virtue and understanding, to him appeared as hopeful as his own children—this discovery would give him an opportunity to consider whether he was attached to any interest distinct from the interest of those children. Some of us have estates sufficient for our children and for as many more to live upon did they all employ their time in useful business and live in that plainness consistent with the character of true disciples of Christ, and have no reason to believe that our children after us will apply them to benevolent purposes more than some poor children who we are acquainted with would, if they had them; and yet, did we believe that after our decease these estates would go equally between our children and an equal number of these poor children, it would be likely to give us uneasiness. This may show to a thoughtful person that to be redeemed from all the remains of selfishness, to have a universal regard to our fellow creatures, and love them as our Heavenly Father loves them, we must constantly attend to the influence of his Spirit.

When our hearts are enlarged to contemplate the nature of this divine love, we behold it harmonious; but if we attentively consider that moving of selfishness which would make us uneasy at the apprehension of that which is in itself reasonable, and which being separated from all previous conceptions and expectations will appear so, we may see an inconsistency in it, for the subject of such uneasiness is in future, and would not affect our children till we were removed into that state of being where there is no possibility of our taking delight in any thing contrary to the pure principle of universal love.

As that natural desire of superiority in us, being given way to, extends to such our favourites whom we expect will succeed us, and as the grasping after wealth and power for them adds greatly to the burdens of the poor and increaseth the evil of covetousness in this age, I have often desired in secret that in looking toward posterity we may remember the purity of that rest which is prepared for the Lord's people, the impossibility of our taking pleasure in any thing distinguishable from universal righteousness, and how vain and weak a thing it is to give wealth and power to such who appear unlikely to apply it to a general good when we are gone.

As Christians, all we possess are the gifts of God. Now in distributing it to others we act as his steward, and it becomes our station to act agreeable to that divine wisdom which he gracious gives to his servants. If the steward of a great family, from a selfish attachment to particulars, takes that with which he is entrusted and bestows it lavishly on some to the injury of others and to the damage of him who employs him, he disunites himself and becomes unworthy of that office.

The true felicity of man in this life, and that which is to come, is in being inwardly united to the fountain of universal love and bliss. When we provide for posterity and make settlements which will not take effect till after we are centered in another state of being, if we therein act contrary to universal love and righteousness, such conduct must arise from a false, selfish pleasure in directing a thing to be done wrong, in which it will be impossible for us to take pleasure at the time when our directions are put in execution. For if we, after such settlement and when too late for an alteration, attain to that purified state which our Redeemer prayed his Father that his people might attain to—of being united to the Father and the Son—a sincere repentance for all things done in a will separate from universal love must precede this inward sanctification; and though in such depth of repentance and reconciliation all sins are forgiven and sorrows removed, that our misdeeds heretofore done could no longer afflict us, yet our partial determinations in favour of such whom we loved in a selfish love could not afford us any pleasure. And if after such selfish settlement our wills continue to stand in opposition to the fountain of universal light and love, there will be an unpassable gulf between the soul and true felicity, nor can anything [24] heretofore done in this separate will afford us pleasure.

Chapter Eight

[MS., p. 162]

To labour for an establishment in divine love where the mind is disentangled from the power of darkness is the great business of man's life. Collecting of riches, covering the body with fine-wrought, costly apparel, and having magnificent furniture operates against universal love and tends to feed self, that to desire these things belongs not to the children of the Light.

He who sent ravens to feed Elijah in the wilderness, and increased the poor widow's small remains of meal and oil, is now as attentive to the necessities of his people as ever, that when he numbers us with his people and saith, "Ye are my sons and daughters" [2 Cor. 6:18]—no greater happiness can be desired by them who know how gracious a Father he is.

The greater part of the necessaries of life are so far perishable that each generation hath occasion to labour for them; and when we look toward a succeeding age with a mind influenced by universal love, we endeavour not to exempt some from those cares which necessarily relate to this life, and give them power to oppress others, but desire they may all be the Lord's children and live in that humility and order becoming his family. Our hearts being thus opened and enlarged, we feel content in a use of things as foreign to luxury and grandeur as that which our Redeemer laid down as a pattern.

By desiring wealth for the power and distinction it gives and gathering it on this motive, a person may properly be called a rich man, whose mind is moved by a draft distinguishable from the drawings of the Father and cannot be united to the heavenly society, where God is the strength of their life, before he is delivered from this contrary drawing.

"It is easier," saith our Saviour, "for a camel to go through a needle's

24. The MS. actually reads "and thing." That this is clearly an error in writing is substantiated by Woolman's having erased "any" before "pleasure," apparently to avoid repetition. This is perhaps the only instance in which the present editor has felt justified in changing a word Woolman wrote—a decision substantiated by MS. W, which reads "anything."

eye than for a rich man to enter the kingdom of God" [Mk. 10:25]. Here our Lord uses an instructing similitude, for as a camel considered under that character cannot pass through a needle's eye, so a man who trusteth in riches and holds them for the sake of the power and distinction attending them cannot in that spirit enter the kingdom. Now every part of a camel may be so reduced as to pass through a hole as small as a needle's eye, yet such is the bulk of the creature, and the hardness of its bones and teeth, that it could not be completed without much labour. So man must cease from that spirit which craves riches, and be reduced into another disposition, before he inherits the kingdom, as effectually as a camel must cease from the form of a camel in passing through the eye of a needle.[25]

When our Saviour said to the rich youth, "Go sell that thou hast and give to the poor" [Mk. 10:21], though undoubtedly it was his duty to have done so, yet to confine this of selling all as a duty on every true Christian would be to limit the Holy One. Obedient children who are entrusted with much outward substance wait for wisdom to dispose of it agreeable to his will, in whom "the fatherless findeth mercy" [Hos. 14:3]. It may not be the duty of every one to commit at once their substance to other hands, but rather from time to time to look round amongst the numerous branches of the great family, as his stewards who said, "Leave thy fatherless children; I will preserve them alive; and let thy widows trust in me" [Jer. 49:11]. But as disciples of Christ, however entrusted with much goods, they may not conform to sumptuous or luxurious living.[26] For if possessing great treasures had been a sufficient reason to make a fine show in the world, then Christ our Lord, who had an unfailing storehouse, and in a way surpassing the common operations in nature supplied thousands of people with food, would not have lived in so much plainness.

What we equitably possess is a gift from God to us; but by the Son all things were created. Now he who forms things out of nothing—who creates and, having created, doth possess—is more truly rich than he who possesseth by receiving gifts from another. If depth of knowledge and a high title had been sufficient reasons to make a splendid show, he would have made it. He told the woman of Samaria sundry things relative to her past life, made mention of the decease of Lazarus, and answered the scribe

25. Inserted with a caret: "before he inherits the kingdom."
26. The first edition omits a long passage starting in the next sentence and continuing to near the end of the chapter: "if possessing . . . to him; and."

who accounted him a blasphemer, without information, and having the
spirit without measure knew what was in man. The title of Lord he
owned, nor was it ever more justly given to any—that in riches and
wisdom and greatness there was none on earth equal to him; and as he
lived in perfect plainness and simplicity, the greatest in his family cannot
by virtue of their station claim a right to live in worldly grandeur without contradicting his doctrine who said: "It is enough for the disciple to
be as his master" [Mt. 10:25].

Chapter Nine

[MS., p. 165]

When our eyes are so single as to discern the selfish spirit clearly, we
behold it the greatest of all tyrants.[27] Many thousand innocent people
under some of the Roman emperors, being confirmed in the truth of
Christ's religion from the powerful effects of his Holy Spirit upon them,
and scrupling to conform to heathenish rites, were therefore, by various
kinds of cruel and lingering torments, put to death, as is largely set forth
by Eusebius.[28] Now if we single out Domitian, Nero, or any other of
these persecuting emperors, the man, though terrible in his time, will
appear a tyrant of small consequence compared with the selfish spirit. For
though his bounds were large, yet a great part of the world were out of
his reach; and though he grievously afflicted the bodies of those innocent
people, yet the minds of many were divinely supported in their greatest
agonies, and being faithful unto death were delivered from his tyranny.
His reign though cruel for a time was soon over, and he, considered in
his greatest pomp, appears to have been a slave to the selfish spirit. Thus
tyranny, as applied to a man, rises up and soon hath an end. But if we
consider the numerous oppressions in many states and the calamities occasioned by nation contending with nation in various parts and ages of
the world, and remember that selfishness hath been the original cause of
them all; if we consider that such who are finally possessed with this selfish

27. For no apparent reason, the first edition fails to indicate the beginning of
Chapter 9, but includes it as part of Chapter 8. As a result, Chapter 10 is designated
as Chapter 9, and throughout the rest of the essay the designations are one number
behind in the sequence.

28. Eusebius (ca. 263–ca. 340), Bishop of Caesarea, was (next to St. Luke) the
most eminent historian of the early church, and is chiefly known for his *Ecclesiastical
History*.

spirit not only afflict others but are afflicted themselves and have no real quietness in this life nor in futurity, but according to the saying of Christ have their portion in that uneasy condition "where the worm dieth not, and the fire is not quenched" [Mk. 9:48]; under all these circumstances how terrible does this selfishness appear? [29]

If we consider the havoc that is made in this age, and how numbers of people are hurried on, striving to collect treasures to please that mind which wanders from perfect resignedness, and in that wisdom which is foolishness with God are perverting the true use of things, labouring as in the fire, contending with one another even unto blood, and exerting their power to support ways of living foreign to the life of one wholly crucified to the world; if we consider what great numbers of people are employed in different kingdoms in preparing the materials of war, and the labour and toil of armies set apart for protecting their respective territories from the incursions of others, and the extensive miseries which attend their engagements; while many of those who till the lands and are employed in other useful things—in supporting themselves, supporting those employed in military affairs, and some who own the soil—have great hardships to encounter through too much labour; while others in several kingdoms are busied in fetching men to help labour from distant parts of the world, to spend the remainder of their lives in the uncomfortable condition of slaves, and that self is at the bottom of these proceedings—amidst all this confusion, and these scenes of sorrow and distress, can we remember the Prince of Peace, remember that we are his disciples, and remember that example of humility and plainness which he set for us, without feeling an earnest desire to be disentangled from everything connected with selfish customs in food, in raiment, in houses, and all things else; that being of Christ['s] family and walking as he walked, we may stand in that uprightness wherein man was first made, and have no fellowship with those inventions which men in the fallen wisdom have sought out.[30]

In the selfish spirit standeth idolatry. Did our blessed Redeemer enable his family to endure great reproaches, and suffer cruel torments

29. Inserted with carets: "real" and "in this life nor."

30. What follows, from this point to the end of the chapter, is written on a sheet pasted into the MS. This was probably attached after MS. W (which lacks it) was written, making MS. Plea later at this point. Other evidence suggests that Woolman did not consciously prepare either version as his final one.

even unto death, for their testimony against the idolatry of those times; and can we behold the prevalence of idolatry though under a different appearance, without being jealous over ourselves lest we unwarily join in it?

Those faithful martyrs refused to cast incense into the fire, though by doing it they might have escaped a cruel death. Casting sweet-scented matter into the fire to make a comfortable smell—this considered separate from all circumstances—would appear to be of small consequence; but as they would thereby have signified their approbation of idolatry, it was necessarily refused by the faithful. Nor can we in any degree depart from pure universal righteousness and publicly continue in that which is not agreeable to the Truth, without strengthening the hands of the unrighteous and doing that which in the nature of the thing is like offering incense to an idol.[81]

Origen, a primitive Christian, it is reported of him that in a time of unwatchfulness, being under great difficulty, he took incense into his hand, and a certain heathen to forward the work took hold of his hand and cast the incense into the fire on the altar, and that through thus far complying, he was released from his outward troubles, but afterward greatly bewailed his condition as one fallen from a good estate to that which was worse.[82] Thus it appears that a small degree of deliberate compliance to that which is wrong is very dangerous, and the case of Origen carries in it an admonition worthy of our notice.

Chapter Ten

[MS., p. 167]

"Are not two sparrows sold for a farthing, and one of them shall not fall on the ground without your Father" [Mt. 10:29].

The way of carrying on wars, common in the world, is so far distinguishable from the purity of Christ's religion that many scruple to join in them. Those who are so redeemed from the love of the world as to possess nothing in a selfish spirit, their "life is hid with Christ in God"

31. Inserted with a caret: "publicly."
32. Origen (ca. 185–ca. 254), a native of Alexandria, ranks with Augustine as a leading scholar, theologian, and teacher of the early church. His prolific writings reflect a thorough knowledge of Greek philosophy. He survived three major periods of persecution, during the last of which (A.D. 250) he was imprisoned and tortured.

[Col. 3:3], and these he preserves in resignedness, even in times of commotion. As they possess nothing but what pertains to his family, anxious thoughts about wealth or dominion hath little or nothing in them to work upon, and they learn contentment in being disposed of according to his will who, being omnipotent and always mindful of his children, causeth all things to work for their good. But where that spirit which loves riches works, and in its working gathers wealth and cleaves to customs which have their root in self-pleasing, this spirit, thus separating from universal love, seeks help from that power which stands in the separation; and whatever name it hath, it still desires to defend the treasures thus gotten. This is like a chain where the end of one link encloses the end of another. The rising up of a desire to attain wealth is the beginning. This desire being cherished moves to action, and riches thus gotten please self, and while self hath a life in them it desires to have them defended.

Wealth is attended with power, by which bargains and proceedings contrary to universal righteousness are supported; and here oppression, carried on with worldly policy and order, clothes itself with the name of justice and becomes like a seed of discord in the soil; and as this spirit which wanders from the pure habitation prevails, so the seed of war swells and sprouts and grows and becomes strong, till much fruits are ripened. Thus cometh the harvest spoken of by the prophet, which is "a heap in the day of grief, and of desperate sorrow" [Is. 17:11].

Oh, that we who declare against wars and acknowledge our trust to be in God only, may walk in the Light and therein examine our foundation and motives in holding great estates! May we look upon our treasures and the furniture of our houses and the garments in which we array ourselves and try whether the seeds of war have any nourishment in these our possessions or not. Holding treasures in the self-pleasing spirit is a strong plant, the fruit whereof ripens fast. A day of outward distress is coming and divine love calls to prepare against it! [33] Harken then, Oh ye children who have known the Light, and come forth! Leave everything which our Lord Jesus Christ does not own. Think not his pattern too plain or too coarse for you. Think not a small portion in this life too little, but let us live in his spirit and walk as he walked, and he will preserve us in the greatest troubles.

33. At this point, at the bottom of page 168, MS. *Plea*, Woolman wrote: "the end. Chap 11." Then he erased this note and at the top of page 169 repeated the last sentence from page 168: "A day . . . against it." Then he wrote what follows, through "troubles," after which he wrote, "the end is here."

Chapter Eleven

[MS., p. 171]

"The heavens, even the heavens, are the Lord's, but the earth hath he given to the children of men." Ps. 115:16.

As servants of God, what land or estate we hold, we hold under him as his gift; and in applying the profits it is our duty to act consistent with the design of our benefactor. Imperfect men may give on motives of misguided affection, but Perfect Wisdom and Goodness gives agreeable to his own nature. Nor is this gift absolute, but conditional, for us to occupy as dutiful children and not otherwise, for he alone is the true proprietor. "The world," saith he, "is mine, and the fullness thereof." Ps. 24:1.

The inspired Lawgiver directed that such of the Israelites who sold their inheritance should sell it for a term only, and that they or their children should again enjoy it in the Year of Jubilee, settled on every fiftieth year. "The land shall not be sold forever, for the land is mine," saith the Lord, "for ye are strangers and sojourners with me" (Lev. 25:23), the design of which was to prevent the rich from oppressing the poor by too much engrossing the land. And our blessed Redeemer said: "Till heaven and earth pass, one jot or one tittle shall in no wise pass from the law till all be fulfilled" [Mt. 5:18].

Where divine love takes place in the hearts of any people, and they steadily act on a principle of universal righteousness, there the true intent of the Law is fulfilled, though their outward modes of proceeding may be distinguishable from one another. But where men are possessed by that spirit hinted at by the prophet, and looking over their wealth, say in their hearts, "Have we not taken to us horns by our own strength?" [Amos 6:13] [34]—here they deviate from the divine law and do not account their possessions so strictly God's, nor the weak and poor entitled to so much of the increase thereof, but that they may indulge their de-

---

34. Woolman originally wrote all of Chapter 11 except the last paragraph on pages 169 and 170 of the MS. He then crossed it out and wrote his final version on pages 171 and 172. Although most of his changes were minor, two are of interest, as indicated here and in note 35. At this point in the original version (after "by our own strength") he added: "Have we not attained by lawful means a clear, uncontested right to the estate we possess? And may we not, within the bounds of the laws of our country, use the profits thereof agreeable to our heart's desire?"

sires in conforming to worldly pomp.[35] And thus where house is joined to house and field laid to field till there is no place, and the poor are thereby straitened, though this be done by bargain and purchase, yet, so far as it stands distinguished from universal love, so far that woe prefixed by the prophet will accompany their proceedings.[36]

As he who first formed the earth out of nothing was then the true proprietor of it, so he still remains; and though he hath given it to the children of men, so that multitudes of people have had sustenance from it while they continued here, yet he hath never aliened it; but his right to give is as good as at the first, nor can any apply the increase of their possessions contrary to universal love, nor dispose of lands in a way which they know tends to exalt some by oppressing others, without being justly chargeable with usurpation.

Chapter Twelve

[MS., p. 173]

If we count back one hundred and fifty years and compare the inhabitants of Great Britain with the natives of North America on the like compass of ground, the natives I suppose would bear a small proportion to the others. On the discovery of this fertile continent, many of those thick-settled inhabitants coming over,[37] the natives generally treated them kindly at the first, and as those brought iron tools and a variety of things convenient for man's use, these gladly embraced the opportunity of traffic and encouraged these foreigners to settle. I speak only of improvements made peaceably.

35. The original version reads: "indulge their inclinations in conforming to the expensive, showy customs of the world."

36. At this point Woolman wrote a paragraph which he later crossed out. In the margin he wrote, "let this be left out." The deleted paragraph reads: "When God promised the land of Canaan to Abraham, he said, 'To thee will I give it and to thy seed forever.' Gen. 13:15. To Jacob he said, 'The land which I gave Abraham and Isaac, to thee will I give it, and to thy seed after thee will I give the land.' Gen. 35:12. The way of expressing is here very instructive. The Lord speaks of giving as a thing doing and to be done, and not as a thing finished. In rehearsing to Jacob the gifts he made to Abraham and Isaac, he mentions the same land as his own, and though he promiseth it to Jacob, he still retains the property in himself, to give to others in futurity: 'To thy seed after thee will I give the land.' "

37. Woolman first wrote: "inhabitants came." When he changed "e" to "ing," he neglected to change "a" to "o." Hence it now reads "caming," but in MS. W it is naturally copied as "coming."

Thus our gracious Father, who at the same time beholds the situation of all his creatures, hath opened a way from a thick-settled land and given us some room on this. Now if we attentively consider the turning of God's hand in thus far giving us room on this continent, and that the offspring of those ancient possessors of the country (in whose eyes we appear as newcomers) are yet owners and inhabiters of the land adjoining to us; and that their way of life, requiring much room, hath been transmitted to them from their predecessors and probably settled by the custom of a great many ages; under these considerations we may see the necessity of cultivating the lands already obtained of them and applying the increase consistent with true wisdom, so as to accommodate the greatest number of people it is capable of, before we have any right to plead, as members of the one great family, the equity of their assigning to us more of their possessions and living in a way requiring less room.

Did we all walk as became the followers of our blessed Saviour, were all those fruits of our country retained in it which are sent abroad in return for such strong drink, such costly array, and other luxuries which we should then have no use for, and the labour and expense of importing and exporting applied to husbandry and useful trades, a much greater number of people than now reside here might with the divine blessing live comfortably on the lands already granted us by these ancient possessors of the country.

If we faithfully serve God, who hath given us some room on this land, I believe he will make some of us useful amongst them, both in publishing the doctrines of his Son our Saviour, and in pointing out to them the advantages of replenishing the earth and subduing it.

Some I expect will be careful for such poor people abroad who earn their bread in preparing and trading in those things which we, as true disciples living in a plainness like our Heavenly Pattern, should have no use for. But laying aside all superfluities and luxuries, while people are so much thicker settled in some parts than in others, a trade in some serviceable articles may be to mutual advantage and carried on with much more regularity and satisfaction to a sincere Christian than the trade now generally is.

One person in society continuing to live contrary to true wisdom commonly draws others into connection with him; and where these embrace the way this first hath chosen, their proceedings are like a wild vine which, springing from a single seed and growing strong, the branches extend, and their little twining holders twists round all herbs and boughs of trees where they reach, and are so braced and locked in that without much labour or great strength they are not disentangled. Thus these customs, small in their beginning, as they increase they promote business and traffic, and many depend on them for a living. But as it is evident that all business which hath not its foundation in true wisdom is unbecoming a faithful follower of Christ, who loves God not only with all his heart, but with all his strength and ability to labour and act in the world; and as the Lord is able to, and will, support those whose hearts are perfect toward him, in a way agreeable to his unerring wisdom; it becomes us to meditate on the privileges of his children, to remember that where the spirit of the Lord is, there is liberty, and that in joining to customs which we know are wrong, there is a departing from the purity of his government and a certain degree of alienation from him.

To lay aside curious, costly attire, and use that only which is plain and serviceable, to cease from all superfluities and too much strong drink, are agreeable to the doctrines of our blessed Redeemer, and if in the integrity of our hearts we do so, we in some degree contribute toward lessening that business which hath its foundation in a wrong spirit; and as some well-inclined people are entangled in such business and at times desirous of being freed from it, such our ceasing from these things may be made helpful to them; and though for a time their business fail, yet if they humbly ask wisdom of God and are truly resigned to him, he will not fail them nor forsake them. He who created the earth and hath provided sustenance for millions of people in past ages is now as attentive to the necessities of his children as ever. To press forward toward perfection is our duty, and if herein we lessen some business by which some poor people earn their bread, the Lord who calls to cease from these things will take care of those whose business fails by it, if they sincerely seek to him.

If the connections we have with the inhabitants of those provinces and our interest considered as distinct from others engage us to promote plain living in order to enrich our own country, though a plain life is in itself best, yet by living plain in a selfish spirit we advance not forward in true religion. Divine love, which enlarges the heart toward mankind universally, is that alone which can rightly stop every corrupt stream and open those channels of business and commerce where nothing runs that is not pure, and so establish our goings that when in our labour we meditate on the universal love of God and the harmony of holy angels, this serenity of our minds may never be clouded in remembering that some part of our employment tends to support customs which have their foundation in the self-seeking spirit.

Chapter Thirteen

[MS., p. 176]

While our minds are prepossessed in favour of customs distinguishable from perfect purity, we are in danger of not attending with singleness to that Light which opens to our view the nature of universal righteousness.

In the affairs of a thick-settled country are variety of useful employments besides tilling the earth: that for some men to have no more land than is necessary to build on and to answer the occasions relative to the family may consist with brotherhood; and from the various gifts which God hath bestowed on those employed in husbandry, for some to possess and occupy much more than others may likewise. But where any on the strength of their possessions demands such rent or interest as necessitates those who hire of them to a closer application to business than our merciful Father designed for us, this puts the wheels of perfect brotherhood out of order and leads to employments the promoting of which belongs not to the family of Christ, whose example in all parts being a pattern of wisdom, so the plainness and simplicity of his outward appearance may well make us ashamed to adorn our bodies in costly array or treasure up wealth by the least degree of oppression.

The soil yields us support and is profitable for man; and though some possessing a larger share of these profits than others may consist with the harmony of true brotherhood, yet that the poorest people who are honest, so long as they remain inhabitants of the earth, are entitled to a certain portion of these profits, in as clear and absolute a sense as those who inherit much, I believe will be agreed to by those whose hearts are enlarged with universal love.

The first people who inhabited the earth were the first who had possession of the soil. The gracious Creator, and owner of it, gave the fruits thereof for their use. And as one generation passed away, another came and took possession; and thus through many ages, innumerable multitudes of people have been supplied by the fruits of the earth. But our gracious Creator is as absolutely the owner of it as he was when he first formed it out of nothing, before man had possession of it. And though by claims grounded on prior possession great inequality appears amongst men, yet the instructions of the great proprietor of the earth is necessary to be attended to in all our proceedings as possessors or claimers of the profits of the soil.

"The steps of a good man are ordered by the Lord" [Ps. 37:23], and those who are thus guided, whose hearts are enlarged in his love, give directions concerning their possessions agreeable thereto; and that claim which stands on universal righteousness is a good right, but the continuance of that right depends on properly applying the profits thereof.

The word *right* is commonly used relative to our possessions. We say a *right* of propriety to such a dividend of a province or a clear, indisputable *right* to the land within such certain bounds. Thus this word is continued as a remembrancer of the original intent of dividing the land by boundaries, and implies that it was designed to be equitably or rightly divided, to be divided according to righteousness. In this—that is, in equity and righteousness—consists the strength of our claims. If we trace an unrighteous claim and find gifts or grants to be proved by sufficient seals and witnesses, this gives not the claimant a *right*, for that which is opposite to righteousness is wrong, and the nature of it must be changed before it can be *right*.

Suppose twenty free men, professed followers of Christ, discovered an island unknown to all other people, and that they with their wives, independent of all others, took possession of it, and dividing it equitably, made improvements and multiplied. Suppose these first possessors, being generally influenced by true love, did with paternal regard look over the increasing condition of the inhabitants, and near the end of their lives gave such directions concerning their respective possessions as best suited the convenience of the whole and tended to preserve love and harmony, and that their successors in the continued increase of people generally followed their pious examples and pursued means the most effectual to keep oppression out of their island. But [suppose] that one of these first settlers, from a fond attachment to one of his numerous sons, no more deserving than the rest, gives the chief of his lands to him, and by an instrument sufficiently witnessed strongly expresses his mind and will. Suppose this son, being landlord to his brethren and nephews, demands such a portion of the fruits of the earth as may supply him and his family and some others; and that these others, thus supplied out of his store, are employed in adorning his buildings with curious engravings and paintings, preparing carriages to ride in, vessels for his house, delicious meats, fine-wrought apparel, and furniture, all suiting that distinction lately arisen between him and the other inhabitants; and that having this absolute disposal of these numerous improvements, his power so increaseth that in all conferences relative to the public affairs of the island, those plain, honest men who are zealous for equitable establishments find great difficulty in proceeding agreeable to their righteous inclinations while he stands in opposition to them. Suppose he, from a fondness for one of his sons, joined with a desire to continue this grandeur under his own name, confirms chief of his possessions to him, and thus for many ages, on near a twentieth part of this island there is one great landlord and the rest generally poor oppressed people; to some of whom from the manner of their education, joined with a notion of the greatness of their predecessors, labour is disagreeable; who therefore by artful applications to the weakness, unguardedness, and corruption of others, in striving to get a living out of them increase the difficulties amongst them; while the inhabitants of the other parts who guard against oppression and with one consent train up their children in plainness, frugality, and useful labour live more harmonious.

If we trace the claim of the ninth or tenth of these great landlords down to the first possessor and find the claim supported throughout by instruments strongly drawn and witnessed, after all we could not admit a belief into our hearts that he had a *right* to so great a portion of land, after such a numerous increase of inhabitants.

The first possessor of that twentieth part held no more we suppose than an equitable portion; but when the Lord, who first gave these twenty men possession of this island unknown to all others, gave being to numerous people who inhabited this twentieth part, whose natures required the fruits thereof for their sustenance, this great claimer of the soil could not have a *right* to the whole, to dispose of it in gratifying his irregular desires; [38] but they, as creatures of the Most High God, possessor of heaven and earth, had a *right* to part of what this great claimer held, though they had no instruments to confirm their *right*.

Thus oppression in the extreme appears terrible, but oppression in more refined appearances remains to be oppression, and where the smallest degree of it is cherished it grows stronger and more extensive: that to labour for a perfect redemption from this spirit of oppression is the great business of the whole family of Christ Jesus in this world.

38. Added with a caret: "to dispose . . . desires." Copied smoothly into MS. W.

Chapter Fourteen

ON SCHOOLS

[MS., p. 181]

When we are thoroughly instructed in the kingdom of God, we are content with that use of things which his wisdom points out, both for ourselves and our children, and are not concerned to learn them the art of getting rich, but are careful that the love of God and a right regard for all their fellow creatures may possess their minds, and that in all their learning their improvements may go forward in pure wisdom.[39] Christ our Shepherd being abundantly able and willing to instruct his family in all things proper for them to know, it remains to be our duty to wait patiently for his help in teaching our families and not seek to forward them in learning by the assistance of that spirit from which he gave his life to redeem us.[40]

It was his own saying that the children of this world are in their generation wiser than the children of Light, and it appears by experience that in awakening and cherishing the spirit of pride and the love of praise in children they may sometimes be brought on in learning faster than they would otherwise; but while in learning any art or science they accustom themselves to disobey the pure Spirit and grow strong in that wisdom which is foolishness with God, they must have the painful labour of unlearning a part of what they thus learned, before they are adopted into the divine family. It is therefore good for us in schools and in all parts of

39. The fourth word of this sentence was spelled "througly" by Woolman. Apparently he intended it to be "throughly," as it is in the first line of the fourth paragraph of this chapter and in the first line of the next to the last paragraph of Chapter 16. In Woolman's day "throughly" was a word in common use, one meaning of which—as given by the *Oxford English Dictionary*—was "thoroughly." To avoid confusion, we have rendered it "thoroughly" in these instances as well as in Chapter 4, above. Cf. note 1 to *Considerations on Keeping Negroes: Part Second*.

In the outer margin opposite this sentence Woolman wrote "See page 194." This is the page on which the *Journal* is resumed with his account of the statement made by the aged John Smith at the Philadelphia Yearly Meeting of 1764. Mr. Smith deplored the gradual increase of worldliness and the corresponding decrease in humility and adherence to Quaker principles which he had noted in the Society during the previous sixty years. This testimony is found near the start of Chapter 9 of the *Journal*. See Addendum, par. 5, for explanation of the note: "See page 194."

40. Inserted with a caret: "patiently."

education to attend diligently to the principle of universal Light, and patiently wait for their improvement in the channel of true wisdom, without endeavouring to get help from that spirit which seeks honour from men. (It is through a deviation from the pure Light that people desire help from the spirit of this world in pushing forward their children in learning, that they may save out of their education to support ways of life less plain and simple than what our Holy Pattern has laid down for us.) [41]

Children in an age fit for schools are in a time of life that requires the careful and patient attendance of their tutors, and such a diligent observation of their several tempers and dispositions as that they may be enabled rightly and seasonably to administer to each individual.

Were we thoroughly weaned from the love of wealth and fully brought out of all superfluities in living, employments about vanities being finished and labour wanted only for things consistent with a humble, self-denying life, there would on a reasonable estimate be so much to spare on the education of our children that a plain, humble man with a family like himself might be furnished with a living for teaching and overseeing so small a number of children that he might properly and seasonably administer to each individual, and gently lead them on as the Gospel Spirit opened the way, without giving countenance to pride or evil emulation amongst them.

The management of children being sometimes committed to men who do not live under the seasoning virtue of Truth is a case that requires our serious consideration, for that it is our indispensable duty to use our utmost endeavours in their education to bring them into an acquaintance with the inward work of grace; and where a tutor is not experienced in this work, their spirit and conduct in directing and ordering the children does often make impressions on their tender, inexperienced minds to their great disadvantage.

Again, where pious men enter into this employ, they sometimes find it difficult to support their families without taking charge of so great a number that they cannot so fully attend to the spirit and disposition of each individual as would be profitable to the children. A large number of children in a school is often a heavy weight on the mind of an honest

---

41. This sentence is partly surrounded by a line, which may have meant that it was to be omitted or subordinated. Generally Woolman marked very clearly what he wished to omit, but there are exceptions in this essay. In the next sentence Woolman inserted with a caret: "and patient."

tutor, and when his thoughts and time are so much taken up in the more outward affairs of the school that he cannot so attend to the spirit and temper of each individual as to administer rightly and seasonably in the line of true judgment, there the minds of children often suffer and a wrong spirit gains strength, which frequently increases difficulties in a school and like an infection spreads from one to another.

A man influenced by the spirit of Truth, employing his time in tutoring children, while he hath only such a number that the manifestation of divine strength in him is superior to the instability in them, this good spirit in which he governs does measurably work on their minds and tends to bring them forward in the Christian life. But where the straitness of a man's circumstances, joined with the small wages set on teaching children, proves a temptation and so enters into his heart that he takes charge of too many for the measure of his gift, or where the desire for wealth so corrupts the heart of any that they take charge of too many, here the true order of a Christian education is lost.[42] But where a man hath charge of a number too great for that degree of strength with which the Lord hath endowed him, he not only suffers as to the state of his own mind, but the children suffer also;[43] and government not being supported in the true Christian spirit, the pure witness is not reached in the minds of the children.

To educate children in the way of true piety and virtue is a duty incumbent on all of us who have them;[44] and our Heavenly Father requires no duties of us but what he gives strength to perform, as we humbly seek to him: that though to the eye of reason the difficulties appear great in many places which attend instructing our children in useful learning, yet if we obediently attend to that wisdom which is from above, our gracious Father will open a way for us to give them such an education as he requires of us.

And here I may say that my mind hath been sorrowfully affected on account of some who from a desire for wealth, a desire to conform in living to those ways distinguishable from the true Christian spirit, exert themselves in things relating to this life, and do not enough lay to heart

42. At this point Woolman wrote, rearranged, and then crossed out the following succinct summary of his chief thesis: "I believe it will be granted by all pious people that to watch the spirit of children in school and labour to bring them on as lambs in the flock of Christ is of greater moment than their improvement in the knowledge of letters."

43. "The Lord" replaces Woolman's original "divine providence."

44. Added with a caret: "and virtue."

the suffering condition of youth in many places, through want of pious examples and tutors whose minds are seasoned with the spirit of Truth.[45]

Are great labours performed to gain wealth for posterity? Are many supported with wages to furnish us with delicacies and luxuries?

Are monies expended for colours to please the eye, which renders our garments less serviceable? Are garments of a curious texture purchased at a high rate, for the sake of their delicacy?

Are there various branches of workmanship only ornamental—in the building of our houses, hanging by our walls and partitions, and to be seen in our furniture and apparel? And amidst all these expenses which the pure Truth does not require of us, do we send our children to men to get learning who we believe are not influenced by the spirit of Truth, rather than humbly wait on the Lord for wisdom to direct us in their education?

To commit children to the tuition of men who we believe are not rightly qualified to lead them on in the true Christian life, I believe no pious man will say is required of us as a duty. To do evil that good may come of it is contrary to the doctrine of Christianity; that when times are so cloudy that we cannot go forward in the way of clearness and purity, it behooves us in the depth of humility to wait on the Lord to know his mind concerning us and our children.

Chapter Fifteen

ON MASTERS AND SERVANTS

[MS., p. 186]

"Servants, be obedient to them that are your masters according to the flesh, with fear and trembling, in singleness of your heart, as unto Christ." Eph. 6:5.

It is observable in several places where the apostle writes to servants that he labours to direct their minds to the true Light, that in labouring in the condition of servants they might as the apostle expresseth it, "do the will of God from the heart" (Eph. 6:6),[46] that their labours might not be like those of men-pleasers, but in singleness of heart fearing God, and that

45. "And tutors . . . Truth" is written over an erasure, the last part of which can be deciphered as "in the way of holiness."
46. Lacking in MS. M: "(Eph. 6:6)."

in whatsoever they did they might "do it heartily, as to the Lord, and not unto men." Col. 3:23.

As the pure principle of righteousness is the foundation whereon the pure in heart stand, so their proceedings are consistent herewith; [47] and while they encourage to an upright performance of every reasonable duty on one hand, they guard on the other against servants actively complying with unrighteous commands, doing service "as to the Lord and not unto men" (verse 7), by which we are instructed in the necessity of a humble walking before God, that by faithfully attending on the leadings of his Holy Spirit, our senses may be "exercised to discern both good and evil" (Heb. 5:14). And that as the righteous commands of masters ought to be obeyed because they were righteous, so on the contrary, such commands of men which could not be performed without disobeying God were not sufficient authority for a servant of Christ to proceed upon, but herein we ought to obey God rather than men.

The present concern of my mind is that all who are in the station of masters may seriously consider this subject and demand nothing of servants which is unreasonable, or that in the performance of which they must necessarily act contrary to universal righteousness. [48]

A pious father hath a conscientious care for his children, that by his labours they may be rightly educated and have some things which necessarily relate to their first settling in the world. But where a man seeth his righteous intentions perverted and his labours made to serve purposes which are not equitable and hath no hopes of a remedy, his case is very grievous; for here however disposed to labour, he cannot labour "heartily as to the Lord and not unto men."

To comply with demands which are not equitable is afflicting to a well-disposed mind, and for a man in power to demand service of another without proposing an equitable reward appears to me to have the spirit of persecution in it. Upright men labouring in temporal affairs have in view to do good thereby; they labour because they are convinced it is their duty. But where labours not equitably due are required of them to gratify the covetous, luxurious, or ambitious designs of others, this lays

47. Variant readings in this paragraph: (1) In which MS. M is apparently later: "pure in heart" was copied, then changed to "men of God"; added after "other": "hand"; omitted: "(verse 7)"; "attending on" changed to "attending to"; "could not" changed to "can not"; "were not" changed to "are not." (2) In which MS. *Plea* is apparently later: crossed out before "masters": "our"; "are righteous" changed to "were righteous."

48. MS. M variants: In this paragraph: "stations"; in line 31 of this page: "such labour."

conscientious men under great difficulty. If they comply not, they are liable to punishment, and if they do that which they believe is not right for them to do, they wound their own souls.

Chapter Sixteen

[MS., p. 188]

To keep Negroes as servants till they are thirty years of age and hold the profits of the last nine years of their labour as our own, on a supposition that they may sometime be an expense to our estates, is a way of proceeding which appears to admit of improvement.

REASONS OFFERED

1. Men of mature age who have walked orderly and made no contract to serve—that they are entitled to freedom I expect is generally agreed to, and to make them serve as slaves nine years longer may be to keep them slaves for term of life. They may die before that age and be no expense to us, and may leave children to whom, with reason, they might in their last sickness desire to give the monies they had earned after they had paid for their own education.

2. The labour of a healthy, industrious Negro man for nine years, I suppose at a moderate computation, may not be less than fifty pounds proclamation money, besides his diet and clothing. Now if this money be earned either in the service of the man who educated him or laid by in yearly proportion under the care of the said man, and put out at a moderate interest for the Negro's use, and to be applied to his future necessities or to such honest purposes as he by his last will might direct, this would appear to us a more brotherly way of proceeding were we in the Negro's condition.

3. Pure goodness tendeth to beget its own likeness; and where men are convinced that the conduct of those who have power over them is equitable, it naturally yields encouragement for them to provide against old age. The pure witness being reached, a care is thereby incited that they may not become a burden on the estates of those whom they have found to be honest men and true friends to them. But where men have laboured without wages nine years longer than is common with other men amongst whom they dwell, and then set free, and at going off are assured that those

who so detained them are largely in their debt, but expect not to recover the debt except they become needy when unable to help themselves—such would naturally be induced to think this treatment unbrotherly, to think of the reasonableness of their wages being some time paid, to think that the estate in which they laboured might reasonably assist them in old age, and thus be tempted to decline from a wise application to business.

4. If I see a man want relief and know he hath money in my hands which must some time be paid with reasonable use, either to him or to others by his direction, there appears in this case no temptation to withhold it at the time I saw that he wanted it. But if selfishness so far prevailed in me that I looked upon the money which I had in trust with a desire to keep it from the true owner, and through the strength of desire joined with expectation, at length so far considered it a part of my estate as to apply it in promoting myself or my family in the world, and therewith entered into expenses which a humble follower of Christ might have shunned—here, by joining with one temptation there is great danger of falling into more, and of not attending to the wants of the man who had monies in my hands with that care and diligence as I might have done had the tempter found no entrance into my mind.

5. If we righteously account for the monies which we have in security, with a reasonable use thereon, and frugally expend the whole in relieving the man who earned it; and more being wanted, the public refuseth to bear any part of the expense; if our estates have not been benefited aforetime by the labours of his fathers nor ancestors, this appears to be a case wherein the righteous suffer for the testimony of a good conscience, and from which if faithfully attended to they might in time, I trust, hope for relief.

6. The Negroes have been a suffering people, and we as a civil society are they by whom they have suffered. Now where persons have been injured as to their outward substance and died without having recompense, their children appear to have a right to that which was equitably due to and detained from their fathers. My heart is affected with sorrow while I write on this subject, on account of the great injuries committed against these Gentiles, and against their children who have been born in that captivity which is an unrighteous captivity. When the ancestors of these people were imported from Africa, some I believe bought them with intent to treat them kindly as slaves. They bought them as though those violent men had a right to sell them, but I believe without weightily considering the nature and tendency of such a bargain, and thus building on

an unrighteous foundation, a veil was gradually drawn over a practice very grievous and afflicting to great numbers of the Gentiles. A care is now reviving in many places that this veil may be yet further removed, and that this disorder may be searched to the bottom; and my concern is that we may not only bear in mind that the Negroes have been a suffering people under us as a civil society, but that we may in true humiliation feel for that pure influence which alone is able to guide us in the way where healing and restoration is experienced.[49]

6. Having thus far spoken of the Negroes as equally entitled to the benefit of their labour with us, I feel it on my mind to mention that debt which is due to many Negroes of the present age. Where men within certain limits are so formed into a society as to become like a large body consisting of many members, here whatever injuries are done to others not of this society by members of this society, if the society in whose power it is doth not use all reasonable endeavours to execute justice and judgment, nor publicly disown those unrighteous proceedings, the iniquities of individuals becomes chargeable on such civil society to which they remain united. And where persons have been injured as to their outward substance and died without having recompense, so that their children are kept out of that which was equitably due to their parents, here such children appear to be justly entitled to receive recompense from that civil society under which their parents suffered.

My heart is affected with sorrow while I write on this subject, on account of the great injuries committed against these Gentiles and against their children born in captivity. Had the active members in civil society when those injuries were first attempted united in a firm opposition to those violent proceedings, had others in a selfish spirit attempted the like afterward and met with a firm opposition, and been made to do justice to the injured persons till the prospect of gain by such unrighteous proceedings appeared so doubtful that no further attempts had been made—how much better had it been for these American colonies and islands?

Some, I believe, bought those poor sufferers with intent to treat them kindly as slaves. They bought them as though these violent men had had a right to sell them, but, I believe, without entering deep enough into the

49. Woolman drew a large bracket down the left-hand margin, including all of this first of two sections with the number 6 (from "The Negroes have" through "is experienced.") Then he pasted in a note, which folds over part of the bracketed portion. Its contents are reproduced in the section of the Appendix dealing with major extant manuscripts. Woolman did not necessarily intend to exclude the first section 6. Hence both sections are included here.

consideration of the consequence of such proceedings. Others, I believe, bought them with views of outward ease and profit; and thus those violent men found people of reputation who purchased their booty and built on that purchase as a foundation to exercise the authority of masters, and thus encouraged them in this horrible trade, till their proceedings were so far approved by civil society as to consider those men as members without proceeding to punish them for their crimes; and hence a veil was in some measure drawn over a practice the most foreign to righteousness, and the face of things so disguised that under the most lamentable injustice but few appeared to be alarmed at it or zealously labour to have justice done to the sufferers and their posterity.

These poor Africans were people of a strange language and not easy to converse with, and their situation as slaves too generally destroyed that brotherly freedom which frequently subsists between us and inoffensive strangers. In this adverse condition, how reasonable is it to suppose that they would revolve in their distressed minds the iniquities committed against them and mourn!—mourn without any to comfort them? [50]

Though through gradual proceedings in unrighteousness dimness hath come over many minds, yet the nature of things are not altered. Long oppression hath not made oppression consistent with brotherly love, nor length of time through several ages made recompense to the posterity of those injured strangers. Many of them lived and died without having their suffering case heard, and determined according to equity; and under a degree of sorrow on account of the wantonness, the vanity, and superfluity too common amongst us as a civil society, even while a heavy load of unrighteous proceedings lies upon us, do I now under a feeling of universal love and in a fervent concern for the real interest of my fellow members in society, as well as the interest of my fellow creatures in general, express these things.

Suppose an inoffensive youth, forty years ago, was violently taken from Guinea, sold here as a slave, laboured hard till old age, and hath children who are now living.[51] Though no sum may properly be mentioned as an equal reward for the total deprivation of liberty, yet if the sufferings of this man be computed at no more than fifty pounds, I expect candid men will suppose it within bounds, and that his children have an equitable right to it.

50. The second "mourn" is inserted with a caret.
51. Inserted with a caret: "laboured hard till old age."

Fifty pounds at three percent, add-ing the interest to the principal once in ten years appears in forty years to make upward of one hundred and forty pounds.

Principal £ 50 50
Interest 10 year at 3 percent ... 15
                                                   ——
                                                   65
Interest 10 year 19
                                                   ——
                                                   84
Interest 10 year 25
                                                   ——
                                                   109
Interest 10 year 32
                                                   ——
                                                   141

Now when our minds are thoroughly divested of all prejudice in relation to the difference of colour, and the love of Christ in which there is no partiality prevails upon us, I believe it will appear that a heavy account lies against us as a civil society for oppressions committed against people who did not injure us, and that if the particular case of many individuals were fairly stated, it would appear that there was considerable due to them.[52]

I conclude with the words of that righteous judge in Israel: "Behold here I am; witness against me before the Lord and before his anointed: whose ox have I taken? or whose ass have I taken? or whom have I defrauded? whom have I oppressed? or of whose hand have I received any bribe to blind mine eyes therewith? and I will restore it to you." 1 Samuel 12:3.

52. Erased after "due to them": "from such."

Appendix A

RATIONALE FOR THE PRESENT EDITION OF THE *JOURNAL*

THIS EDITION OF the *Journal* was undertaken only after a long period of study and writing about Woolman convinced the present editor that it was urgently needed. In the nearly two hundred years since Woolman's death many editions have appeared, including the famous one with an introduction by John Greenleaf Whittier, issued in 1871. Twice in the twentieth century new editions were brought out. Why, then, is another one necessary? The answer is that every printed edition to date has differed at literally hundreds of points from the final manuscript Woolman prepared for the printer. The two twentieth-century editions were intended to remedy this situation, but (in addition to other limitations) they were based on a major error, the consequences of which are evident on every page. To amplify these statements a brief analysis of the major editions is in order.

I. First Edition (1774)

As noted in the list of major extant manuscripts (see Appendix B), Woolman wrote two complete manuscripts of the first ten chapters—in addition to provisional drafts of certain sections. His preliminary manuscript (MS. A) was writtten over a period of about fourteen years (1756–1770). Before he sailed for England in 1772, working from MS. A, he prepared MS. B as his final copy for publication. On shipboard and in England he wrote two additional chapters (11 and 12), the final version of which is now designated MS. S.

After Woolman's death the Quaker Meeting for Sufferings in Philadelphia appointed a committee to prepare the *Journal* for the printer. As intended by the author, the committee based the first ten chapters of this first edition on his final copy (MS. B). They rightly based the last two chapters (11 and 12) on MS. S, which had been sent from England. The *Journal* came from the press of Joseph Crukshank, a Philadelphia printer, in 1774. The committee and the printer did a careful, accurate job. By the standards of present-day editorial scholarship, however, the first edition is seriously defective on two counts:

A. At hundreds of points the committee revised Woolman's copy. These revisions can usually be detected by the darker ink, finer lines, and different handwriting. Although most of the changes are minor, some definitely affect the meaning.

B. Several important passages were omitted. These include Woolman's accounts of dreams he had had; three mathematical illustrations introduced for emphasis; an instance of torture by Indian warriors; a mention of the running down of pedestrians by English stagecoaches; a reference to an occasion on which Woolman resorted to a law court; the author's recorded opposition to smallpox inoculation; and an expression of concern about the impure air of cities, in contrast to "pure country air."

Although these revisions and omissions do not preclude a reasonably sound understanding of Woolman, they present a serious handicap to the careful scholar.

II. Editions Printed Between 1775 and 1921

With one exception, the many later editions (up to 1922) were based exclusively on the first or on subsequent printed editions rather than on the original MSS. Later editions perpetuated and compounded the defects of the first one. The one version (Philadelphia, 1837) whose editors, John Comly and Samuel Comfort, may have consulted Woolman's holographs, failed to restore the omitted portions noted above and produced even more deviations from Woolman than the first edition. The Whittier edition of 1871 was neither new nor revised. It was a verbatim copy of a defective 1840 edition, plus a few footnotes and an extended introduction—whose perceptiveness, along with Whittier's reputation, was doubtless responsible for its having been accepted as the standard edition for about fifty years.

III. The Gummere Edition of 1922

In 1922 *The Journal and Essays of John Woolman*, edited by Amelia Mott Gummere, was published. It included an illuminating biography of

Woolman, along with a new edition of the *Journal*, other Woolman essays and papers, and a number of supplementary data in footnotes and appendices. To this, the most comprehensive collection of Woolman papers ever printed, the present editor and all students of Woolman are deeply indebted. In it, the major passages omitted from previous editions of the *Journal* were restored. It was inadequate, however, in the following respects:

A. Although Mrs. Gummere consulted both holographs, she made the crucial error of identifying Woolman's preliminary MS. (A) as his final one, and accordingly based the first ten chapters of her edition on it rather than on MS. B. Because the two differ at many points, her edition does not represent Woolman's final intention.

B. The text contains a large number of minor errors and undocumented variant readings. For example, the following deviations from MS. A occur in the first five pages of the Gummere edition of the *Journal*; the incidence is about the same throughout. The numerals refer to pages.

MS. A	Gummere edition
2: turned	151: drawn *
2: was	151: were
2: in reading it	151: in the reading of it
2: [phrase lacking]	151: by the way *
2: there	152: their
3: [tilde over "sumer,"]	152: [tilde over "comonly"]
3: full of strength and resolution	152: [phrase lacking]
4: sixteen years	153: sixteen
4: repentance to repentance	153: repentance
6: the day	155: a day
6: from all those	156: from those

The variants marked with an asterisk were taken from MS. B. Although the Gummere edition is based on MS. A, occasionally phrases have been taken from MS. B, without any indication of the source.

C. The editorial methods are inconsistent. More often than not, Woolman's spelling and capitalization have been retained. Yet in places they have been modernized for no apparent reason. On page 2 of MS. A, for example, Woolman twice wrote "seting." The Gummere edition renders this as "seting" the first time and "sitting" the second (pages 151 and 152). On the same two pages, lower-case letters have been substituted for Woolman's capitals in "seven," "soon," "as," "religious," and "books." Brackets are used for varying purposes. Although usually Woolman's words have been transcribed in preference to revisions by the original editorial committee, in some instances the phrasing of the committee has been selected. Since the variations have not been documented or explained, the result is confusing.

Edwin H. Cady, Professor of English, Indiana University, in his volume *John Woolman*, writes of Mrs. Gummere's "valiant but unprofessional efforts":

> Great intelligence, years of devoted work, and the profit of extraordinary inside knowledge and contacts went into this landmark work of a gifted amateur. Not always consistent or accurate, the text . . . restored hundreds of original Woolman readings. . . . The long and authoritative (if sometimes inchoate) "Biographical Sketch" reprints almost all known Woolman letters and other basic documents. . . . Altogether, the indispensable Woolman reference.
>
> (128, 174)

IV. The Whitney Edition of 1950

In 1950 *The Journal of John Woolman* was published as edited by Mrs. Janet Whitney, the distinguished author of *John Woolman, Quaker*, among other books. Because she followed Mrs. Gummere in supposing Woolman's preliminary holograph to be the final one, Mrs. Whitney also based the first ten chapters primarily, but not entirely, on MS. A. Her aim and method were "to present John Woolman's own words and phrases in full and verbatim. . . . When any differences occur . . . between the rival versions, . . . the choice has been made with the desire to present Woolman's own thought in its most arresting expression" (xii, xiii). Her edition is a mosaic of MSS. A, B, C, S, and T, plus some of the revisions made by the original editorial committee and (on practically every page) minor revisions of her own, which often serve to improve the style.

Two instances in which Mrs. Whitney has included revisions made by the committee are found on page 35: "the main" has been substituted for "that side the water," and "returned" for "came on." Other examples could be cited, though in general this edition rightly ignores the changes made by the committee.

A typical example of Mrs. Whitney's own revision is found on page 60 (line 3). MSS. A and B both read: "From thence to the head of Little River on a First Day, where was a crowded meeting and I believe was through divine goodness made profitable to some." The Whitney edition reads: "This was also the case at the head of Little River, where we had a crowded meeting on a First Day." On page 159 are several deviations from MSS. A and B. For example, MSS. A and B read: "But I felt no inclination at that time to speak with him." The Whitney edition reads: "I felt no inclination to speak with the latter."

At several points, curious omissions occur. On page 21, after Woolman's opening paragraph about his sister's character and death, a long passage has been omitted. On page 36, twenty-seven words have been left out of the closing sentence of the first paragraph. A similar omission occurs on page 46. In each of these cases, the missing material appears in both MS. A and MS. B. On the other hand, the Whitney edition includes, on pages 58 and 74, sections that Woolman had indicated in MS. A were to be left out, and which he had left out of MS. B.

Several errors in documentation may be noted in passing. A footnote on page 167 states that the first thirty-one lines of Chapter 11 come from the "Swarthmore manuscript." This is presumably a reference to MS. S; yet the lines do not appear there (or in MS. T). They were probably taken from an earlier printed edition; the original manuscript source seems to have been lost. A note on page 21 locates the end of MS. C about fifteen lines above its actual conclusion. Similarly, on page 178 the end of MS. T1 has been designated at the wrong point; it actually contains an additional short page. On the whole, little documentation appears in the Whitney edition; the various sources, omissions, and revisions have not been indicated.

Nevertheless, the Whitney edition is very fluent and conveys the essential spirit of Woolman. Like the Gummere edition, it restores most of the sections previously omitted. It was the first edition to include Woolman's dream of visiting a dictator on a mission of peace, which is described in MS. R2. It is also the first in which the variant readings of MS. T have been taken into account.

The limitations of previous editions have been spelled out in order to explain why a new one is needed. Edwin H. Cady was undoubtedly right when he declared, after recognizing the merits of the Gummere and Whitney editions, that there was need for "a definitive edition by modern and professional bibliographical means" (128).

V. Evidence that MS. A was Woolman's Preliminary Holograph
and that MS. B Was the Final Copy He Intended for the Printer

Any doubt as to the need of a new edition was dispelled in the summer of 1966. The present editor then made the startling discovery that (except for sixteen pages) MS. B, rather than MS. A, was the final copy of Chapters 1–10 which Woolman prepared for the printer. Both Mrs. Gummere and Mrs. Whitney viewed MS. A as Woolman's final copy; believing that the first printed edition was based on it, they accordingly based their own editions primarily on it (Gummere, x, xi, xii, xviii, 114; Whitney, xi, xii, xiii).*

The crucial question is: Which of the two MSS. was Woolman's final version, the one intended by him for the printer? It is illuminating to note first the judgment of those in the best position to know. On which of the two MSS. did the original editorial committee and the printer actually base the first printed edition?

The answer to this question is clear. Although the original editorial committee had both MSS. and made some revisions in both, MS. B was the one they prepared for the printer. In the printed edition, each chapter is preceded by a summary of its contents. These summaries are written on separate slips of paper that have been pinned or stitched into place at the heads of the chapters in MS. B—though some are missing, apparently having been lost. The handwriting of those extant is that of the penman for the editorial committee. The name of Israel Pemberton, a member of the committee, appears on the back of one of the slips. In MS. B, Roman numerals for each chapter have also been supplied, as though to make it ready for the printer. In MS. A, such summaries are completely lacking and Roman numerals have been supplied for only two chapters.

On page 324 of MS. B (at the very end of Chapter 9) appears this significant note by the original editors: "A paragraph dated 9/10/69 in bound book folio 212 should come in here." The paragraph in question was duly copied by the committee from MS. A (the bound book folio), page 212. Then the note was crossed out. Woolman had omitted the paragraph in the copying process; the editors believed it should be included.

The original editorial committee clearly had both MSS. at hand. Some-

---

* It may be noted in passing that the Gummere edition in one place (xviii) refers to MS. C as "MS. B," and vice versa.

times they revised MS. A to make it accord with MS. B, as though recognizing MS. B as the norm. They never seem to have changed MS. A simply to improve it, without reference to MS. B. Often, however, they changed MS. B, with the evident purpose of preparing it for the printer, and usually without bothering to change MS. A. For example, on page 67 of MS. B the committee has written: "Leave this dream out in printing." They made no such note in MS. A, although they crossed out the description of the dream in both MSS.

Although the printer apparently had access to MS. A, he followed MS. B in all (or almost all) of the hundreds of cases in which the MSS. differ. Here are typical examples from the opening pages:

MS A	*MS. B and first edition*
p. 2: my mind was turned	my mind was drawn
what I had read I believed	what I had read and heard
p. 4: placed that in the human mind	placed a principle in

Pages 61–66 of MS. B contain twenty-three points of difference from MS. A. Other differences abound throughout the manuscripts, as may be noted in comparing page 224 of MS. B with page 118 of MS. A. Page 200 of MS. A contains an unimportant paragraph that is missing from the parallel passage on page 209 of MS. B. In all of these instances the printer followed MS. B instead of MS. A.

Notwithstanding the assumptions on which the Gummere and Whitney editions are based, a mass of detailed textual evidence bears witness that both committee and printer, while having access to MS. A, used MS. B as the basis for the first edition. Of course, they could both have been mistaken. Hence we must ask: was MS. B really the final copy that Woolman intended for the printer? In all but two short sections (see Appendix C and notes to Chapter 9), the evidence is conclusive that it was, as careful analysis will reveal.

In many passages where the two MSS. read exactly alike, it may be noted that MS. A bears the marks of considerable revision. Sections have been erased, leaving gaps in the copy. Words have been inserted with carets. Interpolated lines have been crowded between those that are regularly spaced. Sentences have been written in the margin and keyed to the text. In MS. B, on the other hand, the text proceeds smoothly. The same words as in MS. A appear with no gaps, carets, or inserted lines—as would be expected if Woolman had revised these portions of MS. A and then copied them as portions of MS. B. At some points comparison is less

easy because of additional changes made by Woolman as he copied into
MS. B, or by the the editorial committee. However, instances of considerable revision in MS. A and of a smoothly flowing copy in MS. B, the
phrasing being alike, are found frequently in the manuscripts, as for example in the following parallel passages: A 47–48 and B 100–102; A 100
and B 185; A 3 and B 6; A 64 and B 132–133. If Woolman had copied
from MS. B to MS. A for the sake of the printer he might have done some
revising in the process, using carets, etc. But then the two copies would
not read alike. If he had then gone back and revised B so as to read the
same way, marks of revision would be evident in B. It is scarcely possible to
imagine Woolman copying from a smoothly flowing MS. B to MS. A for
the sake of the printer—making insertions, deliberately leaving gaps, etc.,
but ending up with exactly the same words. It thus becomes evident that
he copied from MS. A to MS. B, and not vice versa.

Further clear evidence is found at several other points. At the end of
page 36 in MS. A, Woolman directs the reader first to pages 41 and 42,
then back to pages 37–40, and finally to page 43. It is obvious that after
composing this section he had rearranged the order. In MS. B the entire
passage is written consecutively according to the rearranged order—as
would be expected in a later copy. It is hardly conceivable that the writer
would have copied from MS. B to MS. A and scrambled that order
deliberately. On page 162 of MS. B, Woolman omitted four lines found on
page 89 of MS. A ("alleging that . . . these people"). Later he pasted in a
slip of paper containing the missing lines (keyed to the text), at the bottom of which he wrote: "This was occasioned by an omission in copying."

Such instances prove conclusively that Woolman copied from MS. A
to MS. B. Less conclusive individually, but quite convincing as a whole,
are bits of evidence found at many other points. On page 30 of MS. A is
a drawing, in the margin of which is written: "I do not want this figure
printed. John Woolman." On page 70 of MS. A is another note by Woolman. "If this journal be printed let all the quotation from J. Churchman's notes be left out." The drawing and the quotation are simply
omitted from MS. B—as would be expected if (years later) he had copied
it for the printer. On page 61 of MS. A, Woolman wrote in the margin
of a paragraph: "Let this be left out." In MS. B (page 127) he copied half
a line of this paragraph, then apparently noticed that it was to be omitted,
and erased it so as to leave out the whole paragraph. After page 97 of
MS. A, Woolman pasted in a printed copy of the Philadelphia Yearly

Meeting Epistle of 1759. When he reached the same point in MS. B, he first wrote: "Here take in the printed epistle of 1759." Later he added: "1772. I am easy that that epistle be left out. J. W." The epistle does not appear in MS. B. On page 91 of MS. B is Woolman's note: "Copy bound book 43." At that point Woolman copied a letter appearing on page 43 of MS. A. These notes by Woolman and their implementation in the MSS. accord with the conclusion that MS. B is the final copy, but not with the opposite belief.

It is significant that Woolman's *A Plea for the Poor* occupies pages 148–193 of the bound volume containing MS. A, which is interrupted on page 147 and resumed at the top of page 194. If MS. A had been prepared in a comparatively short time for the printer, it is unlikely that MS. *Plea* would have been inserted here. But if MS. A is viewed as having been written over a longer period (as a diary) the interruption is comprehensible, since the dates of the entries before and after MS. *Plea* are more than a year apart.

A final consideration is that where the two versions differ, the literary style of MS. B is often notably superior to that of MS. A. It is seldom, if ever, clearly the reverse. Here are examples:

MS. A	MS. B
p. 26: which we had the command of	p. 61: of which we had the command
26: he that night desired me	62: that night he desired me
28: And in the winter ensuing	64: And in the next winter
35: such more especially who	73: more especially of such who

It is more reasonable to assume that awkward expressions in MS. A have been improved in MS. B than that he changed felicitous phrases in MS. B to cumbersome ones in MS. A.

VI. The Need for a Critical Treatment of Chapters 11 and 12

Further evidence of the need for a new edition of Chapters 1–10 could be adduced but is probably unnecessary. No less essential is a critical edition of Chapters 11 and 12. The value of MSS. T1 and T2 was recognized in the introduction to the Whitney edition, but heretofore no thorough collation of these with MS. S has been made. The many variations between the two MSS. account for the heavy documentation of Chapter 11 in the present edition. In preparing Chapter 12, account has also been taken of MS. Y. At several points MSS. T1, T2, and Y have proved valuable in clarifying the wording of sections of MS. S, the document on which Chapters 11 and 12 of the present edition are based.

VII. Summary and Conclusion

Editions of Woolman's works published before this century, although based on the right manuscripts, have been inadequate because they incorporated hundreds of editorial changes and omitted many significant passages. The twentieth-century editions, while restoring most of the omissions, have not reproduced Woolman's narrative with sufficient accuracy, consistency, or sound documentation, and in both, the first ten chapters have been based on the wrong manuscript. No previous editions have dealt thoroughly with the preliminary manuscripts on which Chapters 11 and 12 are based.

To reconstruct the history of the manuscripts and the process by which MS. B was ultimately produced is a complex task. At some points Woolman worked back and forth between MSS. A and B. Sometimes, after making his final revision of MS. B he changed MS. A accordingly; more often he did not. To complicate matters, as noted above, two of the eleven sections of MS. B are preliminary versions, of which MS. A does, in fact, contain revisions made later. Moreover, the changes made by (at least two) members of the original editorial committee cannot always be identified with certainty, and Woolman's writing is occasionally unclear or illegible. After working on the project for several years and receiving considerable guidance from leading authorities, the present editor realizes that not all of the mysteries encountered in the manuscripts have been, or are likely ever to be, resolved.

Appendix B

MAJOR EXTANT MANUSCRIPTS

THE MANUSCRIPTS LISTED below are all portions of the *Journal* except MSS. G, H, M, *Plea*, and W. All are holographs except MSS. G, H, and Y. The holographs of *Some Considerations on the Keeping of Negroes* and *Considerations on Keeping Negroes, Part Second* are missing.

MS. A Composed of 175 pages, 8 × 12¼ inches, covering the years 1720–1770 (Chapters 1–10). Woolman started writing this version at age 36, and kept adding to it until 1770. It is his preliminary draft of the ten chapters, and is in a bound volume that also contains holographs of *A Plea for the Poor* and other essays, together with copies of his letters and miscellaneous notations. In addition, it contains a copy of MS. S (see below) made by Samuel Comfort in 1839. MS. A is now in the Manuscript Department of the Historical Society of Pennsylvania.

MS. B Composed of sheets folded once, not bound, but stitched together with thread, totalling 348 pages that vary from 6 to 7 inches in width and from 7½ to 8 inches in height. These sheets were grouped by Woolman into eleven sections of varying lengths. For the most part these sections are unrelated to the chapter divisions made by the original editorial committee and retained in the present edition.

Woolman definitely wrote nine of these sections in preparation for publication of the *Journal*, after completing MS. A. The other two sections (7 and 9) total only sixteen pages in MS. B. Woolman apparently intended them also for the printer, although the parallel portions of MS. A are later revisions of these sections (cf. Chapter 9, notes 2–16 and 30–46). Except at these two points, after Woolman revised MS. A he copied it to produce MS. B, his final version for the printer, making additional changes in the process. This work was apparently done between early 1770 and his departure for England in 1772. It is certain that MS. B (all eleven sections) was the one the original editorial committee revised for the printer in 1773 and 1774. From this revised copy of MS. B plus a similarly revised copy of MS. S (see below), J. Crukshank printed the first edition in 1774. MS. B is now in the Friends Historical Library of Swarthmore College.

MS. C Composed of forty-eight pages measuring about 6½ × 8 inches, not bound, but stitched together, covering the years 1720–1747 (all of Chapter 1 and the first part of Chapter 2, through "educated in the way of the Presbyterians"). This, the earliest holograph of this portion of the *Journal,* was apparently written at some time between 1747 and 1756. Woolman prepared the first part of MS. A from it, revising extensively as he did so. MS. C is now in the Friends Historical Library of Swarthmore College.

MS. G A longhand copy of Chapters 1–13 of *A Plea for the Poor,* headed: "Extract from . . . *A Word of Remembrance and Caution to the Rich* by John Woolman . . ." and [apparently added later] "Compared since with the printed copy . . . it not being in print when this was written." In the Grubb Collection, Friends Historical Library, Dublin, Ireland.

MS. H A longhand copy of the first thirteen chapters of *A Plea for the Poor,* bearing the initials of the copyists, "J. H. and F. W.," in Waterford, Ireland, and dated January, 1793. This copy bears the title: *A Word of Remembrance and Caution to the Rich.* Correspondence with Henry J. Cadbury (Haverford, Pa.), Olive Goodbody (Dublin), and William M. Glynn (Waterford) has produced two suggestions as to the identity of "J. H."—the names of Joseph Hoyland and John Hancock, prominent Irish Quakers in 1793. In Box 1005A of the Gummere papers in the Quaker Collection at Haverford College Library.

MS. M Composed of two folded sheets with writing on both sides, constituting a total of eight pages. This is stitched together with two more folded sheets that comprise MS. P. Enclosing both MSS. is a cover bearing the inscription: "Manuscript in the handwriting of John Woolman." The cover measures 8¾" high by 6½" wide, the pages being slightly smaller—the same size as those of MS. B.

MS. M is basically a fair copy of Chapter 15 of MS. *Plea.* This is attested by internal evidence, particularly several instances in which revised passages in MS. *Plea* are transcribed smoothly into MS. M. A few substantive changes were made in the process of copying. Yet at certain points MS. *Plea* seems to have been revised after MS. M was copied. Chapter 15 of MS. *Plea* is here reproduced, with all variant MS. M readings indicated in footnotes.

MS. P consists of eight pages, of which the fourth and eighth are blank. The seventh page contains the following statement, which apparently refers to both MS. M and MS. P: "This manuscript is in the handwriting of John Woolman, and some of it is inserted in his *Journal*—and for the sake of the pious author it has been carefully preserved and now left at Friends Library.— T.M.P."

MSS. M and P are in Box R. S. 565 of the Department of Records of the Philadelphia Yearly Meeting, 302 Arch Street, Philadelphia.

MS. P For the physical characteristics and location of MS. P, see MS. M above. This MS. parallels the material in Chapter 9 of the *Journal* from "11th day, 6th month" to the end of the chapter. The wording is almost identical with that of the same section of MS. A as it was before being revised by erasures and insertions. It is practically certain that Woolman first wrote this portion of MS. A, then copied MS. P from it, and later revised MS. A. It is certain that here, as in eight other sections, MS. B was based on the revised MS. A (cf. Chapter 9, notes 56–62).

MS. *Plea*. This is a holograph of *A Plea for the Poor*. Comprising part of the bound volume containing MS. A of the *Journal*, it interrupts the *Journal* near the beginning of Chapter 9. On page 147 of the *Journal* Woolman completed his description of the incident of the magician or juggler, which occurred in 1763; then he wrote: "Journal continued on p. 194." *A Plea for the Poor* appears on pages 148–193. At the top of page 194 Woolman wrote: "Journal continued." The *Journal* then resumes with his comments concerning the Yearly Meeting at Philadelphia in 1764.

Assuming that Woolman wrote MS. A as the events occurred, this location of MS. *Plea* would imply that it had been composed (or at least copied into this volume) in the interval between the appearance of the magician and the Yearly Meeting. On page 191, however, Woolman pasted a note referring to a numbered section in the last chapter of MS. *Plea*: "Note 6 the second was chiefly written some months ago and 6 the first was entered in this book like an abstract from it, but now the 9th day, 10th month, 1769, seriously looking over it, I could not be easy without entering it at large nearly as I had wrote it at first in an unbound book." This seems to mean that most of the original draft of 6 the second (no longer extant) was written ("some months ago") in early 1769. The shorter version (6 the first) was entered in the existing volume some time later, and the original draft was copied into the book (with little alteration) October 9, 1769. Although this part of the essay can thus be dated to 1769, the question of when the earlier parts were composed remains unanswered.

Chapters 1-13 (pages 148–180) were probably written in 1763 and 1764, pages 181–193 being left blank. The continuation of the *Journal* (on p. 194) may have proceeded shortly after the events described (in 1764), Chapters 14–16 of MS. *Plea* being added later on the blank pages.

MSS. R1, R2, and R3. Three fragments written on pages of the same size as those in MS. B. MS. R1 is an extract from two portions of John Churchman's *Journal*, which was copied onto these pages by Woolman (from the author's manuscript before it was published). Woolman later copied it in condensed form into Chapter 5 of MS. A. It does not appear in MS. B but is included in the present edition of the *Journal*.

MS. R2 recounts Woolman's dream of visiting a dictator on a mission of peace. It appears nowhere else in Woolman's extant holographs. It is included in Appendix E of this volume.

MS. R3 is one of three accounts Woolman wrote of a journey to the western shore of Maryland that began in April, 1767. It corresponds to a portion of Chapter 9 of the *Journal*, starting with "Through the humbling dispensations of divine providence" and continuing through "reverent thankfulness to him." The wording is almost identical with that in MS. A before Woolman revised the latter by making erasures and insertions. It is practically certain that Woolman first wrote this portion of MS. A, then copied MS. R3 from it, and later revised MS. A. It is certain that here, as in eight other sections, MS. B was based on the revised MS. A. MS. R3 thus stands in the same relation to MSS. A and B as does MS. P (cf. notes 47–54 to Chapter 9 of the *Journal*, above.)

All three MS. R fragments are in the Rutgers University Library.

MS. S Composed of seventy pages measuring 4 × 6½ inches, contained in a small booklet, the pages of which were stitched together after the writing on them was complete. This is the final version of two extant accounts Woolman wrote of the sea voyage, plus the only extant account in his hand of the English journey. Along with MS. B, these accounts of the sea voyage and English journey (MS. S) were revised by the original editorial committee. They were then printed as Chapters 11 and 12 of the first edition of the *Journal*.

In addition to these chapters of the *Journal*, the booklet contains quotations Woolman copied from books he had read, memoranda he dictated during his illness, a copy of a letter he had written, miscellaneous notations by Woolman and others, and several blank pages. A few entries cannot be certainly identified as belonging in the *Journal*. One for September 28, 1772, has been omitted from all previous editions, although Mrs. Gummere includes it elsewhere in her volume, along with eulogies and documents concerning Woolman's death. Its inclusion in the present edition seems justified by a note at the top of the page where it begins: "Take this in after page 60." This note has been written and then crossed out, and is in a handwriting that cannot be identified. Page 60 contains a letter to a "beloved Friend" dated September 22, which appears in practically all editions. Incidentally, some editions contain an essay on the ministry, which is not in MS. S but was apparently written in England. The present editor has included what seemed most appropriate to him, but a valid case could be made for a slightly different selection.

MS. S is now in the Friends Historical Library at Swarthmore College.

MSS. T1 and T2. These are the two sections of Woolman's preliminary account of his sea voyage, which comprises Chapter 11 of the *Journal*. The first section, up to "24th day, 5th month," is here designated as MS. T1. It is at the Mount School, York, England. The second part, starting where the first ends and continuing to the end of the chapter, is known as the Luke Howard manuscript, after a former owner, and is here designated as MS. T2. It is in the Friends Library, London.

MS. W See Introduction to the Essays, and Addendum.

MS. Y A copy, probably in the handwriting of William Tuke, of that portion of MS. S dealing with Woolman's English journey (Chapter 12 of the *Journal*). It was apparently made before MS. S was sent to America, where the latter was revised by the original editorial committee. Now in the possession of Guy Worsdell, 17 Bedford Gardens, London, W. 8.

Appendix C

Woolman wrote most of MS. B on sheets that he folded once, thus producing four pages. Occasionally he covered both sides of a sheet half as large, which he did not fold, to produce two pages. In either instance the pages were about 6⅛" wide by 7½" high. Woolman grouped the sheets into eleven sections (so designated by the present editor, not Woolman). Starting anew in each section, he numbered or lettered the sheets consecutively; thus every fourth page was so marked (except for a few instances noted below).

The entire manuscript has been stitched together (by whom is unknown) in chronological order, according to Woolman's dates. It corresponds to MS. A, a bound volume in which the pages cannot be rearranged. The pages have been numbered consecutively from beginning to end. The color of ink, width of lines, and style of writing indicate rather clearly that this numbering was done by the original editorial committee.

Under the section headings below are the page numbers (in brackets) corresponding to Woolman's symbols. Also indicated are the notes made by Woolman and the editorial committee on the first pages of several sections. What they refer to cannot always be determined.

As indicated in Appendix A, all but three short sections of MS. B constitute Woolman's latest revised holograph. However, the passages in MS. A corresponding to sections 7 and 9, and parts of the MS. A parallel to section 8, were revised after those portions of MS. B. The latter are preliminary drafts comparable to MSS. R3 and P (see Appendix B). But Woolman did not, as in those instances, make additional clear copies from MS. A (or if he did make them, they were lost). As nearly as can be determined, he left these sections of MS. B (along with the other, final ones) with the original editorial committee for the printer. At least the committee and printer included them in the published volume.

Perhaps Woolman intended to replace these sections with later copies (or to incorporate in them the revisions he made in MS. A) but was unable to do this before leaving for England. Or he may have felt that the wording of the two versions was so much alike (although MS. A was smoother) that to make extra copies was unneccessary. And he may have wished to avoid the confusion involved in referring the committee to MS. A at these points and back to MS. B for the rest; these sections could be fitted into the final document, whereas MS. A was a bound volume from which sheets could not be removed. Or, upon reflection, he may have decided that he preferred the preliminary versions to the final ones.

The editorial problem here was whether to follow Woolman's apparent intentions and print MS. B as a unit, or shift to the MS. A parallels of sections 7, 9, and parts of 8 and then back to MS. B. The present editor decided to print MS. B as a unit, including these sections, while supplying in footnotes and appendix all variant readings in MS. A which were written later. Thus both versions are available to the reader.

Concerning section 7 of MS. B, the present editor cannot determine with certainty whether it was written before or after the *first* draft of its MS. A parallel. At one time they were essentially alike. Then MS. A was revised by erasures and insertions, including a passage pasted in. These revisions were not made in this section of MS. B; it retains the deleted words and lacks the insertions. That Woolman worked back and forth between these two manuscripts adds to the complexity. It is clear, however, that Woolman's latest revision of this passage is in MS. A. Footnotes 2 through 16 of Chapter 9 describe the chief evidence for these conclusions and cite the most significant variant readings in MS. A. The entire MS. A parallel is printed in this section of the Appendix (see below).

For the most part, section 8 of MS. B is later than its MS. A parallel. At some points, however, MS. A is later. Either way, the later passage is essentially a transcription of the other. Hence the two versions read nearly alike. Footnotes 17 through 29 of Chapter 9 indicate every difference in wording, specifying which version seems later at that point. Thus the reader can readily reconstruct Woolman's final words.

Regarding section 9 of MS. B: This was written before the MS. A parallel and then revised. Later it was copied into MS. A with little further revision, producing a very smooth copy. Since all variations are given in footnotes 30 through 46 of Chapter 9, the MS. A parallel can be readily reconstructed.

It is interesting that only in relation to Chapter 9 do we find later passages in MS. A, extra holographs closely related to MS. A (MSS. R3 and P), and an account which never found its way into the *Journal* (cf. Appendix E). This part of MS. A may have been composed in the late 1760's (possibly on the basis of earlier records), not long before MS. B was transcribed for the printer. This would tend to explain his working back and forth between the two holographs more than he did in the earlier chapters, where the dates of composition were more widely separated.

Here follows an outline of the sections plus the MS. A parallel to section 7:

Section 1

Notation by Woolman in margin of page 1: "First."
In his alphabetical designation, here as elsewhere, Woolman omitted "J."
Half-size sheet (in contrast to the others, which are folded): "O."
Woolman's letters, with the corresponding page numbers in brackets: A[1–4], B[5–8], C[9–12], D[13–16], E[17–20], F[21–24], G[25–28], H[29–32], I[33–36], K[37–40], L[41–44], M[45–48], N[49–52], O[53–54].

Section 2

Two notations, apparently by Woolman, in the margin of page 55, each of which has been crossed out, apparently by the original editorial committee: "Second," "Page 23." The parallel narrative in MS. A begins on page 23.
Woolman's numbers, with the corresponding page numbers in brackets: 1[55–58], 2[59–62], 3[63–66], 4[67–70], 5[71–74], 6[75–78], 7[79–82], 8[83–86], 9[87–90], 10[91–94], 11[95–98], 12[99–102], 13[103–106], 14[107–110], 15[111–114], 16[115–118], 17[119–122], 18[123–126], 19[127–130], 20[131–134], 21[135–138].

Section 3

Notations, apparently by Woolman, in margin of page 139: "Third" (crossed out, apparently by Woolman), "Second," "page 68." Page 68 of

MS. A begins at this point, as does Chapter 5 (established by the original editorial committee and followed by all subsequent editors).

Half-size sheet: "C."

Woolman's letters, with the corresponding page numbers in brackets: A[139–142], B[143–146], C[147–148].

Section 4

Half-size sheets: "c" and "l."

Woolman's letters, with the corresponding page numbers in brackets: a[149–152], b[153–156], c[157–158], d[159–162], e[163–166], f[167–170], g[171–174], h[175–178], i[179–182], k[183–186], l[187–188].

Section 5

Notations, apparently by Woolman, in margin of page 189: "Fourth" (crossed out, apparently by the committee), "102," and "5." Page 102 of MS. A begins at this point, as does Chapter 7.

Pages 190–221 inclusive are numbered in pencil, whereas the others are numbered in black ink. The handwriting in all appears to be the same.

Half-size sheets: "13" and "18," the latter written on one side only.

Woolman's numbers, with the corresponding page numbers in brackets: 5[189–192], 6[193–196], 7[197–200], 8[201–204], 9[205–208], 10[209–212], 11[213–216], 12[217–220], 13[221–222], 14[223–226], 15[227–230], 16[231–234], 17[235–238], 18[239].

Section 6

Notation by the committee in margin of page 240: "(Third part) containing 118 pages."

Woolman's numbers, with the corresponding page numbers in brackets: 1[240–243], 2[244–247], 3[248–251], 4[252–255], 5[256–259], 6[260–263], 7[264–267], 8[268–271], 9[272–275], 10[276–279], 11[280–283], 12[284–287].

Section 7

Notations and deletion, apparently by Woolman, in margin of page 288: "Sixth" (crossed out) and "fourth."

The paper used for this section, and for sections 8 and 9, is of a different texture from that in the preceding sections. Page 292 is a half page, pasted in. A detailed comparison reveals clearly that the corresponding section of MS. A (pp. 194–196), as revised, is later than this section of MS. B (see explanation above).

Woolman's numbers, with the corresponding page numbers in brackets: 1[288–291], not numbered [292].

Section 8

The color of the ink is darker here than in the preceding or the following sections. For the most part this section is clearly later than the corresponding pages of MS. A, but a few revisions made by Woolman in MS. A were not incorporated into this section of MS. B.

Half-size sheet: "B."

Woolman's letters, with the corresponding page numbers in brackets: A[293–296], B[297–298].

Section 9

Notations and deletion, apparently by Woolman, in margin of page 299: "Eighth" (crossed out) and "fifth."

Like section 7, this section of MS. B is not as late a version as the revised parallel passage in MS. A.

Page 310 is blank.

Woolman's letters, with the corresponding page numbers in brackets: A[299–302], B[303–306], C[307–310].

Section 10

Except for a short paragraph, this section is paralleled by MSS. P and R3, which are unquestionably earlier drafts, as is MS. A. The paper used in this section and the next is softer and of larger dimensions (7" wide and 7⅞" high) than in the rest of MS. B.

Half-size sheet: "B."

Woolman's letters, with the corresponding page numbers in brackets: A[311–314], B[315–316], C[317–320], D[321–324].

Section 11

Chapter 10 starts at page 325.

Half-size sheets: pages 341–342 (page 342 is blank), and also 6.

Woolman's numbers, with the corresponding page numbers in brackets:

1[325–328], 2[329–332], 3[333–336], 4[337–340], not numbered [341–342], 5[343–346], 6[347–348].

Transcription of MS. A Parallel to Section 7

Notes at our Yearly Meeting at Philadelphia in the 9th month, 1764.

John Smith of Chester County, aged upward of eighty years, a faithful minister though not eloquent, in our meeting of ministers and elders on the 25th, stood up and appearing to be under a great exercise of spirit informed Friends that he had been a member of the Society upward of sixty years, and well remembered that in those early times Friends were a plain, lowly-minded people and that there was much tenderness and contrition in their meetings; that at the end of twenty years from that time the Society increasing in wealth and in some degree conforming to the fashions of the world, true humility decreased and their meetings in general were not so lively and edifying; that at the end of forty years many in the Society were grown rich and that wearing of fine costly garments and silver watches, with fashionable furniture, became customary with many, and with their sons and daughters; and as these things prevailed in the Society and appeared in our meetings of ministers and elders, so the powerful overshadowings of the Holy Spirit were less manifested amongst us; that there had been an increase of outward greatness till now, and that the weakness amongst us in not living up to our principles and supporting the testimony of Truth in faithfulness was matter of much sorrow.

He then mentioned the uncertainty of his attending Yearly Meetings in future [Woolman's footnote keyed to this point: "It was the last Yearly Meeting he attended."], expecting his dissolution was near. And as pious parents, finally departing from their families, express their last and fervent desires for their good, so did he most tenderly express his concern for us, and signified that he had seen in the true light that the Lord would bring forth his people from that worldly spirit into which too many were thus degenerated, and that his faithful servants must go through great and heavy exercises before this work was brought about.

The 29th day. The committee appointed by the Yearly Meeting sometime since to visit the Quarterly and Monthly Meetings now made report in writing in which they signified that in the course of their proceedings they had been apprehensive that some [Note by Woolman: "Get the report," followed by blank space of about seven lines].

After this report was read an exercise revived on my mind which at times had attended me several years, and inward cries to the Lord were raised in me that the fear of man might not hinder me from doing what he required of me; and so standing up in his dread, I spake in substance as follows:

"I have felt a tenderness in my mind toward persons in two circumstance mentioned in that report—that is, toward such active members who keep slaves and them who are in those offices in government—and have desired that Friends in all their conduct may be kindly affectioned one toward another. Many Friends who keep slaves are under some exercise on that account and at times think about trying them with freedom, but find many things in their way; and the manner of living and annual expenses of some of them are such that it is impracticable for them to set their slaves free without changing their own way of life.

"It has been my lot to be often abroad, and I have observed in some places at Quarterly and Yearly Meetings and at some stages where travelling Friends and their horses are often entertained that the yearly expense of individuals therein is very considerable. And Friends in some places crowding much on persons in these circumstances for entertainment hath often rested as a burden on my mind for some years past, and I now express it in the fear of the Lord, greatly desiring that Friends now present may duly consider it."

And I may here add what then occurred to me though I did not mention it, to wit: In fifty pounds are four hundred half crowns; if a slave be valued at fifty pounds and I with my horse put his owner to half a crown expense, and I with many others for a course of years repeat these expenses four hundred times without any compensation, then on a fair computation this slave may be accounted a slave to the public under the direction of the man he calls master.

Appendix D

THE DISCOVERY OF A MISSING FRAGMENT

IN CHAPTER 6 of the *Journal*, instead of the brief statement introducing the Epistle of the Philadelphia Yearly Meeting of 1759, Woolman originally wrote the following, which he then crossed out: "A short-time before I went to this Yearly Meeting, I felt a weight on my mind in respect to writing on some subjects then before me, whereupon I wrote an essay of a general epistle which, being examined and corrected by the committee on the epistle, was signed by a number of Friends in behalf of the meeting, and is as follows." In MS. A, Woolman wrote and crossed out a statement that reads the same, except that "opened" appears after "then." He inserted the same substitute sentence. The original sentence establishes Woolman's authorship of the epistle. Two additional notes by Woolman appear in MS. B (but not in MS. A). The first (written twice) reads: "Here take in the printed epistle of 1759." The second is dated, probably to indicate that it is Woolman's final suggestion: "1772. I am easy that that epistle be left out. J. W."

· Although the epistle itself does not appear either in MS. B or in MS. A (as it is at present), it is printed in the first edition. Also printed in the first edition are the four paragraphs that follow the epistle (through "in his work"). Although these paragraphs appear in MS. B, they are missing from MS. A. This curious omission has been previously noted, but no explanation for it has been forthcoming.

In 1967 the present editor made an interesting discovery among the Woolman manuscripts in the Friends Historical Library at Swarthmore College. It consisted of a four-page folder, on the first three pages of which is printed the Epistle of the Philadelphia Yearly Meeting of 1759. On the fourth page appear the four paragraphs by Woolman that are missing from MS. A. At the bottom of the page is the word "Compar'd," written by a member of the original editorial committee (as had been done at several points in MS. A, to indicate that MS. A had been compared with MS. B in preparing the latter for the printer).

At the top of the first page of the epistle, the following had been written by Woolman and later crossed out, presumably by the original editorial committee: "Do not print this epistle. The substance of it is other [ways?] published. John Woolman." Along the inner margin of this first page is red paste like that used elsewhere by Woolman. Along the inner margin of page 97 of MS. A are clear traces of paste of the same color. It is evident that these pages containing the epistle and Woolman's four paragraphs were pasted into MS. A so as to appear between pages 97 and 98. They fit into this context perfectly. How they were separated from the remainder of the manuscript and came to rest in a different library can only be conjectured.

The four paragraphs (like the rest of MS. A) have been revised by Woolman, some words having been crossed out and others inserted. As elsewhere in copying from MS. A, Woolman incorporated these changes smoothly into MS. B. Although the changes are all minor, four are worth noting. In the second paragraph after the epistle, discussing his vocation, he crossed out "secret" before "draught." In the next paragraph he made three changes that improved the style and lessened the emphasis on the severity of his trials. "Sad and sorrowful" became simply "sad." He removed "great" from "in times of great trial," and "hard and painful" became simply "hard."

Appendix E

WOOLMAN'S DREAM OF A PEACE MISSION

THE FOLLOWING account of a significant dream recorded by Woolman is designated as R₂ in the list of extant manuscripts (see Appendix B). Like MSS. P and R₃, it would fit chronologically into Chapter 9. Since it does not appear in either MS. A or MS. B, however, it is reproduced here rather than in the *Journal* proper:

26th day, 7th month, 1764. At night I dreamed I was abroad on a religious visit beyond the sea and had been out upward of two months, and that while I was out on the visit the people of the country where I was and those of a neighbouring kingdom, having concerns together in affairs abroad, had difference which arose so high that they began to fight; and both parties were preparing for a general war. I thought there was no sea between them, but only bounded by a line, and that the man who was chief amongst the other people lived within a day's journey of where I was.

I, being troubled at these things, felt a desire in my mind to go and speak with this chief man and try to prevail on him to stop fighting, that they might enquire more fully into the grounds of their disagreement and endeavour to accommodate their difference without shedding more blood. So I set off, having one man with me as a pilot; and after travelling some time in the woods, we came in sight of a few of those people at labour, having guns with them. I being foremost came near them before they saw us, and as soon as they discovered that we were from their enemies' country they took up their guns and were preparing to fire on us, whereupon I hastily approached them, holding up both my arms to let them see that I had no warlike weapons. So I shook hands with them and let them know the cause of our coming, at which they appeared well pleased. In the surprise at our meeting, my pilot held forth a small gun he had with him, which I knew not of before; but they so soon understood our business that none fired, after which I saw my pilot no more.

But one of these people offering to conduct me to their chief man, he and I set forward and travelled along a path through woods and swamps near southeast; and on our way my new pilot, who

297

could talk broken English, spake to me with an agreeable countenance and desired that when I came before their chief I would speak my mind freely, and signified their salutation at meeting was to speak to each other but not to shake hands. At length we came to the house of this chief man, whom I thought had the command of the soldiers and was at the head of the affairs of their country, but was not called a king. His house stood by itself, and a good garden with green herbs before the door, in which garden I stood while my pilot went to tell this chief man that I wanted to speak with him. As I stood alone in the garden my mind was exercised on the affair I came upon, and presently my pilot returned, and passing by me said he had forgot to tell me that I had an invitation to dinner. Soon after him came the chief man, who having been told the cause of my coming looked on me with a friendly countenance, and as I was about to enter on the business I awoke. JOHN WOOLMAN.

Appendix F

INSERTION AT THE BEGINNING OF CHAPTER 11

A MYSTERY at the beginning of Chapter 11 is that the original editorial committee crossed off the heading "Memorandum . . . Visit" and put in a sign (#) indicating that an insertion was to be made before "My beloved friend Samuel Emlen, Jr." Such an insertion appears in the first printed edition. The present editor has been unable to locate its source, or to ascertain whether it was written by Woolman or by the original editorial committee. Quite probably it was written by Woolman on a loose sheet that was used by the printer and then lost. The pages of MS. S were sewed together at some time after the committee revised and numbered the pages—as can be seen by an examination of page 395, where the stitching goes through writing added in the margin by the committee. Incidentally, in the following paragraph the date of the certificate was printed as "8th month," and the error corrected with a pen (as it probably was in all copies of the first edition) to read "3rd month." The insertion follows:

Having been some time under a religious concern to prepare for crossing the seas in order to visit Friends in the northern parts of England, and more particularly in Yorkshire, after weighty consideration I thought it expedient to inform Friends at our Monthly Meeting at Burlington of it, who, having unity with me therein, gave me a certificate. And I afterwards communicated the same to our Quarterly Meeting. And they likewise certified their concurrence therewith, some time after which, at the General Spring Meeting of Ministers and Elders, I thought it my duty to acquaint them of the religious exercise which attended my mind, with which they likewise signified their unity by a certificate dated the 24th day of the 3rd month, 1772, directed to Friends in Great Britain.

In the 4th month following, I thought the time was come for me to make some inquiry for a suitable conveyance, being apprehensive that as my concern was principally toward the northern parts of England, it would be most proper to go in a vessel bound to Liverpool or Whitehaven. And while I was at Philadelphia deliberating on this occasion, I was informed that [my beloved friend Samuel . . .]

Appendix G

A GLOSS ON A MATHEMATICAL CALCULATION

WOOLMAN frequently used mathematical calculations to prove or illustrate a statement. One such calculation is found in Chapter 6 of *A Plea for the Poor*. In connection with it, Woolman several times revised the first paragraph of Chapter 6. The three passages he rejected (themselves the products of revision) are as follows:

1. Written first, on page 156 of the MS. (following "to revive them"):

That portion of [At this point are two lines that have been obliterated by an insert Woolman pasted over them.] . . . What labouring men buy, being dear, their wages are necessarily high, and thence a large portion of labour expected from them. Were more men employed in preparing the real necessaries of life, these necessaries being more plenty might be sold cheaper, and labouring men having them at a low rate might ask less for a day's labour, or a certain piece of work; and they working for low wages, their employers might be satisfied with having less done in a day or a week. Thus labourers being plenty and real necessaries plenty,"

The final word "plenty" connects with the last part of the paragraph Woolman retained, so that it is followed immediately by "a small portion" (see the first paragraph of Chapter 6).

2. At the top of the insert pasted in by Woolman (after "that portion of"):

the necessaries of life answerable to a day's labour is such that those who support their families by day's labour find occasion to labour hard; and many of them think strong drink a necessary part of their entertainment.

3. At the bottom of the same insert:

For if four men working eight hours in a day raise and clean three hundred bushels of grain (or twelve hundred pounds of flax) with sixty days labour, then five men working six hours and twenty-four minutes in a day would at that rate do the same business in the same time.

Appendix H

WOOLMAN'S FINAL ILLNESS AND DEATH

DURING HIS FINAL ILLNESS Woolman stayed at Almery Garth, the home of Thomas and Sarah Priestman,* just outside the city of York. Here he was cared for chiefly by Esther (Mrs. William) Tuke.* William Tuke * also spent many hours with him. Priestman and Tuke (and perhaps others) made a careful record of those last days, from which the following account was composed, very likely by Priestman. (It has been transcribed from a photostatic copy in the Quaker collection at the Haverford College Library. The present editor has spelled out and capitalized days of the week to distinguish them from the days of the month.)

✤ ✤ ✤ ✤

Some Account of His Illness and Death

He came to the city of York the 21st day of the 9th month and Second Day of the week, and having been poorly in health for some time before, apprehended the like feverish disorder he usually had at that season of the year was coming upon him.

The Quarterly Meeting of Ministers and Elders was held in the evening of Third Day, and the sittings of the Quarterly Meeting for business and meetings for worship on Fourth and Fifth Days, all which he was enabled to attend except the parting meeting for worship. He appeared in the ministry greatly to the comfort and satisfaction of Friends, the spring of the gospel flowing through him with great purity and sweetness. His last testimony was in a meeting for discipline, on the subject of the slave trade, remarking that as Friends had been solicitous for, and obtained relief from, many of their sufferings, so he recommended this oppressed part of the creation to their notice, that they may in an individual capacity, as way may open, remonstrate their hardships and sufferings to those in authority, especially the legislative power in this kingdom.

His illness growing upon him, some spots appeared upon his face, like the smallpox, on Seventh Day; and the next day it appeared beyond a doubt that was his disorder. As he had seldom eaten flesh for some time, and from the symptoms at first, there was hopes he would have had the disorder favourably, but a great quantity of spots began to appear the 3rd and 4th days, so that he was pretty full, and though not so loaded as many, yet for the most part was greatly afflicted, but bore it with the utmost meekness, patience, resignation, and Christian fortitude, frequently uttering many comfortable and instructive expressions, some of which being minuted down or remembered are as follows: [Marginal note keyed to this point]—He often said it was hid from him whether he should recover or not, and he was not desirous to know it, but from his own feeling of the disorder and his feeble constitution, thought he should not. [End of note]

First Day, 27th of 9th month. His disorder appearing to be the small-pox, being asked to have a doctor's advice, he signified he had not liberty in his mind so to do, standing wholly resigned to his will who gave him life and whose power he had witnessed to heal him in sicknesses before, when he seemed nigh unto death; but if he was to wind up now, he was perfectly resigned, having no will either to live or die, and did not choose any should be sent for to him. But a young man of our Society, an apoth-ecary, coming of his own accord the next day and proposing to do something for him, he said he found freedom to confer with him and the other Friends about him, and if anything should be proposed as to medi-cine that did not come through defiled channels or oppressive hands, he should be willing to consider and take it so far as he found freedom.

The next day said he felt the disorder affect his head, so that he could think little and but as a child, and desired if his understanding should be more affected, to have nothing given him that those about him knew he had a testimony against.

The same day, he desired a Friend to write, and brake forth as follows:

"O Lord my God! The amazing horrors of darkness were gathered around me and covered me all over, and I saw no way to go forth. I felt the depth and extent of the misery of my fellow creatures separated from the divine harmony, and it was heavier than I could bear, and I was crushed down under it. I lifted up my hand and I stretched out my arm, but there was none to help me. I looked round about and was amazed in the depths of misery. O Lord! I remembered that thou art omnipotent, that I had called thee Father, and I felt that I loved thee; and I was made quiet in thy will and I waited for deliverance from thee. Thou hadst pity upon me when no man could help me. I saw that meekness under suffering was showed unto us in the most affecting example of thy Son, and thou wast teaching me to follow him; and I said, 'Thy will, O Father, be done.' "

Fourth Day morning. Being asked how he felt himself, he meekly answered, "I don't know that I have slept this night. I feel the disorder making its progress, but my mind is mercifully preserved in stillness and peace." Sometime after, he said he was sensible the pains of death must be hard to bear, but if he escaped them now, he must sometime pass through them, and did not know he could be better prepared, but had no will in it. Said he had settled his outward affairs to his mind, had taken leave of his wife and family as never to return, leaving them to the divine protection, adding, "and though I feel them near to me at this time, yet I freely give them up, having an hope they will be provided for," and a little after, said, "This trial is made easier than I could have thought, by my will being wholly taken away, for if I was anxious as to the event, it would be harder, but I am not, and my mind enjoys a perfect calm."

At another time he said he was a little uneasy, lest any should think he had put himself into the hands of the young man and another apothecary, who of their own choice attended him, and desired Friends might be informed, and he would inform the young man, upon what bottom they attended him, being of the same judgment his friends in America and some here knew he had been of, but that he found a freedom to confer with them, finding nature needed support during the time permitted to struggle with the disorder—that he had no objection to use the things in the creation for real use and in their proper places, but any thing that came through defiled channels or oppressive hands he could not touch with, having had a testimony to bear against those things, which he hoped to bear to the last.

He lay for a considerable time in a still, sweet frame, uttering many broken expressions, part of which were thus: "My soul is poured out unto thee like water, and my bones are out of joint. I saw a vision in which I beheld the great confusion of those that depart from thee—I saw their horror and great distress—I was made sensible of their misery. Then was I greatly distressed—I looked unto thee; thou wast underneath and supported me. I likewise saw the great calamity that is coming upon this disobedient nation."

In the night, a young woman having given him something to drink, he said, "My child, thou seemest very kind to me, a poor creature; the Lord will reward thee for it." A while after, he cried out with great earnestness of spirit, "O my Father! My Father! How comfortable art thou to my soul in this trying season!" Being asked if he could take a little nourishment, after some pause he replied, "I cannot tell what to say to it. I seem nearly arrived where my soul shall have rest from all its troubles."

After giving in something to be put into his journal, he said, "I believe the Lord will now excuse me from exercise of this kind, and I see now no work but one, which is to be the last wrought by me in this world; the messenger will come that will release me from all these troubles, but it must be in the Lord's time, which I am waiting for. I have laboured to do whatever was required, according to the ability received, in the remembrance of which I have peace; and though the disorder is strong at times and would come over my mind like a whirlwind, yet it has hitherto been kept steady and centered in everlasting love, and if that's mercifully continued, I ask nor desire no more."

At another time said he had long had a view of visiting this nation and some time before he came, had a dream in which he saw himself in the northern parts of it, and that the spring of the gospel was opened in him much as in the beginning of Friends, such as George Fox and William Dewsbury. And he saw the different states of the people as clear as ever he had seen flowers in a garden; but in his going on he was suddenly stopped, though he could not see for what end, but looked towards home and thereupon fell into a flood of tears which waked him. At another time said, "My draught seemed strongest to the north, and I mentioned in my own Monthly Meeting that attending the Quarterly Meeting at York, and being there, looked like home to me."

Fifth Day night. Having repeatedly consented to take a medicine with a view to settle his stomach, but without effect, the Friend then waiting on him said, through distress, "What shall I do now?" He answered with great composure, "Rejoice evermore, and in everything give thanks," but added a little after, "This is sometimes hard to come at."

Sixth Day morning early. He brake forth in supplication on this wise, "O Lord! It was thy power that enabled me to forsake sin in my youth, and I have felt thy bruises since for disobedience, but as I bowed under them, thou healedst he; and though I have gone through many trials and sore afflictions, thou hast been with me, continuing a father and a friend. I feel thy power now and beg that in the approaching trying moments, thou wilt keep my heart steadfast unto thee."

Upon giving the same Friend directions concerning some little things, she said, "I will take care, but hope thou mayest live to order them thyself." He replied, "My hope is in Christ, and though I may now seem a little better, a change in the disorder may soon happen and my little strength be dissolved; and if it so happen, I shall be gathered to my everlasting rest."

On her saying she did not doubt that, but could not help mourning to see so many faithful servants removed at so low a time, he said, "All good cometh from the Lord, whose power is the same, and can work as he sees best." The same day after giving her directions about wrapping his corpse, and perceiving her to weep, he said, "I had rather thou wouldst guard against weeping and sorrowing for me, my sister. I sorrow not, though I have had some painful conflicts; but now they seem over and matters all settled, and I look at the face of my dear Redeemer, for sweet is his voice and his countenance comely."

First Day, 4th of 10th month. Being very weak and in general difficult to be understood, he uttered a few words in commemoration of the Lord's goodness to him, and added, "How tenderly have I been waited on in this time of affliction, in which I may say in Job's words, Tedious days and 'wearisome nights are appointed to me' [Job 7:3]; and how many are spending their time and money in vanities and superfluities, while thousands and tens of thousands want the necessaries of life, who might be relieved by them, and their distress at such a time as this in some degree softened, by the administering of suitable things."

Second Day morning. The apothecary not in profession with us, who also appeared very anxious to assist him, being present, he queried about the probability of such a load of matter being thrown off his weak body; and the apothecary making some remarks implying he thought it might, he spake with an audible voice on this wise, "My dependence is in the Lord Jesus Christ, who I trust will forgive my sins, which is all I hope for. And if it be his will to raise up this body again, I am content, and if die [sic], I am resigned. And if thou canst not be easy without trying to assist nature in order to lengthen out my life, I submit."

After this, his throat was so much affected that it was very difficult for him to speak so as to be understood, and frequently wrote, though blind, when he wanted anything.

About the 2nd hour on Fourth Day morning, he asked for pen and ink and at several times, with much difficulty, wrote thus, "I believe my being here is in the wisdom of Christ; I know not as to life or death." A little before six the same morning, he appeared to fall into an easy sleep, which continued about half an hour. Then seeming to awake, he breathed a few times with a little more difficulty, and so expired without sigh, groan, or struggle.

Thus, this patient and faithful servant of the Lord finished a life of deep exercise and many sorrows, at the house of his friend Thomas Priestman,* aforementioned, the 7th day of the 10th month, 1772, and was interred in Friends burying ground the 9th of the same, after a large and solid meeting held on the occasion in the great meeting house.

✤ ✤ ✤ ✤

According to a letter written by William Tuke * to Reuben Haines on October 26, 1772, during his final illness Woolman told Tuke "that he was not willing to have the coffin of oak, because it is a wood more useful than ash for some other purposes." He then dictated the following to Tuke, which Woolman then signed:

> YORK, 29th of 9th month, 1772. An ash coffin made plain without any manner of superfluities—the corpse to be wrapped in cheap flannel, the expense of which I leave my wearing clothes to defray, as also the digging of the grave; and I desire that William Tuke may take my clothes after my decease and apply them accordingly. JOHN WOOLMAN

Biographical Notes

THE NAMES LISTED HERE are those marked with an asterisk in the text. They include Woolman's travelling companions, persons mentioned more than once in his writings, and a few others who figure prominently in his experiences. With one exception, all those listed were contemporaries of Woolman; other persons mentioned have been identified in footnotes. Additional information concerning those listed below can be obtained by consulting the index. In preparing this data the editor has depended primarily on the typewritten "Dictionary of Quaker Biography" in the Haverford College Library.

ANDREWS, ISAAC (?-1775). For many years Isaac and his brothers Jacob and Peter were close neighbors of Woolman in Mount Holly. Their father was converted through the preaching of Thomas Chalkley, a noted Quaker. As a youth, Isaac also had a striking conversion experience. He was prominent in his home congregation and frequently visited other Quaker meetings.

ANDREWS, JACOB (?-?). A farmer for a time, he later founded the village of Jacobstown and operated a general store. He was active in the Quaker ministry.

ANDREWS, PETER (1707-1756). A minister recorded at the same time as Woolman, he travelled not only through the American colonies but also to England, where he spent the last year of his life.

BENEZET, ANTHONY (1713-1784). Born in France, he went to England, where he became a Quaker. He migrated to America at the age of eighteen. A teacher in Quaker schools for most of his life, and a close associate of Woolman, he was a prolific writer of tracts and carried on a voluminous correspondence with notable people in England and France. His widely distributed writings were very influential in the growing antislavery movement.

CASEY, JOHN (1695-1767). A prominent Newport Quaker, he served several years as clerk of the meeting for ministers and elders and as a member of the committee to revise the New England Discipline. According to Mrs. Gummere (236), he may have been the "ancient Friend" to whom Woolman spoke with too little charity during the debate about lotteries (Chapter 7).

CHILAWAY, JOB (?-1796). An Indian with a fluent command of English, he frequently served as guide and interpreter for government and army officials. He was a convert to the Moravian church and a friend of Papunehang at Wyalusing. He played a prominent role in complicated negotiations over land involving the Indians, the government, and the Bethlehem Synod of the Moravian church.

CHURCHMAN, JOHN (1705-1775). An influential Quaker, he shared a number of Woolman's attitudes and concerns. He declined the position of justice of the peace because "God called him to avoid worldly cumber." He travelled widely as a minister in America and Europe. With Woolman he visited slaveowners in 1759 to confront them with the implications of their practice.

COX, WILLIAM (?-1782). An emigrant from England, he settled in Maryland, where his home became a lodging place for travelling Quakers. He opposed the payment of war taxes. He was apparently a slaveholder and may have been involved in the slave trade. In his last illness he expressed regret that he had not always lived up to the light given him, particularly in regard to plain and simple living.

EASTBURN, SAMUEL (1702-1785). Busy in several Quaker affairs, he shared many of Woolman's concerns, including opposition to war taxes.

EMLEN, SAMUEL (1730-1799). Raised in a wealthy Philadelphia household, he was well educated and an able linguist. He travelled through the southern colonies and visited the British Isles several times as a Quaker minister. He was well known and highly regarded both within and beyond Quaker circles.

FARRINGTON, ABRAHAM (ca. 1691-1758). A native of Bucks County, Pa., he became a resident of Burlington, N. J., in 1733. He carried on a business as a real estate agent and administrator of property in Philadelphia. He also travelled in the Quaker ministry, and died in England after an extensive journey through the northern counties.

FOULKE, SAMUEL (1718-1797). His grandfather had emigrated from Wales to Pennsylvania in 1698, and his father had settled in Richland, Bucks County. Samuel served for thirty-seven years as clerk of the Richland Monthly Meeting, and for seven years was a member of the Pennsylvania Assembly.

FRANKLIN, MATTHEW (ca. 1699-1780). A native of Long Island, he was active there in Quaker affairs, and took a special interest in distributing Woolman's writings.

GAUNTT, ANN (Ridgway) (1710-?). A native of Little Egg Harbor, N. J., she began preaching while she was in her teens and was still active at the age of seventy-seven. Her husband, whom she married at twenty, was a noted local wit, besides being a highly respected Friend and a man of wealth and influence in the community.

HALLETT, RICHARD (1691-1769). A native of Newtown, Long Island, he was a recorded minister—the only member of his family who was a Friend. Married twice, he had five children. His home was often visited by travelling Friends, including Thomas Chalkley, who noted the occasion in his journal.

HORNE, WILLIAM (1714-1772). Born in England, he emigrated to Philadelphia and later settled in Darby. He travelled as a minister throughout the middle colonies and New England, returning to England for a stay of over a year (1763-64). Woolman was twice a guest in his home, which was a center of entertainment for passing Friends.

HOSKINS, JANE (FENN) (1693-1770). Born in London, she travelled to Philadelphia as an indentured servant at the age of nineteen. Later she was employed as tutor and housekeeper in several Quaker homes. Becoming an itinerant minister, she sailed first to Barbados and then to England. After her marriage at the age of forty-five, she made a voyage to the British Isles and continued travelling as a minister in the colonies.

HUNT, WILLIAM (1733-1772). The son of William Hunt of Bucks County, Pa., and Mary Woolman, he was a cousin of John Woolman. Another cousin, John Hunt, kept a journal, which has been published in *Friends' Miscellany*, X (Philadelphia, 1837). Throughout most of his life William Hunt lived at Guilford, North Carolina. He had eight children. After extensive travels as a minister in America, he embarked for England exactly a year before Woolman did. They were together at the London Yearly Meeting in June, 1772. Hunt died of smallpox at Newcastle-upon-Tyne, England, September 9, 1772.

JONES, BENJAMIN (1728-1791). He accompanied Woolman on at least four of his trips. Otherwise little is known of his career.

KINSEY, JOHN III (1693-1750). The son of a Speaker of the New Jersey Assembly, he was appointed Chief Justice of the Pennsylvania Supreme Court, and later became Speaker of the Assembly of Pennsylvania. He also served as clerk of the Philadelphia Yearly Meeting for over twenty years. After his death his reputation was marred by evidence that he had misappropriated public funds.

NAYLER, JAMES. No information about the "lad" is available. However, the "uncle to his father" is the famous James Nayler (ca. 1618-1660), a former quartermaster in the British army, who was converted to the Quaker faith. He became one of the most prominent early Friends, and his powerful preaching led his followers to venerate him as though he were Christ himself. For accepting their homage, he was punished by the government and disowned by the Quakers, who reinstated him after he repented. He is best known in the twentieth century for a saying attributed to him shortly before his death: "There is a spirit . . . that delights to do no evil . . ."

NICHOLS, JOSEPH (1730-ca. 1774). Apparently a very effective speaker, he was one of the first men to preach against slaveholding in Maryland and Virginia. His followers (called "Nicholites" or "New Quakers") attended Quaker meetings until they founded their own sect in 1774. Their beliefs remained very similar to those of the Friends: they emphasized simplicity (plain furniture, undyed clothing, etc.) and opposed slavery, war, and oath-taking. They laid particular stress upon the immanence of the Holy Spirit. By 1780 slaveholding had been prohibited among their members. By 1800, practically all of the sect were again members of the Society of Friends and had transferred their corporate property to it.

PAPUNEHANG (ca. 1705-1775). A chief of the Delaware Indians, he was a spiritual leader of his people both before and after becoming a Christian.

He was converted by David Zeisberger (see *Journal*, Chapter 8, note 16). He represented his tribe in meetings with other tribes, with colonial officials, and with the Quakers. His gentle disposition and spiritual sensitivity greatly impressed the white Christians who knew him.

PARVIN, BENJAMIN (1727–?). Born and educated in Ireland, he was named for his grandfather, who had been imprisoned for his Quaker beliefs. After emigrating to America his father eventually settled in Berks County, Pa., serving as county coroner, and later becoming a member of the Pennsylvania Assembly. Benjamin remained in Berks County, where he was a surveyor and also served as coroner.

PEMBERTON, ISRAEL (1715–1779), JAMES (1723–1809), and JOHN (1727–1795). The Pemberton brothers were prominent Quakers and civic leaders in Philadelphia. They were all well educated, successful in business, and inclined toward philanthropy. During the French and Indian War they sought to establish closer and more friendly relations with the Indians. Because of their pacifism, they were arrested and imprisoned in Virginia during the Revolutionary War. Israel seems to have advised Woolman on financial matters. All three served on the original committee that edited the *Journal*.

POWELL, AMOS (1700–1749). A native of Long Island, he never married. When Woolman and Samuel Eastburn travelled in the ministry through New England, Powell joined them on Long Island and rode with them for at least the three days they spent in Connecticut.

PRIESTMAN, THOMAS (1736–1812). He followed the business of his father, a tanner. In 1766 he married Sarah Proctor, with whom he settled the next year at Almery Garth on the outskirts of York. Here the Priestmans and Tukes ministered to Woolman during his final illness (see Appendix H).

RECKITT, WILLIAM (1706–1769). A weaver in England, he had nine children. A dedicated minister, he travelled in England, Ireland, and Wales. On a voyage to America during the Seven Years War (1756) he was seized by the French and imprisoned for six months. He returned to England, where he stayed only four weeks before again setting out for America. He travelled to England again in 1759 and once more in 1764, this time remaining two years. His journal (*Some Account of the Life . . . William Reckitt*) was published at Philadelphia in 1783.

REDMAN, MERCY (DAVIS) (1721–1778). A resident of Haddonfield, N.J., where both she and her husband (Thomas) were itinerant ministers. Their only child died in infancy.

SCARBOROUGH, JOHN (1704–1769). A member of the Buckingham, Pa., Monthly Meeting and active in the affairs of the Philadelphia Yearly Meeting, he also served as an itinerant minister. His grandfather (with the same name) was an early settler in Bucks County, Pa.

SLEEPER, JOHN (1731–?). His parents were said to have emigrated to New Jersey from New England because of the persecution of Quakers there. He and his wife were raised in Burlington County. They had ten children. A carpenter in Mount Holly, he owned land near that owned by Woolman, and the two were lifelong friends.

SMITH, ELIZABETH (1724-1772). A native of Burlington, where her father and four brothers were active in civic and political affairs, she was a close friend of John Woolman. Remaining unmarried, she served as a Quaker minister in the vicinity of her own home, and also travelled through the middle colonies and New England. She had planned to visit England at about the same time as Woolman, but was prevented by the illness from which she died. Woolman signed her certificate for the journey, after which he wrote her a tender, affectionate letter expressing "a reserve which I then . . . felt as to the exemplariness of those things amongst thy furniture which are against the purity of our principles."

SMITH, JOHN (1681-1766). He was born in Massachusetts of Presbyterian parents, who later became Quakers. At twenty-two he was imprisoned for his testimony against war. Two years later he went to England, where he was "pressed" aboard a man-of-war and imprisoned for six weeks. He later married and lived forty years in East Marlborough, Pa., where for a time the Quakers held their meetings in his home.

SMITH, JOHN (1722-1771). His father was a merchant at Burlington and a long-time member of the Assembly of New Jersey. At nineteen, John went to sea in one of his father's vessels. Then he settled in Philadelphia as a merchant, engaging in extensive commerce with England, Ireland, Portugal, Madeira, and the West Indies. He married Hannah Logan, a daughter of James Logan, who was William Penn's secretary. He was active in civic affairs, as a founder of the Pennsylvania Hospital, as founder and executive officer of an insurance company, and as a member of the Assembly, a justice of the peace, and a county judge. When Gilbert Tennent of Philadelphia preached a sermon in December, 1747, entitled "The Lawfulness of a Defensive War," Smith wrote a reply to it. He helped establish the Loganian library, consisting of books assembled by his wife's father. After his wife died in 1762, he retired to Burlington.

STANLEY, WILLIAM (1729-1807). He was the son of James Stanley, of Cedar Creek, Virginia, with whom Woolman lodged on one of his journeys. He was imprisoned at Winchester, Virginia, because of his refusal to bear arms on the side of the British in the French and Indian War.

STANTON, DANIEL (1708-1770). He was an itinerant Quaker minister for over forty years. His experiences are recounted in A Journal of the Life . . . Daniel Stanton . . . . (Philadelphia and London, 1799). He travelled to the West Indies and to Great Britain, as well as through many of the American colonies. Like Woolman, he sought to establish more friendly relations with the Indians and (at the behest of the Philadelphia Yearly Meeting) remonstrated with slaveholders.

STORER, JOHN (1725-1795). A native of Nottingham, England, he was in the wool-stapling trade. He became a Quaker at age twenty-three, and four years later began his itinerant ministry. Having visited America in 1759-60, he returned in 1785 with two companions—the first Quakers to make the journey after the Revolutionary War. He is given special approbation in the epistle sent by the New England Yearly Meeting to London in 1760 and in the journal of John Hunt.

SYKES, JOHN (1682-1771). A Quaker minister, he was a frequent travelling companion and financial adviser to Woolman, who was thirty-eight years his junior.

TUKE, WILLIAM (1732-1822), and ESTHER (MAUD) (1727-1794). The ancestors of William Tuke had been tea merchants for many generations; he successfully carried on the same business. A native of York, England, he founded "The Retreat," devoted to humane treatment of the insane. This prominent Quaker is said to have taken part in fifty consecutive Yearly Meetings. With Esther, his second wife, he organized a school for girls, of which Esther served as headmistress. The present "Mount School," established in 1831, is its successor. Esther ministered to Woolman in his final illness. Letters written by the Tukes describing his last days and commenting upon his character are very illuminating. Esther's letter to Samuel Emlen, published by Mrs. Gummere (145-148), is especially perceptive.

WHITE, JOSEPH (1712-1777). Born in Bucks County, Pa., he began his itinerant ministry at the age of twenty. In 1758 he went to the British Isles, where he remained for three years. Both Woolman and John Churchman refer in their journals to visiting his wife and children in his absence.

WILSON, RACHEL (ca. 1721-1775). The daughter of John and Deborah Wilson of Kendal, England, she married Isaac Wilson. They had nine children. An eloquent Quaker preacher, she traversed the British Isles, where she was on friendly terms with George Whitefield. In 1768 and 1769 she travelled on horseback through the American colonies. At the Philadelphia Yearly Meeting of 1769, she interrupted her testimony to speak directly to Woolman, who was then undecided as to whether to visit the West Indies. Woolman had a high regard for her and her son John (see *Journal*, Chapter 12, note 20).

WOOLMAN, ELIZABETH, JR. (1715-1747). John's sister, and the oldest child in the family, she never married. She moved in 1740 to Haddonfield, N.J., where she was successful as a tailor. She is the only one of his siblings to whom John refers in his *Journal* by name.

WOOLMAN, SAMUEL (1690-1750) and ELIZABETH (BURR) (1695-1773). Samuel, John Woolman's father, lived his entire life at the homestead he inherited on the Rancocas River in Burlington County, N.J. He accumulated additional land and performed many legal functions—in real estate transactions, as executor of estates, and in settling claims. The books in his sizable library dealt chiefly with religion, law, and navigation. Elizabeth, who came from a well-known family, was noted for her hospitality despite the duties involved in raising a family of thirteen children.

WOOLMAN, SARAH (ELLIS) (1721-1787). Wife of John Woolman; sometimes called "cousin" by Woolman and his siblings, although not a blood relative. Her father, an emigrant from England, disappeared (apparently having been lost at sea) shortly after her birth. Her mother died when she was seventeen. She spent much of her life with relatives within a few miles of Mount Holly, where she and Woolman were members of a rather large circle of friends and relatives. Although not in robust health, she survived her husband by fifteen years, during which she served as an officer and committee member of the Mount Holly Monthly Meeting.

WOOLMAN, URIAH (1728–1804). A younger brother of John, at the age of twenty-seven he moved to Philadelphia, where he successfully engaged in business. At forty-one he married a first cousin, Susanna Burr, whose father was Surveyor-General of West Jersey. They had no children. His death notice in Poulson's "American Daily Advertiser" described him as "a respectable member of the Society of Friends," but he appears not to have been a notably active one.

Glossary

THE TERMS LISTED HERE are those that may puzzle a twentieth-century reader. For the most part they are used by Woolman in ways not customary today. The aim here is simply to provide the reader with an understanding of what Woolman meant by them. Examples are generally not provided, since the *Journal* itself illustrates their use.

Awful. Inspiring awe. It does not mean "terrible" or "bad."

Baptize. To initiate; to acquaint; to make aware; to enrich spiritually—generally implying that the awareness or enrichment is brought about through a trying experience.

Comfortable. Satisfactory; fruitful; enriching. Spiritual or inward comfort in this sense is that occasioned by an experience according with one's higher values or conscience, but not necessarily comfortable in the physical sense.

Drawings. A sense of guidance or mission; a "vocation," usually to a particular act rather than to a lifelong occupation. Hence, to be "drawn" is to experience this sense.

Easy. At ease with one's conscience; inwardly free. This meaning does not necessarily imply "without difficulty."

Exercise. Inner turmoil; concern; awareness of a burden or obligation. The word has many nuances of meaning, all of which concern intellectual or spiritual, as distinguished from physical, exertion.

Nearly. Directly; closely; intimately.

Odds. Difference; distinction.

Opening. Revelation; guidance; leading.

Outward. External; material; physical; worldly—the opposite of internal or spiritual.

Singular. Peculiar; odd; unusual; different.

Society (capitalized). Religious sect or denomination; usually refers to the Society of Friends.

Stock. Supply of money or capital; treasury.

Sunk. Financed; paid for.

Truth (capitalized). Ultimate spiritual reality; divinity. This usage is to be distinguished from reference to particular truths, such as creedal affirmations. In the text it has been capitalized to indicate this special meaning, except where it is used in conjunction with a similar term, as in the phrase "truth and righteousness."

Weighty. Serious; heavy (referring to a mental burden); influential; important.

Selected Bibliography

THE LIST BELOW is limited almost entirely to books of major importance (including editions of Woolman's works) that are readily available. See also the list of major extant manuscripts in Appendix B; each of the depositories indicated there contains primary source materials in addition to those described.

A. EDITIONS OF WOOLMAN'S WORKS

BEARDSLEY, WILLIAM A., ed. *The Works of John Woolman*, 1774 (a reprint in the American Literature and Culture Series). New York: Garrett Press, 1970. This is a clear photographic reproduction of the first edition, consisting of the *Journal* and the *Works*, including the major essays, except *A Plea for the Poor*. An eleven-page Foreword by the editor is well done. See Appendix A of the present volume for a discussion of the first edition.

GUMMERE, AMELIA MOTT, ed. *The Journal and Essays of John Woolman*. New York: The Macmillan Company, 1922. This edition is discussed in Appendix A of the present volume. It remains by far the most complete source of material by and about Woolman.

SCUDDER, VIDA, ed. *The Journal and Other Writings of John Woolman* (Everyman's Library). London and New York: J. M. Dent and E. P. Dutton, 1910. A reprint of the first English edition, published in London by Thomas Letchworth in 1775. Members of the London Yearly Meeting prepared this volume by eliminating some forty pages from the first American edition. The omitted pages dealt with Woolman's visions and with his scruples regarding such things as payment of war taxes, the use of dyes, luxurious living, the oppression of stagecoach drivers, and the corrupt environment of apprentice sailors. As a result, this is a very unsatisfactory volume.

TOLLES, FREDERICK B., ed. *The Journal of John Woolman and A Plea for the Poor* (The American Experience Series). New York: Corinth Books, 1961. A reprint in paperback of the Whittier edition, including Whittier's footnotes but omitting the introduction and other items. The brief introduction by Tolles is first-rate. A hard-cover reprint of this edition has been issued by Peter Smith, Gloucester, Mass.

WHITNEY, JANET, ed. *The Journal of John Woolman*. Chicago: Henry Regnery Co., 1950. This very readable edition is treated at length in Appendix A of the present volume. A paperback edition, also published by Regnery, lacks the introduction, Chapters 11 and 12, the "Account of Woolman's Death," and the appendices; otherwise the contents (including footnotes) are the same.

WHITTIER, JOHN G., ed. *The Journal of John Woolman.* Boston: J. R. Osgood and Co., 1871. This edition is described in Appendix A of the present volume. Whittier's introduction and footnotes are well worth reading. Following the *Journal* it contains an abbreviated account of Woolman's final illness and death, plus testimonies about him published by the Yorkshire Quarterly and Burlington Monthly Meetings. *A Plea for the Poor* (here entitled *A Word of Remembrance and Caution to the Rich*) is also included, but lacks the last three chapters.

B. SECONDARY SOURCES

ALTMAN, W. FORREST. "John Woolman's Reading." Publication 23,971, University Microfilms. Ph.D. dissertation, Florida State University, 1957. A good exposition and analysis of the books Woolman read or (in some cases) may have read, set in the context of Quakerism and of the religious and literary currents of Woolman's day. Sections are devoted to Woolman's use of the Bible and to his reading of non-religious books. Altman also considers the relation between the books Woolman read and his literary style, his theological ideas, his mystical tendencies, and his humanitarian concerns.

BARBOUR, HUGH. *The Quakers in Puritan England.* New Haven: Yale University Press, 1964. Although primarily concerned with the early years of Quakerism (1652-1665), this excellent study offers a many-faceted illumination for the study of later periods.

BENTON, JOSEPHINE M. *John Woolman: Most Modern of Ancient Friends.* Philadelphia: Friends General Conference (1520 Race St.), 1952. Each of the sixteen chapters in this useful study guide consists of three or four pages of quotations and comment on one aspect of Woolman's teaching, plus a list of "Topics for Consideration."

BRONNER, EDWIN B. *William Penn's "Holy Experiment": The Founding of Pennsylvania, 1681-1701.* New York: Temple University Publications (distributed by Columbia University Press), 1962. This impressive work shows how the foundations were laid among Pennsylvania Quakers for religious toleration, opposition to war, and concern for the welfare of the Indians—all characteristic of Woolman.

CADBURY, HENRY J. *John Woolman in England: A Documentary Supplement.* London: Friends Historical Society. An authoritative account of the last four months of Woolman's life, scheduled for publication in 1971.

CADY, EDWIN H. *John Woolman* (Great American Thinkers). New York: Washington Square Press, 1965. Cady portrays Woolman's spiritual ancestry, without taking sides on the question of whether the early Quaker movement was rooted primarily in Puritanism or in continental mysticism. Woolman is pictured as exemplifying central aspects of both the Quaker and American traditions. The author skillfully weaves together significant aspects of his life and work. His discussion of the literary genre to which the *Journal* belongs is stimulating, and his summaries of Woolman's writings are useful.

DRAKE, THOMAS E. *Quakers and Slavery in America.* New Haven, Conn.: Yale University Press, 1950. Reprint, Gloucester, Mass.: Peter Smith, 1965. Woolman's influence is revealed in this careful examination of the role played by the Quakers in the American antislavery movement from its beginnings until the Civil War.

JAMES, SYDNEY V. *A People Among Peoples: Quaker Benevolence in Eighteenth-Century America.* Cambridge, Mass.: Harvard University Press, 1963. A study of Quaker social service and action, in which the prominent role of Woolman is evident, by an authority on American colonial history.

JONES, RUFUS (assisted by Isaac Sharpless and Amelia Mott Gummere). *The Quakers in the American Colonies.* London: The Macmillan Company, 1911. Reprint, New York: W. W. Norton and Co., 1966. This perceptive study, part of a comprehensive series dealing with Quaker history, is still the standard work on its subject. A group of scholars is now preparing three volumes which to a large degree will supersede this one. However, the insights of Rufus Jones will never become obsolete.

PEARE, CATHERINE O. *John Woolman: Child of Light.* New York: Vanguard Press, 1954. An interesting, well-written biography intended primarily for young people.

POWYS, LLEWELLYN. *Thirteen Worthies.* New York: American Library Service, 1923. Reprint, Freeport, New York: Books for Libraries Press, 1966. The brief chapter on Woolman in this book consists of a beautiful portrayal of his spirit and character.

REYNOLDS, REGINALD. *The Wisdom of John Woolman: With a Selection from His Writings as a Guide to the Seekers of Today.* London: George Allen and Unwin, 1948. A vivid sketch of Woolman's life and background, followed by a thoughtful correlation of Woolman's insights and methods with perennial ethical issues and mid-twentieth-century social problems. Well-chosen extracts from Woolman's writings round out this very useful book.

ROSENBLATT, PAUL. *John Woolman* (United States Authors Series). New York: Twayne Publishers, 1969. A good summary of Woolman's life and thought, based on the biographies of Gummere and Whitney, as well as on the *Journal.* Particular attention is given to literary aspects of the *Journal.* The chief value of this volume is in the light it sheds on Woolman by comparison with such figures as St. Augustine, Jonathan Edwards, Benjamin Franklin, the Transcendentalists, and Walt Whitman. The annotated bibliography is quite useful in calling attention to essays not often referred to by writers on Woolman.

SHEA, DANIEL B. *Spiritual Autobiography in Early America.* Princeton: Princeton University Press, 1968. After a survey of Quaker autobiographical literature, the author devotes a chapter to Woolman's *Journal,* and to the qualities that make it unique. In discussing the revisions Woolman made in the *Journal,* Shea is led into errors (76 and 77) by his reliance on the Gummere edition. Otherwise, the study is a sound one and its interpretation of Woolman's thought is stimulating.

SHORE, W. T. *John Woolman: His Life and Our Times.* London: Macmillan and Company, 1913. The chief value of this book is in its descriptions of the geographical settings of Woolman's home and travels, the social life and commerce of the day, and the attitudes of his predecessors and contemporaries towards problems with which he grappled. The book is marred by a pedestrian style and the absence of documentation.

Steere, Douglas V. *Doors Into Life: Through Five Devotional Classics.* New York: Harper and Row, 1948. A twenty-five-page introduction to Woolman's *Journal* is exceptionally valuable.

Tolles, Frederick B. *Quakers and the Atlantic Culture.* New York: The Macmillan Company, 1960. This collection of essays sheds light on several aspects of Woolman's life and times.

Trueblood, D. Elton. *The People Called Quakers.* New York: Harper and Row, 1966. A clear and balanced chapter on Woolman is central to this well-written account of the history and present-day relevance of Quakerism.

Whitney, Janet. *John Woolman: American Quaker.* Boston: Little, Brown, and Company, 1942. Some readers may be repelled by the occasional sentimentalism and the imaginative liberties taken in reconstructing events in this biography. Yet it is a discerning account, based upon impressive research, buttressed by useful appendices.

———. *John Woolman: Quaker.* London: George Harrap and Co., 1943. The contents of this and the preceding volume are the same, except for some of the illustrations and the absence of some notes and appendices in this one.

Addendum Regarding

A PLEA FOR THE POOR
OR
A WORD OF REMEMBRANCE AND CAUTION TO THE RICH ETC.

In the Introduction to the Essays, the newly-discovered MS. W is discussed briefly. It remains to indicate its relation to, and its substantive variations from, MS. *Plea*.

Aside from possible preliminary drafts of which we lack knowledge, we may reconstruct the approximate processes of composition as follows. First Woolman composed MS. *Plea*, revising it continuously as he did so. Additional revisions were made later, judging by the different color of the ink and the nature and location of the revisions.

Then he copied MS. W from MS. *Plea*, making relatively few emendations in the process. Occasionally phrases or longer sections are omitted; additions are rare. The numerous complex revisions in MS. *Plea* are almost invariably transcribed smoothly into MS. W with no alteration of phraseology. It is difficult to conceive of the reverse process: copying from MS. W to create MS. *Plea*, replete with interlining, insertions with carets, writing over erasures, and marginal additions—with identical wording. In Chapter 11 of MS. *Plea* he composed two pages, then revised and renumbered the paragraphs, after which he copied the result (with the new paragraph order) on the succeeding pages. In MS. W the final product is smoothly and accurately transcribed. One can scarcely imagine Woolman copying from MS. W, changing many phrases and the order of paragraphs, and then changing it all back again as he recopied it! A detailed examination of numerous other points, including several where he improved his style in process, confirms that he copied from MS. *Plea* to MS. W—not vice versa. The few minor instances where revision has occurred

319

in MS. W but not in MS. *Plea* can be readily explained as incidental to the copying process.

Later Woolman made several identical changes in both manuscripts: using carets, erasing and writing over passages, etc. He also made further revisions in MS. *Plea* but not in MS. W. At these points MS. *Plea* constitutes the later version. The reason for not making these changes in MS. W can only be conjectured.

Chapters 1–13 in MS. *Plea* seem to constitute a distinct unit. The final sentence of Chapter 13 is a fitting close. A gap then appears (not typical of previous chapter divisions), and Chapter 14 begins on the next page (181) in ink of a different color. The writing is also more generously spaced, with fewer words to the line and lines to the page. In the margin (page 181) is the note: "See page 194," apparently written when the intervening pages were blank—to refer the reader to the place where the *Journal* is resumed. Chapter 14 is also the first to bear a title. A line across the page at the conclusion of Chapter 14 may indicate that Woolman considered it the end of the essay and that Chapter 15 was added still later. It is illuminating also that in Chapter 16 the writing becomes increasingly smaller, as if he were trying to cram it all in before reaching page 194, where the *Journal* had been resumed. Moreover, a note attached to section 6 of Chapter 16 dates the writing of that portion to "some months" before October 9, 1769.

All of this tends to imply that the reason MS. W lacks Chapters 14–16 is that MS. *Plea* did not yet contain them. (It should be noted, however, that Chapters 14–16 appear on consecutive pages in the same volume, that the chapters are numbered in Woolman's handwriting, and that the subject matter is all related to the general topic of poverty and affluence.) It seems also reasonable to conjecture that some or all of the revisions in the earlier chapters that were not copied into MS. W were made while Woolman was writing, or after he had concluded, the last three chapters.

Whether Woolman intended MS. W as a printer's copy is not clear. Certain minor revisions tend to imply that he did. The editorial emendations made in MS. W by another person are not conclusive proof of Woolman's intent. In any event, he may have decided later to consider MS. *Plea* his final copy. Certain revisions and additions found only in MS. *Plea* tend to support this view. At a few points in MS. *Plea* (but never in MS. W) he wrote directions, such as: "Let this be left out." But whether these were for his own future guidance or for the printer is not certain. At two points in MS. *Plea* where Woolman revised and rearranged passages, he did not cross out the rejected portions as clearly and decisively as he did in MS. B (and as one would expect in a document intended for the printer). Noting the inconclusive nature of the evidence, and leaving aside the possibility that he made a third copy (since lost), we may conjecture that he died without having finally prepared either manuscript for the printer.

Relevant to this issue is the question of the title. At the beginning of MS. *Plea* Woolman wrote *A plea for the poor*, in small, lower-case letters (except for the initial "A"). It is written a bit off center, with a blank space below it, as though he might have considered adding another title. The longer title, on the cover of MS. W, is written in large letters, the main words being capitalized. Although this is probably in Woolman's handwriting, the "A" and "C" are sufficiently atypical of his customary usage to leave room for doubt. Moreover, if he intended *A Word . . . Rich* as his title, and if he intended MS. *Plea* for the printer, why did he not write that title in the large blank space at the top of MS. *Plea?* Since the pages of the present volume have already been set in type, and in view of this element of doubt, the editor is content to allow *A Plea for the Poor* to stand as the main title, the reader being free to prefer the other.

A good case could be made for printing a composite of MSS. *Plea* and W, using at each point what the editor considers Woolman's final intention. The differences in terminology are few, however, the major points of variance being omissions in MS. W. Everything considered, it has seemed best to print the latest revision of MS. *Plea* and to record all substantive variants in MS. W, analyzing those of special significance. Thus we shall provide the reader with all relevant evidence. To this we now turn.

Textual Notes and Variant Passages

Note: The figures in the left-hand column refer to location in the present volume. Before the decimal is the page; after it is the line. In counting the lines, chapter headings, MS. page numbers, and mathematical calculations are ignored. A half bracket separates the word or phrase in MS. *Plea* (to the left) from its parallel in MS. W (to the right). The word *ditto* means that the passage reads the same in both MSS. A pair of square brackets identifies editorial comment.

The intent of the editor has been to cite every point in MS. W at which a substantive variation from MS. *Plea* occurs for which Woolman is responsible. "Substantive" refers to word, word order, or grammar, as distinguished from "accidentals" (spelling, punctuation, capitalization, and paragraphing). When emendations made in MS. W by someone other than Woolman are noted, their author is referred to as "editor." Where no comment by the present editor is provided, significant complicating factors are not evident.

In addition to noting variant readings, the present editor has commented on a sampling of typical passages that clarify the relation of MS. *Plea* to MS. W. Unless otherwise indicated, references to numbers (such as, "see 242") are to pages in this volume. The present editor uses "smooth" or "smoothly" to mean: with identical wording and without such evidence of revision as carets, erasures, or interlinings. Additional textual comment is provided in the footnotes to *A Plea for the Poor*.

239.1   possessions] estates

239.22   creation, we are] creation, are [The process here seems to have been: Woolman originally had the same sentence in both MSS. Then he made the same revisions in both, using the margin of MS. *Plea* and interlining in MS. W. Later Woolman (or possibly someone else) added "we" in MS. *Plea*, but not in MS. W, at the same time writing "while we, etc., etc." in MS. *Plea* to clarify (perhaps for a printer?) the point where the marginal note belonged. See 239, n. 2.]

239.26   faithfully] *ditto* [In MS. W, Woolman carefully touched up this word (which had been written over an erasure) to make it clear—possibly with the printer in mind.]

240.5   proceedings] proceeding

240.28   ages] age

240.29   they may more] they more ["may" has been inserted in MS. W by someone—other than Woolman—who has edited the whole MS. carefully, adding and eliminating letters and words, as if in preparation for the printer. The first known printed edition (1793) follows enough of these emendations to indicate that the printer had access to MS. W or a copy which took these changes into account. However, the 1793 edition varies at scores of points from both Woolman and the editor—adding, subtracting, and substituting words and phrases. This and other observations too complex to discuss here suggest that a currently unknown copy of this essay may have existed in 1793, to which the printer and the scribe of MS. G had access. Whether or not the unknown document was a holograph can only be conjectured.]

241.1–3   [In MS. W, four times in these three lines Woolman carefully changed "his" to "His," thus making his practice in this part of the manuscript consistent. (Several unchanged instances of "his"—referring to deity—occur later.) Could he have done this for the printer?]

241.25   towards] toward

241.31   case, not] case, as not

242.2   and to pay] and pay

242.4   to improve] and improve

242.11   rents] rent

242.26   selfish] *ditto* [Following the directions in MS. *Plea*, Chap. 4 of MS. W ends here with no indication of any revision. See 242, n. 8.]

243.7   to sympathy] *ditto* [MS. W reads "sympathize," but the change appears to have been made by editor. See 243, n. 9.]

243.13   means] means [Underlining may have been done by editor.]

244.10   sight to support them and] sight and

244.18   relent, or] relent? or

244.20   inconvenience?] *ditto* [MS. W omits the remaining line and a half in Chapter 5, which was squeezed into MS. *Plea* after the heading to Chapter 6 was written.]

244.24   [The situation here is very complex. Woolman revised this first sentence in Chap. 6 of MS. *Plea*. This revised sentence is copied into MS. W ("drink" being changed to "liquor," however). Then follows a passage which is crossed out of MS. *Plea* and duly omitted from MS. W. (This passage is reproduced in point 1 of Appendix G of this volume.) Woolman pasted an insert into MS. *Plea* to replace the rejected passage. The insert consisted of three sentences, all of which were copied into MS. W. The first and third of these sentences were crossed out of MS. *Plea*. (These sentences are reproduced in points 2 and 3 of Appendix G.) But they were never crossed out of MS. W. The probable explanation is that they had not been crossed out of MS. *Plea* at the time MS. W was written. That is, MS. *Plea* was apparently revised not only before MS. W was written but also afterwards, and hence constitutes Woolman's final version at this point. Incidentally, in copying the three sentences from the insert into MS. W, Woolman made several changes that should be noted. In the first sentence, "day's labour" is changed to "day's work." In the second, "food or raiment" is changed to "food and raiment." In the third, "pounds" is changed to "pound," and "with sixty day's labour" is changed to "in sixty days."]

245.5   Question . . . time] [This question and the mathematical calculation which follows it are omitted from MS. W, perhaps because they were marginal notations. But the reason may be that they were not there at the time. Woolman may have added them later—to replace the sentences crossed out at this approximate point. See preceding entry.]

245.8   in these colonies] in our country

245.9   nor may we suppose that . . . this liquor can be drank] nor can . . . this liquor be drank [Originally this passage in MS. *Plea* was the same as it now stands in MS. W. Then it was changed to its present form. It is more likely that it was changed after MS. W was written—than that Woolman rejected the change and reconstructed the original version while copying.]

245.16   motion in the heat and] motion and ["in the heat," inserted with a caret in darker ink,was evidently added after MS. W was written.]

245.17   for serious thinking and divine] for divine

245.20   custom requires our serious thoughts] custom is strongly supported [See 245, n. 16. MS. *Plea* was probably changed after MS. W was written. His failure clearly to cross out "is strongly supported" tends to imply he did not prepare MS. *Plea* for the printer.]

246.4   [See 246, n. 17.]

246.7   [See 246, n. 18.]

246.8   people crave] nature craves [In MS. *Plea* Woolman crossed out "nature craves" and substituted "people crave," apparently at the same time as he added "the spirits are exhausted and." It is not clear why MS. W made the addition but not the substitution.]

246.10   Holy Spirit] Celestial Influence [Here again MS. *Plea* apparently reflects Woolman's final intention. See 246, n. 19.]

246.13   is acceptably worshipped] is worshipped [The insertion of "acceptably" with a caret was probably made after MS. W was written. The different color of the ink implies a significant time gap between the writing of "acceptably" and the rest of the sentence.]

247.19   for the propagating] for propagating

247.23   wisdom will be evident, thereby to be directed] *ditto* [At this point is a typical instance of complex revision in MS. *Plea*: "will be evident" is inserted with a caret; "directed" is written over an erasure; the two words that originally followed "directed" ("and supported") are crossed out. The final wording is transcribed smoothly into MS. W.]

248.12   suffice twenty] suffice for twenty ["for" erased in MS. *Plea*, probably after MS. W was written.]

248.26–27 our children and an equal number of these poor children, it] *ditto* [In MS. *Plea*, written over an erasure: "our children"; inserted with a caret: "and an equal"; between "children" and "it": a half line erasure. The changes are all copied accurately and smoothly into MS. W. Instances of this kind are innumerable—in the same direction, from MS. *Plea* to MS. W.]

248.27 likely to give] likely give

248.32 contemplate the] contemplate on the ["on" erased in MS. *Plea*]

249.8 succeed] *ditto* [In neither MS. is it clear whether Woolman intended "succeed" or "succeeds."]

249.14 and how vain and weak a thing it is to give] *ditto* [In MS. *Plea*, all of these words except "weak" and "to" are written over erasures. The whole passage is copied smoothly into MS. W.]

249.17 of God.] of God to us.

249.18 steward] stewards

249.19 gracious] graciously

250.4 afford] give

250.9 that to desire these things belongs not to the children of the Light] that it belongs not to the children of the Light to desire these things

251.2 instructing] instructive

251.22 preserve]*ditto* [In MS. W, Woolman wrote "keep," then crossed it out and wrote "preserve" above it. In this context it would be natural to write "keep." MS. *Plea* shows no revision.]

251.25 treasures] treasure

252.7 doctrine]*ditto* [In MS. W, Woolman first wrote "example" (a natural error in this context) and then replaced it with "doctrine." MS. *Plea* shows no revision.]

252.17 appear a] appear as a

253.13 employed in different kingdoms in preparing] employed in preparing

253.28 Christ] Christ's

253.31 [See 253, n. 30.]

254.26–27 is so . . . Christ's religion] *ditto* [This is probably the most complex passage in MS. W which is rendered smoothly in MS. *Plea*; "so" is inserted with a caret, and an erasure appears before "Christ's." These can be explained as copying errors. Moreover, this passage in MS. W has not been revised nearly as much as have many passages in MS. *Plea* that are smooth in MS. W.]

255.6–7 spirit which loves riches works] spirit works which loves riches

255.19–20 seed of war swells, and sprouts and grows and becomes] seeds of war swell and sprout and grow and becomes [In MS. W, "s" has been erased from "swell," "sprout," and "grow." The "s" on "be-comes" has been crossed out by editor. The erasures were probably made by Woolman. He erased rather frequently, whereas editor customarily crossed out undesired items.]

255.22   and of desperate] and desperate

255.30   against it!] *ditto* [MS. W omits the rest of the chapter. This could have been done inadvertently, since the rest of the chapter is on the next page, most of which Woolman had crossed out. See 255, n. 33, re-garding Woolman's marginal directions in MS. *Plea*.]

256.1–257.5   [See 256, n. 34; and 257, nn. 35 and 36. Here is the in-stance, referred to earlier in this Addendum, where Woolman copied smoothly into MS. W the results of his extensive revision in MS. *Plea*. He also copied into MS. W a paragraph (following the revised section) which has been crossed out of both MSS. by Woolman. This paragraph is printed on 257, n. 36. The marginal direction quoted there appears only in MS. *Plea*.]

256.10   Ps. 24:1] [MS. W lacks "Ps. 24:1." The Leviticus reference is in both MSS. The Matthew and Amos references are in neither.]

257.18   caming] coming [See 257, n. 37. The original passage in MS. *Plea* read: "came over, and the natives." It is more likely that he changed this and then copied the result ("coming over, the") into MS. W, than that he copied from MS. W into MS. *Plea*, in the process changing "com-ing over, the" to "came over and"—and later changed it back again. Many similar instances tend to confirm that he copied from MS. *Plea* to MS. W —not vice versa.]

257.21   these] those [In MS. W, Woolman started to copy "these," and then changed it to "those"—an obvious improvement, one of several he made in the copying process.]

258.3–4   [In MS. W, the words between the first "this" and the second "this" are interlined, the location before "continent" being marked with a caret. As he looked back and forth in copying, his eye apparently caught the wrong "this," a common type of error. Checking the copy later, he noted the error and rectified it.]

258.6–7   adjoining to us] adjoining us [Another slight improvement made in copying]

258.24   I believe] I believe I believe [This type of error is more likely to occur (and remain unrectified) in a manuscript copied from another, than in an original composition from which a copy is made.]

258.36   with him] with them [This is perhaps the only instance where it seems to the present editor that the original word in MS. *Plea* is more apt than the substitute in MS. W. There is no indication that the word in MS. *Plea* was added later.]

258.38 the branches] their branches [In MS. *Plea* "ir" has been erased from "their," but is still visible.]

259.30 those] these ["those" bears the marks of revision.]

259.31ff. [In these final eleven lines of Chapter 12 are the following revisions in MS. *Plea*: six words ("interest . . . others") written over an erasure; a gap (erasure) of about seven words between "spirit" and "we"; "in true religion" written over an erasure; "Divine" over an erasure; "runs" over an erasure; "we meditate" over an erasure; a gap (erasure) of about seven words between "angels" and "this"; a three-word gap (erasure) between "be" and "clouded"; "employment" written over erased "business." The parallel passage in MS. W is entirely smooth, except for a slight change of one word. The final wording of the two manuscripts is identical. One can readily imagine Woolman laboring over the MS. *Plea* passage and later copying it into MS. W. One can hardly picture him first composing MS. W, then writing a much different version in MS. *Plea*, and then making numerous alterations, resulting in a passage just like the one with which he started. Several similar examples exist for each one cited in these notes.]

260.33 nothing, before man had possession of it. And] nothing. And

261.20 follows] followers

262.4 those] these

262.6–7 inclinations while he stands in opposition to them. Suppose] inclinations. Suppose

262.10–11 rest generally poor] rest poor

262.17 in plainness, frugality] in frugality

Index

CPSIA information can be obtained
at www.ICGtesting.com
Printed in the USA
FFOW05n0514201117